COLLECTED WORKS

OF

COUNT RUMFORD

VOLUME IV

COLLECTED WORKS
OF
COUNT RUMFORD

EDITED BY SANBORN C. BROWN

VOLUME IV

LIGHT AND ARMAMENT

THE BELKNAP PRESS OF
HARVARD UNIVERSITY PRESS
CAMBRIDGE, MASSACHUSETTS
1970

PREFACE

The two areas of physics in which Count Rumford made significant contributions were the fields of heat and light. His published papers in the theory and practice of light and illumination are brought together in this volume. Before Rumford's day very little had been done to put measurements in these fields on a quantitative basis. In inventing instruments and defining standards, Rumford not only designed a shadow photometer which is still known by his name, but defined a standard candle which survived as a unit of luminous intensity into the twentieth century. The papers describing these developments are to be found here.

The common use of the viscous animal and vegetable oils for fuel in lamps turned the attention of many eighteenth- and nineteenth-century inventors toward improvements that would render lamps both more efficient and more uniform in luminous intensity. Rumford solved the annoying problem of the light output decreasing as the oil level sank in the then ordinary type of lamp by introducing reservoirs that stored the oil at the same level as the wick.

After carrying out a series of investigations to prove that translucent diffusing screens did not markedly decrease the luminous efficiency of a flame, Rumford described in papers included in this volume a large number of variations of what he called his illuminators. These studies also led him to demonstrate that the use of ground-glass window panes increased rather than decreased the illumination of a room shielded from direct sunlight.

As might be expected, Count Rumford was attracted to any experiment that might show the similarities or differences between heat and light. Two papers included in this volume, his "Inquiry concerning the Chemical Properties that have been attributed to Light" and his "Experiments on the Production of Air from Water, exposed with various Substances to the Action of Light," both led him to the conclusion that heat and light were different in their interaction with material substances.

Not connected with Rumford's studies of light and illumination were those on gunpowder. These were the experiments that first attracted attention to him as a scientist and won him fellowship in the Royal Society of Great Britain. He felt at the time he was engaged with them that these studies might prove to be theoretically useful in his search for the nature of heat. The fact that they did not in no way lessened their usefulness to military technology, and his conclusions and techniques were widely adopted both in England and on the continent of Europe. Since these papers are unrelated to most of Rumford's other work they are included here at the end of his scientific contributions.

Sanborn C. Brown

CONTENTS

Experiments on the Relative Intensities of the Light emitted by Luminous Bodies   1

An Account of some Experiments on Coloured Shadows   53

Conjectures respecting the Principles of the Harmony of Colours   65

An Inquiry concerning the Chemical Properties that have been attributed to Light   73

Of the Management of Light in Illumination   97

Observations on the Dispersion of the Light of Lamps by Means of Shades of unpolished Glass, Silk, &c.; with a Description of a new Lamp   206

An Inquiry concerning the Source of the Light which is manifested in the Combustion of Inflammable Bodies   229

Experiments on the Production of Air from Water, exposed with various Substances to the Action of Light   251

An Account of some Experiments Upon Gunpowder   293

Experiments to determine the Force of Fired Gunpowder   395

A Short Account of some Experiments made with Cannon, and also of some Attempts to Improve Field Artillery   473

Facts of Publication   495

Index   501

EXPERIMENTS

ON THE

RELATIVE INTENSITIES OF THE LIGHT EMITTED BY LUMINOUS BODIES.

EXPERIMENTS

RELATIVE INTENSITIES OF THE LIGHT EMITTED
BY LUMINOUS BODIES.

———

BEING employed in making a number of experiments to determine, if possible, the most economical method of lighting up a very large workhouse, or public manufactory, which had been erected in the suburbs of Munich under my direction, a method occurred to me for measuring the relative quantities of light emitted by lamps of different constructions, candles, etc., which is very simple, and which I have reason to think perfectly accurate.

Let the two burning candles, lamps, or other lights to be compared, A and B, be placed at equal heights upon two light tables or movable stands, in a darkened room; let a sheet of clean white paper be spread out equally, and fastened upon the wainscot or side of the room, at the same height from the floor with the lights; and let the lights be placed over against this sheet of paper, at the distance of 6 or 8 feet from it, and 6 or 8 feet from each other, in such a manner that a line drawn from the centre of the paper, perpendicular to its surface, shall bisect the angle formed by lines drawn from the lights to that centre; in which case, considering the sheet of paper as a plane speculum, the one light will be precisely in the line of reflection of the other.

This may be easily performed, by actually placing a piece of a looking-glass, 6 or 8 inches square, flat upon the paper, in the middle of it, and observing by means of it the real lines of reflection of the lights from that plane, removing it afterwards as soon as the lights are properly arranged.

When this is done, a small cylinder of wood, about $\frac{1}{4}$ of an inch in diameter and 6 inches long, must be held in a vertical position about 2 or 3 inches before the centre of the sheet of paper, and in such a manner that the two shadows of the cylinder, corresponding to the two lights, may be distinctly seen upon the paper.

If these shadows should be found to be of *unequal densities*, which will almost always be the case, then that light whose corresponding shadow is the densest must be removed farther off, or the other must be brought nearer to the paper, till the densities of the shadows appear to be *exactly equal*, — or, in other words, till the densities of the rays from the two lights are equal *at the surface of the paper;* when, the distances of the lights from the centre of the paper being measured, the squares of those distances will be to each other as the real intensities of the lights in question at their sources.

If, for example, the weaker light being placed at the distance of 4 feet from the centre of the paper, it should be found necessary, in order that the shadows may be of the same density, to remove the stronger light to the distance of 8 feet from that centre, in that case the real intensity of the stronger light will be to that of the weaker as 8^2 to 4^2, or as 64 to 16, or 4 to 1 ; and so for any other distances.

It is well known that, if any quality do proceed from a centre in straight lines in all directions, like the light emitted by a luminous body, its intensity at any given distance from that centre must necessarily be as the square of that distance inversely ; and hence it is evident that the intensities of the lights in question, at their sources, must be to each other as the squares of their distances from that given point *where their rays uniting are found to be of equal density.* For putting $x =$ the intensity of the light A, and $y =$ the intensity of B : if P represent the point where the rays from A and from B, meeting, are found to be of equal density or strength, and if the distance of A from P be $= m$, and the distance of B from the same point $P = n$, then, as the intensity of the light of A at P is $= \frac{x}{m^2}$, and the intensity of the light of B at the same place is $= \frac{y}{n^2}$, and as it is $\frac{x}{m^2} = \frac{y}{n^2}$ by the supposition, it will be $x : y :: m^2 : n^2$.

That the shadows being of equal density at any given point, the intensities of the illuminating rays must also *of necessity* be equal at that point is evident from hence ; that the total absence of light being perfect blackness, and the shadow corresponding to one of the lights in question being *deeper* or *fainter*, according as it is *more* or *less enlightened* by the other, when the shadows are equal the intensities of the illuminating rays must be equal likewise.

In removing the lights, in order to bring the shadows to be of the same density, care must be taken to recede from or advance towards the centre of the paper in a straight line, so that the one light may always be found exactly in the line of reflection of the other; otherwise the rays from the different lights falling upon the paper, and consequently upon the shadows, at different angles, will render the experiment fallacious.

When the intensity of one strong light is compared with the intensities of several smaller lights taken together, the smaller lights should be placed in a line perpendicular to a line drawn to the centre of the paper, and as near to each other as possible; and it is likewise necessary to place them at a greater distance from the paper than when only single lights are compared.

In all cases, it is absolutely necessary to take the greatest care that the lights compared be properly trimmed, and that they burn clear and equally, otherwise the results of the experiments will be extremely irregular and inconclusive. It is astonishing what a difference there is in the quantities of light emitted by the same candle, when it burns with its greatest brilliancy, and when it has grown dim for want of snuffing. But as this diminution of light is progressive, and as the eye insensibly conforms to the quantity of light actually present, it is not always taken notice of by the spectators. It is nevertheless very considerable in fact, as will be apparent to any one who will take the trouble to make the experiment; and so great is the fluctuation in the quantity of light emitted by burning bodies, lamps or candles, in all cases, even under the most favourable circumstances, that this is the source of the greatest difficulties I have met with in determining the relative intensities of lights by the method here proposed.

Since this method of measuring light first occurred to me, I have made many improvements in the apparatus employed in it; and I have now brought the principal instrument to such a degree of perfection that, if I might, without being suspected of affectation, I should dignify it with a name, and call it a *photometer*. I have likewise made a considerable number of experiments, with a view to determining the relative quantities of light produced by lamps and candles of different kinds, and the relative expense of lighting rooms in different ways; but, before I proceed to give an account of them, it will be necessary to describe very particularly the alterations I have found it expedient to make in the instruments employed in making them.

And, in the first place, the shadows, instead of being thrown upon a paper spread out upon the wainscot or side of the room, are now projected upon the inside of the back part of a wooden box, $7\frac{1}{4}$ inches wide, $10\frac{1}{2}$ inches long, and $3\frac{1}{4}$ inches deep, in the clear, open in front to receive the light, and painted black on the inside, in every part except the back, upon which the white paper is fastened which receives the shadows. To the under part of the box is fitted a ball and socket, by which it is attached to a stand which supports it; and the top or lid of it is fitted with hinges, in order that the box may be laid quite open as often as it is necessary to alter any part of the machinery it contains. The front of the box is likewise furnished with a falling lid or door, movable upon hinges, by which the box is closed in front when it is not in actual use.

Finding it very inconvenient to compare two shadows projected by the same cylinder, as these were either too far from each other to be compared with certainty, or when they were nearer they were in part hid from the eye by the cylinder, to remedy this inconvenience I now make use of two cylinders, which being fixed perpendicularly in the bottom of the box just described, in a line parallel to the back part of it, distant from this back $2\frac{2}{10}$ inches, and from each other 3 inches, measuring from the centres of the cylinders,— when the two lights made use of in the experiment are properly placed, these two cylinders project four shadows upon the white paper upon the inside of the back part of the box, which I shall henceforth call *the field* of the instrument, two of which shadows are in contact precisely in the middle of that field; and it is these two alone that are to be attended to. To prevent the attention being distracted by the presence of unnecessary objects, the two outside shadows are made to disappear, which is done by rendering the field of the instrument so narrow that they fall without it, upon a blackened surface, upon which they are not visible.

If the cylinders be each $\frac{4}{10}$ of an inch in diameter, and $2\frac{2}{10}$ inches in height (as they are in the instrument I have lately constructed), it will be quite sufficient if the field be $2\frac{7}{10}$ inches wide; and, as an unnecessary height of the field is not only useless, but disadvantageous, as a large surface of white paper not covered by the shadows produces too strong a glare of light, the field ought not to be more than $\frac{3}{10}$ of an inch higher than the tops of the cylinders.

In order to be able to place the lights with facility and precision, a fine black line is drawn through the middle of the field, from the top to the bottom of it, and another (horizontal) line at right angles to it, at the height of the top of the cylinders. When the tops of the shadows touch this last-mentioned line, the lights are at a *proper height;* and when, further, the two shadows are in contact with each other in the middle of the field, the lights are then in their *proper directions.*

In my new-improved instrument (for I have already caused four to be constructed), the white paper which forms the field is not fastened immediately upon the inside of the back of the box, but it is pasted upon a small pane of very fine ground glass; and this glass, thus covered, is let down into a groove made to receive it in the back of the box. This covered glass is $5\frac{1}{2}$ inches long, and as wide as the box is deep, viz. $3\frac{1}{4}$ inches, but the field of the instrument is reduced to its proper size by a screen of black pasteboard interposed before the anterior surface of this covered glass, and resting immediately upon it. A hole in this pasteboard, in the form of an oblong square, $1\frac{7}{10}$ inches wide and 2 inches high, determines the dimensions, and forms the boundaries of the field. This screen should be large enough to cover the whole inside of the back of the box; and it may be fixed in its place by means of grooves in the sides of the box, into which grooves it may be made to enter. The position of the opening above mentioned is determined by the height of the cylinders, the top of it being $\frac{3}{10}$ of an inch higher than the tops of the cylinders; and as the height of it is only 2 inches, while the height of the cylinders is $2\frac{2}{10}$ inches, it is evident that the shadows of the lower parts of the cylinders do not enter the

field.   No inconvenience arises from that circumstance; on the contrary, several advantages are derived from that arrangement.

Instead of the screen just described, I sometimes
make use of another, which differs from it only in this,
that the hole in it, which determines the form and
dimensions of the field, instead of being quadrangular,
is round, and $1\frac{6}{10}$ inches in diameter.   And, when this
screen is made use of, the shadows are increased in
width (by means which will hereafter be described) in
such a manner as completely to fill the field, appearing under the form of two hemispheres, or rather half
disks, touching each other in a vertical line.   The
object I had in view in reducing the field and the
shadows to a circular form was this: I imagined that
by diminishing the number of objects capable of acting upon the mind, and particularly by removing all
straight lines and angles and all unnecessary varieties
of lights and shades, the attention might be concen-
trated and fixed in such a manner as to render the
sense of sight peculiarly acute in distinguishing any
difference in the simple objects presented to the eye.
But, however plausible this reasoning may appear, I
own the experiment did not answer my expectation.
It is true the apparent densities of two equal hemispheres of shade, in contact with each other, may be
compared with great facility, and when no discernible
difference is to be perceived between them it is more
than probable that they are in fact very nearly equal;
but still I have found by experience that two equal
parallelograms of shade, in contact with each other,
may be compared with the same ease, and, I have
reason to think, with equal certainty, and *that* even

when these united shadows are bounded on three sides by a perfectly white surface, illuminated by the direct rays of two strong lights, — that is to say, when the screen with the quadrangular opening or field is made use of.

In describing the cylinders by which the shadows are projected, I said they were fixed in the bottom of the box; but as the diameters of the shadows of the cylinders vary in some small degree, in proportion as the lights are broader or narrower, and as they are brought nearer to or removed farther from the photometer, in order to be able in all cases to bring these shadows to be of the same diameter, which I have found by experience to be advantageous, in order to judge with greater facility and certainty when the shadows are of the same density, I have rendered the cylinders movable about their axes, and have added to each a vertical wing $\frac{11}{20}$ of an inch wide, $\frac{1}{16}$ of an inch thick, and of equal height with the cylinder itself, and firmly fixed to it from the top to the bottom. This wing commonly lies in the middle of the shadow of the cylinder, and as long as it remains in that situation it has no effect whatever; but, when it is necessary that the diameter of one of the shadows should be increased, the corresponding cylinder is moved about its axis, till the wing just described, emerging out of the shadow and intercepting a portion of light, brings the shadow projected upon the field of the instrument to be of the width or diameter required. In this operation it is always necessary to turn the cylinder outwards, or in such a manner that the augmentation of the width of the shadow may take place on that side of it which is opposite to the shadow corresponding to the other light. The necessity for that precaution will appear evident to any one who has a just idea of the instrument in question and of the manner of making use of it.

It is by means of these wings attached to the cylinders that the widths of the shadows are augmented, so as to fill the whole field of the *photometer*, when the screen with the circular opening is made use of.

As the lower ends of the cylinders, which pass through the holes made to receive them in the bottom of the box, are about $\frac{1}{20}$ of an inch less in diameter than their upper parts, which cast the shadows; and as they not only go quite through the bottom of the box (which is an inch thick), but project near an inch below its inferior surface; and, lastly, as these cylinders are not firmly fixed in these holes, — it is easy, by taking hold of the ends of them which project below the bottom of the box, to turn about the cylinders upon their axes, even without opening the box. I said above that the height of the vertical wing attached to each of the cylinders was equal to the height of the cylinder itself. This must be understood to mean not the total length of the cylinder, comprehending that part of it which passes into and through the bottom of the box, but merely its height above the bottom of the box, or that part of it which projects above the bottom of the box.

As it is absolutely necessary that the cylinders should constantly remain precisely perpendicular to the bottom of the box or parallel to each other, it will be best to construct them of brass, and instead of fixing them immediately to the bottom of the box (which being of wood may warp) to fix them to a strong, thick piece of well-hammered plate brass, which plate of brass may be afterwards fastened to the bottom of the box by means of one strong screw. In this manner two of my best instruments are constructed. And, in order to secure the cylinders still more firmly in their vertical positions, they are furnished with broad flat rings or projections, where they rest upon the brass plate; which rings are $\frac{1}{10}$ of an inch thick, and equal in diameter to the projection of the wing of the cylinder, to the bottom of which they afford a firm support. (See Plate I., Fig. 1.) These cylinders are likewise forcibly pushed, or rather pulled, against the brass plate upon which they rest, by means of compressed spiral springs placed between the under side of that plate and the lower ends of the cylinders.

Of whatever material the cylinders be constructed, and whatever be their forms or dimensions, it is absolutely necessary that they, as well as every other part of the photometer except the field, should be well painted of a deep black, dead colour. That, and that alone, will prevent the inconveniencies which would otherwise arise from reflected light and from the presence of too great a number of visible objects.

In order to move the lights to and from the photometer with greater ease and precision, I provided two long and narrow but very strong and steady tables, in the middle of each of which there is a straight groove, in which a sliding carriage, upon which the light is placed, is drawn along by means of a cord which is fastened to it before and behind, and which passing over pulleys at each end of the table goes round a cylinder, which cylinder is furnished with a winch, and is so placed, near the end of the table adjoining the photometer, that the observer can turn it about, without taking his eye from the field of the instrument. (See Plate III., Fig. 3, and Plate IV., Fig. 4.)

Many advantages are derived from this arrangement: as, first, the observer can move the lights as he finds necessary, without the help of an assistant, and even without removing his eye from the shadows; secondly, each light is always precisely in the line of direction in which it ought to be, in order that the shadows may be in contact in the middle of the vertical plane of the photometer; and, thirdly, the sliding motion of the lights being perfectly soft and gentle, that motion produces little or no effect upon the lights themselves, either to increase or diminish their brilliancy.

These tables, which are 10 inches wide and 35 inches high, and the one of them 12 feet and the other 20 feet long, are placed at an angle of 60° from each other, and in such a situation with respect to the photometer that lines drawn through their middles in the direction of their lengths meet in a point exactly under the middle of the vertical plane or field of the photometer, and from that point the distances of the lights are measured; the sides of the tables being divided into English inches, and a Vernier, showing tenths of inches, being fixed to each of the sliding carriages upon which the lights are placed. (See the Plates III. and IV.)

These carriages are so contrived that they can be raised or lowered at pleasure, which is absolutely necessary, in order that the lights may be always of a proper height; namely, that they may be in the same horizontal plane with the tops of the cylinders of the photometer.

The method of ascertaining when the lights are at the proper height has already been described.

In order that the two long and narrow tables or platforms just described, upon which the lights move, may remain immovable in their proper positions, they are both firmly fixed to a very strong stand which supports the photometer; and in order that the motion of the carriages which carry the lights may be as soft and gentle as possible, they are made to slide upon parallel brass wires, 9 inches asunder, about $\frac{1}{10}$ of an inch in diameter, and well polished, which are stretched out upon the tables from one end to the other. (See Plate III.)

The pane of glass covered with white paper, which, being fixed in a groove in the back of the box, constitutes the vertical plane upon which the shadows are projected, is $5\frac{1}{2}$ inches long and $3\frac{1}{4}$ inches wide, as has already been observed, which is much larger than the dimensions assigned above for the field; namely, $1\frac{7}{10}$ inches wide and 2 inches high. I had two objects in view in this arrangement: first, to render it easier to fix this plane in its proper position; and, secondly, to be able to augment occasionally the dimensions of the field, by removing entirely the black pasteboard screen from before this plane, or making use of another with a larger aperture, which is sometimes advantageous.*

* Since writing the above, I have made a little alteration in the form of the box which contains my photometer. The front of it, instead of being open, is now closed ; and the light is admitted through two horizontal tubes, which are placed so as to form an angle of 60°, their axes meeting at the centre of the field of the instrument. (See Fig. 1, Plate I.) The field of the photometer is viewed through an opening made for that purpose in the middle of the front of the box, between the two tubes above mentioned. The Plates I., II., III., and IV. will serve to give a clearer idea of the instrument, in its present most improved state.

Having now, as I imagine, sufficiently described all the essential parts of these instruments, it remains for me to give some account of the precautions which, from experience, I have found it necessary to employ in making use of them.

And, first, with respect to the distance at which lights whose intensities are to be compared should be placed from the field of the photometer, I have found that, when the weakest of the lights in question is about as strong as a common wax candle, *that light* may most advantageously be placed from 30 to 36 inches from the centre of the field; and when it is weaker or stronger, proportionally nearer or farther off. When the lights are too near, the shadows will not be well defined; and when they are too far off, they will be too weak.

It will greatly facilitate the calculations necessary in drawing conclusions from experiments of this kind, if some steady light, of a proper degree of strength for that purpose, be assumed as a standard by which all others may be compared. I have chosen for that purpose an Argand's lamp, made in London, and very well finished; and though the quantity of light emitted by this or any other kind of lamp is very various, depending in a great measure upon the length to which the wick is drawn out, yet I have found by repeated trials that this lamp, once properly adjusted, continues to emit light more equally for a considerable time than any other lamp, and much more so than any candle whatever.

At the beginning of each experiment I adjust this standard light in the following manner: Having placed the lamp upon its carriage, at the distance of

100 inches from the centre of the field of the photo-meter, measuring from the centre of the circular flame of the lamp, a cylindric wax candle, of known weight and dimensions, and which is kept merely for that purpose, being lighted and trimmed, and made to burn with the greatest possible degree of brilliancy, is placed over against it, at a certain given distance (33 inches), and then the wick of the lamp is drawn out or short-ened, as it is found necessary, till the shadows corre-sponding to the lamp and to the candle are precisely of the same density: this done, the proof candle is ex-tinguished, and laid by for further use, and the pro-jected experiment is immediately commenced.

Here the proof candle is, properly speaking, *the standard;* but the lamp is to be preferred to it, for the experiments, on account of the superior constancy or equality of its light.

The only danger of error in this mode of proceeding arises from the difficulty of procuring proof candles which shall always give precisely the same quantity of light, or of making the same candle burn with exactly the same brilliancy at different times. I flattered my-self at one time that even this cause of error and uncertainty, however insurmountable the difficulty ap-pears, might be in a great measure removed. I con-ceived that if the light from the standard lamp and that of the proof candle, brought to be of the same intensity at the surface of the vertical plane, were really stronger at one time than at another, the equal shadows of the cylinders would be proportionally deeper, and that by comparing at different times the density of those shadows with a painted scale of shades, regularly graduated, any difference in the intensity of the standard light might be discovered and compensated; but upon making the experiment I found, what indeed a little patient reflection would have enabled me to foresee, that the apparent density of the two equal shadows corresponding to the lights compared with a painted scale of shades, *exposed in the same light*, is ever the same, however the intensity of the rays at the surface upon which those shadows are projected may vary.

There is, however, another method by which I think it probable that the standard lamp might be adjusted with the requisite degree of precision. It appears, from a considerable number of experiments, of which I shall hereafter give a more particular account, that the quantity of light emitted by a lamp on any given construction, which burns with a clear flame *and without smoke*, is in all cases as the quantity of oil consumed. If therefore the standard lamp be so adjusted as always to consume a certain given quantity of oil in a given time, there is much reason to suppose that it may then be depended on as a just standard of light.

In order to abridge the calculations necessary in these inquiries, it will always be advantageous to place the standard lamp at the distance of 100 inches from the photometer, and to assume the intensity of its light at its source equal to unity. In this case (calling this standard light A, the intensity of the light at its source $= x = 1$, and the distance of the lamp from the field of the photometer $= m = 100$) the intensity of the illumination at the field of the photometer $(= \frac{x}{m^2}$*$)$ will be expressed by the fraction $\frac{1}{100^2} = \frac{1}{10000}$; and the relative intensity of any other light which is

* See Page 5.

compared with it, according to the directions before given, may be found by the following proportion: Calling this light B, and putting $y =$ its intensity at its source, and $n =$ its distance from the field of the photometer, expressed in English inches, as it is $\frac{y}{n^2} = \frac{x}{m^2}$ (as was before shown), or, instead of $\frac{x}{m^2}$, writing its value $= \frac{1}{10000}$, it will be $\frac{y}{n^2} = \frac{1}{10000}$, and consequently y is to 1 as n^2 is to 10,000; or the intensity of the light B at its source is to the intensity of the standard light A at its source as the square of the distance of the light B from the middle of the field of the instrument, expressed in inches, is to 10,000; and hence it is $y = \frac{n^2}{10000}$.

I have been the more particular in this account of the instruments employed in these inquiries, the manner in which the experiments were conducted, and the principles upon which the conclusions drawn from them are founded, not only because, the subject being new, the most particular information upon all these points is absolutely necessary, to enable others to judge with certainty of the matter submitted to their examination, but also because I was very desirous of affording every information and assistance in my power to those who may be disposed to prosecute these curious and entertaining researches.

Hoping that this apology may be thought sufficient to excuse the prolixity of these descriptions, I shall now proceed to give a short account of such experiments as I have hitherto found leisure to make with this apparatus.

My first attempts were to determine how far it might be possible to ascertain, by direct experiments, the certainty of the assumed law of the diminution of the intensity of the light emitted by luminous bodies;

namely, that *the intensity of the light is everywhere as the squares of the distances from the luminous body inversely.* These experiments appeared to me the more necessary, as it is quite evident that this law can only hold good when the light is propagated in perfectly transparent or unresisting spaces, or where — suffering no diminution whatever from the medium — its intensity is diminished merely in consequence of the divergency of the rays; and as it is more than probable that air, even in its purest state, is far from being perfectly transparent.

For greater perspicuity, I shall arrange all my experiments and inquiries under general heads, and shall begin by prefixing to those which relate to the subject now under consideration the general title of

Experiments upon the Resistance of the Air to Light.

EXPERIMENT No. 1.

Two equal wax candles, well trimmed, and which were found by a previous experiment to burn with exactly the same degree of brightness, were placed *together* on one side before the photometer, and their united light was counterbalanced by the light of an Argand's lamp, well trimmed, and burning very equally, placed on the other side over against them. The lamp was placed at the distance of 100 inches from the field of the photometer, and it was found that the two burning candles (which were placed as near together as possible, without their flames affecting each other by the currents of air they produced) were just able to counterbalance the light of the lamp at the field of the photometer, when they were placed at the distance of 60.8 inches from that field. One of the candles being now taken away and extinguished, the other was brought nearer to the field of the instrument, till its light was found to be just able, singly, to counterbalance the light of the lamp; and this was found to happen when it had arrived at the distance of 43.4 inches.

In this experiment, as the candles burned with equal brightness, it is evident that the intensities of their united and single lights were as 2 to 1, and in that proportion ought, according to the assumed theory, the squares of the distances, 60.8 and 43.4, to be; and in fact $60.8^2 = 3696.64$ is to $43.4^2 = 1883.56$ as 2 is to 1 very nearly.

Again, in another experiment (No. 2), the distances were: —

    With two candles = 54 inches.   Square = 2916.
    With one candle = 38.6   = 1489.96

Upon another trial (Experiment No. 3): —

    With two candles = 54.6 inches.   Square = 2981.16
    With one candle = 39.7   = 1576.09

And in the 4th experiment: —

    With two candles = 58.4 inches.   Square = 3410.56
    With one candle = 42.2   = 1780.84

And taking the mean of the results of these four experiments: —

	Squares of the distances.	
	With two candles.	With one candle.
In the Experiment No. 1,	3696.64	1883.56
No. 2,	2916.	1489.96
No. 3,	2981.16	1576.09
No. 4,	3410.56	1780.84
	4) 13004.36	4) 6730 45
Means	3251.09 and	1682.61

which again are very nearly as 2 to 1.

With regard to these experiments, it may be observed that were the resistance of the air to light, or the diminution of the light from the imperfect transparency of air, sensible within the limits of the inconsiderable distances at which the candles were placed from the photometer, in that case the distance of the two equal lights united ought to be to the distance of one of them single in a ratio less than that of the square root of 2 to the square root of 1. For if the intensity of a light emitted by a luminous body, *in a space void of all resistance*, be diminished in the proportion of the squares of the distances, it must of necessity be diminished in a still higher ratio when the light passes through a resisting medium, or one which is not perfectly transparent; and from the difference of those ratios, — namely, that of the squares of the distances, and that other *higher ratio* found by the experiment, — the resistance of the medium might be ascertained. This I have taken much pains to do with respect to air, but have not as yet succeeded in these endeavours, the transparency of air being so great that the diminution which light suffers in passing through a few inches or even through several feet of it is not sensible.

Having found upon repeated trials that the light of a lamp, properly trimmed, is incomparably more equal than that of a candle, whose wick continually growing longer renders its light extremely fluctuating, I substituted lamps to candles in these experiments, and made such other variations in the manner of conducting them as I thought bid fair to lead to a discovery of the resistance of the air to light, were it possible to render that resistance sensible within the confined limits of my machinery.

Having provided two lamps, the one an Argand's lamp, which I made to burn with the greatest possible brilliancy; the other a small common lamp, with a single, round, and very small wick, which, burning with a very clear, steady flame, and without any visible smoke, emitted only about $\frac{1}{25}$ part as much light as the Argand's lamp, — these lamps being placed over against each other before the field of the photometer, their lights were found to be in equilibrium when, the smaller being placed at the distance of 20 inches from the centre of that field, the greater was removed to the distance of 101 inches. I now concluded that, if the smaller light were to be removed to the distance of 40 inches, it would be necessary, in order to restore the equilibrium of light or equality of the shadows in the field of the photometer, to remove the greater light to the distance of 202 inches; that is to say, if the diminution of the light arising from the imperfect transparency of the air should not be perceptible within the limits of that distance. But if, on the contrary, it should be found upon repeated trials that the equilibrium was restored when the greater light had arrived at a distance *short* of 202 inches, I might thence conclude that such effect might safely be attributed to the imperfect transparency of the air; for notwithstanding that the light of the smaller lamp would of course be diminished as well as that of the greater, yet as there is every reason to suppose that the diminution, whatever it may be, must ever be proportional to the distance through which the light passes in the medium; as the augmentation of the distance through which the light of the smaller lamp passes is no more than 20 inches, while that of the greater is made to pass through an additional distance, amounting to more than 100 inches, it is evident that the diminution of the light of the greater lamp, arising from the imperfect transparency of the medium, must be greater than the diminution of the light of the smaller lamp, arising from the same cause; and consequently that the effects of such diminution would become apparent in the experiment, were they in reality considerable.

The following table will show the results of the experiments which were made with a view to determine that fact : —

Experiments.	Distance of the smaller light.		Distance of the greater light.		Second distance of the greater light, *computed* according to the assumed law of the squares of the distances.	Difference between the result of the experiment and the theory.
		Inches.		Inches.	Inches.	Inches.
No. 5.	First dist.	20	First dist.	101	202	+ 1
	Second dist.	40	Second dist.	203		
No. 6.	First dist.	20	First dist.	100.2	200.4	— 2.1
	Second dist.	40	Second dist.	198.3		
No. 7.	First dist.	20	First dist.	100.8	201.6	+ 0.5
	Second dist.	40	Second dist.	202.1		
No. 8.	First dist.	20	First dist.	101.5	203	+ 1
	Second dist.	40	Second dist.	204		
No. 9.	First dist.	50	First dist.	100	200	— 2
	Second dist.	100	Second dist.	198		
No. 10.	First dist.	50	First dist.	95.5	191	+ 1.2
	Second dist.	100	Second dist.	192.2		
No. 11.	First dist.	50	First dist.	95.1	190.2	+ 1
	Second dist.	100	Second dist.	191.2		
No. 12.	First dist.	50	First dist.	96	192	+ 0.4
	Second dist.	100	Second dist.	192.4		

In the four last experiments, instead of the small lamp above described, a common Argand lamp was made use of, the wick of which was only drawn out so far as to cause it to emit about ¼ part as much light as the other Argand's lamp, burning with its greatest brilliancy, which was placed over against it.

In order that in judging of the equality of the shadows, my mind might be totally unbiassed by my expectations, or by any opinions I might previously have formed with respect to the probable issue of the various experiments, keeping my eye constantly fixed upon the field of the photometer, and causing the light whose corresponding shadow was to be brought to be of equal density with the standard to move backwards and forwards, by means of the winch which I had constantly in my hand, — as soon as the shadows appeared to me to be perfectly equal, I gave notice to an assistant to observe, and silently to write down, the distance of the lamp or candle, so that I did not even know what that distance was till the experiment was ended, and till it was too late to attempt to correct any supposed errors of my eyes by my wishes or by my expectations, had I been weak enough to have had a wish in a matter of this kind. I do not know that any predilection I might have had for any favourite theory would have been able to have operated so strongly upon my mind and upon my senses as to have made *black* and *white* appear to me otherwise than as they really were; but this I know, that I was very glad to find means to avoid being *led into temptation.*

But to return to the foregoing experiments : the results of them, so far from affording means for ascertaining the resistance of the air to light, do not even indicate any resistance at all; on the contrary, it might almost be inferred from some of them that the intensity of the light emitted by a luminous body in air is diminished in a ratio *less* than that of the squares of the distances ; but as such a conclusion would involve an evident absurdity, namely, that light moving in air, its absolute quantity, instead of being diminished, actually goes on to *increase*, that conclusion can by no means be admitted.

Besides the experiments above mentioned, I made a great number of others, similar to them, and with the same view; but, as their results were all nearly the same, I have not thought it worth while to lengthen this paper by inserting a particular account of them. In general, they all conspired to show that the resistance of the air to light was too inconsiderable to be perceptible, and that the assumed law of the diminution of the intensity of the light may with safety be depended on.

That the transparency of air in its purest state is very great is evident from the very considerable distances at which objects, and such even as are but faintly illuminated, are visible ; and I was by no means surprised that its want of transparency could not be rendered sensible in the small distance to which my experiments were necessarily confined. But still I think means may be found for rendering its resistance to light apparent, and even of subjecting that resistance to some tolerably accurate measure.

An accurate determination of the relative intensity of the sun's or moon's light, when seen at different heights above the horizon, or when seen from the top and from the bottom of a very high mountain, in very clear weather, would probably lead to a discovery of the real amount of resistance of the air to light.*

Of the Loss of Light in its Passage through Plates or Panes of different Kinds of Glass.

In these experiments I proceeded in the following manner. Having provided two equal Argand's lamps, A and B, well trimmed, and burning with very clear bright flames, they were placed over against each other before the photometer, each at the distance of 100 inches from the field of the instrument, and the light of B was brought to be of the same intensity as that of A, or the shadows were brought to be of the same density, which was done by lengthening or shortening the wick of the lamp B, as the occasion required. This done, and the two lamps now burning with precisely the same degree of brilliancy, a pane of fine, clear, transparent, well-polished glass, such as is commonly made use of in the construction of looking-glasses, six inches square, placed vertically upon a stand, in a small frame, was interposed before the lamp B at the distance of about four feet from it, and in such a position that the light emitted by it was obliged to go perpendicularly through the middle of the pane, in order to arrive at the field of the pho-

---

* This method of ascertaining the diminution of light in passing through the atmosphere was proposed, and put in practice, many years ago, by an ingenious French philosopher, M. Bouguer, of the Royal Academy of Sciences. See Traité d'Optique pour la Gradation de la Lumière: Ouvrage posthume de M. Bouguer, de l'Académie Royale des Sciences, etc. Published at Paris by the Abbé de la Caille, in the year 1760.

When this paper was written, I had not seen that most ingenious and learned dissertation. It did not come into my hands till a few months ago (in November, 1801) when, being at Paris, my worthy and respectable friend the Senator Laplace procured it for me.

tometer. The consequence of this was that, the light of the lamp B being diminished and weakened in its passage through the glass, the illuminations of the shadows in the field of the photometer were no longer equal, the shadow corresponding to the lamp A being now less enlightened by the light of the lamp B than the shadow corresponding to the lamp B was enlightened by the undiminished light of the lamp A.

To determine precisely the exact amount of this diminution of the light of the lamp B (which was the main object of the experiment), nothing more was necessary than to bring this lamp nearer to the field of the photometer, till its light passing through the glass should be in equilibrium with the direct light of the lamp A, or, in other words, till the equality of the shadows should be restored; and this I found actually happened when the lamp B from 100 inches was brought to the distance of 90.2 inches from the field of the photometer.

Now, as it has already been shown that the intensities of the lights are as the squares of their distances from the field of the photometer, the illuminations being equal at that field, it is evident that the light of the lamp B was diminished, in this experiment, in its passage through the pane of glass, in the ratio of 100^2 to 90.2^2, or as 1 to .8136; so that no more than .8136 parts of the light which impinged against the glass found its way through it, the other .1864 parts being dispersed and lost.

To assure myself that the lamps still continued to emit the same relative quantities of light as at the beginning of the experiment, I now removed the pane of glass, and found that the equality of the shadows was again restored, when the lamp B arrived at its former station, 100 inches from the field of the photometer.

This experiment I repeated no less than 10 times, and found the loss of light in its passage through this pane of glass, taking a mean of all the experiments, to be .1973 parts of the whole quantity that impinged against it; the variations in the results of the various experiments being from .1720 to .2108.

In four experiments, with another pane of the same kind of glass, the loss of light was .1836, .1732, .2056, and .1853; mean, .1869.

When the two panes of this glass were placed before the lamp B at the same time, but without touching each other, and the light made to pass through them both, the loss of light in four different experiments was .3089, .3259, .3209, and .3180; mean, .3184.

With another pane of glass of the same kind, but a little thinner, the mean loss of light in four experiments was .1813.

With a very thin, clean pane of clear white or colourless window-glass, not ground, the loss of light in four experiments was .1324, .1218, .1213, and .1297; mean, .1263. When the experiment was made with this same pane of glass a very little dirty, the loss of light was more than doubled.

Might not this apparatus be very usefully employed by the optician, to determine the degree of transparency of the glass he employs, and direct his choice in the provision of that important article in his trade?

In making these experiments, a great deal of the trouble may well be spared, for there is no use whatever in bringing the two lamps A and B to burn with the same degree of brilliancy; all that is necessary being to bring the shadows to be of the same density with the glass and without it, noting the distance of the lamp B in each case (the lamp A remaining immovable in its place); for the relative quantity of light lost will ever be accurately shown by the ratio of the squares of those distances, whatever be the relative brilliancy with which the two lamps burn. The experiment is more striking, and the consequences drawn from it rather more obvious, when the lamps are made to burn with equal flames; otherwise that equality is of no real advantage.

Of the Loss of Light in its Reflection from the Surface of a plane Glass Mirror.

In these experiments the method of proceeding was much the same as in those just mentioned. The lamps A and B burning with clear, bright, and steady flames were placed before the field of the photometer, and one of them was moved backwards and forwards till the illuminations of the shadows in the field of the instrument were found to be precisely equal. The distance of the lamp B being then noted, this lamp was removed; and a mirror being put in its place, but nearer the field of the photometer, the lamp was so placed that its rays, striking the centre of the mirror, were reflected against the field of the photometer, where, by bringing the lamp nearer to or removing it farther from the mirror, the illumination of the field by those reflected rays was now brought to be in equilibrium with the illumination of the standard lamp, and then the distance of the lamp from the centre of the mirror, and the distance from thence to the centre of the field, were carefully measured and noted. These two distances added together was the real distance through which the rays passed in order to arrive at the field of the photometer.

Now, as there is always a loss of light in reflection, it is evident that the reflected rays must come to the field of the photometer weakened, and that in order to illuminate this field by these reflected rays as strongly as it was illuminated by the direct rays of the same lamp, the lamp must be brought nearer to the field. It is likewise evident, from what has already been said, that the ratio of the squares of those distances of the lamp when its rays pass on directly, and when they arrive after having been reflected are found to illuminate equally the field of the photometer, will be an accurate measure of the loss of the light in reflection.

The following table will show the results of five experiments with a small but most excellent glass mirror made by Ramsden. This mirror, which makes part of an optical instrument I caused to be constructed in London about twelve years ago, is 7 inches long and $5\frac{1}{2}$ inches wide, and I suppose is as perfect as ever glass mirror was of that size.

To facilitate the comparison of the results of the experiments, the lamp B at the beginning of each experiment (when the intensity of its direct rays was compared with the intensity of the standard lamp) was placed at the distance of 100 inches, the standard lamp being occasionally moved, in order to produce an equality of the shadows.

Experiments.	The angle of incidence.	Distance of the centre of the mirror from the centre of the field.	Distance of the lamp from the centre of the mirror.	Real distance of the lamp, or length of the reflected rays.	Light lost in the reflection.
		Inches.	Inches.	Inches.	Parts.
1	60°	40	40.8	80.8	.3472
2	85°	—	41.	81.	.3439
3	45°	—	41.5	81.5	.3358
4	60°	—	39.5	79.5	.3680
5	70°	—	40.5	80.5	.3520

The mean of these five experiments gives for the loss of light .3494; and from hence it appears that more than $\frac{1}{3}$ part of the light which falls upon the best glass mirror that can be constructed is lost in reflection.

The loss with mirrors of indifferent quality is still more considerable. With a very bad common looking-glass the loss, in one experiment, appeared to be .4816 parts; and with another looking-glass it was .4548 parts in one experiment, and .4430 in another. I should certainly have made an experiment to determine the loss of light in its reflection from the surface of a plane metallic mirror, but I had no such mirror at hand.

The difference of the angles of incidence at the surface of the mirror, within the limits mentioned, namely, from 45° to 85°, did not appear to affect in any sensible degree the results of the experiments. I also found upon trial that the effect produced by the difference of the angles at which light impinges against a sheet of transparent glass through which it passes is, within the limits of 40° or 50° from the perpendicular, but very trifling.

Of the relative Quantities of Oil consumed and of Light emitted by an Argand's Lamp, and by a Lamp on the common Construction, with a Riband Wick.

The brilliancy of the Argand's lamp is not only unrivalled, but the invention is, in the highest degree, ingenious, and the instrument useful for many purposes; but still, to judge of its real merits, as an illuminator, it was necessary to know whether it gives more light than another lamp *in proportion to the oil consumed.* This point I determined in the following manner.

Having placed an Argand's lamp, well trimmed, and burning with its greatest brilliancy, before my photometer, and over against it a very excellent common lamp with a riband wick, about an inch wide, and which burned with a clear bright flame without the least appearance of smoke, I found the intensities of the light emitted by the two lamps to be to each other as 17956 to 9063; the densities of the shadows being equal when the Argand's being placed at the distance of 134 inches, the common lamp was placed at the distance of 95.2 inches, from the field of the photometer.

Both lamps having been very exactly weighed when they were lighted, they were now (without being removed from their places before the photometer) caused to burn with the same brilliancy just 30 minutes; when they were extinguished, and weighed again, and were found to have consumed of oil, the Argand's lamp $\frac{253}{8192}$, and the common lamp $\frac{163}{8192}$, of a Bavarian pound.

Now as the quantity of light produced by the Argand's lamp in this experiment is to the quantity produced by the common lamp as 17956 to 9063, or as 187 to 100, while the quantity of oil consumed by the former is to that consumed by the latter only in the ratio of 253 to 163, or as 155 to 100, it is evident that the quantity of light produced by the combustion of a given quantity of oil in an Argand's lamp is greater than that produced by burning the same quantity in a common lamp, in the ratio of 187 to 155, or as 100 to 85.

The saving, therefore, of oil which arises from making use of an Argand's lamp, instead of a common lamp, in the production of light, is evident; and it appears from this experiment that that saving cannot amount to less than 15 per cent. How far the advantage of this saving may, under certain circumstances, be counterbalanced by inconveniences that may attend the making use of this improved lamp, I will not pretend to determine.

Of the relative Quantities of Light emitted by an Argand's Lamp and by a common Wax Candle.

I have made a considerable number of experiments to determine this point, and the general result of them is that a common Argand's lamp, burning with its usual brightness, gives about as much light as *nine good wax candles;* but the sizes and qualities of candles are so various, and the light produced by the same candle so fluctuating, that it is very difficult to ascertain with any kind of precision what a common wax candle is, or how much light it ought to give. I

once found that my Argand's lamp, when it was burning with its greatest brilliancy, gave twelve times as
much light as a good wax candle ¾ of an inch in diameter, but never more.

Of the Fluctuations of the Light emitted by Candles.

To determine to what the ordinary variations in the
quantity of light emitted by a common wax candle
might amount, I took such a candle, and lighting it
placed it before the photometer, and over against it an
Argand's lamp, which was burning with a very steady
flame; and measuring the intensity of the light emitted
by the candle from time to time, during an hour, the
candle being occasionally snuffed when it appeared to
stand in need of it, its light was found to vary from
100 to about 60. The light of a wax candle of an
inferior quality was still more unequal, but even this
was but trifling compared to the inequalities of the
light of a tallow candle.

An ordinary tallow candle, of rather an inferior
quality, having been just snuffed and burning with
its greatest brilliancy, its light was as 100; in eleven
minutes it was but 39; after eight minutes more had
elapsed, its light was reduced to 23; and in ten minutes more, or twenty-nine minutes after it had been
last snuffed, its light was reduced to 16. Upon being
again snuffed, it recovered its original brilliancy, 100.

Of the relative Quantities of Beeswax, Tallow, Olive Oil, Rape Oil, and Linseed Oil, consumed in the Production of Light.

In order to ascertain the relative quantities of beeswax and of olive oil consumed in the production of

light, I proceeded in the following manner. Having provided an end of a wax candle of the best quality, .68 of an inch in diameter, and about 4 inches in length, and a lamp with five small wicks, which I had found upon trial to give the same quantity of light as the candle, I weighed very exactly the candle and the lamp filled with oil, and then placing them at equal distances (40 inches) before the field of the photometer I lighted them both at the same time; and after having caused them to burn with precisely the same degree of brightness *just one complete hour*, I extinguished them both, and weighing them a second time I found that 100 parts of wax and 129 parts of oil had been consumed.

Hence it appears that the consumption of *beeswax* is to the consumption of *olive oil* in the production of the *same given quantity of light* as 100 is to 129.

In this experiment no circumstance was neglected that could tend to render the result of it conclusive. Care was taken to snuff the candle very often with a pair of sharp scissors, in order to make it burn constantly with the same degree of brilliancy; and the light of the lamp was, during the whole time, kept in the most exact equilibrium with the light of the candle, which was easily done by occasionally drawing out a little more or less one or more of its five equal wicks. These wicks, which were placed in a right line perpendicular to a line drawn from the middle wick to the middle of the field of the photometer, were about $\frac{1}{10}$ of an inch in diameter each, and $\frac{1}{4}$ of an inch from each other, and when they were lighted their flames united into one broad, thin, and very clear white flame, without the least appearance of smoke.

In order to ascertain the relative consumption of olive oil and rape oil in the production of light, two lamps like that just described were made use of; and, the experiment being made with all possible care, the consumption of *olive oil* appeared to be to that of *rape oil*, in the production of the same quantity of light, as 129 is to 125.

The experiment being afterwards repeated with *olive oil* and very pure *linseed oil*, the consumption of olive oil appeared to be to that of the linseed oil as 129 to 120.

The experiment being twice made with *olive oil* and with *a tallow candle,* — once when the candle, by being often snuffed, was made to burn constantly with the greatest possible brilliancy, and once when it was suffered to burn the whole time with a very dim light, owing to the want of snuffing, — the results of these experiments were very remarkable.

When the candle burned with a clear bright flame, the consumption of the olive oil was to the consumption of the tallow as 129 is to 101; but, when the candle burned with a dim light, the consumption of the olive oil was to the consumption of the tallow as 129 is to 229. So that it appeared from this last experiment that the tallow, instead of being nearly as productive of light in its combustion as beeswax, as it appeared to be when the candle was kept constantly well snuffed, was now, when the candle was suffered to burn with a dim light, by far less so than oil.

But this is not all: what is still more extraordinary is that the very same candle, burning with a long wick and a dim light, actually consumed *more tallow* than when, being properly snuffed, it burned with a clear, bright flame, and gave near *three times as much light !*

To be enabled to judge of the relative quantities of light actually produced by the candle in the two experiments, it will suffice to know that, in order to counterbalance this light at the field of the photometer, it required in the former experiment the consumption of 141 parts, but in the latter only the consumption of 64 parts of olive oil.   But in the former experiment 110 parts, and in the latter 114 parts of tallow, were actually found to be consumed.   These parts were 8192ths of a Bavarian pound.

From the results of all the foregoing experiments it appears that the relative expense of the under-mentioned inflammable substances, in the production of any given quantity of light, is as follows : —

		Equal parts in weight.
Beeswax.	A good wax candle, kept well snuffed, and burning with a clear bright flame	100
Tallow.	A good tallow candle, kept well snuffed, and burning with a bright flame	101
	The same tallow candle burning very dim for want of snuffing	229
Olive oil.	Burned in an Argand's lamp	110
	The same burned in a common lamp, with a clear bright flame, without smoke	129
Rape oil.	Burned in the same manner	125
Linseed oil.	Likewise burned in the same manner	120

I should have been very glad to have made the experiment with whale oil, but there was none to be had in the country I inhabited at that time (Bavaria).

With the foregoing table, and the prices current of the therein-mentioned articles, the relative *prices of light* produced by those different materials may very readily be computed.

The light of a wax candle, for instance, costs just

nine times more at Munich than the same quantity of
light produced by burning rape oil in an Argand's
lamp.

Of the Transparency of Flame.

To ascertain the transparency of flame or the measure of the resistance it opposes to the passage of
foreign or extraneous light through it, I placed before
the photometer, over against the standard lamp, two
burning wax candles, well trimmed; and putting them
near together, sometimes by the sides of each other,
and sometimes in a straight line behind each other, I
found that, when their distances from the field of the
photometer were the same, the intensity of the illumination was to all appearance the same, whether the
light of the one was made to pass through the flame of
the other or not. And the same held good, with very
little variation, when three and even when four candles
were made use of in the experiment, instead of two.

I even caused a lamp to be constructed with nine
round wicks, placed in a horizontal line, and just so
far asunder as to prevent their flames uniting, and no
farther. And I found, upon repeating the experiment
with this lamp, that the result was much the same as
with the candles; the intensity of the illumination at
the field of the photometer being very nearly the same,
whether these nine lights were placed so as to cover
and pass through each other, or not.

But I afterwards found means to demonstrate the
very great transparency of flame by a still more simple
experiment. Suspecting that the only reason why
bodies are not visible through a sheet of vivid flame is

that the light of the flame affects the eye in such a manner as to render it insensible to the weaker light emitted by or reflected from the objects placed behind it, I conceived that a very strong light would not only be visible through a weak flame, but also (as all transparent bodies are invisible) that it might perhaps cause the flame totally to disappear.   To determine that fact, I took a lighted candle, at mid-day, the sun shining moderately bright, and holding it up between my eye and the sun I found the flame of the candle to disappear entirely.   It was not even necessary, in order to cause the flame to become invisible, to bring it to be directly between the eye and the body of the sun: it was sufficient for that purpose to bring it into the neighbourhood of the sun where the light was very strong; even in a situation in which the light was not so strong as to dazzle the eye so much as to prevent its seeing very distinctly the body of the candle and the wick, not the least appearance of flame was discernible, though the candle actually burned the whole time very vigorously.

DESCRIPTION OF THE PLATES.

Plate I., Fig. 1.   This represents a plan, or rather the outlines of a bird's-eye view of the photometer, upon its stand, together with the ends adjoining to the stand of the long and narrow tables on which the carriages run which support the lights: *a*, *b*, *c*, *d*, *e*, *f*, *g*, *h*, *i*, *k*, is the plan of the photometer properly so called, which is a box of wood, painted black within and without, with two projecting, horizontal, quadrangular tubes, *e*, *f*, *g*, *h*, and *i*, *k*, *a*, *b*, through which the light is admitted.   The part of the figure which is bounded by the three straight lines *g*, *h*, — *h*, *i*, — and *i*, *k*, and the curved line *k*, *g*, is merely a projection of the board which forms the bottom of the box.   It is of no real use, serving only to give a more elegant form to the instrument.

Dotted lines drawn through the axes of the two horizontal tubes above-mentioned meet at the surface of a vertical plane consisting of a piece of sheet glass covered with white paper, which plane constitutes the field of the instrument on which the shadows are projected.

Two small circles through which those dotted lines pass represent the ground plans of the two cylinders of brass, painted black, by which the shadows are thrown on the field of the photometer.   On one side of each of these cylinders there is a projecting wing, a plan of which is represented in the figure.

Each of the small circles which represent the plans

PLATE I.

Fig. 1.

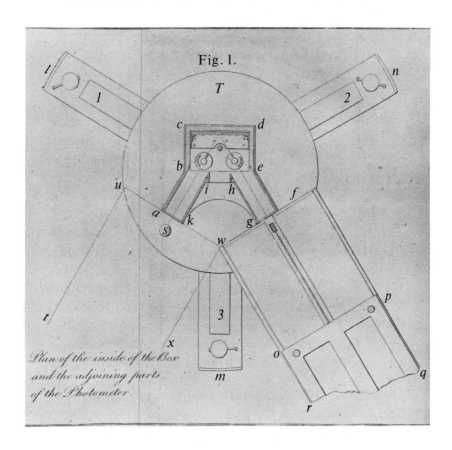

Plan of the inside of the Box
and the adjoining parts
of the Photometer.

or horizontal sections of the cylinders is surrounded by another circle, about three times as large, which represents a flat horizontal circular plate of brass, about $\frac{1}{10}$ of an inch thick, on which the cylinder stands, and to which it is firmly fastened by solder. These circular plates are placed on an oblong horizontal plate of brass, through which the cylinders which are continued below the circular plates pass in two holes in the oblong plate which are made to receive them.

To the lower ends of each of the cylinders which, passing through the bottom of the wooden box which constitutes the body of the photometer, project downward, about an inch below it is fixed a thumb-piece or handle (visible in the Fig. 2, Plate II.).

These thumb-pieces serve for turning the cylinders about their axes, which is done occasionally in order to bring the shadows of the two cylinders which are thrown on the field of the instrument to be of the same width. The manner in which this is effected will be evident, if we consider that, as long as the vertical wing which is annexed to each of the cylinders remains in the shadow of its cylinder, it cannot add to the width of the shadow cast on the vertical plane which constitutes the field of the photometer; but, as soon as by turning the cylinder about its axis that wing is made to emerge from the shadow of the cylinder on one side, the width of the shadow on the field of the instrument will be increased. By these means the widths of the two shadows which are compared may at any time be made equal; and they should be so, in order that their intensities may be compared with greater facility and accuracy. As often as the two lights, which are the subjects of an ex-

PLATE II.

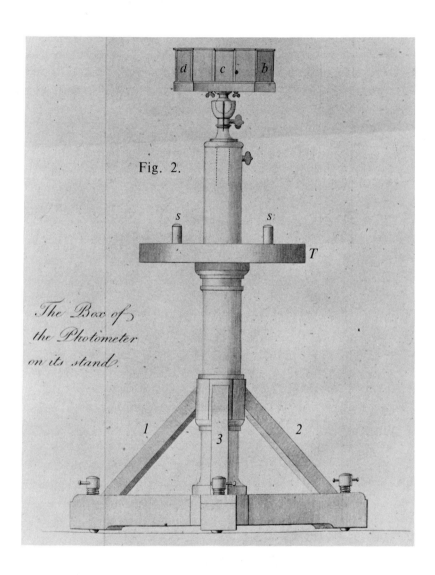

Fig. 2.

The Box of
the Photometer
on its stand.

periment, are placed at different distances from the field of the photometer, the shadows of the two equal cylinders, unassisted by their projecting wings, will of course be of unequal widths. To bring their widths to be equal was the sole object of the contrivance we have been describing.

l, *m*, *n* (Fig. 1, Plate I.), are the three strong feet which support the photometer, and also a round table on which one end of each of the long narrow tables rests that support the sliding carriages which carry the lights. In each of these feet there is a screw (represented more distinctly in the Fig. 2, Plate II.) by means of which the stand or pillar which supports the photometer may be brought into a position exactly vertical.

A ground plan of a part of one of the long and narrow tables (that on the right hand) is represented in this figure; and a part also of one of the carriages which carry the lights is seen at *o*, *p*, *q*, *r*. The top of the pulley is also seen, and the line which passing over it draws the carriage on which the light stands. The place occupied by one end (that next to the photometer) of the other long table is represented by the dotted lines *t*, *u*, *w*, *x*. The place of the strong pin which, passing through a hole made to receive it, near the end of the table, is represented (in a ground plan) at *s*. These pins are shown very distinctly at *s*, *s*, in the Fig. 2, Plate II.

1, 2, 3, Figs. 1 and 2, are three strong braces which assist in supporting the pillar, on the top of which the photometer is placed.

T in the Figs. 1 and 2 is a strong circular table on which one end of each of the long narrow tables is

PLATE III.

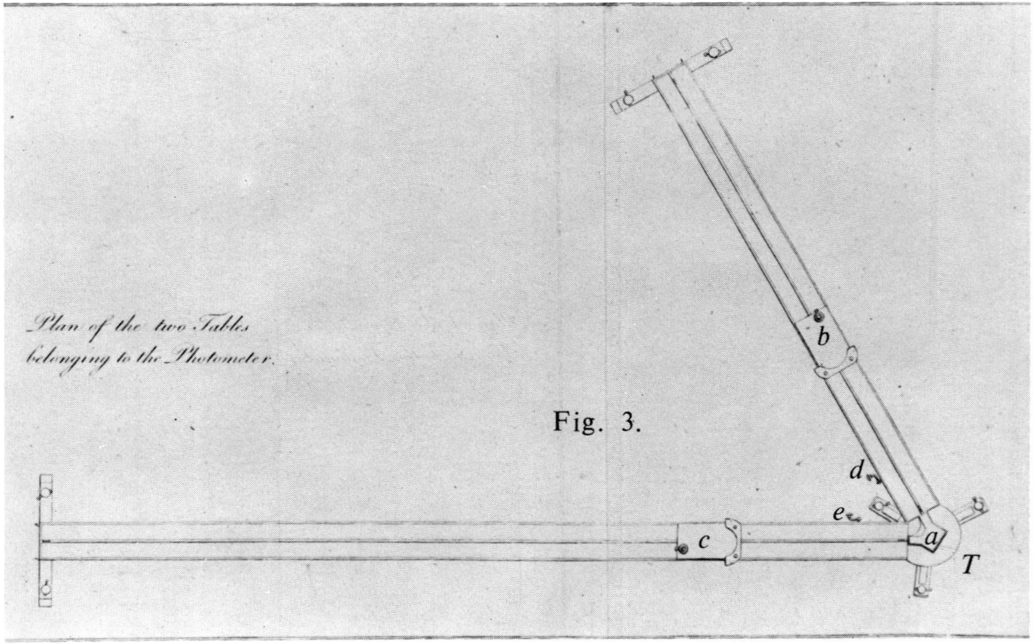

Fig. 3.

Plan of the two Tables
belonging to the Photometer.

b

d

e

a

T

c

supported. This circular table, through the centre of which the pillar of the photometer passes, is supported on a strong flange or shoulder in the pillar which is made for it to rest upon.

The box of the photometer is fixed to its stand or pillar by means of a ball and socket. In the Fig. 2, this box is represented shut up by three sliding wooden doors, *a*, *b*, and *c*. Through the door-way on the left at *a*, and through that on the right at *b*, light is admitted into the photometer; and that in the middle, at *c*, is opened in order to observe the shadows cast on the field of the instrument.

The places occupied by these three sliding-doors in the ground plan of the photometer (see Fig. 1) are as follows. The first (*a*) fills the opening from *a* to *k;* the second (*b*) that from *f* to *g;* and the third (*c*) that from *i* to *h*.

Plate III., Fig. 3. This figure represents a plan, or rather the outlines of a bird's-eye view of the whole of the apparatus, drawn to a small scale.

a is the box of the photometer, which is represented as being closed above with its lid or wooden cover.

b and *c* are the two sliding carriages on which the lights are placed, which are the subjects of the experiments. There is a movable stage or platform belonging to each of these carriages, which, by means which will presently be described, can be placed higher or lower. It is upon these platforms, and not on the bottoms of the carriages, that the lights are placed; and, as they are movable upwards and downwards, the lights to be compared can easily be placed exactly at the same height, which is always necessary. Each of the pieces of board which form these platforms has three holes through it, in which three cylindrical pillars pass, which stand on the bottom of the carriage, and are firmly fixed in it. The platform is attached to these three pillars at any height above the bottom of the carriage, by means of small horizontal screws, which can be made to press against the pillars. These screws are fixed in large hollow knobs of wood which are fixed to the platform, just over the holes, in such a manner that each pillar passes through the axis of one of these knobs.

One of these knobs, together with the end of the screw by which it is fastened to the pillar, is represented in the bird's-eye view of the carriage *b*, and another in that *c*, Fig. 3. The reason why the other two knobs belonging to each of these carriages are not seen is this: they are hid by a flat narrow piece of wood (represented in the figure) which, passing from the top of one of the two front pillars of the carriage to the other, serves to make those pillars more steady. A front view of the three knobs belonging to each of the carriages may be seen in the next figure.

d and *e* are the winches by means of which the sliding carriages, *b* and *c*, are occasionally brought nearer to and carried farther from the field of the photometer. The strong wires stretched along upon each side of each of the long tables on which the carriages slide are represented in this figure, as also the cord stretched along the middle of each table, and passing over pulleys at each end of it, and round the cylinder of the winch, which serves for drawing the carriage backwards and forwards.

The two ends of this cord are united under the table, forming of the whole a kind of band, which is kept at a proper degree of tension by a weight under the table which is fixed to a pulley. This weight is seen in the next figure (Plate IV.) suspended by the cord under one of the tables. T is the circular table, which is represented on a much larger scale in the Figs. 1 and 2.

In this figure (3) and in the next, the brackets are seen which support the ends of the long tables which are farthest from the stand of the photometer. Each of these brackets is furnished with two screws, distinctly represented in the figure, which serve for setting the table on a true horizontal level.

Plate IV., Fig. 4. This figure is an elevation of the whole of the machinery, seen in the direction of the length of one of the long tables. The two tables are supposed to be so placed as to form an angle of 60°, in which situation they are also represented in the last figure. As in this figure (4) one end of one of the long tables is represented as standing immediately before the stand of the photometer, the sliding carriage belonging to that table obstructs the view of the upper part of the stand, and of the box of the photometer, and renders the appearance of the machinery in that part of the plate rather confused; but by a careful examination the different parts of it may be distinguished.

The platforms on which the lights are placed are represented as being both fixed at the same horizontal level; and all the six hollow knobs of wood are distinctly seen, by which they are fastened to the slender pillars which support them. The lights themselves are not represented in any of these figures. The handles of the winches, by means of which the lights are moved backwards or forwards, by an observer who

PLATE IV.

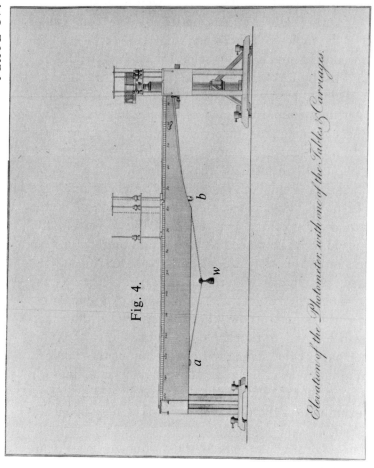

Fig. 4.

Elevation of the Photometer, with one of the Tables & Carriages.

is sitting before the photometer and looking at the shadows, are both represented in this figure.

Care must always be taken, in making the experiments, to place the two lights and the centre of the field of the photometer in the same plane.

The frames of the long tables are constructed of strong deal boards placed edgeways, and the two long boards which form the two sides of each table are made narrower at that end of them which is next to the stand of the photometer, in the manner represented in the Fig. 4.

This is done to give more room to the observer, when he is sitting before the instrument to observe the shadows. The winches are so placed that he can conveniently keep one of them in each hand, and turn them about while his eye remains fixed on the field of the instrument.

In order that the weight w, by which the cord is kept properly stretched, may be forced to remain in its proper place, the cord is made to pass over two additional pulleys at a and b. The manner in which these pulleys act will be evident from a bare inspection of the figure.

The upper edges of the two long boards which constitute the insides of the frames of the two long tables are divided in feet and inches, which greatly facilitates the ascertaining of the distances of the lights from the field of the photometer.

At the ends of the long tables the pins are seen by means of which the wires are stretched on which the carriages of the lights slide.

AN ACCOUNT OF SOME EXPERIMENTS
ON COLOURED SHADOWS.

WHILE I was employed in the prosecution of my experiments on the intensities of light, I was struck with a very beautiful and what I then considered as a new appearance. Desirous of comparing the intensity of the light of a clear sky, by day, with that of a common wax candle, I darkened my room, and letting the daylight from the north (coming through a hole near the top of the window-shutter) fall at an angle of about 70° upon a sheet of very fine white paper, I placed a burning wax candle in such a position that its rays fell upon the same paper, and, as nearly as I could guess, in the line of reflection of the rays of daylight from without; when, interposing a cylinder of wood, about half an inch in diameter, before the centre of the paper, and at the distance of about two inches from its surface, I was much surprised to find that the two shadows projected by the cylinder upon the paper, instead of being merely shades, *without colour*, as I expected to find them, the one of them — that which, corresponding with the beam of daylight, was illuminated by the candle — was *yellow;* while the other, corresponding to the light of the candle, — and consequently illuminated by the light of the heavens, — was of the most beautiful *blue* that it is possible to imagine.

This appearance, which was not only unexpected, but was really in itself in the highest degree striking and beautiful, I found, upon repeated trials and after varying the experiment in every way I could think of, to be so perfectly permanent that it is absolutely impossible to produce *two shadows* at the same time from the same body, the one answering to a beam of daylight and the other to the light of a candle or lamp, without these shadows being coloured, the one *yellow* and the other *blue*.

The experiment may very easily be made at any time by day, and almost in any place, and even by a person not in the least degree versed in experimental researches. Nothing more is necessary for that purpose than to take a burning candle into a darkened room in the daytime, and open one of the window-shutters a little, about half or three quarters of an inch, for instance; when, the candle being placed upon a table or stand, or given to an assistant to hold, in such a situation that the rays from the candle may meet those of daylight from without at an angle of about 40°, at the surface of a sheet of white paper, held in a proper position to receive them, any solid opaque body, a cylinder, or even a finger held before the paper at the distance of two or three inches, will project two shadows upon the paper, the one blue and the other yellow.

If the candle be brought nearer to the paper, the blue shadow will become of a deeper hue, and the yellow shadow will gradually grow fainter; but, if it be removed farther off, the yellow shadow will become of a deeper colour, and the blue shadow will become fainter; and, the candle remaining stationary in the same place, the same varieties in the strength of the tints of the coloured shadows may be produced merely by opening the window-shutter a little more or less, and rendering the illumination of the paper by the light from without stronger or weaker. By either of these means the coloured shadows may be made to pass through all the gradations of shade, from the deepest to the lightest, and *vice versa;* and it is not a little amusing to see shadows thus glowing with all the brilliancy of the purest and most intense prismatic colours, then passing suddenly through all the varieties of shade, — preserving in all the most perfect purity of tint, — growing stronger and fainter, and vanishing and returning at command.

With respect to the causes of the colours of these shadows, there is no doubt but they arise from the different qualities of the light by which they are illuminated; but how they are produced does not appear to me so evident.* That the shadow corresponding to

* I ought to inform the reader that when the above was written I had not the smallest recollection of what, many years before, I had read concerning coloured shadows, in Priestley's History of Optics. It may perhaps be thought (by others, as well as by myself) that it was a fortunate circumstance that I had forgotten what I had read ; for it left my mind in perfect freedom to pursue, in my own way, the investigation of the causes of the phenomena which presented themselves to my observation, without my being biassed by the opinions of others, who, before me, had attempted to explain them. Had I recollected what others had done, I should not, most probably, have given myself the trouble of engaging in the prosecution of these inquiries.

But although *at the time when this paper was written* I had really no remembrance whatever of what had been written and published before on this subject, yet soon after the paper was finished, and some time before it was sent to England to be laid before the Royal Society, I was, by an accidental circumstance, made to recollect what I had so entirely forgotten. Shall I confess what the motives were which induced me to expose myself to the danger of being thought *ignorant*, or something worse, by suffering my paper to go out of my hands without alteration? When the glow of the sudden blush which I felt on discovering my danger had passed off, and I had taken time to reflect coolly on all the circumstances of the case, I concluded that it might be *useful* the beam of daylight, which is illuminated by the yellow light of a candle, should be of a yellowish hue, is not surprising; but why is the shadow corresponding to the light of the candle, and which is illuminated by no other light than the apparently white light of the heavens, *blue?* I at first thought that it might arise from the blueness of the sky; but finding that the broad daylight, reflected from the roof of a neighbouring house covered with the whitest new-fallen snow, produced the same blue colour, and if possible of a still more beautiful tint, I was obliged to abandon that opinion.

To ascertain with some degree of precision the *real colour* of the light emitted by a candle, I placed a lighted wax candle, well trimmed, in the open air, at mid-day, at a time when the ground was deeply covered with new-fallen snow, and the heavens were overspread with white clouds; when the flame of the candle, far from being white, as it appears to be when viewed by night, was evidently of a very decided *yellow colour*, not even approaching to whiteness.

The flame of an Argand's lamp, exposed at the same time in the open air, appeared to be of the same yellow hue. But the most striking manner of showing the yellow hue of the light emitted by lamps and candles is by exposing them in the direct rays of a bright meridian sun. In that situation, the flame of an

to permit my paper to go forth into the world in its original state. I conceived that it would show, in a very striking manner, if not the advantages which sometimes result from forgetting what we have read, at least the very great importance of preserving the mind totally unbiassed by the speculative opinions of others when we are in search of truth.

An ardent lover of science will not hesita e to expose himself to *personal danger*, when he perceives that by so doing he has a chance of promoting useful investigation.

Argand's lamp, burning with its greatest brilliancy, appears in the form of a dead yellow semi-transparent smoke. How transcendently pure and inconceivably bright the rays of the sun are, when compared to the light of any of our artificial illuminators, may be gathered from the result of this experiment!

It appearing to me very probable that the *difference in the whiteness of the two kinds of light* which were the subjects of the foregoing experiments might, somehow or other, be the occasion of the *different colours of the shadows*, I attempted to produce the same effects by employing two artificial lights of different colours; and in this I succeeded completely.

In a room previously darkened, the light from two burning wax candles being made to fall upon the white paper at a proper angle in order to form two distinct shadows of the cylinder, these shadows were found not to be in the least coloured; but upon interposing a pane of yellow glass, approaching to a faint orange colour, before one of the candles, one of the shadows immediately became *yellow* and the other *blue*.

When two Argand's lamps were made use of instead of the candles, the result was the same: the shadows were constantly and very deeply coloured, the one yellow approaching to orange, and the other blue approaching to green. I imagined that the greenish cast of this blue colour was owing either to the want of whiteness of the one light, or to the orange hue of the other, which it acquired from the glass.

When equal panes of the same yellow glass were interposed before *both* the lights, the white paper took an orange hue, but the shadows were to all appearance *without the least tinge of colour;* but *two* panes of the yellow glass being afterwards interposed before *one of the lights*, while only *one* pane remained before the other, the colours of the shadows immediately returned.

The results of these experiments having confirmed my suspicions that the colours of the shadows arose from the *different degrees of whiteness* of the two lights, I now endeavoured, by bringing daylight to be of the same yellow tinge with candlelight, by the interposition of sheets of coloured glass, to prevent the shadows being coloured when daylight and candlelight were together the subjects of the experiment; and in this I succeeded. I was even able to *reverse* the colours of the shadows, by causing the daylight to be of a *deeper yellow* than the candlelight.

In the course of these experiments, I observed that different shades of yellow, given to the daylight, produced very different and often quite unexpected effects: thus one sheet of the yellow glass, interposed before the beam of daylight, changed the yellow shadow to a lively violet colour, and the blue shadow to a light green; two sheets of the same glass nearly destroyed the colours of both the shadows; and three sheets changed the shadow which was originally yellow to blue, and that which was blue to a purplish yellow colour.

When the beam of daylight was made to pass through a sheet of blue glass, the colours of the shadows — the yellow as well as the blue — were improved and rendered in the highest degree clear and brilliant; but, when the blue glass was placed before the candle, the colours of the shadows were very much impaired.

In order to see what would be the consequence of

rendering the candlelight of a still deeper yellow, I interposed before it a sheet of yellow or rather orange-coloured glass, when a very unexpected and most beautiful appearance took place: the colour of the yellow shadow was changed to orange, — the blue shadow remained unchanged, — and the whole surface of the paper not covered by the shadows appeared to be tinged of a most beautiful violet colour, approaching to a light crimson or pink, — almost exactly the same hue as I have often observed the distant snowy mountains and valleys of the Alps to take about sunset.

Is it not more than probable that this hue is, in both cases, produced by nearly the same combinations of coloured light? In the one case, it is the white snow illuminated at the same time by the purest light of the heavens and by the deep yellow rays from the west; and in the other, it is the white paper illuminated by broad daylight and by the rays from a burning candle, rendered still more yellow by being transmitted through the yellow glass.

The beautiful violet colour which spreads itself over the surface of the paper will appear to the greatest advantage, if the pane of orange-coloured glass be held in such a manner before the candle that only a part of the paper — half of it, for instance — be affected by it, the other half of it remaining white.

To make these experiments with more convenience, the paper, which may be about 8 or 10 inches square, should be pasted or glued down upon a flat piece of board, furnished with a ball and socket upon the hinder side of it, and mounted upon a stand; and the cylinder should be fastened to a small arm of wood or of metal, projecting forward from the bottom of the board for that purpose. A small stand, capable of being made higher or lower, as the occasion requires, should likewise be provided for supporting the candle; and, if the board with the paper fastened upon it be surrounded with a broad black frame, the experiments will be so much the more striking and beautiful. For still greater convenience, I have added two other stands, for holding the coloured glass through which the light is occasionally made to pass, in its way to the white surface upon which the shadows are projected. It will be hardly necessary to add that, in order to the experiments appearing to the greatest advantage, all light which is not absolutely necessary to the experiment must be carefully excluded.

Having fitted up a little apparatus according to the above directions, merely for the purpose of prosecuting these inquiries respecting the coloured shadows, I proceeded to make a great variety of experiments, — some with pointed views, and others quite at random, and merely in hopes of making some accidental discovery that might lead to a knowledge of the causes of appearances, which still seemed to me to be enveloped in much obscurity and uncertainty.

Having found that the shadows corresponding to two like wax candles were coloured, the one blue and the other yellow, by interposing a sheet of yellow glass before one of them, I now tried what the effect would be when *blue* glass was made use of instead of yellow, and I found it to be the same: the shadows were still coloured, the one blue and the other yellow, with this difference however, that the colours of the shadows were *reversed;* that which, with the yellow glass, was before yellow, being now blue, and that which was blue being yellow.

I afterwards tried a glass of a bright amethyst colour, and was surprised to find that the shadows still continued to be coloured blue and yellow. The yellow, it is true, had a dirty purple cast; but the blue, though a little inclining to green, was nevertheless a clean, bright, decided colour.

Having no other coloured glass at hand to push these particular inquiries farther, I now removed the candles, and opening two holes in the upper parts of the window-shutters of two neighbouring windows, I let into the room, from above, two beams of light from different parts of the heavens; and, placing the instrument in such a manner that two distinct shadows were projected by the cylinder upon the paper, I was entertained by a succession of very amusing appearances.

The shadows were tinged with an infinite variety of the most unexpected and often most beautiful colours, which continually varying, sometimes slowly and sometimes with inconceivable rapidity, absolutely fascinated the eyes, and, commanding the most eager attention, afforded an enjoyment as new as it was bewitching.

It was a windy day, with flying clouds, and it seemed as if every cloud that passed brought with it another complete succession of varying hues and most harmonious tints. If any colour could be said to predominate, it was purples; but all the varieties of browns, and almost all the other colours I ever remembered to have seen, appeared in their turns, and there were even colours which seemed to me to be perfectly new.

Reflecting upon the great variety of colours observed in these last experiments, many of which did not appear to have the least relation to the apparent colours of the light by which they were produced, I began to suspect that the colours of the shadows might in many cases, notwithstanding their apparent brilliancy, be merely an optical deception, owing to contrast or to some effect of the other *real* and neighbouring colours upon the eye.

To determine this fact by a direct experiment, I proceeded in the following manner. Having, by making use of a flat ruler instead of the cylinder, contrived to render the shadows much broader, I shut out of the room every ray of daylight, and prepared to make the experiment with two Argand's lamps, well trimmed, and which were both made to burn with the greatest possible brilliancy; and having assured myself that the light they emitted was precisely of the same colour, by the shadows being pefectly colourless which were projected upon the white paper, I directed a tube of about 12 inches long and near an inch in diameter, lined with black paper, against the centre of one of the broad shadows; and looking through this tube with one eye, while the other was closed, I kept my attention fixed upon the shadow, while an assistant repeatedly interposed a sheet of yellow glass before the lamp whose light corresponded to the shadow I observed, and as often removed it.

The result of the experiment was very striking, and fully confirmed my suspicions with respect to the fallacy of many of the appearances in the foregoing experiments.

So far from being able to observe any change in the shadow upon which my eye was fixed, I was not able even to tell when the yellow glass was before the lamp and when it was not; and, though the assistant often exclaimed at the striking brilliancy and beauty of the blue colour of the very shadow I was observing, I could not discover in it the least appearance of any colour at all. But as soon as I removed my eye from the tube, and contemplated the shadow with all its neighbouring accompaniments, — the other shadow rendered *really* yellow by the effect of the yellow glass and the white paper, which had likewise from the same cause acquired a yellowish hue, — the shadow in question appeared to me, as it did to my assistant, of a beautiful blue colour.

I afterwards repeated the same experiment with the apparently blue shadow produced in the experiment with daylight and candlelight, and with exactly the same result.

How far these experiments may enable us to account for the apparent blue colour of the sky and the great variety of colours which frequently adorn the clouds, as also what other useful observations may be drawn from them, I leave to philosophers, opticians, and painters to determine. In the mean time I believe it is a new discovery — at least it is undoubtedly a very extraordinary fact — that our eyes are not always to be believed, *even with respect to the presence or absence of colours.*

I cannot finish this paper without mentioning one circumstance, which struck me very forcibly in all these experiments upon coloured shadows, — and that is, the most perfect harmony which always appeared to subsist between the colours — whatever they were — of the two shadows; and this harmony seemed to me to be full as perfect and pleasing when the shadows were of different tints of brown as when one of them was blue and the other yellow. In short, the harmony of these colours was in all cases not only very striking, but the appearances altogether were quite enchanting; and I never found anybody to whom I showed these experiments whose eyes were not fascinated with them. It is, however, more than probable that a great part of the pleasure which these experiments afforded to the spectators arose from the continual changes of colour, tint, and shade with which the eye was amused and the attention kept awake.

We are used to seeing colours fixed and unalterable, — hard as the solid bodies from which they come, and just as motionless, — consequently *dead, uninteresting, and tiresome to the eye;* but in these experiments all is *motion, life,* and *beauty.*

It appears to me very probable that a further prosecution of these experiments upon coloured shadows may not only lead to a knowledge of the *real nature of the harmony of colours,* or the peculiar circumstances upon which that harmony depends, but that it may also enable us to construct instruments for producing that harmony for the entertainment of the eyes, in a manner similar to that in which the ears are entertained by musical sounds. I know that attempts have already been made for that purpose ; but, when I consider the means employed, I am not surprised that they did not succeed. Where the flowing tide, the varying swell, the *crescendo* is wanting, colours must ever remain hard, cold, and inanimate masses.

I am very sorry that my more serious occupations do not at present permit me to pursue these most entertaining inquiries. Perhaps at some future period I may find leisure to resume them.

CONJECTURES RESPECTING THE PRINCIPLES
OF THE HARMONY OF COLOURS.

SINCE the foregoing paper was written, I have at different times repeated most of the experiments therein described, and have made a variety of others, with a view to the farther investigation of this curious subject; and from the results of these inquiries I have been enabled to form some conclusions and conjectures which may perhaps be thought not altogether uninteresting.

Whenever a beam of *coloured light* of any species, and a beam of *white* or *colourless light* of equal intensity, arriving in different directions and at equal angles of incidence at a plane white surface, illuminate that surface together, if a solid opaque body of any kind be placed in each of these beams of light, just before the illuminated plane, in such a manner that the two shadows cast on the plane by these opaque bodies may be near each other, the intensities of these shadows will be equal, and they will both appear to be coloured, but of very different hues. That which is illuminated by the *coloured light* will be of the colour of that light, — which is what would naturally be expected to happen by a person who had never seen the experiment, — but that which is illuminated by the *colourless light*, and by that alone, instead of appearing colourless, will *appear* to be as deeply coloured as the other, but of a different hue.

The two colours exhibited by the two shadows appear in all cases to harmonize in the most perfect manner, or, in other words, to afford the most pleasing contrast to the view.

These two colours are always such that, if they could be intimately mixed together, the result of that mixture would be *perfect whiteness;* and, as whiteness results from the mixture of all the different colours in certain proportions, the two shadows may be considered as containing all the colours in their just proportions, and the colour of the one shadow may with propriety be said to be the *complement* of the other.

Two neighbouring colours are then, and only then, in perfect harmony when the intimate mixture of both would produce perfect whiteness; and hence it appears that, when two colours harmonize, one of them at least must necessarily be a compound colour.

In the experiment of the coloured shadows, the colour exhibited by one of the shadows only is real, that of the other is *imaginary*, being an optical deception, occasioned in some way unknown to us by the colour actually present and by the effects of the different lights and shades. The *imaginary colour*, which may be said to be *called up in the mind* by the other *real colour*, does not, however, appear to be at all inferior to the real colour either in lustre or in the distinctness of its hue.

Any two harmonizing coloured shadows may be produced indifferently, either with one of the given colours, or with the other of them and white light: *pink* and *green*, for instance, are harmonizing colours;

and two shadows of these two colours, equally bright, may be produced either with a beam of pink-coloured light, or with a beam of green light, crossed by a beam of white light, according to the method above described.

A beam of coloured light may readily be produced for making these experiments by causing white light to pass through coloured glass or any other coloured transparent substance.

To every colour without exception, whatever may be its hue or shade, or however it may be compounded, there is another in perfect harmony to it, which is its complement, and may be said to be its companion. It may be *called up* and exhibited to view in the following manner. Let white light be made to pass through the coloured body, or, if it be opaque, let it be reflected from it: with this light so coloured, and with pure white light, make the experiment of the two shadows, and the colour in question will appear *with its companion by its side.*

By experiments of this kind, which might easily be made, ladies may choose ribbons to their gowns; or those who furnish rooms may arrange their colours upon principles of the most perfect harmony and of the purest taste.

The advantages that painters might derive from a knowledge of these principles of the harmony of colours are too obvious to require illustration.

Upon a careful examination of the works of the great masters of the art of colouring, it will appear that they have frequently practised upon these principles, though it is not likely that they were acquainted with the scientific foundation of their practice. They have certainly produced *appearances* of colours or tints, when their pictures are viewed in a proper light and at a proper distance, which we search for in vain upon the canvas. This may well be called the "*magic of colouring;*" for it is in fact calling up, as by enchantment, and presenting to the mind colours the most pure and vivid, which have no real existence.

As it might very naturally be suspected that the colours called up by means of shadows owe their existence to *something peculiar to shadows*, and that similar effects could not be produced without shadows, by means of coloured pigments, to remove all doubts on that subject, I made the following decisive experiment.

Having found that when a beam of deep red light and a beam of white or colourless light, of equal intensity, arrive in different directions at a plane white surface, and illuminate it, that a blue shadow, nearly approaching to green, is called up by the red shadow, I attempted to imitate this experiment with a coloured pigment.

On the middle of the floor of a spacious room I laid down a very large sheet of black paper, and on the middle of this I placed a circular piece of crayon paper, which, in order that it might supply the place of the illuminated plane surface on which the shadows were projected in my experiments, I covered or coloured it with such a mixture of red lead (*minium*) and pure white lead, both finely powdered and well mixed together as brought it to be of the same tint, as nearly as possible, with the surface illuminated by the red and by the white light. I then took two oblong slips of crayon paper, half an inch wide and two inches long each: then, colouring one of them as highly as possible with red lead, in a dry powder, and covering the other with a powder composed of white lead and lamp-black, in such proportions that the quantities of light reflected from the two slips so prepared should be equal, I placed these slips in contact with each other, in the middle of the circular piece of paper on the floor; when retiring backwards a few steps, and look-ing through my hand with one eye, to exclude all other objects, I had the pleasure to perceive that the slip of paper which was covered with a gray powder now appeared to be of a beautiful greenish blue colour, while the other was of the most vivid red.

This experiment was first made at an inn at Flor-ence, in the year 1793; and in order that I might assure myself that my expectations had not deceived me, by imposing upon my senses, I called two of my friends who happened to lodge in the house (Lord and Lady Palmerston) into the room, and without letting them into the secret simply asked them, with a feigned air of indifference, which of the two colours they saw in the centre of the circular piece of paper on the floor they thought the brightest.

After looking at them for some time, and going round to view them from different sides, one of them answered: " I don't know which of them is the bright-est. The red is very bright, and so is the blue. But why do you ask us that question?"

When I told them there was no blue there, and that what they took to be blue was merely a deception, they did not believe me; but they were much surprised, and convinced that what I told them was true, when they saw on my removing the red slip that its companion, which was left behind, instantly *faded* and *lost its colour*.

In attempts to call up colours in this way, many precautions are necessary, to which the most scrupulous attention must be paid, otherwise the experiments will not succeed. Care must be taken to exclude all coloured light in illuminating the slips of paper; and, in preparing that slip which is designed for exhibiting the *imaginary* colour, the quantities of black and of white powder that are mixed must be so adjusted to each other that, when the surface of the slip is covered with it, the *quantity* of light reflected from it to the spectator's eye must be precisely equal to that reflected from the surface of the other *coloured slip*, for this equality is essential to the purity and brilliancy of the colour called up. But this equality can only be found by actual trials with several slips of deeper and lighter shades. That slip which takes the clearest and brightest colour is to be chosen.

When experiments of this kind are attempted to be made with oil colours, other and still greater difficulties will occur; for the oil used for fixing the colours diminishes in so great a degree both the brilliancy and the purity of the light reflected from the surfaces of coloured pigments that the light reflected from an oil painting cannot be expected to produce the same brilliant appearances which are exhibited by the mixtures and contrasts of the uncontaminated and brilliant colours of pure light.

But although it may be impossible for painters, with *their imperfect colours*, to produce effects that will bear a close comparison with those magic appearances of which we have been giving an account, yet there can be no doubt but that the knowledge of those facts, and of the theory by which they are explained, may be very useful to them.

The impossibility of producing perfect whiteness by any mixture of painters' colours is a proof of the want of purity of those colours, and of the difficulty of imitating by means of them any of those very striking effects which are exhibited in experiments with the pure prismatic colours.

There is one most important advantage which painters may certainly derive from a knowledge of the principles of the harmony of colours: it will enable them, on sound philosophical principles, to contrast their colours in such a manner as to give to their pictures, or rather to what they choose to make the prominent parts of them, a great degree of force and brilliancy. For, if any and every simple and compound colour has such a power on objects near it as to cause a neighbouring *colourlesss shadow* to assume the appearance of a colour, there can be no doubt but that if, instead of the shadow a *real colour*, nearly of the same tint and shade as that so *called up*, be substituted in its place, *this colour will appear to great advantage*, or will assume an uncommon degree of strength and brightness.

The science of painting is a most curious and interesting subject of philosophical investigation; and until it is more cultivated the art of colouring must continue to be very obscure, uncertain, and imperfect. Genius will be condemned to waste its energy in tedious mechanical experiments, instead of being employed, as it ought to be, in tracing with a rapid pencil the beautiful conception of a sublime imagination.

AN INQUIRY

CONCERNING THE

CHEMICAL PROPERTIES THAT HAVE BEEN ATTRIBUTED TO LIGHT.

IN the second part of my Seventh Essay (on the Propagation of Heat in Fluids) I have mentioned the reasons which had induced me to doubt of the existence of those chemical properties in light that have been attributed to it, and to conclude that all those visible changes which are produced in bodies by exposure to the action of the sun's rays are effected, not by any chemical combination of the matter of light with such bodies, but merely by the heat which is generated or excited by the light that is absorbed by them.

As the decision of this question is a matter of great importance to the advancement of science, and particularly to chemistry, and as the subject is in many respects curious and interesting, it has often employed my thoughts in my leisure hours; and I have spent much time in endeavouring to contrive experiments, from the unequivocal results of which the truth might be made to appear. Though I have not been so successful in these investigations as I could wish, yet I cannot help flattering myself that an account of the results of some of my late experiments will be thought

sufficiently curious and interesting to merit the attention of those who take pleasure in the cultivation of
experimental philosophy.

Having found that gold or silver might be melted
by the heat (invisible to the sight) which exists in the
air, at the distance of more than an inch above the
point of the flame of a wax candle (see my Seventh
Essay, Part II., page 350*), I was curious to know
what effect this heat would produce on the oxides of
those metals.

Experiment No. 1. — Having evaporated to dryness
a solution of fine gold in nitro-muriatic acid, I dissolved the residuum in just as much distilled water as
was necessary in order that the solution (which was
of a beautiful yellow colour) might not be disposed to
crystallize; and wetting the middle of a piece of white
taffeta ribbon, $1\frac{1}{2}$ inch wide and about 8 inches long,
in this solution, I held the ribbon (with both my hands)
stretched horizontally over the clear, bright flame of a
wax candle; the under side of the ribbon being kept
at the distance of about $1\frac{1}{2}$ inch above the point of the
flame. The result of this experiment was very striking.
That part of the ribbon which was directly over the
point of the flame began almost immediately to emit
steam in dense clouds; and in about 10 seconds, a circular spot about $\frac{3}{4}$ of an inch in diameter having become
nearly dry, a spot of a very fine purple colour, approaching to crimson, suddenly made its appearance in the
middle of it, and spreading rapidly on all sides became,
in one or two seconds more, nearly an inch in diameter.

By moving the ribbon, so as to bring in their turns
all the parts of it which had been wetted with the solu-

* See Vol. I., page 252.

tion to be exposed to the action of the current of hot vapour that arose from the burning candle, all those parts which had been so wetted were tinged with the same beautiful purple colour.

This colour, which was uncommonly brilliant, passed quite through the ribbon; and I found the stain to be perfectly indelible. I endeavoured to wash it out; but nothing I applied to it appeared in the smallest degree to diminish its lustre. The hue was not uniform, but varied from a light crimson to a very deep purple, approaching to a reddish brown.

I searched but in vain for traces of revived gold in its reguline form and colour; but, though I could not perceive that the ribbon was gilded, it had all the appearance of being covered with a thin coating of the most beautiful purple enamel, which in the sun had a degree of brilliancy that was sometimes quite dazzling.

Experiment No. 2. — A piece of the ribbon which had been wetted with the aqueous solution of the oxide was carefully dried in a dark closet, and was then exposed dry over the flame of a burning wax candle. The part of the ribbon which had been wetted with the solution (and which on drying had acquired a faint yellow colour) was tinged of the same bright purple colour as was produced in the last-mentioned experiment, when the ribbon was exposed wet to the action of the heat.*

Experiment No. 3. — A piece of the ribbon which had been wetted with the solution, and dried in the dark, was now wetted with distilled water and exposed *wet* to the action of the ascending current of hot

* We shall hereafter find reason to conclude that the success of this experiment, or the appearance of the purple tinge, was owing to the watery vapour or steam which existed in the hot current of vapour that ascended from the flame of the candle.

vapour which arose from the burning candle: the purple stain was produced as before, which extended as far as the ribbon had been wetted with the solution, but no farther.

I afterwards varied this experiment in several ways, sometimes using paper, sometimes fine linen, and sometimes fine cotton cloths, instead of the silk ribbon; but nearly the same tinge was produced, whatever the substance was that was made to imbibe the aqueous solution of the metallic oxide.

Similar experiments and with similar results were likewise made with pieces of ribbon, fine linen, cotton, paper, etc., wetted in an aqueous solution of nitrate of silver: with this difference, however, that the tinge produced by this metallic oxide, instead of being of a deep purple inclining to a crimson, was of a very dark orange colour or rather of a yellowish brown.

In order to discover whether the purple tinge, in the experiments with the oxide of gold, was occasioned by the *heat* communicated by the ascending current of hot vapour or by the *light* of the candle, I made the following experiment, the result of which I conceive to have been decisive: —

Experiment No. 4. — A piece of ribbon was wetted with the aqueous solution of the oxide of gold, and held vertically by the side of the clear flame of a burning wax candle, at the distance of less than half an inch from the flame.

The ribbon was dried, but its colour was not in the smallest degree changed.

When it was held a few seconds within about $\frac{1}{8}$ of an inch of the flame, a tinge of a most beautiful crimson colour, in the form of a narrow vertical stripe, was produced.

The heat which existed at that distance from the flame, *on the side of it* where this coloured stripe was produced, was sufficiently intense, as I found by experiment, to melt very fine silver wire, flatted, such as is used in making silver lace.

The objects I had in view in the following experiments will be too evident to require any particular explanation : —

Experiment No. 5. — Two like pieces of ribbon were wetted at the same time in the solution, and suspended while wet in two thin phials, A and B, of very transparent and colourless glass, the mouths of the phials being left open. Both these phials were placed in a window which fronted the south ; that distinguished by the letter A being exposed naked to the direct rays of a bright sun, while B was enclosed in a cylinder of pasteboard, painted black within and without, and closed with a fit cover, and consequently remained in perfect darkness.

In a few minutes, the ribbon in the phial A began sensibly to change its colour, and to take a purple hue ; and at the end of five hours it had acquired a deep crimson tint throughout.

The phial B was exposed in the window, in its dark cylindrical cover, three days ; but there was not the smallest appearance of any change of colour in the silk.

Experiment No. 6. — Two small parcels of *magnesia alba*, in an impalpable powder (about half as much in each as could be made to lie on a shilling), were placed in heaps in two china plates, A and B, and thoroughly moistened with the before-mentioned aqueous solution of the oxide of gold. Both plates were placed in the same window; the moistened earth in the plate A being exposed naked to the sun's rays, while that in the plate B was exactly covered with a teacup, turned upside down, which excluded all light.

The *magnesia alba* in the plate A, which was exposed to the strong light of the sun, began almost immediately to change colour, taking a faint violet hue, which by degrees became more and more intense, and in a few hours ended in a deep purple; while that in the plate B, which was kept in the dark, retained the yellowish cast it had acquired from the solution, without the smallest appearance of change.

Experiment No. 7. — A small parcel of *magnesia alba* placed on a china plate, having been moistened with the aqueous solution of the oxide of gold, and thoroughly dried in a dark closet, was now exposed, *in this dry state*, to the action of the direct rays of a very bright sun.

It had been exposed to this strong light above half an hour, before its colour began to be *sensibly changed;* and at the end of three hours it had acquired only a very faint violet hue.

Being now thoroughly wetted with distilled water, it changed colour very rapidly, and soon came to be of a deep purple tint, approaching to crimson.

Experiment No. 8. — A piece of white taffeta ribbon, which had been wetted with the solution, and thoroughly dried in the dark, was suspended in a clean dry phial of very fine transparent glass; and the phial, being well stopped with a dry cork, was exposed to the strong light of a bright sun.

After the ribbon had been exposed in this manner to the action of the sun's direct rays about half an hour, there were here and there some faint appearances of a change of its colour; but it showed no disposition to take that deep purple hue which the ribbon had always acquired, when exposed to the light in the preceding experiments.

On taking the ribbon out of the phial, and wetting it thoroughly with distilled water, and exposing it again *while thus wetted* to the sun's rays, it almost instantaneously began to change colour, and soon became of a deep purple tint; but, though I examined the surface of the ribbon with the utmost care and with a good lens, both during the experiment and after it, I could not perceive the smallest particle of *revived gold*, nor did I see any vestige remaining that appeared to indicate that any had in fact been revived.

This experiment was repeated several times, and always with results which led me to conclude (what indeed was reasonable to expect) that light has little effect in changing the colour of metallic oxides, *as long as they are in a state of crystallization.*

The heat which is generated by the absorption of the rays of light must necessarily, *at the moment of its generation* at least, exist in almost infinitely small spaces; and consequently it is only in bodies that are *inconceivably small* that it can produce durable effects in any degree indicative of its extreme intensity.

Perhaps the particles of the oxide of gold dissolved in water are of such dimensions; and it is very remarkable that the colours produced in some of my experiments on white ribbons, by means of an aqueous solution of the oxide of gold, are precisely the same as are produced from the oxide of that metal by enamellers, in the intense heat of their furnaces.

As the colouring substance is the same, and as the colours produced are the same, why should we not conclude that the effects are produced in both these cases by the same means, — that is to say, by the agency of heat? or, in other words, and to be more explicit, by exposing the oxide in a certain temperature, at which it becomes disposed to vitrify or to undergo a change in regard to the quantity of oxygen with which it is combined?

But the results of the following experiments afford still more satisfactory information respecting the intensity of the heat generated in all cases where light is absorbed, and the striking effects which under certain circumstances it is capable of producing.

The facility with which most of the metallic oxides are reduced, in the dry way, by means of charcoal, shows that, at a certain (high) temperature, oxygen is disposed to quit those metals, in order to form a chemical union with the charcoal, or at least with some one of its constituent principles, if it be a compound substance; and hence I concluded that gold might be revived, *in the moist way*, by means of charcoal, from a solution of its oxide in water, were it possible under such circumstances to communicate to the charcoal and to the oxide *at the same time* a degree of heat sufficient for that purpose.

To see if this might not be done by means of light, I made, or rather repeated, the following very interesting experiment: —

Experiment No. 9. — Into a thin tube of very fine colourless glass, 10 inches long and $\frac{6}{10}$ of an inch in diameter, closed hermetically at its lower end, I put as many pieces of charcoal, about the size of large peas, as filled the tube to the height of two inches; and, having poured on them as much of the aqueous solution of nitro-muriate of gold as nearly covered them, exposed the tube, with its contents, to the action of the direct rays of a very bright sun.

In less than half an hour, small specks of revived gold, in all its *metallic splendour*, began to make their appearance here and there on the surface of the charcoal; and in six hours the solution, which at first was of a bright yellow colour, became perfectly *colourless*, AND AS CLEAR AND TRANSPARENT AS THE PUREST WATER.

The surface of the charcoal was in several places nearly covered with small particles of revived gold; and the inside of the glass tube, in that part where it was in contact with the upper surface of the contained liquid, was most beautifully gilded.

This gilding of the tube was very splendid, when viewed by reflected light; but, when the tube was placed between the light and the eye, it appeared like a thin cloud, of a greenish blue colour, without the smallest appearance of any metallic splendour.

From the colour and apparent density of this cloud, I was induced to conclude that the gilding on the glass was less than *one millionth part of an inch* in thickness.

This interesting experiment was repeated six times, and always with nearly the same result. The gold was completely revived in each of them, and the solution left perfectly colourless: in most of the experiments, however, the sides of the glass were not gilded, all the revived gold remaining attached to the surface of the charcoal.

In two of these experiments, I made use of pieces

of charcoal which had been previously boiled several hours in a large quantity of distilled water, and which were introduced *wet* and *hot* into the tube, and immediately covered by the solution, to prevent them from imbibing any air; and in different experiments the solution was used of different degrees of strength.

I plainly perceived that the experiment succeeded best — that is to say, that the gold was *soonest revived* — in those cases in which the solution was *most diluted*: one of the experiments, however, and which succeeded perfectly, was made with the solution so much condensed that it was nearly at the point at which it became disposed to crystallize.*

On examining with a good microscope the particles of revived gold which remained attached to the surface of the charcoal after it had been dried, I found them to consist of an infinite number of small scales, separated from each other, not very highly polished, but possessing the true metallic splendour, and a very deep and rich gold colour.

The gold which attached itself to the inside of the glass tube was in the form of a ring, about $\frac{1}{10}$ of an inch wide (badly defined, however, below), and adhered to the glass with so much obstinacy as not to be removed by rinsing out the tube a great number of times with water. It had, as has already been observed, a very high polish, when seen by reflected light.

Those who enter into the spirit of these investigations will easily imagine how impatient I must have

* This agrees perfectly with the results of similar experiments made by the ingenious and lively Mrs. Fulhame. (See her Essay on Combustion, page 124.)

It was on reading her book that I was induced to engage in these investigations ; and it was by her experiments that most of the foregoing experiments were suggested.

been, after seeing the results of these experiments, to find out whether gold could be revived from this aqueous solution of its oxide by means of charcoal, *without the assistance of light*, and merely by such a degree of equal heat as could be given to it in the dark. To determine that important question, the following experiment was made: —

Experiment No. 10. — A cylindrical glass tube, $\frac{6}{10}$ of an inch in diameter and 10 inches long, closed hermetically at its lower end, and containing a quantity of a diluted aqueous solution of the oxide of gold mixed with charcoal in broken pieces, about the size of large peas, was put into a fit cylindrical tin case, which was nicely closed with a fit cover; and the glass tube, with its contents so shut up in the dark, was exposed two hours in the temperature of 210° of Fahrenheit's scale.

On taking the glass tube out of its tin case, I found the solution *perfectly colourless*, and the revived gold adhering to the surface of the charcoal.

On repeating the experiment, and using the solution nearly saturated with the oxide, the result was precisely the same; the solution being found perfectly colourless, and the revived gold adhering to the surface of the charcoal.

I own fairly that the results of these last experiments were quite contrary to my expectations, and that I am not able to reconcile them with my hypothesis respecting the causes of the reduction of the oxide, in the foregoing experiments; but, whatever may be the fate of this or of any other hypothesis of mine, I hope and trust that I never shall be so weak as to feel pain at the discovery of truth, however contrary it may be to my expectations; and still less to feel a secret wish to suppress experiments, merely because their results militate against my speculative opinions.

It is proper I should observe that the charcoal used in this last-mentioned experiment had been boiled two hours in distilled water, by which means its pores had been so completely filled with that fluid that the pieces of it that were used were specifically heavier than water, and sunk in it to the bottom of the containing vessel.

Having been so successful in my attempts to reduce the oxide of gold by means of charcoal, *in the moist way*, I lost no time in making similar experiments with the oxide of silver.

Experiment No. 11. — A solution of fine silver in nitrous acid was evaporated to dryness, and the residuum dissolved in distilled water.

A portion of this solution (which was perfectly colourless), diluted with twice as much distilled water, was poured into a phial containing a number of small pieces of charcoal; and the phial, being well closed with a new cork stopple, was exposed to the action of the sun's rays.

In less than an hour small specks of revived silver began to make their appearance on the surface of the charcoal; and at the end of two hours these specks became very numerous, and had increased so much in size that they were distinctly visible to the naked eye at the distance of more than three feet. They were very white, and possessed the metallic splendour of silver in so high a degree that, when enlightened by the sun's beams, their lustre was nearly equal to that of very small diamonds.

The phial, which was in the form of a pear, and

about $1\frac{1}{2}$ inch in diameter at its bulb, was very thin, and made of very fine colourless glass; the aqueous solution was also perfectly transparent and colourless; and, when the contents of the phial were illuminated by the direct rays of a bright sun, the contrast of the white colour of these little metallic spangles with the black charcoal to which they were fixed, and their extreme brilliancy afforded a very beautiful and interesting sight.

As the air had been previously expelled from the charcoal by boiling it in distilled water, it was specifically heavier than the aqueous solution of the metallic oxide, and consequently remained at the bottom of the bottle.

Experiment No. 12. — A phial as nearly as possible like that used in the last experiment, and containing the same quantity of diluted aqueous solution of nitrate of silver and also of charcoal, was enclosed in a cylindrical tin box, and exposed one hour to the heat of boiling water, in an apparatus used for boiling vegetables in steam for the table.

The result of this experiment was uncommonly striking. The surface of the charcoal was covered with a most beautiful *metallic vegetation;* small filaments of revived silver, resembling fine flatted silver wire, pushing out from its surface in all directions!

Some of these metallic filaments were above one tenth of an inch in length. On agitating the contents of the phial, they were easily detached from the surface of the charcoal, to which they seemed to adhere but very slightly.

These experiments were repeated several times, and always with precisely the same results.

When the oxide of gold was reduced in this way, the revived metal appeared under the form of small scales, adhering firmly to the surface of the charcoal, as has already been observed.

The following experiments, which were first suggested by an accident, were made with a view to investigate still farther the causes of those effects which have been attributed to the supposed chemical properties of light.

Having accidentally put away two small phials, each containing a quantity of aqueous solution of the oxide of gold and sulphuric ether, in each of which the ether had extracted the gold completely from the solution, as was evident by the yellow colour of the solution having been transferred to the ether, and the solution being left colourless, — in one of the phials which happened to stand in a window, in which there was occasionally a strong light (though the direct rays of the sun never fell upon it), I found, in about three weeks, the oxide of gold was almost entirely reduced; the revived gold, appearing in all its metallic splendour in the form of a thin pellicle, swimming on the surface of the aqueous liquor in the phial, and the colour of the ether which reposed on it having become quite faint; while no visible change had been produced in the contents of the other phial, which had stood in a dark corner of the room.

As these appearances induced me to suspect, or rather strengthened the suspicions I had before conceived, that the separation of gold from ether under its metallic form, when a solution of its oxide is mixed with that fluid, is always effected by a reduction of the oxide by means of light, I made the following experiment, with a view to the farther investigation of that matter : —

Experiment No. 1 3. — Into a small pear-like phial, of very fine transparent glass, I put equal quantities of an aqueous solution, a crystallized oxide of gold, and of sulphuric ether; and the phial, which was about half filled, being closed with a good cork, well secured in its place, was exposed to the action of the direct rays of a bright sun.

A pellicle of revived gold in all its metallic splendour began almost immediately to be formed on the surface of the aqueous liquid, and soon covered it entirely ; and at the end of two hours the whole of the oxide was completely reduced, as was evident from the appearance of the ether, which became *perfectly colourless.*

On shaking the phial, the metallic pellicle which covered the surface of the aqueous liquid was broken into small pieces, which had exactly the appearance of leaf gold, possessing the true colour and all the metallic brilliancy of that metal.

On suffering the phial to stand quiet, the aqueous liquor and the ether separated, and most of the broken pieces of the thin sheet of gold descended to the bottom of the phial. The remainder of them floated on the surface of the aqueous liquid, and the ether as well as the aqueous liquid appeared to be perfectly transparent and *colourless.*

By the length of time which was required for the ether and the aqueous liquid to separate, I thought I could perceive that the ether had lost something of its fluidity; but, as this was an event I expected, it is the more likely, on that account, that I was deceived, when I imagined I saw proofs of its having taken place.

On removing the cork, after the contents of the bottle had been suffered to cool, there was no appearance of any considerable quantity of air, or other permanently elastic fluid, having been either generated or absorbed during the experiment.

Finding that the oxide of gold might be so completely and so expeditiously reduced by means of ether, I conceived it might be possible to perform that chemical process *in the moist way*, by means of essential oils; and this conjecture proved to be well founded.

Experiment No. 14. — Upon a quantity of a diluted aqueous solution of nitro-muriate of gold, in a small pear-like phial, about $1\frac{1}{2}$ inch in diameter at its bulb, was poured a small quantity of ethereal oil of turpentine, just as much as was sufficient to cover the aqueous solution to the height of $\frac{2}{10}$ of an inch; and the phial being closed with a good cork, well secured in its place, it was exposed one hour to the heat of boiling water in a steam-vessel.

The gold was revived, appearing in the form of a splendid pellicle of a bright gold colour, which floated on the surface of the aqueous liquid. The oil of turpentine, which at the beginning of the experiment was as pale and colourless as pure water, had taken a bright yellow hue; and the aqueous fluid on which it reposed had entirely lost its yellow colour.

On shaking the phial, its contents were intimately mixed; but, on suffering it to stand quiet, the oil of turpentine soon separated from the aqueous liquid, retaining its bright yellow hue, and leaving the aqueous liquid colourless.

On shaking the phial *before it had been exposed to the heat*, and mixing its contents, and then suffering it to stand quiet, the oil of turpentine, on taking its place at the top of the aqueous solution, was not found to have acquired any colour; nor was the bright gold colour of the solution found to be at all impaired. When sulphuric ether was used instead of the oil of turpentine, the effect was in this respect very different.

To find out whether the oil of turpentine used in this experiment, and which had acquired a deep yellow colour, had lost that property by which it effected the reduction of the metallic oxide, I now poured an additional quantity of the aqueous solution of the oxide into the phial, and shaking the phial exposed it, with its contents, to the heat of boiling water.

After it had been exposed to this heat about two hours, I examined it, and found that though a considerable quantity of gold had been revived, yet the aqueous liquid still retained a faint yellow colour.

The oil of turpentine had acquired a deeper and richer gold colour, approaching to orange.

To the contents of the phial I now added about half as much distilled water, and mixing the whole by shaking I exposed the phial again, during two hours, to the heat of boiling water; when the remainder of the oxide was reduced, and the aqueous liquid left perfectly *colourless*.

On repeating this experiment with oil of turpentine, and varying it by using a solution of the oxide of *silver* (an aqueous solution of nitrate of silver) instead of that of *gold*, the result was nearly the same. The metal was revived, and the oil of turpentine acquired a faint greenish yellow colour.

I also revived the oxides of gold and of silver with *oil of olives* by a similar process, with the heat of boiling water. The oil of olives used in these experiments lost its transparency, and became deeply coloured; that used in the reduction of the oxide of silver taking a very deep dirty brown colour approaching to black, and that employed in reducing the oxide of gold being changed to a yellowish brown with a purple hue.

In the experiment with the oxide of silver, the inside of the phial in the region where the oil reposed on the aqueous solution was beautifully silvered, the revived metal forming a narrow metallic ring extending quite round the phial; and in both experiments small detached pellicles of revived metal were visible in the oil, and adhered in several places to the inside of the phial, forming bright spots, in which the colour of the metal and its peculiar splendour were perfectly conspicuous.

Experiment No. 15.—As *carbon* is one of the constituent principles of spirit of wine, as well as of essential oils and sulphuric ether, I thought it possible that I might succeed in the reduction of the oxide of gold, by mixing alcohol with an aqueous solution of nitromuriate of gold, and exposing the mixture, in a phial well closed, to the heat of boiling water; but the experiment did not succeed.

By pouring upon this mixture a small quantity of oil of olives and exposing it again to the heat of boiling water, the gold was revived.

Is it not probable that the reason why the oxide was not reduced by alcohol is the mobility of those elements, which ought to act on each other, in order that the effect in question may be produced? There is reason to think the oxide would be reduced, could the alcohol be made to rest on the surface of the aqueous solution, without mixing with it.

I wished to have been able to collect and examine the elastic fluids which probably were formed in most of the preceding experiments; but my time was so much taken up with other matters that I had not leisure to pursue these investigations farther.

In order to see what effects would be produced by the heat generated at the surface of an opaque body, of a nature different from those hitherto used in the reduction of the metallic oxides, and one that is little disposed to form a chemical union with oxygen (*magnesia alba*) when, being immersed in an aqueous solution of the oxide of gold, the rays of the sun were made to impinge on it, I contrived the following experiment: —

Experiment No. 16. — I took four small thin phials, A, B, C, and D, of very fine glass; and, putting into each of them about five grains of dry *magnesia alba*, I filled the phial A nearly full with a saturated aqueous solution of the oxide of gold.

I filled the phial B in like manner with some of the same solution, diluted with an equal quantity of distilled water; and the phials C and D were filled with the solution still farther diluted.

These phials, open or without stoppers, were exposed one whole day to the action of the direct rays of a bright sun, their contents being often well mixed together during that time by shaking.

The contents of all these phials changed colour more or less, but they acquired very different hues. The contents of the phial A became of a very deep rich *gold colour* approaching to *orange*, the earthy sediment being throughout of the same tint.

The contents of the phial B, which were at first of a light straw colour, first changed to a light green and then to a greenish blue. The phial having been suffered to stand quiet several days, in an uninhabited room, in a retired part of the house, the solution became nearly colourless, and the sediment was found to be of a dirty olive colour.

The colour of the contents of the phials C and D was changed nearly in the same manner; and having been suffered to stand quiet two or three days to settle, the solution was found to be quite colourless, and the sediment to be deeply coloured. There was, however, a very remarkable difference in the hues of the contents of the two phials; that of the phial C being of a light greenish blue, while that in the phial D was indigo, and of so deep a tint that it might easily have been taken for black.

These appearances were certainly very striking, and well calculated to excite curiosity. I wish that what I have done may induce others to pursue these interesting investigations.

SUPPLEMENT.

SINCE the foregoing paper was presented to the Royal Society, I have had an opportunity of prosecuting these inquiries a little farther; and the results of two of my late experiments were so remarkable that I have thought them deserving of being made known to the public.

Experiment No. 17.— Into a thin globe of fine colourless glass, about $1\frac{1}{2}$ inches in diameter, with a short cylindrical neck, I put equal parts of a weak solution of gum arabic in water and of a diluted aqueous solution of the oxide of gold; and filling the globe about two thirds full with these liquids, which being well mixed together by shaking, the globe was suspended to a nail, by its neck, near a window in an unfrequented room fronting the north, where by accident it happened to remain undisturbed and unobserved six weeks.

When the globe was examined, it exhibited a very curious appearance. The glass was beautifully tinged in every part where it had been in contact with the liquid, but the hues were very different in different parts. The part of the globe in contact with the upper surface of the liquid was of a very faint purple, but this tinge gradually became of a deeper colour as it descended by the sides of the globe, and ended below in a rich gilding, which had all the metallic splendour of pure gold.

Experiment No. 18.—Having provided a thin slip of ivory, about half an inch wide and 3 inches long, I introduced it into a small phial with a wide mouth, nearly filled with a diluted solution of nitrate of silver, where it was suffered to remain in a dark closet till the ivory had acquired a bright yellow colour. The slip of ivory was then taken out of the phial, and immersed in a tumbler of pure water, and immediately exposed in the water to the direct rays of a bright sun.

The instant the sunbeams fell upon the ivory it began to change colour, and in less than two minutes from being of a very beautiful yellow it became quite black.

The rapidity with which this change of colour takes place is very striking, and renders the experiment uncommonly interesting. On examining the ivory, its surface was found to be covered with a fine coaly substance, which was easily rubbed off with the hand.

On removing this coaly substance, after the ivory had been suffered to remain two or three hours exposed in water to the action of the sun's light, the surface of the ivory was found to be completely silvered over, so as perfectly to resemble a slip of metal.

Although this coating of revived metal which covers the surface of the ivory is very thin, yet, if the ivory be well soaked in the solution of nitrate of silver, the oxide of that metal will penetrate the ivory to a considerable depth; and as fast as the silvering wears off from the surface of the ivory, the oxide below it being uncovered and exposed to the light, a new coating of revived metal will be formed to replace it, and the surface of the ivory will not lose its metallic appearance.

I tried by a similar process to gild a slip of ivory with gold, but in this attempt I did not succeed as well as I could have wished. A slip of ivory which had been soaked in a diluted solution of oxi-muriate of gold did not at first acquire a metallic appearance on being exposed in water to the action of the sun's rays; but I found, on examining one of these slips after it had been laid by for several months, that its surface was slightly gilded.

I think it highly probable that means may be devised for expediting this process, and gilding ivory and perhaps some other substances in this way, which would be a valuable acquisition to the arts.

This method of silvering ivory, which is not only expeditious, but very economical, might no doubt be employed with advantage in many cases for ornamental purposes. The process is certainly curious, when considered merely as a philosophical experiment; and I know of no experiment by which the visible and permanent effects produced by light, without apparent heat, can be so expeditiously and so distinctly exhibited.

OF THE MANAGEMENT OF LIGHT IN
ILLUMINATION.

CHAPTER I.

An Investigation of the Principles of the Art of Illu-
mination. — Of the Circumstances which contri-
bute to render Vision distinct. — Of the Dispersion
of Light. — Of the bad Effects of Cross-Lights. —
Descriptions of several new Illuminators of differ-
ent Forms and Dimensions.

THE art of illumination, although it is undoubtedly
one of the most useful that has been invented
by man, and contributes perhaps more than any other
to his comfort and convenience in all countries and in
every class of society, has nevertheless been little cultivated: it has not even been considered as an art; for
the technical terms have not yet been invented which
are indispensably necessary in order to render it possible to treat of it in a clear and satisfactory manner.

My attention was first turned to this interesting subject in the year 1789, when, being actively engaged in
the public service of the late Elector Palatine, reigning
Duke of Bavaria, I was employed by His Most Serene
Highness in establishing Houses of Industry for the
poor, in the cities of Manheim and Munich. In lighting up these spacious establishments, I first learned to

know how much room there was for improvement in the art of illumination; and since that time the subject has frequently been the object of my meditations, and of a variety of experimental researches.

It was with a view to the prosecution of these investigations that I contrived the photometer for measuring the relative intensities of the light emitted by luminous bodies, which is described in the first volume of my Philosophical Papers, page 270.* With the assistance of that instrument I determined the relative quantities of light that are emitted in the combustion of the various inflammable substances most commonly used in procuring light; viz., of beeswax, tallow, and several of the fat oils. An account of the results of these experiments was read before the Royal Society the 6th February, 1794, and was afterwards published in the Philosophical Transactions, and also in the first volume of my Philosophical Papers.

Having found, from the results of these and of other experiments, that the purest light and most beautiful illumination may be obtained by means of lamps properly constructed for less than one eighth part of the price that the same quantity of light would cost if it were furnished by wax candles, and consequently for about half the sum it would cost when furnished by tallow candles, I saw that very great advantages could not fail to result to the public from such improvements in lamps as should render them neat and elegant, and prevent their being any longer liable to those disgusting accidents to which they have hitherto been exposed.

Animated by a strong conviction of the importance

* See also page 7 of this volume.

of the subject to society, I took great pains to make myself thoroughly acquainted with lamps, and with the causes of their imperfections; and I made a great many experiments with a view to improve them. These researches employed my attention occasionally during several years, and in the prosecution of them I actually caused to be constructed more than one hundred lamps (all differing from each other more or less), as I found to my no small surprise on counting them, as they were taken away from a store-room to be carried into another house, on changing my lodgings.

I mention this circumstance merely to show that the subject I have undertaken to treat in this Essay has not been taken up hastily, but that it has long been an object of my meditations, and that I have spared neither pains nor expense in its investigation. If I have not published the results of my numerous experiments, it is because those results were not sufficiently important to merit the attention of the public. They were useful to me, for they made me acquainted with facts with which it was necessary that I should be acquainted, in order to be duly qualified to propose improvements in the construction of lamps; but their details could not fail to be tiresome to readers in general.

By far the greater number of the lamps I caused to be constructed in the course of my experiments were, however, rather rude sketches than finished contrivances. They were designed for making particular experiments, and never could have been employed for any other purpose.

The results of these experimental investigations enabled me to contrive two lamps, for different purposes, which came into very general use in Bavaria; but, as both these are inferior in many respects to the lamps I shall recommend in this Essay, I have not thought that it would be useful to publish any description of them.

As it is a duty incumbent on those who publicly recommend new improvements, not only to show their utility in the clearest manner, but also to explain the principles on which they are grounded, — in treating of illumination, I must first investigate the principles on which that art must be established, and must then point out the particular objects which must be had in view in all attempts to improve the instruments employed in the practice of it.

As artificial light is employed to illuminate surrounding objects to the end that they may be easily and distinctly seen, it is necessary to inquire what circumstances are favourable to distinct vision, and also what circumstances are unfavourable to it.

If the facility with which objects are distinguished by the eye depended solely on the intensity of the light by which they are illuminated, this particular inquiry would be superfluous; but that is very far indeed from being the case.

We can see objects, and even very distinctly, when they are illuminated by light of very different degrees of intensity.

It is a well-known fact that a book may be read at night by the light of the full moon, when the air is very clear; and everybody knows that it may be read when illuminated by the direct rays of a bright meridian sun. The differences of the intensities of the light in these two cases is truly astonishing: the intensity of the light of the sun is to that of the full moon, at the surface of the earth, as *three hundred thousand* to *one*.

But notwithstanding this astonishing power of accommodation possessed by the organ of sight, yet, when the eye passes suddenly from a strong light to one much more feeble, and *vice versa*, nothing can be distinctly seen for some moments. It is true that the eye soon recovers from these momentary derangements, and that habit has rendered them so familiar to us that we seldom take any notice of them; but it is nevertheless most certain that they not only injure the eye very much, and weaken it in such a manner as to impair its faculties at a very early period of life, but that they also render it impossible to see surrounding objects so distinctly as they might be perceived, *even with much less light*, were the illumination established on better principles.

The facility with which we see objects distinctly depends much on their shadows. When the lights and shades are simple and distinct, they are necessarily well defined, and we see distinctly; but when the light arrives in several directions at the same time, the luminous points of the object and its shadows are so blended and confused that distinct vision is impossible, whatever may be the intensity of the light present.

A portrait painter never permits light to come into his room but through one single window; and those who are desirous of having their apartments illuminated at night in the pleasantest manner possible must contrive to have all the light come from one source. If every sudden change in the intensity of the light that strikes the eyes is injurious to them, the direct rays which proceed from the flames of lamps and candles must necessarily fatigue them very much, and render it impossible to see distinctly any objects that may happen to be near those dazzling sources of brightness. A near view of the naked flame of an Argand lamp is quite insupportable, as is well known; but the advantages which would result from masking those flames, and all others used in domestic illumination, have never been justly estimated. That subject has never been properly investigated.

The only way in which the flames of lamps and candles can be masked, without occasioning a great loss of light, is to cover them by screens composed of such substances as disperse the light without destroying it. Ground glass, thin white silk stuffs, such as gauze and crape, fine white paper, horn, and various other substances, may be used for that purpose, and have been used very often.

This contrivance has been in use several years, in most parts of Europe, for moderating the too powerful brightness of Argand's beautiful lamp; but so many important advantages would be derived from the general use of it in all cases, and it would give rise to so many elegant improvements in the forms of illuminators, that too much pains cannot be taken to recommend it.

This system of illumination has been universally practised by the Chinese for many ages; and so wise and so economical a nation could not have continued to practise it so long, had it not been found to be really advantageous. But, without depending on this authority, the utility of the system can be demonstrated by direct and decisive experiments.

As there can be no difference of opinion respecting

the immediate advantage, for the preservation of the eyes and for facilitating vision, which must necessarily be derived from the protection of the eyes from the too powerful action of the direct rays which proceed from the flames of lamps and candles, the only objection that can be made to the proposal for masking those flames by screens must be founded on a supposition that those screens must necessarily destroy a great deal of the light. Now that this is not the case in fact I learned more than twenty years ago, from the result of the following experiment.

Two wax candles, of the same size, and burning with the same degree of vivacity, were placed on two tables, at the distance of about 8 feet from each other, in two tall cylindrical glass jars, about 6 inches in diameter, made of fine transparent glass; the polish of the surface of one of them having been taken off by grinding it with emery. At the distance of about 16 feet from these lights, a sheet of white paper was presented to them, in a vertical position; and a small cylinder of wood, about a quarter of an inch in diameter, held in a vertical position, was placed before the paper, at the distance of about 2 inches.

This cylinder caused two shadows to be cast on the paper; and as these shadows were reciprocally illuminated by the two burning wax candles, if that placed in the transparent glass jar had emitted considerably more light than that placed in the jar of ground glass, the two shadows could not have been of the same density. They were, however, very nearly of the same density; which, as it proved evidently that there was little or no loss of light in its passage through ground glass, as this was contrary to my expectation, it surprised me not a little; but, after meditating more attentively on the subject, I perceived that there was nothing in this result that could not easily be explained.

Although ground glass appears to us to be opaque, it cannot be so in fact. In the operation of grinding it, its surface, which was smooth and even, is so ploughed and broken up as to present an assemblage of asperities which are invisible to the naked eye on account of their extreme smallness, but which have all their sides smooth and shining, as may be seen by examining them with a microscope.

Now it is quite evident that a ray of light which arrives at the smooth surface of one of those little asperities must enter the glass with the same facility (at the same angle of incidence) as it would penetrate the surface of the largest sheet of polished glass ; and it is likewise evident that the ray, having passed through the surface, must continue its course in the glass, and pass out of it on the other side, in the same manner in the one case as in the other.

If a collection of parallel rays of light, forming a small cylindrical bundle, fall perpendicularly on the polished surface of a large sheet of glass, they will pass through the glass in straight lines, and will continue their courses without suffering any change in their direction; but, if these rays fall on a sheet of ground glass, they will be dispersed, and having passed through it they will diverge in all directions.

The final direction of each individual ray will depend on the refractions it will have experienced in passing into the glass and in passing out of it; and these refractions will depend on the positions of the planes of those infinitely small portions of the broken surface of the glass where the rays happen to pass.

If the flame of a burning candle be placed in the centre of a large globe of very fine transparent glass, its rays will pass through the glass without suffering any sensible alteration, either in their direction or in their intensity; and the form and dimensions of the flame will be seen so distinctly through the glass that, at a little distance, the globe might easily escape observation. But if, instead of placing the candle in a globe of transparent glass, it be placed in the centre of a globe of ground glass, the rays of light will be so dispersed in passing through it that from each visible point of its external surface rays will be sent off in all directions, which will render the surface of the globe *luminous.* The flame of the candle will no longer be seen through it, but surrounding bodies will not be less illuminated on that account.

The globe will be the only luminous body which will be visible; and as the intensity of the light at its surface may be diminished without any loss, merely by increasing that surface by augmenting the diameter of the globe, it is evident that by a judicious arrangement of screens of ground glass, or of other fit substances, the too vivid light of lamps may be so dispersed and softened without any considerable loss as to protect the eyes from injury, and at the same time render the illumination infinitely more mild, tranquil, and agreeable.

But if screens can be found which do not sensibly diminish the light employed to render them luminous, and if their forms and dimensions can be varied without inconvenience, there can be no longer any difficulty

in introducing an entirely new system of domestic illumination, which must necessarily be far more beautiful,
and at the same time more pleasant and more economical, than any of the methods hitherto put in practice.

All that is ugly and disgusting in a lamp may be
concealed: the shadows projected by its solid parts
may be obliterated, and the luminous object presented
to the view may at the same time be of an elegant
form, and have a surface sufficiently large to dispense
a great deal of mild light, without being so brilliant as
to dazzle and injure the eyes.

One of my first attempts to put these principles in
practice was made in the year 1800, in lighting the
reading-rooms and lecture-room of the Royal Institution. Argand lamps, with several burners suspended
from the ceiling or elevated on stands, were so covered
by large screens of white gauze, in the form of a flat
dome or truncated cone, as to conceal the lamps
entirely from the view, and at the same time, by dispersing the light over the whole surface of the dome,
to moderate the too intense brilliancy of the flames.

This experiment succeeded even beyond my expectation; and the lighting of these rooms met with such
universal approbation that I was encouraged to proceed in my endeavours to improve the art of illumination.

My next attempt was to light a large dining-room in
my house at Paris, by a single luminous dome suspended over the middle of the dining-table; and, in
order to prevent cross-lights, I ventured to place a cluster of burners, on Argand's principles, in the axis of
this dome, and so near together as to touch each other,
and to feed them with oil from a circular reservoir, in

the form of a hollow flat ring, on which the dome was supported.

By this contrivance I got rid of the inconveniences that attend the use of inverted reservoirs; and I got rid also of all shadows proceeding from the lamp, for that of the flat circular reservoir was entirely effaced at the distance of a few inches from the reservoir (as I expected it would be) by the light emitted by the luminous dome. The shadows of the burners were likewise so completely effaced that there was no appearance of any shadow proceeding from them to be perceived either immediately under the lamps or anywhere else.

The circular reservoir was very convenient for supporting the dome; but one disagreeable circumstance attended this arrangement. As the tops of the burners could not be raised above one inch higher than the level of the bottom of this reservoir, without preventing the oil from flowing freely to the wicks, when the reservoir was suspended at the height of six or seven feet above the floor, the naked flames might be seen under it. To remedy that imperfection, a hoop of white gauze, 4 inches wide and just equal in diameter to the external diameter of the circular reservoir, was suspended from the bottom of the reservoir, or rather from the lower part of a strong brass hoop on which it was placed. This hoop of gauze effectually prevented the naked flames from being seen under the reservoir (except when pains were taken to see them), and when this hoop was ornamented on the outside with festoons of cut glass it became a very elegant object.

All the dishes and plates on the table were illuminated by the direct rays from the burners, but the eyes

of those who were seated round the table were de-
fended from those direct rays by the hoop of gauze
just described. The room was lighted quite sufficiently, and in a most agreeable manner, by the
luminous dome and the hoop of gauze below it. It
was on these principles that the illuminator was constructed which I presented to the first class of the
National Institute of France, on the 24th March, 1806.

A description of it was published in the Memoirs of
the Institute for the next year, and a short account of
it was also published by Mr. Nicholson in his Journal
of Natural Philosophy; but as its usefulness has now
been sufficiently established by the experience of several years, and as it is getting fast into general use on
the Continent, I have thought it right not to postpone
any longer the publication of such a particular description of it as may make it better known in England,
where I am very desirous that it should be found
useful.

As lamps in general have hitherto been so filthy,
and liable to so many disagreeable accidents, that the
name can hardly be pronounced or heard without calling up several disgusting ideas, on that account I am
desirous that my new illuminator may be called an
Illuminator.

As a description of it would be of little use, unless
it were sufficiently detailed and precise to enable an
intelligent workman to execute it, even without having
seen it, I must take the liberty to be very particular in
my account of it. The reader will pass over such of
the details as may appear to him to be tiresome.

As one of the objects principally had in view in contriving this illuminator was to light a room sufficiently

with *one single luminous body* (in order to avoid the bad effects of cross-lights), it was necessary to construct illuminators of different sizes and also of different forms.

There are three varieties of them in use which have all been found to answer very well the different purposes for which they were particularly designed.

1. The *Balloon Illuminator*, which is a luminous globe of 18, 20, or 22 inches in diameter, suspended from the ceiling at the height of 7 or 8 feet, designed for lighting saloons, drawing-rooms, ball-rooms, etc.

2. The *Dining-Room Illuminator*, which serves likewise for lighting a billiard-room in great perfection. This is likewise suspended from the ceiling; but its screen, instead of being globular, is in the form of a dome, with a hoop about four or five inches in width suspended from the bottom of it.

3. The *Table Illuminator*, which is covered by a hemispherical screen or dome, is placed on a stand or foot about twenty inches high, and is used for lighting a dining-table or reading or working table; and it lights the room at the same time quite sufficiently, if the room be not large.

All these illuminators have circular horizontal reservoirs for the oil, which have all the same depth, — viz., one eighth of an inch, — but which are of different widths and diameters, according to the number of burners which they are destined to supply.

These burners, whatever may be their number, are all placed close together, in a cluster, in the centre of the reservoir, and so near as to touch each other. They have hitherto been constructed on Argand's principles, and each of them is furnished with its separate chimney; but from a discovery I have lately made I think it very probable that an important improvement will soon be made, by employing one burner with several wicks, instead of several separate burners.

The most powerful balloon illuminators that have yet been made have had six Argand burners; their reservoirs are $22\frac{1}{2}$ inches in diameter externally, and $2\frac{1}{4}$ inches in width; and their light has been found to be quite sufficient for illuminating very spacious saloons in the most complete manner.

Those most generally used at Paris for lighting drawing-rooms are such as have *three* or *four* burners, which have reservoirs of 17 and $19\frac{1}{2}$ inches in diameter.

All the pendulous dining-room illuminators that have yet been constructed have either *three* or *four* burners; and those used for lighting billiard-rooms have all had *four*.

All the table illuminators hitherto made have had single burners, and their circular reservoirs have had 10 inches in diameter externally, and about 1 inch in width; but there is no reason why illuminators of this kind should not be constructed with *two* and even with *three* burners. When placed on stands of about 24 or 26 inches in height, they would be found very convenient for lighting large dining-tables in dining-rooms which are not high enough to allow a pendulous illuminator to be properly suspended.

From what has been said a general idea may be formed of the construction and use of these illuminators. I shall now proceed to give particular descriptions of their different parts, with full directions for the management of them; together with such occasional remarks as may be necessary, in order to illustrate the principles on which they have been constructed.

When new inventions are recommended to the public, calculated to produce a total change in habits long established, no hope can reasonably be entertained of their being adopted, unless pains be taken to show their utility in the plainest and most convincing manner.

I shall first give an account of the means that have been used for suspending the pendulous illuminators; and, as there is nothing either new or complicated in this machinery, it may be described in a few words.

A strong hoop of brass, of about 1 inch in width, is suspended from the ceiling of the room in a position perfectly horizontal, by means of six chains attached to six arrows of brass, of about 0.4 of an inch in diameter and 6.9 inches in length, which project horizontally from the outside of the hoop, to which they are firmly fixed. These chains, which are each about 30 inches in length, are all fixed above to the bottom of an ornamented baldaquin, which is a hoop of brass in the form of a crown, of about 9 inches in diameter; which hoop is suspended in a horizontal position by means of a double cord, which passes over two pulleys fixed in a small block, which is attached by means of a hook to a staple fixed in the ceiling. This cord descends and is attached to a counterpoise of lead in the form of a large tassel, ornamented by gilding. This tassel being made hollow, the cord by which the illuminator is suspended passing through it, is kept in its place.

The length of the cord is such that, when the illuminator is at a proper height, the heavy tassel, which serves as a counterpoise to it, has descended so low as nearly to touch the top of the crown or ornamented ring where the six chains unite; and the weight of the counterpoise is such that the friction of the cord and pulleys is sufficient to prevent the illuminator from either ascending or descending, except when force is employed to raise it or to lower it.

The crown (baldaquin) to which the chains are attached above is of an elegant form, and it is commonly ornamented more or less with cut glass. The chains are likewise very richly ornamented, by fixing in each of their oblong links of gilt brass an oblong diamond of cut glass, of about 2 inches in length and 1 inch in width in the middle, cut into facets. These are called olives in France; and they cost at Paris six sous apiece. To hide the cords, they are loosely wrapped round with thin silk stuff, of the same kind and colour with that used for the curtains of the windows. This is placed loose about them, and in such a manner as not to prevent the free action of the pulleys.

The large horizontal hoop and the arrows that project from it, which together weigh about $5\frac{1}{2}$ lbs. avoirdupois, are sometimes gilt; and they are sometimes painted white or of a dark bronze colour.

This hoop has a rim about half an inch wide, even with the level of its under side, and projecting inwards, which serves two important purposes: it strengthens the hoop and prevents its shape from being altered; and it forms a convenient support for the circular reservoir of the illuminator, which reposes on it.

The diameter of the hoop should be about a quarter of an inch greater than the diameter of the circular reservoir which it is destined to receive, in order that the reservoir may be removed and replaced without difficulty. This reservoir is always removed and taken away and carried into another room, when the illuminator is cleaned and replenished with oil.

The reservoir is a hollow, flat, horizontal ring made of tin (tinned iron), just 0.8 of an inch in thickness or depth, and from 1 inch to $2\frac{1}{4}$ inches in breadth, according to the number of burners it is destined to supply. These burners are fixed in its centre in a cluster, as has already been observed; and their openings above are just 1 inch above the level of the bottom of the reservoir. Each burner is supplied with oil from the reservoir by a small tube, a quarter of an inch in diameter, which, descending obliquely from the inside of the reservoir, enters the burner on one side of it, and at such a distance below its upper extremity as is just sufficient to allow the glass chimney of the burner to be fixed in its proper place.

Each of the burners is cylindrical; and it is fixed in the axis of a cylindrical tube, 1.88 inch in diameter and 5 inches in length. This vertical tube receives the glass chimney into its opening above. The wick, which is in the form of a tube, is moved either by a rack or by a vertical endless screw, concealed in the interior of the vertical tube just described, and attached to the side of the burner. When this last contrivance is used, the small horizontal wheel, by means of which the screw is turned, should not be made flat, as they are *commonly* made, but *dishing*, in order that the oil, which sometimes finds its way through the collars in which this screw turns and runs down slowly on the axis of the wheel, may not be able to spread on the wheel, so as to arrive at its periphery, where it is touched by the finger in turning it, in moving the wick. The introduction of this small improvement has, I am persuaded, contributed very much to the approbation universally bestowed on the table illuminator and to its rapid introduction into general use.

In the table illuminator the small quantity of oil which occasionally leaks out of the burner below descends immediately into the column on which the illuminator is placed, consequently it is never seen, and may easily be removed as often as shall be found necessary.

For receiving and at the same time concealing the leakage of the burners of pendulous illuminators, a shallow globular dish of tin, painted white and varnished, about 4 inches in diameter and 1 inch in depth, is fixed, by means of a strong screw passing through its centre, immediately under the lower extremities of the burners. The bottom of this dish is ornamented below by a large gilt knob in the form of an acorn, which gives it the appearance of having been placed there for the sole purpose of giving an elegant finish to the balloon below or to cover the ends of the burners, and for presenting a convenient handle for taking hold of the illuminator in moving it up or down.

There is a circular opening in the under part of the balloon, of about 2 inches in diameter, through which the brass knob projects downwards; and there is also a circular opening, of about 4 or 5 inches in diameter, in the middle of the hemispherical screen which forms the upper half of the balloon or the dome, through which opening the ends of the glass chimneys project, which belong to the burners; but neither of these openings is much noticed when the illuminator is in its proper place, and that above is indeed never seen, so that the form of the illuminator when lighted is always simple and elegant.

The lower hemispherical screen of the balloon illuminator is attached to the brass hoop by means of a hinge, and it is fastened to the opposite side of it by a hook; but the upper hemispherical screen of all the illuminators is merely laid down on the top of the reservoir, and may be taken away whenever it is necessary.

These screens, notwithstanding that their openings both above and below are circular, are not of a spherical form, though when seen at a little distance they appear to be globular. They are composed of skeletons made of strong iron wire, wound round with narrow thin white silk ribbon, and covered with thick white gauze or white crape. The wire is so disposed as to form nine or twelve vertical ribs, according to the size of the screen; and, where ornament is required, these ribs are covered on the outside, and entirely concealed from the view, by rows of brilliants of cut glass, gradually diminishing in size from what may be called the equator of the balloon towards its two poles. These brilliants, being perforated with small holes at each of their extremities, are easily attached to the ribs by screwing.

By covering the whole of the surface of the balloon in this manner with cut glass, a most beautiful and splendid effect may be produced without sensibly diminishing the light or disturbing the agreeable mildness and tranquillity of the illumination. One balloon illuminator has already been ornamented in this manner under the direction of M. Ravrio, and has been much admired. It was made to occupy the middle of

a very superb lustre. But I must return to more hum·
ble but not less important details.

Having by means of luminous screens, properly disposed, contrived to conceal all that was disgusting
in the appearance of lamps, — to obliterate all their
shadows which rendered them so gloomy and melan-
choly, to disperse the too powerful brightness of their
flames without destroying their light, and to unite a
sufficient quantity of mild light in one place to illuminate large rooms from one source, — a difficulty still
remained, which, if means had not been found to sur-
mount it, must for ever have prevented these improvements from coming into general use. The spilling of
the oil in transporting lamps from one place to another
is an accident which is so very disagreeable, and yet
so common, that no person of taste or feeling can,
without considerable repugnance, permit a lamp to be
brought into an elegant apartment; and it is easy to
perceive that, when oil is put into large circular reservoirs, the danger of its being thrown out of them on
the least motion is so great that the accident could
not fail to happen very often if the most effectual
means were not used to prevent it.

I was so fortunate as to hit upon a very simple contrivance for preventing the oil from being spilled in the
management of my illuminators; and the means employed are so effectual that the accident is evidently all
but impossible. The person who has sold more than
200 of them in Paris assures me that this accident has
never once happened, to his knowledge, during the six
years he has been engaged in the fabrication and sale
of them; and he is so persuaded that it cannot happen
that he does not hesitate to place pendulous illumi-

nators directly over the middle of the most elegant billiard-tables, even where he has no reason to suppose that the servants into whose hands they come are particularly careful.

This contrivance, which is extremely simple, can easily be described. The reservoir for the oil, which, as has already been observed, is a flat, hollow ring, has three openings above at equal distances from each other. They are short, vertical brass tubes, of about half an inch in height and three quarters of an inch in diameter internally, which are soldered to the upper part of the reservoir. Each of them is furnished with a brass stopper, which closes it hermetically; and each of the stoppers is perforated in its axis, and receives a screw of about a quarter of an inch in diameter and three quarters of an inch in length, which by means of a collar of leather closes this aperture completely when the screw is screwed down fast in its place. But these screws are not entire: about one third part of the substance of each of them is filed away, from the shoulder which supports the collar of leather quite down to the lower end of the screw. This neither prevents the screw from moving regularly in the female screw, nor from closing hermetically the opening in the brass stopper when it is screwed down fast in its place; but, when the screw is turned backwards one or two turns, a passage is opened by which air can pass freely in or out of the reservoir.

When the illuminator is lighted, a passage for the air to enter the reservoir must be opened by unscrewing one of these screws, otherwise the oil cannot flow to the burners; but at all other times all these screws must be kept screwed fast down, which will most

effectually prevent the oil from being spilled in transporting the illuminator from place to place.   It would
even be very difficult to make it run out at the openings of the burners, for the pressure of the external air
would prevent it.

As the reservoirs of the table illuminators are small,
two openings above, opposite to each other, have been
found to be sufficient; but, when the reservoir is much
larger, three openings are useful, as they afford the
means of seeing when the reservoir is placed horizontally, as also when it is completely filled with oil.
There never can be any use in opening more than one
of the passages for the admittance of air into the reservoir when the illuminator is lighted, and that is to be
opened which happens to be nearest at hand.

A very important advantage has been obtained by
making the reservoirs of those illuminators large and
shallow; for, as the level of the oil in the reservoir
varies so little, the burners are always well supplied,
without employing any of those complicated contrivances which have been used for preserving the level
of the oil in Argand's lamp.   As all these methods are
connected more or less with the elastic force exerted
by the air, and as that force varies with heat and cold,
these contrivances are liable to many inconveniences,
not to mention the awkward and complicated forms
they give to lamps, and the disagreeable nature of the
operation of filling their reservoirs with oil.

If a lamp with an inverted reservoir, after having
burned some time, be extinguished and suffered to
cool, it must be filled anew before it can be lighted
again: otherwise the air which has found its way into
the upper part of the inverted reservoir, on being

heated by the flame of the lamp, will press on the oil below it with an increased force, which will cause a part of it to descend and overflow the burner and run out into the room; and these accidents frequently happen even without lighting the lamp a second time, and sometimes without its having been lighted at all, merely in consequence of the ordinary changes which take place in the temperature of the air, especially in rooms which front the south, where these occasional variations of temperature are most considerable.

As people in general are not aware of the danger to which they are exposed, when lamps with fountain reservoirs, partly filled with oil, are left several days hung up in the rooms which they are destined to illuminate, it may be useful to explain this matter at some length.

When a lamp with an inverted reservoir has burned for some time, the oil in the reservoir becomes warm, and the air which now occupies the upper part of it is warm likewise; but, as soon as the lamp is extinguished and begins to cool, the elasticity of the air in the reservoir begins to be diminished. And, as the pressure of the atmosphere without remains the same, a part of the oil in the burner and in the canal which leads to it is forced back into the reservoir by the pressure of the external air.

If the quantity of air in the reservoir is considerable, and the cooling process continues, so much of the oil in the burner and in the canal leading to it will be forced to return into the reservoir that its level will at length be so much lowered that the opening of the inverted reservoir (which is at its lower extremity) will cease to be submerged in this oil; and, as the cooling goes on, a portion of atmospheric air will make its way into the reservoir by this opening; and the more the cold increases, the greater will be the quantity of air which will thus find its way into the reservoir.

As long as the cold continues, this air will produce no bad effects; but as soon as the lamp becomes sensibly warmed, either in consequence of its being lighted or of a change of temperature in the surrounding atmosphere, the elasticity of the air confined in the upper part of the reservoir will be increased, and will cause a part of the oil below it to be driven out of the reservoir, which will overflow the burner and run out of the lamp. Various attempts have been made to remedy this capital defect of lamps with inverted reservoirs, but none of them have been completely successful. None of them that I have been acquainted with have rendered it possible to light one of these lamps a second time (without emptying and filling it anew), without danger of having some of the oil forced out of the lamp by the expansion of the air in the reservoir, on its being warmed.

This accident is always very disagreeable; and I took special care to avoid it in my illuminators, by avoiding the use of inverted reservoirs.

As every new contrivance, however simple it may be in its construction, is in the greatest danger of being put out of order and spoiled by the ignorance and awkwardness of those into whose hands it comes, it is indispensably necessary that the most particular practical directions should accompany every proposal for the introduction of new improvements. On that ground I hope to be excused for giving the following very particular directions for the management of my illuminators.

One of the six chains by which the pendulous illuminators are suspended must be attached to its corresponding arrow by means of a hook, in order that it
may be unhooked below, and laid aside occasionally
in order to open a passage between the two neighbouring chains for removing the reservoir or the upper
hemispherical screen.

As six chains are employed in suspending the brass
hoop on which the reservoir reposes, this hoop remains suspended, even when one of these chains is
unhooked and laid aside; and as these chains are not
attached immediately to the hoop, but at some distance (3½ inches) from it, to arrows which project horizontally from the outside of it, the opening between
the two neighbouring chains which remain after the
movable chain has been unhooked and laid back on
one of them is so wide that the reservoir or the hemispherical screen can pass between them, without touching either of them.

As these pendulous illuminators will burn well eight
or nine hours without being replenished, it will seldom
be necessary to refresh them with oil while they are in
actual use. If, however, that should be necessary, it
may easily be done, even without extinguishing them
and without danger. But, in general, the reservoir is
always to be taken away and carried out of the room
when it is to be filled, and the burners cleaned and
trimmed.

In removing the reservoir, the following precautions
are necessary: first, the burners having been extinguished, the illuminator must be lowered down to that
height which is most convenient for lifting the reservoir out of its place; or, in case the height of the room

be not sufficient to allow the counterpoise to rise high enough to permit this to be done, a light stand with steps, such as are used in libraries, may be employed to get up to a proper height to perform that operation, without lowering the illuminator. When rooms are so low as to render the use of steps necessary in this operation, as there will be no longer any use for pulleys, the illuminator may be suspended from the ceiling by a simple cord, or by a thin rod of iron, having a hook at each end of it.

The first thing to be done in preparing to remove the reservoir is to unhook the movable chain and lay it aside; the upper part of the balloon (the dome) is then to be lifted up and taken away, care being taken not to derange the chimneys of the burners; the screw belonging to the opening by which air is admitted into the reservoir is next to be screwed down fast, *and this precaution must never be omitted.*

As soon as this is done, the reservoir may be lifted up and taken away, as there will be no longer any danger of the oil being thrown out of it in carrying.

If the illuminator be suspended by pulleys, a weight must be at hand equal to the weight of the reservoir, which must be hung to the brass hoop which supports the reservoir. This is necessary, in order to prevent the hoop from being suddenly drawn upwards by the descent of the counterpoise on the removal of the reservoir.

A temporary stand, about 6 or 8 inches in height, must be provided in the room where the illuminator is cleaned and arranged, on which the reservoir can be placed in a situation perfectly horizontal. In this situation it remains placed on a table, while its burners are cleaned and trimmed, and till its reservoir has been filled with oil. In filling it, care must always be taken to remove the three stoppers which close its three openings above, in order that the air may escape out of it with the greater facility, and that it may be seen when it is properly filled with oil.

As soon as the reservoir is full of oil, the openings above must be closed by their stoppers, and all the screws must be screwed fast, and no passage must be opened for the air to enter the reservoir till after it shall have been carried back and set down in its horizontal brass hoop.

As table illuminators are liable to be removed frequently from place to place when they are not lighted, the screw which closes the passage for the admittance of air into their reservoir should not be opened till the moment when they are lighted; but as the reservoir of this illuminator is not large, and as the tube is narrow which conveys the oil from it to the burner, there is very little danger of the oil being spilled in removing it from place to place, either when it is lighted or when it is not lighted, even though the passage for the air should be left open. I never knew the accident to happen, and it is evidently so unlikely to happen that most people never give themselves the trouble to close that passage on any occasion. By closing this passage with a hollow, conical brass stopper, similar to that used in my *portable lamps* which will be described hereafter, the accident in question would be most effectually prevented. But to return to the pendulous illuminators.

When one of these is to be lighted, the following operations must be performed: —

The illuminator must first be pulled down to a convenient height, or, if it be not suspended by pulleys, steps must be used for getting up to it. The movable chain must then be unhooked and laid aside, and the upper part of the balloon or the dome taken away. When this has been done, one of the screws which close the passages for admitting air into the reservoir must be a little raised, if this should not have been done before.

If it be a balloon illuminator, the under part of the balloon is to be unhooked, in order that it may fall down and hang suspended by the hinge by which it is attached to the horizontal brass hoop which supports the reservoir.

The burners are then to be lighted, one after the other, and their glass chimneys fixed in their places.

As soon as all the wicks are well on fire, they are to be shortened, by drawing them back into their cylindrical burners by means of their racks or endless screws, till their flames are reduced so as to become very short and almost on the point of being extinguished. This is *absolutely necessary*, in order to prevent the upper half of the balloon or the dome from being scorched and perhaps set on fire by the heat, in being passed over the ends of the chimneys of the burners, over which it must pass in order to its being put down into its place.

As soon as this upper half of the balloon or the dome is in its place, the movable chain may again be hooked to the arrow to which it belongs; after which the wicks may be raised, one after the other, till the flames are brought to be of a proper height. When this has been done, the under half of the balloon may be again fixed in its place, and the illuminator may be fitted up and fixed at its proper elevation.

These directions may perhaps be thought tedious; but I have been acquainted with so many accidents, that such particular instructions would probably have prevented, that I dare not venture to suppress them. By following them strictly, I am quite certain that no disagreeable accident whatever can happen in the management of these new illuminators.

It still remains for me to give a more particular account of the table illuminator; and, as it appears to me to be probable that this invention will soon come into general use, I shall be very particular in describing it. The Fig. 1 (Plate V.), which represents a vertical section of it, may serve to give an idea of its general form and appearance; and it will no doubt be very useful to workmen who may be employed to make these illuminators.

In this figure the contour of the dome is indicated by dotted lines, and also the form of its little gallery made of japanned tin, which serves as a handle for taking it on and off. The form of the reservoir is likewise distinctly seen by a vertical section of it.

It will be observed that a circular groove is made on the top of the reservoir for receiving the dome and keeping it in its proper place, and that the inside of the reservoir is made sloping. It was made of this form, in order that it might less obstruct the light, and that its internal surface might serve as a reflector.

The oil is conveyed to the burner by one of the two branches seen in the figure, by which the reservoir is fixed to the burner. These two branches are a little curved, in order to give the illuminator a more elegant

PLATE V.

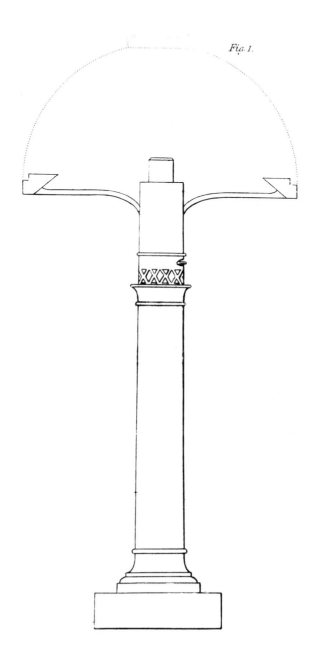

Fig. 1.

appearance. These branches are three-cornered tubes, having one of their flat sides uppermost.

The openings by which the air enters the burner are distinctly seen just above the level of the projecting rim of the column ; and just above these openings the projecting edge of the vertical wheel is seen, which is turned round in lowering or raising the wick.

Just above this wheel is a moulding; but the illuminator would have a more simple and more elegant appearance if, by lowering the moulding to the level of the wheel, this might appear to make a part of the moulding.

The openings for the admission of the oil and for the passage of the air in and out of the reservoir are not represented in this figure. The foot on which the column is placed is 5.4 inches square and 1.5 inch thick. It is usually painted and japanned so as to resemble a piece of marble or granite.

On this square foot the plinth of the column is fixed, which is 3.35 inches square and 0.4 of an inch thick ; and on the plinth the column is placed, which is ornamented with mouldings, and often gilded and japanned. It is 1.88 inches in diameter above and 2.1 inches in diameter below, and at its upper extremity it has a rim which projects outwards 0.4 of an inch. This rim is very useful in transporting the illuminator from place to place, as it affords a firm support for the hand.

The column is made of strong tin; and it is closed below, that it may the more conveniently serve as a reservoir for the oil which may occasionally leak out of the burner.

The burner, properly so called, is a cylinder of tin, 3.8 inches in length and 1.05 inch in diameter, constructed on Argand's principles. It is fixed in a vertical position in the axis of a larger cylinder, which is 1.88 inch in diameter and 5.8 in length, in the opening of which above the glass chimney is fixed. The lower part of this cylinder enters 1.5 inch within the column, and is firmly attached to it by means of a projecting metallic knob, situated on the inside of the column near its upper extremity. A vertical slit or opening, on one side of the cylinder, about a quarter of an inch wide and an inch and a quarter long, permits the cylinder to enter the column, notwithstanding its projecting knob; and when the cylinder has been forced down into the column so low that this knob comes to strike against the upper part of this vertical opening, on turning round the cylinder, the column being held fast, the knob is forced into a horizontal opening, by which means the cylinder and the column are locked together, in a manner similar to that employed for fixing a bayonet to its musket. This horizontal opening in the side of the cylinder, into which the knob passes in fastening the cylinder to the column, may be about one inch in length; and, instead of making it everywhere of the same width, it will be best to make it a little narrower towards its extremity, in order that the knob may fill it completely in that part, and on being forced into it, like a wedge, may hold the faster.

As it will seldom be found necessary to separate the reservoir from its stand (once a month, perhaps, just to pour out any small quantity of oil that may have leaked out of the burner and fallen down into the column), it will be very desirable that the reservoir should be fixed to the column in the most solid manner, in order to prevent their being separated by any accident, while the illuminator is in use.

The square foot on which the column is placed may be made of tin, and it may be filled with sand in order to give it sufficient weight. To prevent its scratching the table on which it is placed, a very simple contrivance has been used. Two pieces of hammered sole leather, each 1 inch square, being cut diagonally, they form four triangular pieces; each of which being riveted by three rivets to a triangular piece of strong tin of the same form and size, care being taken to sink the heads of the rivets below the surface of the leather, on soldering these triangular pieces to the bottom of the square foot of the column, one at each of its four corners, these pieces of leather prevent the bottom of the stand from touching the table. Horn or wood might be made use of instead of leather for this purpose.

A considerable expense might be saved by making the column and its foot of one piece of cast iron. As it might be japanned and gilded as easily as tin or plate iron, it might be as highly finished, and its form might more easily be made correct and elegant.

I have a table illuminator in my house, which is placed on a gilt Ionic column, which is furnished with its capital and all its members, in just proportion; and it is really a very beautiful object. But, as it is chiefly made of gilt brass, it comes high; but it might be made nearly as beautiful of cast iron, and probably at one quarter of the expense.

A little ornament, well chosen and well placed, often produces a very fine effect. I had a striking proof of this in the effect produced by covering the ribs of the dome belonging to this illuminator with artificial diamonds of fine cut glass, and placing a gallery or circular balustrade of cut glass, about an inch in height, round the opening (3 inches only in diameter) at the top of this dome, through which the end of the chimney of the burner passes.

As this gallery is illuminated by the direct rays of the flame, it produces a beautiful effect, which is the more striking on account of the mild light which is diffused by the luminous dome on which it stands.

Some of these table illuminators have been constructed with hemispherical screens below as well as above, which gives them the appearance of a luminous balloon placed on a column and surrounded horizontally by a narrow hoop (about half an inch wide, japanned and gilded), the apparent external circumference of their reservoirs.

When arranged in this manner, the illuminator is very beautiful, especially when seen at a little distance; but, for illuminating objects placed on a table, the dome screen is preferable, on account of the shadows of objects being more distinct and better defined when the light is less diffused.

In examining minute objects, it is always advantageous that they should be illuminated by the direct rays which proceed from bodies that are intensely luminous; but great care must be taken to prevent the eyes being exposed to those rays. No artificial illumination can be so advantageous for nice observations as that of daylight when the sun is high and shines bright; but nobody in those circumstances can look at the sun with impunity.

But that kind of illumination which is most favourable to very distinct vision is not that which is most agreeable; nor is it the most favourable to the beauty of objects in general, or to human beauty. Lines strongly marked are always hard, and some uncertainty is necessary in order that the imagination may have room to play.

No decayed beauty ought ever to expose her face to the direct rays of an Argand lamp; nor should she ever look at herself in her glass with her spectacles on.

That mysterious light which comes from bodies moderately illuminated is certainly most favourable to female beauty, and ought on that account to be preferred by all persons who are wise; but I must not indulge in these pleasing speculations.

In all cases where rooms are lighted by illuminators, all other lights must be excluded; for the admission of either lamps or candles burning with naked flames would greatly disturb that pleasing tranquillity which reigns where the light is mild and uniformly distributed, and instead of being advantageous to distinct vision would, by dazzling the eyes and introducing a confusion of lights and shades, render it much more difficult to see objects distinctly.

As the light of an Argand lamp is so exceedingly vivid that when it is near at hand it may often be found to be too powerful to be agreeable, even when placed behind the screens, in that case I would recommend a very simple contrivance which I often use, and which effectually defends the eyes without darkening the room or sensibly diminishing the beauty of the illumination. A hoop, made of strong white writing paper, of about $2\frac{1}{2}$ inches in width, is so fitted to the outside of the dome of the table illuminator below as to embrace it exactly, and in such a manner as to be supported by it.

The use of this additional paper screen is so far from impairing the illumination of objects placed on the table that it improves it, and it never fails to render vision much more distinct by preventing the eyes from being fatigued and injured; and although objects in distant parts of the room will, in some places, be somewhat less illuminated, yet even there they will be seen distinctly, for the eye will be better prepared to perceive them.

Most of the table illuminators that have been made and sold at Paris have, in addition to their domes of white gauze, been furnished with conical screens or reflectors, made of tin, painted white and varnished on the inside, and painted on the outside of the same colour as the column; but these painted reflectors occasion so great a loss of light, and give so dismal a tinge to the small quantity they reflect, that I never make use of them, and certainly shall never recommend them to others. Lamp-makers and dealers in tin may wish to keep up their credit; but I must say that I think them perfectly useless, and it is evident that they are often embarrassing.

I cannot finish my account of this table illuminator without recommending it in a very particular manner to the studious, and to all those who are in the habit of reading and writing by candlelight. As it gives a great deal of mild light, about six times as much as a good wax candle, it illuminates sufficiently without being near; and, as its stand is considerably higher than a common candlestick, it may be so placed as not to be seen by those who are reading, writing, or working by its light, which circumstance renders the illumination uncommonly mild and agreeable, and tends much to the preservation of the eyes.

I was long of opinion that no lamp would ever be contrived that would be preferable to wax candles for lighting the interior of a private apartment; but I am now convinced that this illuminator gives a pleasanter light than wax candles, and that it is much less liable to disagreeable accidents, and many persons of good taste, to whom I have recommended it, all concur with me in this opinion. That it is more economical than even tallow candles will be shown hereafter.

As the public have a right to expect that those who propose new improvements should give some information respecting the prices that may reasonably be asked by manufacturers for the objects recommended, I feel it to be my duty to mention the prices at which the different kinds of illuminators here described have been sold at Paris.

The table illuminators, elegantly painted and japanned, with two domes, one of thick white gauze, the other of thinner gauze, with a conical reflector of tin, painted white and varnished within, and painted, gilded, and japanned without, have been sold at 55 francs. Those placed on handsome Ionic columns, furnished with their capitals, cost 60 francs. When the columns, with or without capitals, are entirely gilded, they cost no more than when they are painted to imitate marble or granite, and japanned. With each table illuminator sold at these prices are given two glass chimneys and six circular wicks.

These illuminators, or rather imperfect imitations of them, have been sold in some of the shops in Paris as low as 36 francs; but I have so seldom found it to be advantageous to make purchases in cheap shops that I generally avoid them myself, and never recommend them to others.

A dining-room illuminator of the simplest construction, suspended from the ceiling by a metallic rod, with its six chains made of strong links of gilt wire, without being enriched with cut glass, may cost from 200 to 250 francs.

Those most commonly sold at Paris for lighting elegant dining-rooms have had their chains richly ornamented with large artificial diamonds of an oblong form, called olives, made of fine cut glass, and the broad hoop of gauze suspended below the dome covered on the outside with cut glass arranged in festoons. When ornamented in this manner and suspended by pulleys, they cost from 300 to 350 francs.

Balloon illuminators, with three or four burners, for drawing-rooms, ornamented in the same manner, and the ribs of their balloons covered with small diamonds of cut glass, are sold at different prices according to their sizes, and according to the richness and profusion of their ornaments. Very elegant ones with four burners may now be had for 300 francs, which two years ago could not be had for less than 350 francs. As their prices are lowering every day, as the number of manufacturers employed in making and selling them increases, I imagine they will be sold for 10*l.* or 12*l.* sterling in a year or two, and perhaps still lower.

By constructing the hoop by which the reservoir is suspended of strong tin, or of sheet iron painted and japanned, instead of making it of brass and gilding it in the fire, and by making the arrows out of strong iron wire painted and japanned, instead of making them of gilt brass, the price of these pendulous illuminators might be greatly reduced, without making them less useful or much less ornamental.

Their reservoirs are always painted white and ja-panned; and if the hoop which supports the reservoir and its six projecting arrows were also painted white and ornamented modestly, by gilding the two borders of the hoop and the feathers of the arrows, the illuminator would perhaps be quite as beautiful as it now is, when this hoop and its arrows have the appearance of burnished gold.

A considerable expense might be saved, without occasioning any considerable inconvenience, by suspending all pendulous illuminators by metallic rods, instead of suspending them by means of cords passing over pulleys.

Small pendulous balloon illuminators, with one single burner, have lately been introduced at Paris; and they light a boudoir or any other small room in so very elegant a manner that they deserve to be just mentioned. Their circular reservoirs are $12\frac{3}{4}$ inches in diameter on the outside, and about $1\frac{1}{4}$ inch in width; and their balloons are ornamented with cut glass. When the hoop, which supports the reservoir, and its six arrows are made of strong tin, painted of a bronze colour and varnished, this illuminator is sold for 80 francs. They are suspended at the height of about $6\frac{1}{2}$ feet above the floor; and, as the surface of the balloon is very large in proportion to the quantity of light by which it is rendered luminous, the light it diffuses is very mild, and the balloon may be viewed without any injury to the eyes.

Several pendulous balloon illuminators with two burners have also been constructed, which have been sold as low as 120 francs.

CHAPTER II.

Description of a Portable Lamp.

AS vegetable oils, purified by means of the sulphuric acid, burn without either smoke or smell
and give a great abundance of pure white light in their
combustion, and as they cost considerably less than
tallow by the pound and give more light, great advantages would be derived from the general use of them
for domestic illumination; but, to render this possible,
lamps must be made portable. As they have hitherto
been constructed, the danger of spilling the oil is so
great, and that accident is so very disagreeable, that
nobody who can avoid it will make use of them,
except in cases where they can be stationary. Where a
light is wanted that must be continually moved about
from place to place, candles are universally preferred,
though many inconveniences attend the use of them.

Perceiving that great advantages could not fail to be
derived from the introduction of a good *portable lamp*
for common use, to supply the place of tallow candles,
I have taken a good deal of pains to contrive such a
lamp, and after many experiments I have at length
succeeded in this undertaking.

This lamp, which is not inelegant in its appearance,
is liable to none of those disagreeable accidents to
which lamps in general are exposed. It is so perfectly
neat and cleanly that it never spills a drop of oil nor
even lets it come into view; and, when properly arranged, it never smokes or diffuses any disagreeable
smell, not even when it is extinguished. Its flame,

being covered and protected by its glass chimney, burns so steadily that it is not in the least deranged either by the wind or in being moved about from place to place; and the flame of this lamp is so immovably fixed in the axis of its chimney, by the ascending current of air, that it does not quit it, even when the chimney is considerably inclined, so that the flame very seldom touches the glass.

This lamp has one quality which no other ever possessed before in the same perfection. It may be made to furnish any quantity of light required, from that of the smallest bed-chamber lamp or feeblest taper to that furnished by three or four candles all burning together; and these alternate variations in the quantities of light emitted by it may be repeated at pleasure, without any trouble, merely by turning a button which moves a rack that is concealed in the body of the lamp, or rather in the column on which it is placed.

I shall first endeavour to give an idea of the general form of this lamp, and shall then proceed to describe its various parts more particularly.

In order to render these descriptions more satisfactory, I have given a figure of the lamp (Plate VI., Fig. 2) drawn to a scale of half its real size. *a*, Fig. 2, is a circular reservoir which surrounds the upper end of the vertical tube *b*, in the axis of which the burner is placed.

The end of the burner appears above the circular reservoir, and its flame is confined in the glass chimney *g*, which, for want of room, is represented broken off, just above the point of the flame.

The vertical tube *c* is the stand which supports the

PLATE VI.

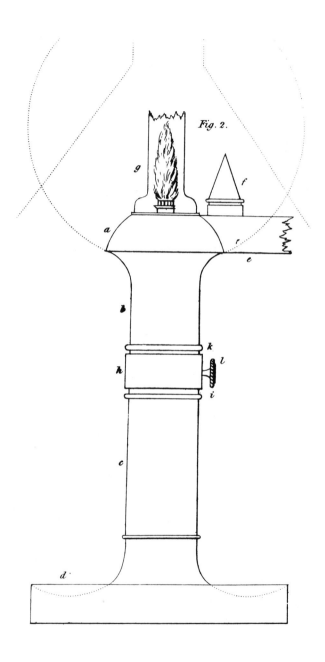

Fig. 2.

lamp. It has a circular foot *d*, and it ends above at the moulding *i*, which belongs to it, and forms what may be considered as its brim. Into the opening of the tube *c*, the lower extremity of the tube *b* enters at about one inch; and it is firmly fixed in it by means of a contrivance similar to that used for fixing a bayonet to its musket.

About one inch and a half above the lower extremity of the tube *b*, this tube is perforated by a circular row of air-holes, which goes quite round it. These holes are concealed by the hoop *h*, which is fastened to the tube *b* by means of three vertical projections, made of pieces of wire soldered to the tube at equal distances from each other. The hoop being afterwards soldered to the ends of these wires, it is supported by them in its place, and the air passing between the inside of the hoop and the outside of the tube enters the air-holes.

The use of this hoop is to screen the air-holes, and prevent the flame of the lamp from being disturbed by sudden gusts of wind; and the mouldings *i* and *k* are placed above and below this hoop for the same purpose.

l is a button which is used for moving a rack (concealed in the inside of the tube *b*), which serves for elevating and lowering the wick. *e* is the handle of the lamp, which projects horizontally from the side of the circular reservoir *a*. It is hollow, and about six inches in length; and it serves at the same time as a handle and as a secondary reservoir for containing the oil. For want of room, it is represented in the figure as being broken off.

f is the stopper which closes the opening by which oil is poured into the lamp.

Fig. 3, Plate VII., represents a vertical section, of the full size, through the middle of the upper part of the lamp, and in a line passing through the middle of its handle.

The vertical tube *b* is 5 inches in length and $1\frac{1}{2}$ inches in diameter. The burner *m, n*, is fixed in the axis of this tube by means of the short horizontal tubes *o, p*, which are soldered to the burner, and likewise to the inside of the tube *b*.

The rack which serves to move the wick is placed within the tube *b*, by the side of the burner; but it is not represented in the figure.

The glass chimney is placed in the upper part of the tube *b;* and, in order that it may be firmly fixed in its place, an elastic hoop, made of tin covered on both sides with soft leather, is first pushed down into the opening of the tube *b*, and the lower extremity of the glass chimney is forced down into this hoop. This hoop is one inch wide; and, when it is in its place, it rests on the tubes *o, p*. The hoop of tin is not soldered together; and, in order to render it more elastic, it has a number of vertical slits, which extend from the upper side of the hoop to within one quarter of an inch of the lower side of it.

This hoop, covered on both sides with soft leather (such as is used for making ladies' gloves), is about one tenth of an inch in thickness, so that its diameter within is one inch and three tenths, which is also the diameter of the glass chimneys below, or of that portion of them which enters the hoop.

The tube *b* is made larger than otherwise would be necessary, in order to receive this elastic hoop, which has been found to be very useful for fixing the glass chimney firmly in its place.

PLATE VII.

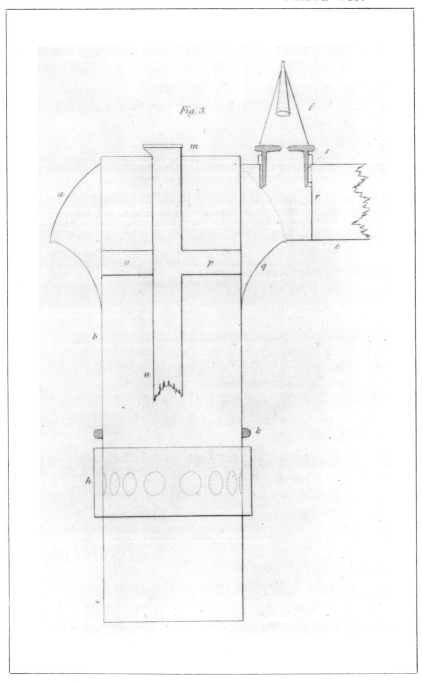

Fig. 3.

The circular reservoir is composed of two pieces of tin, *a* and *q*, formed under the hammer, which are soldered to each other and to the tube *b*. That which forms the upper part of the reservoir is convex: the other, *q*, is in the form of the large end of a trumpet.

The oil passes from this reservoir into the burner through a very small hole made in the side of the tube *b*, which opens into the interior of the short tube *p*.

The greatest diameter of the circular reservoir is two inches and a half; and its depth, measured from the level of the highest part of its sloping bottom, is 0.8 of an inch. The vertical height of this sloping bottom *q* is also 0.8 of an inch, which makes the greatest depth of this reservoir 1.6 inch; but the lower part of it being very narrow holds very little oil.

The hoop *h*, which serves as a screen to the air-holes in the tube *b*, is three fourths of an inch in width and 1.7 inch in diameter.

Before this hoop was used, the flame of the lamp was liable to be deranged, not only by sudden blasts of wind blowing directly into these air-holes, but also by sudden jerks accidentally given to the lamp in carrying it; but the hoop has been found to be an effectual security against both these accidents.

The rings *k* and *i*, Fig. 2 (Plate VI.), which have the appearance of being introduced for mere ornament, serve two important purposes. They prevent the air from being forced into the air-holes in such a manner as to derange the flame in moving the lamp very suddenly, or with a jerk, either upwards or downwards; and they also prevent the air within the tube *b* from passing too freely out of it, by a retrograde motion, on every puff of wind that may blow down into the top of the glass chimney.

In order more effectually to defend this lamp against those descending blasts, and also from being blown out by the air forced into the opening of the chimney above, on lifting up the lamp very suddenly, the top of the chimney is covered by a small conical roof, made of thin sheet iron, two inches in diameter below and about one inch and a quarter in height. This roof is fixed in its place by means of three narrow vertical slips of sheet iron, a quarter of an inch in width and an inch and a half in length, which are riveted above to the inside of the conical roof. These slips, which are elastic, on being forced together, enter the glass chimney, and by pressing against its sides keep the roof fixed in its place.

It might have been apprehended that this roof would have so checked the ascending current of air in the chimney as to diminish the rapidity of the com- bustion and impair the brilliancy of the light; but this has not been found to be the case. The three slips of sheet iron by which the roof is fixed in its place are so arranged that the level of the lower part of the roof is about one tenth of an inch higher than the extremity of the glass chimney; and a greater height has not been found to be necessary to give a free passage to the air.

These different contrivances defend the lamp so effectually against both wind and rain, that the lamp may without any risk be used in the open air instead of a lantern, and even in stormy weather.

The use of the roof is not absolutely necessary

within doors, but when the lamp is exposed to the wind in the open air it will stand in need of its protection; and it is also very useful when the lamp is carried about from place to place, to prevent its being extinguished by sudden jerks.

I shall now endeavour to describe every essential part of this lamp, and one which, more than any other, distinguishes it from all other lamps: this is its *secondary reservoir.*

This is a rectangular flat tube, which projects horizontally from one side of the circular reservoir already described. It is 1.25 in width, 0.8 of an inch in depth, and 6 inches in length, and it is closed at its farther end. It serves at the same time as a secondary reservoir and as a handle for holding the lamp when it is carried about from place to place. Instead of being made of a prismatic form, it is frequently swelled out at its sides and rounded off at its extremity (farthest from the lamp); and it is always painted black and japanned. This is done in order to give it the appearance of being merely a handle.

As there was not room to introduce it entire in either of the Figs. 2 and 3, it is in both shown broken off at the distance of about an inch and a half from the circular reservoir.

It is on the upper part of this secondary reservoir, where it projects horizontally over the upper part of the circular reservoir, that the opening is placed by which this lamp is filled with oil; and this opening is closed by a perforated brass stopper *k*, on which a hollow cone is placed that serves to give a passage to the air which enters the reservoir.

In the Fig. 3 (Plate VII.) a vertical section through

the middle of this stopper and its hollow cone is distinctly represented, the brass stopper being distinguished by diagonal lines. The short brass tube *s* is likewise shown, which receives the stopper. This tube, which is half an inch in diameter above internally, and somewhat smaller below, is 0.35 of an inch in length, and descends a quarter of an inch into the cavity of the reservoir.

The brass stopper, which is hollow, has a small hole in its axis which opens a communication between the circular reservoir and the conical chamber above the stopper; and in the upper part of this conical chamber a small hollow truncated cone is so fixed as to be suspended in it. It is through this small cone that the air passes in and out of the reservoir.

The smaller cone is fixed in the larger by soldering them together before the larger cone is soldered to the brass stopper.

The secondary reservoir is separated from the circular reservoir by means of a vertical partition *r*, which is situated immediately behind the short brass tube *s*, which forms the opening by which the lamp is filled with oil.

Through this partition the extremities of two long horizontal tubes pass, which are concealed in the secondary reservoir and which form the communication between the two reservoirs. The one is situated immediately on the flat bottom of the secondary reservoir, and extends from the partition *r* to within about a quarter of an inch of the extremity of that reservoir. The other, which is of the same length, is fixed to the upper part of the secondary reservoir.

These tubes may be constructed in the following

manner. Two slips of tin, each 0.6 of an inch in width and about 5 inches long, may be formed into two square gutters or spouts, 0.2 of an inch wide and 0.2 of an inch deep. One of them being turned upside down and soldered on both its sides to the flat bottom or floor of the secondary reservoir, in the direction of its length, a square tube or trunk will thus be formed. The other square spout is to be fixed in the same manner to the upper part, or to what may be called the ceiling of the long chamber, which serves as a secondary reservoir.

One of the ends of each of these square tubes must just pass through the vertical partition which separates the two reservoirs, and must be soldered to it; and both these tubes must be open from end to end.

In order to show in a clear and satisfactory manner the various objects had in view in the contrivance of this machinery (if any thing can be called machinery which produces its effect without any motion of its parts), we will suppose the lamp first to be filled with oil, and then lighted.

The upper part of the lamp being united to its stand, and the lamp placed on a table, on removing the stopper *f* and pouring oil slowly into the lamp, the oil will enter the circular reservoir; and, as soon as this is filled to the level of the bottom of the secondary reservoir, it will begin to flow into that also, passing through the long square trunk which is fixed down on its bottom. As the air can escape out of this secondary reservoir through the long square tube which is fixed to its upper side, it is evident that nothing can obstruct the passage of the oil into it, except it be the difficulty that the air in it may find in passing out of

it by a long narrow tube, which perhaps may be sometimes obstructed, more or less, by small parcels of oil
that may remain in it.

As this accident was found to happen sometimes,
another contrivance was used to facilitate the escape
of this air, which has been found to answer perfectly.

A small hole of about three twentieths of an inch in
diameter, which is represented in the figure, has been
made through the side of the vertical brass tube *s*, and
opening directly into the cavity of the secondary reservoir. As the air in this reservoir can escape freely
through this opening, there is no longer any difficulty
whatever in filling the lamp with oil; and when this
operation is ended, as the hole by which the air escapes out of the secondary reservoir is hermetically
closed by the brass stopper, as may be seen in the
figure, no inconvenience whatever has resulted from
the use of this contrivance.

We will now suppose that the lamp, after having
been filled, is lighted.

The oil, passing continually through the small opening in the side of the cylinder *b*, will flow through the
tube *p* into the burner.

As the oil in the circular reservoir passes freely into
the burner, so that in the secondary reservoir passes
freely into the circular reservoir, through the small
square trunk, open at both ends, which is fixed down
on the bottom of the secondary reservoir, so that the
lamp will continue to burn till the last drop of oil is
consumed.

It is very certain that the oil in the secondary reservoir would not flow freely out of it into the circular
reservoir if air could not at the same time enter it

freely to replace that oil; but the long square tube fixed to the top of the secondary reservoir gives a free passage to the air from one of the reservoirs to the other; and as the stopper, which closes the opening by which the oil is poured into the lamp, is perforated at the point of its double cone with a hole sufficiently large to establish the necessary communication between the air in the circular reservoir and that of the surrounding atmosphere, there is nothing in any of these contrivances that can prevent the lamp from burning well, and consuming the whole of its oil.

Suppose now that the lamp, properly arranged and burning well, be taken up by its handle and carried about from place to place in the open air. As it cannot be supposed that those into whose hands this lamp must fall, if it ever gets into general use, will have leisure to pay much attention to their manner of holding it, in carrying it about in the course of their business, if the lamp does not take care of itself it can be of no real value; but a bare inspection of the foregoing figure will be sufficient to show that it cannot be liable to any of those accidents which have hitherto prevented lamps from being portable.

The very small quantity of oil that can be contained in the vertical burner cannot be thrown out of it by any sudden jolts the lamp may receive in being carried in the hand, or on being suddenly set down; and the concussions which the oil in the circular reservoir may receive cannot sensibly affect that in the burner. That accident has been effectually guarded against by causing the oil to pass through a very small hole in its way from the circular reservoir to the burner.

As this small hole is made in the side of a tube

which is vertical, it is not liable to be stopped up by bubbles of air nor by the sediment of the oil; and, if it should ever happen to be stopped up by any accident, it can easily be cleared out by means of a small wire introduced by the opening through which the lamp is filled with oil.

Notwithstanding the smallness of the opening by which the oil passes into the burner, if from careless-ness in carrying the lamp it were held for a consider-able time in such a manner that the extremity of the handle were considerably higher than the level of the top of the burner, so much oil might at length have been forced into the burner as to overflow; but this accident is prevented by the vertical partition which separates the cavities of the two reservoirs. As long as the lamp stands on its foot or is carried in such a manner that its burner is held in a vertical position, the oil flows freely from one reservoir to the other, as we have just seen; but, as soon as the lamp is leaned forward in such a manner as to cause the end of its handle farthest from the burner to be raised up higher than the top of the burner, the oil in the cavity of the handle is thrown forward against the vertical par-tition, which partition will support this oil and prevent its descending into the circular reservoir. The small quantity of oil contained in the lower square trunk belonging to the secondary reservoir will be emptied into the circular reservoir; but no more of the oil in this reservoir can follow it, for the farther end of that tube, and also of the air-tube, will now be elevated above the surface of that oil.

These contrivances effectually prevent the oil from overflowing at the extremity of the burner; but others were necessary to prevent its being thrown out of the lamp by the opening which it was necessary to leave for the air to pass freely in and out of the reservoirs. The most convenient situation for this opening is in the middle of the stopper which closes the passage by which the oil is poured into the lamp; and there I have established it. This stopper is perforated at its centre by a vertical hole of about one tenth of an inch in diameter; and on the top of this stopper, which is flat, there is soldered a thin, hollow, truncated cone, made of tin, half an inch in diameter below, 0.1 of an inch in diameter above, and three fourths of an inch in height, in the axis of which another smaller truncated cone is placed, in such a manner as to remain suspended in it. This smaller cone is 0.15 of an inch in diameter below, 0.5 of an inch in diameter above, and half an inch in height; and it is entirely concealed in the larger cone, except only about 0.1 of an inch in length of its upper end, which comes through the small opening of the larger cone to which it is soldered.

This simple contrivance has proved to be an effectual remedy for an accident which embarrassed me for some time. When the lamp happens to receive any violent jolt, the regurgitation of the oil in the circular reservoir is sometimes such as to cause a small portion of oil to be thrown up through the small hole left for the passage of the air in the centre of the brass stopper; and, although I had taken the precaution to cover this opening by a vertical narrow tube, near an inch long, the oil was, nevertheless, sometimes forced out of the top of this tube by the air which escaped from the secondary reservoir, on its being warmed by the hand;

but, since I have substituted the double cone in lieu of this vertical tube, this accident has never happened, and a bare inspection of the figure is sufficient to show that it never can happen.

Any small quantity of oil on being thrown up into the conical chamber must necessarily spread over the bottom of it, from whence it will afterwards descend slowly; and the air that may happen to follow it immediately into the conical chamber will pass through it and escape by the small interior cone, which is evidently out of the reach of the oil, and therefore cannot be soiled by it.

As the brass tube which forms the opening by which the oil is poured into the lamp descends about a quarter of an inch below the level of the upper part of the circular reservoirs, it is evident that this reservoir cannot be completely filled with oil, for the air cannot all escape out of it. It would have been easy, by piercing this tube on the side of the circular reservoir in the same manner as it is pierced on the opposite side (to facilitate the escape of the air out of the secondary reservoir), to have opened a passage for the escape of all the air out of the circular reservoir; but I have not done it, for I conceived that it might be advantageous to leave some air in the circular reservoir, which on inclining the lamp forward escapes, and makes room for the oil which runs out of the trunk of the secondary reservoir, when the lamp is so inclined.

This precaution could never be of any use except when the lamp, after having been entirely filled with oil, and before any sensible quantity of it should have been consumed, should be so much and so long inclined as to endanger the overflowing of the oil in the burner by the pressure of that in the trunk; and although this accident could seldom have happened, yet I was very glad to have found means to prevent it. Its effects indeed could in no case have been very disagreeable; for, as all the oil that could have possibly overflowed at the extremity of the burner must necessarily have run down on the outside of it, and fallen into the reservoir in the foot of the lamp, it could never have been seen, and much less have been spilled in such a manner as to run out of the lamp. That is an accident which I conceive to be quite impossible to happen with this lamp; and such is my security on that head that I frequently take a portable lamp filled with oil with me in my carriage when I travel, and place it, and not always perfectly upright, in one of the pockets, — not lighted, to be sure, — but ready to light when I arrive at an inn where I mean to spend the night. It is true that in these cases I always take care to draw back the wick and to close the opening of the burner with a fit stopper, but the opening by which the air enters the reservoir is never closed.

The burners of these portable lamps have been made of various forms, and wicks of different kinds have been employed. As it will always be necessary to use glass chimneys with these lamps, in order to prevent their flames from being deranged by the wind, such forms must be chosen for their burners as are well adapted to these chimneys. For common use a form must be chosen which will render the operation of trimming the lamp as easy as possible. A flat wick is the easiest trimmed; but that form is not well adapted to a cylindrical glass chimney, neither is it favourable to the production of light.

A small cylindrical wick, similar to those used in Argand's lamp, gives a great deal of very pure white light; but, as it requires a current of air in the axis of it in order to its performing well, this renders the construction of the burner too complicated, and the operation of changing the wick and trimming it too delicate and difficult for common use. It is, however, most certain that this wick produces a very striking and beautiful effect, and many persons have preferred it to all others.

The wick which has answered best for general use is a flat ribbon wick, about one inch wide, prepared by dipping it into very hot tallow, which, when cooled and cut into proper lengths, is laid by for use. When a new wick is wanted, one of these flat wicks is moulded on a wooden cylinder of about 0.3 of an inch in diameter, and made to take the form of a tube, open on one side from end to end; and in that form it enters the burner, which is so constructed as to receive it, and also to preserve its form till it is quite consumed.

The form of the burner is such that a horizontal section of it is nearly in the shape of a horse-shoe, the open part of it being turned towards the handle of the lamp.

To move the wick, a contrivance has been used, which is not a new invention, but which has been found to be very useful. A strong cylindrical rod of stout wire, a little more than one tenth of an inch in diameter, passing vertically through a collar, formed of several pieces of leather, confined in a small cylindrical brass box soldered to the burner, enters the burner at the bottom of it; and being fixed at its lower extremity to the lower end of a rack which is placed vertically by the side of the burner, and which is moved by means of a pinion, connected with a button (seen at Fig. 1, Plate V.), placed on the outside of the vertical tube, which conceals both the burner and the rack, by turning this button to the right or to the left the cylindrical rod is moved either up or down in the burner, as the occasion may require.

To the upper end of this cylindrical rod is fixed a pair of small elastic nippers with sharp teeth, which hold the lower end of the wick. As long as these nippers are within the burner, they are so pressed together by its two opposite sides that they hold the wick very fast; but, when they are pushed up so high as to come out of the burner, they separate from each other, in consequence of their elasticity.

When they are in this situation, the remains of the old wick may be removed without difficulty; and the end of the new wick being put in their place, in causing the nippers to descend into the burners, they will necessarily draw the new wick after them.

The changing of the wick of a lamp has hitherto been a very disagreeable and filthy operation; but from this description it is evident the wick of this lamp may be changed in an instant, and that there is nothing either difficult or disgusting in that momentary process.

Care must be taken in trimming the new wick, first, to make it descend as far as possible into the burner; then to cut off with a pair of sharp scissors all that projects above the level of the top of the burner; and, when this has been done, the wick must be raised about $\frac{1}{20}$ of an inch, and again cut off level with the top of the burner. If this precaution be neglected, the wick will be too long to be extinguished suddenly, and without smoke, after having been lighted for the first time. If attention be paid to it, no disagreeable smell whatever will be diffused on that occasion, nor on any other.

All the lamps with which I am acquainted diffuse a very noxious, stinking vapour when they are made to burn with a very small flame. Even an Argand lamp, in which the combustion of the oil is usually so complete, if it be so arranged by lowering its wick as to give only about one sixth part of the light it usually furnishes, it will diffuse a smell so very offensive that it will become quite insupportable.

To see clearly into this matter, we have only to consider what the changes are which take place when an Argand lamp, burning with its usual vivacity, is suddenly made to burn with a very feeble flame.

When this lamp burns well, the current of air which passes upwards through its chimney is so strong that the flame of the lamp is forced upwards towards the upper end of the wick; and the burner, being at some distance from the flame, is kept so cool by this strong blast of cold air that it does not become sufficiently hot to decompose the oil with which it is alway in contact; but, as soon as the wick is considerably shortened, the flame being much diminished, the current of air through the chimney becomes very feeble, and the flame, being no longer forced upwards by that current, descends by degrees, till at last it establishes itself on the very brim of the burner. This necessarily heats the top of the burner very hot, however small the flame may be; and, as all the oils which are used in lamps are decomposed and evaporated at a lower temperature than that at which they take fire and burn, the cause of the offensive vapour which is diffused by lamps with metallic burners, when they are made to burn with very small flames, is quite evident.

Conceiving that the evil might be remedied by preventing the flame from coming into contact with the burner, I attempted to do this by giving to the burner a projecting brim, in the form of an inverted truncated cone, and about one tenth of an inch in width; and this contrivance has completely answered the purpose for which it was designed. As the current of air which keeps the flame alive passes upwards in the chimney, it is thrown outwards by the projecting brim of the burner, from whence it returns and falls into the flame in an oblique direction, which prevents the flame from descending so low as to come into contact with the burner.

Since this improvement has been introduced in the construction of the burners of the portable lamps, they have ceased to diffuse a disagreeable smell on being made to burn with a very small flame; and they are now frequently employed as night-lamps (*veilleuses*) in bed-rooms.

They are the better adapted for that use, as they are not liable to be deranged by the wind, or by any other accident, and can always be made to give a very bright light in a moment, as often as such a light is wanted during the night.

For those who have the bad habit of reading in bed, they will be very convenient, and much less dangerous than candles or common lamps. They will likewise be found to be very useful in ante-rooms in great houses, where several of them may be lighted and kept constantly burning with reduced flames, for a very small expense; and at the moment when they are wanted they may be made to furnish their usual quantity of light, and when they are brought back into the ante-room their flames may again be reduced. They would cost much less than wax tapers or bougies, and would be much more cleanly and agreeable.

As the light emitted by these lamps is exceedingly vivid, and especially when they are made to burn with their greatest brilliancy, their flames should always be masked by screens, made of ground glass or of white gauze or crape. The most simple and best form for a screen for this lamp is that of a truncated cone, 6 inches in diameter at its base, $1\frac{1}{2}$ inch in diameter above, and $3\frac{1}{4}$ in perpendicular height, with a gallery above, of about half an inch in height, made of tin japanned, to serve instead of a handle in placing it and removing it. This screen may be fixed in its place by means of a conical tube of tin, attached to the screen on the inside of it, which may be made to receive the cone which is fixed to the stopper which closes the opening by which the lamp is filled with oil.

The handle of the lamp being six inches in length, enough of it will project beyond the lower part of this screen to give a sufficient hold of it in carrying the lamp.

A small balloon screen, of about six inches in diameter, is frequently used with this lamp, and has a very fine effect. This balloon is made of white crape, fixed to vertical ribs of covered wire, and has an opening below of about 2.4 inches in diameter, that it may rest on the widest part of the circular reservoir; and it has also a circular opening above one inch and a half in diameter, to give a passage to the upper end of the glass chimney. This opening at the upper part of the balloon should be surrounded by a gallery of tin, japanned, similar to that on the top of the conical screen, and for the same use.

This balloon screen must also have another opening below, on one side, to make way for the projecting handle of the lamp. The best way of fixing this screen in its place is by means of a conical tube, fastened to it on the inside of it, in the same manner as the conical screen is fixed.

Both these screens are indicated in the Fig. 2 by faint dotted lines.

When this lamp is used as a bed-chamber lamp, and made to burn with a very small flame, its feeble light may be almost entirely concealed by placing a conical screen made of pasteboard over its conical screen of gauze or crape.

Though the principal merit of this lamp is its being portable, yet, as it is not liable to spilling its oil, and gives a clear, bright light, without either smoke or smell, it is perfectly well calculated to serve as a table lamp, even in elegant apartments, and also for lighting dining-tables; but, when it is intended to be used for these purposes, it should be placed on a stand, sufficiently elevated to raise its flame to the height of 12 or 15 inches. This additional height does not prevent its being portable; but, when it is lower, it appears to be better adapted for being carried about in the hand. It must, however, be made about nine inches in height, otherwise there will not be room for the rack to descend sufficiently low to allow of a wick being used of a reasonable length.

Many attempts have been made to improve the light

of lamps by preparing their wicks, and prepared wicks have been sold at high prices; but the secret of the preparation has not to my knowledge been made public.

Having purchased some of these prepared wicks several years ago at Munich, from an itinerant Italian pedlar, I analyzed them. On exposing them to heat, I separated from them a substance which had every appearance of being pure tallow, but to which a strong and not disagreeable scent had been given, probably to conceal the secret of the preparation, which I then considered as being a mere cheat, and paid no farther attention to it. Some time after, on considering the matter more attentively, I found reason to conclude that either tallow or wax, heated very hot, might very probably be used with advantage for preparing wicks for lamps, and also for candles. I can explain my ideas on that subject in a very few words.

In order that a lamp or candle may burn well, it is necessary that the oil, tallow, or wax which supplies the combustion, should *flow freely* over the surface of those minute fibres of the cotton which compose the wick.

Every extraneous body, whether solid or fluid, which remains attached to the surface of those fibres, must necessarily prevent the oil, tallow, etc., from flowing freely over them.

Now it is most certain that a considerable quantity of air, and also of water (moisture), remains attached to the cotton wicks of lamps for a long time after they have been immersed in oil. This may easily be made to appear by exposing the oil with the wick in it under the exhausted receiver of an air-pump, for the surface of the cotton will be quite covered with small bubbles of air in a few minutes; or if the wick of a lamp full of oil, or of a candle full of tallow or of wax, be thrown into melted tallow, so heated as to be almost ready to boil, as this heat is considerably greater than that at which water boils, not only the air, but the moisture also, which remains attached to the cotton, will be suddenly driven out of it. This will occasion a violent effervescence, accompanied by a loud hissing, which, however, will cease entirely in a few moments; and the cotton will sink down to the bottom of the hot melted tallow, where it will remain perfectly quiet, and free from air bubbles.

These appearances afford a decisive proof that air or moisture, or both, remain attached to the wicks of lamps and candles; and it is most certain that they must necessarily be injurious to the wick, by preventing the oil, melted tallow, or melted wax from flowing freely over the minute fibres of the cotton. But this experiment shows us at the same time how this evil may be effectually prevented.

By heating melted tallow till it is nearly boiling hot, on throwing into this hot liquid a parcel of clean dry wicks, the air and the moisture will be expelled in a few moments with a hissing noise, and being replaced by the tallow they will be permanently excluded. As soon as the hissing has ceased, the wicks may be taken out of the melted tallow to drip and cool, and when cold they may be cut into proper lengths; and being wrapped up in clean paper, to preserve them from the dust, they may be preserved for years without change.

The wicks of tallow candles and of wax candles might be prepared by dipping them for *the first time* in melted tallow or melted wax, heated *very hot*, in order more effectually to expel the air and moisture.

Wicks for lamps may be prepared by immersing them in hot melted wax, instead of using melted tallow for that purpose; and many persons who manage their lamps themselves would, no doubt, prefer wax, on account of its greater cleanliness; but, having tried both these substances, I have not found that the wicks which had been prepared with wax burned better than those prepared with tallow.

As dust, and in general every species of soil, is very injurious to a wick, it is necessary that those which are to be prepared be well washed and dried before they undergo this operation.

As oils that are purified by means of the sulphuric acid always retain a certain portion of the acid, notwithstanding all the pains that are taken to separate and remove it, if that residue of the acid attacks the wick and injures it, so as to spoil it entirely if left for a considerable time in the oil, as is generally supposed; as either the tallow or the wax used in preparing the wick will effectually preserve the cotton from the acid till it shall have been displaced by the oil, on being melted in consequence of the lamp being lighted, — it is evident that this mode of preparation must be useful as a preservative against the attacks of the acid, especially when a lamp filled with oil remains some time without being lighted.

The corrosive effects of this acid are so injurious to the burner, especially at its extremity where the heat is considerable, that the burner of an Argand lamp seldom lasts more than two years. To remedy this evil I have lately given directions for the upper end of the

PLATE VIII.

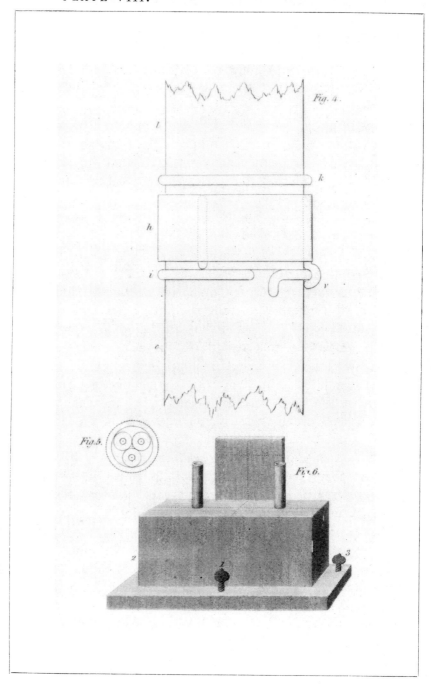

Fig. 4.

Fig. 5.

Fig. 6.

burner (about half an inch in length) to be made of silver instead of tin or copper; and, as this alteration does not occasion an additional expense of more than eighteen pence or two shillings, it must in the end turn out to be very economical. All lamps with vertical burners should be constructed in this manner, especially when they are destined to be used with purified oil.

As I am persuaded that this portable lamp will be found useful, I am anxious that all its essential parts may be so particularly described as to leave no doubt or uncertainty respecting its construction; for unless this be done all my labour will be to little purpose.

Fig. 4, Plate VIII., shows the manner in which the upper part of the lamp is fixed to its stand. *b* is a part of the vertical tube, which is surrounded at its upper extremity by the circular reservoir; *c* is the upper part of the column which serves as a stand for the lamp; *h* is the hoop which serves to mask the air-holes (represented in Fig. 3 by dotted lines), through which the air passes into the tube *b*. This hoop is attached to the vertical tube *b* by means of three vertical wires, which are soldered to the tube. Two of them are represented in this figure. One of them, *v*, descends lower than the under side of the hoop which it supports; and its lower extremity is turned inwards, and forms a hook. The two others descend each about one tenth of an inch below the lower side of the hoop, but they are not bent. *i* is the ring of wire which forms the moulding at the upper extremity of the stand of the lamp. This moulding is interrupted in one part of it, as is clearly shown in the figure.

When the upper part of the lamp is to be fixed to its stand, the lower part of the tube *b* is introduced into the opening of the stand *c*, and is turned round in the tube *c* till the hook *v*, coming to the part of the ring *i* where it is interrupted, descends through that opening. The tube *b*, being then turned round its axis to the left nearly one whole revolution, the hook *v* receiving and embracing the ring *i*, it is at length stopped by a part of this ring, which is turned downwards; and the upper part of the lamp is thus firmly fixed to its stand.

After having tried several contrivances for fixing the lamp to its stand, this appeared to answer best. The hook *v* should be placed nearly under the handle of the lamp, in order that when the lamp is fixed to its stand the opening in the ring *i* may be less in view.

The projecting ends of the vertical wires, by means of which the hoop *h* is fixed in its place, are useful in fixing the lamp to its stand, as they rest on the top of the ring *i*.

Before I finish my account of this portable lamp, I must say a few words more respecting the different forms that may be given to its wick.

As the internal diameter of the glass chimney of this lamp at the level of the lower part of the flame must not be more than eight tenths of an inch, it is necessary that the flame should be placed as exactly as possible in the middle of it, for otherwise there will be some danger of its touching the glass. To avoid that accident, wider chimneys have sometimes been used; but, where this has been done, the beautiful white colour of the flame has always been more or less injured, and the quantity of light sensibly diminished, —

in short, the combustion of the oil has been rendered incomplete.

Those who have attended to the striking effect produced by blowing wood fire with a bellows, in whitening the flame and increasing the light, will easily conceive how much the beauty of the flame of a lamp must depend on the manner in which the air is introduced, which supplies the combustion.

The glass chimney of Argand's lamp is useful, no doubt, in defending the flame and preventing its being agitated by the wind; but it is its usefulness as a blower which renders this contrivance so highly interesting.

I have lately made several experiments with braided wicks in the form of round whip-cords, which have produced a great deal of very pure white light; and I am almost inclined to think that these wicks will be preferable to all others for portable lamps, and perhaps for table lamps also, where not more light is wanted than is emitted by three or four candles.

These cord-wicks should be about *two tenths* of an inch in diameter; and, to stiffen them, they should be braided round a very small cylinder of wood, of about *one twentieth* of an inch in diameter, or round a small slip of cane. This wood, which will be concealed in the middle of the wick, will not only be useful to support that part of the wick which is on fire, but it will also be very useful to prevent the ascent of the oil in the centre of the wick, which will render it possible to use cord-wicks of larger diameter than could otherwise be used without danger of causing the lamp to smoke.

When cord-wicks are employed, three of them must always be used together; and they must be fastened together at their lower extremities, by binding them with a strong thread, to receive them. The burner must of course be cylindrical, and its diameter must be such as just to receive the three cord-wicks without pressing them so as to change their form. This burner must have a rim about one tenth of an inch in width projecting outwards, and obliquely upwards at its upper extremity; and care should be taken to clean this rim every time the lamp is trimmed. The wick being drawn down into the burner by means of the rack, the rim may be cleaned in a moment, with little trouble; *but this must never be neglected.*

These cord-wicks must be previously prepared, by dipping them into melted tallow or melted wax, *heated very hot;* and it will be useful to draw them (in the same manner as wire is drawn) through a round smooth hole, made in a thick plate of iron or of brass, before they become quite cold. This will reduce them to the proper diameter, and will at the same time render them smooth, solid, and stiff, and enable them the better to preserve their cylindrical form when they are bound together in bundles (of three) for use.

It appears to me to be very probable that a very strong-twisted, hard hempen cord, of about one twentieth of an inch in diameter, prepared in a solution of alum, would answer perhaps quite as well as wood for stiffening these cord-wicks, and preventing the oil from rising too freely in the central parts of the cord. There is great reason to suppose that wicks of this kind would be very useful for tallow candles.

Fig. 5, Plate VIII., is a horizontal section of the cylindrical burner of a lamp containing three cord-wicks, each two tenths of an inch in diameter.

The small cylinder of wood (or cane) in the centre of each cord is distinctly represented.

The projecting rim of the burner is indicated by a dotted circle.

The diameter of the cylindrical burner is nine twentieths of an inch.

A wick of this form is easily trimmed; its flame is uncommonly beautiful; it may be made to burn well with a moderate light, or to give a great deal of light. The flame occupies the axis of the glass chimney with great steadiness; and the lamp may be made to burn with a very small flame when necessary, without either smoke or smell.

To all these advantages we may add one more, which on some occasions may be very useful. When the burner is cylindrical, it may easily be closed with a fit stopper of cork; and the lamp, filled with oil, may be carried about in a carriage with the greatest safety, and always be ready to be lighted when wanted, either in the carriage or at inns on the road.

I have more than once carried one of these lamps in one of the pockets of my post-chaise, in travelling, and without ever having had reason to repent of the confidence I placed in its cleanliness, as I have already observed in another place.

It is hardly necessary that I should observe that by means of a trifling alteration in the form of the secondary reservoir of this portable lamp, and the suppression of its foot, it may be made to serve perfectly well on the outside of carriages, instead of the lanterns now in use.

If it should be found to be necessary, a quantity of baked horse-hair, of very fine brass wire, may be put into each of the reservoirs, in order to moderate the too violent concussion of the oil, in the sudden jolts of the carriage ; or the same end may be attained by dividing these reservoirs into a number of small compartments, by means of their vertical partitions of tin, having each two small holes of about one tenth of an inch in diameter, the one on a level with the bottom of the reservoir, and the other on a level with the top of it. These partitions will not prevent the reservoirs from being filled with oil, and they will most effectually prevent the oil from being thrown out of the lamp, in consequence of the jolting and swinging motion of the carriage.

A hint is sufficient for English workmen ; and their ingenuity and address are such that they seldom fail to succeed in what they undertake.

By increasing the size of the portable lamp in all its dimensions, it may without any kind of difficulty be made to contain oil enough to supply a burner on Argand's principles, of the full size ; and by increasing the size of its screen the handle of the lamp may be entirely concealed.

When constructed in this manner, its form becomes perfectly elegant, and such as will render it proper to be used as a table lamp in the most elegant apartments.

The prices at which these portable lamps have been sold at Paris have varied from ten to twenty francs, according to their sizes, and the manner in which they have been ornamented.

CHAPTER III.

Description of an elegant Illuminator for ornamenting the Sides of a Looking-glass. — Additional Observations respecting the Use of Ground Glass. — It is very useful in some Situations for glazing Windows. — Pendulous Illuminators may be made of various Forms. — The Domes of Table Illuminators may be made of Ground Glass, and beautified in various Ways.

IN decorating spacious apartments for balls and assemblies, it may sometimes be desirable to ornament the looking-glasses by placing lights on each side of them. Where this is to be done, I would recommend an illuminator I lately had made for that particular purpose, that produces a very fine effect; and which is not liable to any of those accidents to which lamps in general are exposed. Its construction is extremely simple, and its form is elegant and pleasing, and it has so little of the appearance of being a lamp that it is not easy to discover where any considerable quantity of oil can be concealed. Only one of them has yet been made, and that is in my house at Auteuil, near Paris; but all those who have seen it have thought it very beautiful, and I have no doubt of its meeting with general approbation; and, as it can be afforded at a lower price than any lamp hitherto constructed for the same purpose, it can hardly fail to get soon into common use.

The following descriptions will give a general idea of

the external appearance of this *wall-illuminator*, and of the effect it must produce when lighted.

When it is hung up against the wall, a bracket of an elegant form appears to project horizontally about six inches from the wainscot, and a flambeau to be attached to its extremity, in such a manner as to remain suspended in a vertical position. On the upper end of this flambeau is placed a screen, in the form of a basket, 6 inches in height and 9 inches in width above, formed of ten vertical ribs of wire, covered with white crape, and ornamented with two handsome gilt handles. The ribs of this basket are covered with small diamonds of cut-glass.

As the bracket, which appears to be made of wood, is painted of a dark bronze colour, and the flambeau is so painted and japanned as to represent white porcelain richly gilded, these two objects do not appear to have any farther connection than that one of them is supported by the other. They are, however, very nearly connected; for the bracket, which is made of tin and hollow, is a reservoir from whence the lamp is supplied with oil.

The opening by which the oil is introduced is on the upper side of the bracket, and near its broad end, which is near the wainscot or wall of the room; and this opening is closed by a brass stopper, perforated at its centre, and covered by a hollow truncated cone, 0.8 of an inch in diameter below, 0.3 of an inch in diameter above, and 1 inch in height. This cone is closed above by a screw, similar in all respects to those used to close the passages for the air in the circular reservoirs of the illuminators.

There is a small circular reservoir for the oil, which

appears to be the foot of the basket, and which immediately surrounds the top of the burner; and the hollow
bracket forms a secondary reservoir. These two reservoirs are separated by a vertical partition; and the oil
passes from the secondary reservoir into the circular
reservoir by a long narrow trunk situated at the bottom
of the secondary reservoir, in precisely the same manner
as the oil is conveyed from the secondary reservoir of
the portable lamp into its circular reservoir.

To give a passage for the air to enter the circular
reservoir, and to pass out of it when the lamp is filled
with oil, a narrow horizontal tube, which is concealed
in the secondary reservoir, is fixed to the upper part
of it, and passing through the vertical partition which
separates the two reservoirs opens into the circular reservoir. The other end of this tube is turned upwards
so as to form an elbow, and passing upwards through
the upper part of the secondary reservoir (at the farther
end of it, where it is united to the vertical plate which
rests against the wall of the room, and by which it is
supported), it ends in the open air.

That part of this air-tube which projects vertically
above the secondary reservoir is about $1\frac{1}{4}$ inch in
length, and it is masked and concealed by means of
a hollow cone, similar in all respects to that which is
fixed to the stopper that closes the opening by which
the oil is poured into the lamp. By placing these two
equal cones by the sides of each other, their uses are
the less obvious, and the general appearance of the
lamp is rendered more simple. If it should be thought
more elegant, both these cones may be concealed, by
giving to the vertical plate to which the projecting
bracket is fixed the appearance of being constructed

of a piece of wood, of about one inch in thickness. As brackets are usually constructed in that manner, there will be nothing uncouth in that form.

What appears to be the foot of the basket is a portion of a hoop of tin, painted and gilded like the flambeau, which is attached to the opening of the basket below, where it embraces the circular reservoir. This serves for fixing the basket in its place, and also a handle for removing it when the lamp is trimmed or lighted.

The basket serves for hiding the burner and its glass chimney, and for dispersing and softening the vivid light of the flame. For those purposes an ornamented balloon may be used instead of the basket, if that form should be preferred; but, in all cases where balloons are used, care must be taken that they be sufficiently large, otherwise their surfaces will be too intensely luminous not to injure the eyes.

Globes of ground glass have been in use for some time in France, and elsewhere, no doubt, for masking the flame of Argand's lamp; but their light has been found to be too powerful to be agreeable. This is not owing to any particular quality in ground glass which renders its light dazzling and fatiguing to the eyes, but it is merely owing to the too great intensity of the light at the surface of the visible object, which is owing to the smallness of that surface or to the smallness of the balloon.

As the surfaces of globes are as the squares of their diameters, the surface of a globe of eight inches in diameter is to that of a globe of four inches in diameter as 64 to 16, or as four to one.

Hence we see that the intensity of the light at the surface of a globular screen of ground glass of four inches in diameter is four times greater than it would be if the diameter of the globe were eight inches. Now, as the quantity of light emitted will be the same in both cases, surrounding bodies will be illuminated as much in one case as in the other; but the illumination will be most mild, equal, and agreeable when the larger globe is used, and the eyes will be in much less danger of being fatigued and injured.

As the system of illumination which I have recommended is founded entirely on the supposition that light may be dispersed without being destroyed, I feel it to be necessary to establish that fundamental principle in such a manner as to exclude all doubt. I shall therefore go over the ground again, and shall endeavour to elucidate the subject in the clearest manner.

The experiment which was made with two burning wax candles placed in two glass jars, the one of ground glass and the other of transparent glass, certainly proved that very little light is lost in passing through ground glass, or at least not much more than is lost in passing through the same kind of glass when it is transparent; but there are other experiments by which it may be made quite evident that screens of ground glass, and of other substances, may, under certain circumstances, be so arranged as even to augment the intensity of the illumination of surrounding objects.

If on a dark night a burning candle, fixed in the centre of a cylindrical screen of ground glass, 6 inches in diameter and 6 inches in height, be placed on a small stand in the open air, it will illuminate surrounding objects as much as the same candle would be able to illuminate them if the screen were made of transparent glass.

This is evident from the result of the experiment just mentioned.

If we examine the situation of this lighted candle burning in the centre of the screen of ground glass, we shall find that a considerable portion of its light escapes through the open ends of this screen, and is entirely lost; half of it passing upwards into the clouds; and the other half passing downwards into the earth, so that no part of it is usefully employed in illuminating the surrounding objects.

If now the screen, which is only 6 inches in length, be removed, and another screen of ground glass, of the same diameter and 12 inches in length, be put in its place, the whole of the surface of this taller glass cylinder will become luminous, and the intensity of the illumination of the surrounding objects will of course be increased. A considerable portion of the light which escaped through the open ends of the short cylinder will be arrested by the additional length of the taller cylinder, and will be usefully employed in rendering its surface luminous.

Hence we learn that the tall paper lanterns of the Chinese, and those which are frequently to be met with in the streets of London, in the wheelbarrows of orange-women, may possibly be useful for other purposes than merely for preventing the flame of the candle from being disturbed by the wind.

I am persuaded that they often increase the brightness of the illumination of surrounding objects; and that they would also do so is most certain, if they were properly constructed and arranged for obtaining that end. They always render a service equally important, or even more so; for they defend the eye from the direct rays of the flame, and by preventing its being deranged by them greatly facilitate distinct vision.

In order to be able to form a just idea respecting the manner in which light is dispersed in passing through ground glass and other like substances, it may be useful to examine the matter with some attention; and, as the laws which govern the rays of light in their passage through diaphanous bodies are perfectly known, there is no difficulty whatever in explaining the phenomena in a manner which will be perfectly satisfactory, even to those, I trust, who have not made the science of optics a part of their studies.

Light always passes from luminous bodies in straight lines, and continues to move on in the same direction, without deviation, except when it is reflected or when it is refracted, or drawn out of its straight course, in passing out of one transparent substance into another.

When a ray of light, in passing out of the air into glass, strikes the glass in a direction which happens to be *exactly perpendicular* to that part of the surface of the glass where it arrives, it enters the glass without being at all drawn aside or deranged in respect to the direction of its course, and it continues to move on in the glass in the same straight line; and, farther, if the ray in passing out of the glass happens to arrive at a part of the surface of the glass which is perpendicular to the direction of its course, it will pass directly through it also, and continue its course in the air in the same direction in which it moved before it arrived at the glass.

But when a ray of light in entering glass (or any other transparent substance) meets with a surface which is not perpendicular to the direction in which it moves, the ray will be refracted or its direction will be changed. It will appear to be drawn towards the glass before it arrives at its surface; and its motion in the glass, after it has penetrated through its surface, although it will still be in a straight line, will not be in the same direction in which the ray moved before it approached the glass; and the same change of direction will again take place, in passing out of the glass into the air, if the surface of the glass where it makes its exit should happen not to be perpendicular to the direction in which the ray moves in the glass during its passage through it.

Hence we learn that the direction of a ray of light which has passed through a glass, or any other transparent substance, will depend not only on its original direction, but also on the refractions it has experienced in entering it and in passing out of it; and, as these refractions depend on the angles of inclination which the surface of the glass present to the ray, when the surface of the glass is so broken up by grinding as to present an infinite number of small broken surfaces inclined in all directions, the light which passes through it must necessarily be dispersed.

Every visible point of the surface of the glass, from which the light escapes, will appear to send off rays in all directions, and this is what gives to the glass the appearance of being luminous; and it may indeed be said to be *luminous* without any impropriety of language.

In the memoir which I presented to the French National Institute, on the 24th March, 1806, on the subject of lamps, I made an observation relative to the usefulness of ground glass for windows, which I shall take the liberty to repeat here.

It frequently happens, especially in large towns, that rooms are so situated as to receive no light but what comes through windows which open into narrow streets or very small courts, and are so commanded by high buildings as to receive very little light from above. In all such cases, rooms would be much *more* lighted and much better lighted by windows of ground glass than by windows glazed with the finest transparent glass.

This I have found to be the case by experience, and it may easily be explained.

The rays of daylight which descend from the heavens come down in a direction so nearly perpendicular to the horizon that they impinge against the polished surface of the glass so obliquely that most of the rays are reflected in consequence of the smallness of the angle of incidence; and as those which enter the glass and pass through it come into the room in such a direction that they fall on the floor, where they are mostly absorbed, they are of little use in lighting the room; but when the window is glazed with ground glass, the surface of the glass which is rough being on the outside, the asperities which the glass presents to the descending rays greatly facilitate their entry into the glass, and as in passing through it they are dispersed in all directions the room will be much more equally and more intensely illuminated than when the windows are glazed with polished glass.

The room in which the different classes of the National Institute hold their ordinary weekly meetings is surrounded by very high buildings on every side; and, its walls being covered with books quite up to the ceiling, it was exceedingly dark and gloomy. All the windows have lately been furnished with double sashes; and the new outside sashes, which are nearly even with the outside of the wall, have been glazed with ground glass, the rough side of the glass being on the outside. Since this has been done, the room has become incomparably more light and cheerful, notwithstanding that the light which comes into it from without must now pass through two panes of glass instead of one.

There are many parlours and shops on ground floors in narrow streets, that are so dark at mid-day as to be scarcely habitable, which would be well lighted by the adoption of this simple contrivance; and rooms are so much more warm and comfortable with double windows, and the noise of the street is so effectually excluded by them, that these advantages alone would be sufficient to recommend them; but we see that they may be made to furnish *light* as well as *warmth* and *quiet*.

There are many other situations in which ground glass might be used with great advantage instead of transparent glass; but I must not enlarge on that subject in this place. Perhaps I may find some other occasion of treating it more fully: in the mean time what has been said may be useful as a hint to architects and to those persons who are their own architects.

I have lately made several experiments, in order to see if ground glass could not be used for constructing the screens of large pendulous illuminators; and from the results of these trials I am inclined to think it may be done. But as the large domes of gauze are so beautiful, especially when they are ornamented with cut glass, I shall be cautious how I propose any others till I shall be perfectly sure they are preferable to them.

These pendulous illuminators might, no doubt, be made in a variety of elegant forms, some of which would probably be much less expensive than those I have recommended. The upper hemispherical screen of the balloon illuminator, for instance, might be entirely suppressed, and that below might be made in the form of a large vase, open above; for, as the height at which this illuminator is usually suspended would prevent the flames of the burners being seen above the brim of the vase, the eyes would be as effectually protected by the vase as by the balloon, and the upper part of the walls of the room and the ceiling would be rather more lighted by the former than by the latter; but the circular reservoir would cast a shade on the walls of the room, which would certainly diminish the beauty of the illumination.

That shadow might be removed from the walls of the room to the ceiling, and indeed might be nearly effaced, by fixing a hoop of gauze, about two or three inches in width, on the top of the circular reservoir. By ornamenting this hoop with taste, it might easily be made to appear to be a part of the vase, and the vase might be rendered more beautiful by this addition to its height; and as the illuminator so arranged might, without any inconvenience, be suspended by three chains attached immediately to its circular reservoir, its price might certainly be reduced to about one half of what the balloon illuminators now cost.

But these alterations, and possibly others still more elegant and economical, will no doubt occur to those who may employ their taste and ingenuity in improving these inventions.

Nobody will more sincerely rejoice in their success than I shall do.

There is a very obvious improvement that may easily be made in the construction of the domes of table illuminators, which must occur to everybody. As these domes are not very large, they may be made of blown glass, and after their surface shall have been made rough by grinding they may be ornamented so as to make them very beautiful, when lighted, by painting them on the inside in various ways with white paint. This paint must be mixed up with oil of poppies or with white copal varnish, in order that the figures represented may at night appear through the glass like shades, and without colour. By day they will not be seen.

Glass domes and vases for illuminators might be very elegantly ornamented by etchings made with the fluoric acid; and it is very probable that the surface of the glass might be made rough by means of that acid, and perhaps at a less expense than when its polish is taken off by grinding it with emery.

But I am afraid of being tiresome by dwelling so long on these details.

CHAPTER IV.

Description of a very simple Contrivance for measuring the Intensity of the Light emitted by Lamps and Candles and other luminous Bodies. — Means of estimating of the Light lost in passing through Screens. — Experiments for ascertaining what Substances are most proper for constructing luminous Screens for Lamps and Candles.

A S the art of illumination cannot be cultivated in a satisfactory manner unless means are used for measuring the light which is emitted by luminous bodies, a photometer is indispensably necessary in every experimental inquiry which is undertaken with a view to the improvement of that art and of the various instruments used in the practice of it.

It is likewise necessary to adopt some fixed scale of light to serve as a *standard*, which must be so arranged as to indicate with certainty, by means of numbers, the precise degree of illumination which takes place in any given case, or the relative intensities of the lights which are compared.

This fixed scale of the photometer will be analogous to the scale of the thermometer, but in one respect it will be more perfect and more satisfactory: its intervals, or degrees, may be made to measure very accurately the different degrees of illumination they are designed to indicate, whereas the degrees marked on the scale of thermometers are arbitrary, and afford no satisfactory information respecting the real difference which exists in the various intensities of the heat which they indicate.

In my paper on the relative intensities of light emitted by luminous bodies, which was read before the Royal Society the 6th of February, 1794, and which is published in the Philosophical Transactions, and also in the first volume of my Philosophical Papers, an account is given of the photometer I used in those researches; but I have since found means to simplify the construction of that instrument very much, without injuring it in any respect, and have added to it a *graduated scale*, which indicates the in-

tensities of the light immediately without any calculation.

Fig. 6, Plate VIII., is a perspective view of this new
photometer. (See page 162.)

a is a quadrangular wooden box, turned upside down
and fastened by means of wood screws or nails to the
board *b.*

This board is 10 inches in length, 8 inches in width,
and ¾ of an inch in thickness, and it rests on the lower
ends of three wooden screws, 1, 2, and 3, by means of
which the board may either be placed in a horizontal
position, or inclined a little to the plane of the horizon,
as the occasion may require.   The screw 2 cannot be
seen, being hid by the inverted wooden box. *c* is a
vertical board, which is fastened to the back side of the
box by means of screws, and which projects three inches
above the level of its inverted bottom.

This board, which forms the field of the photometer,
is covered in front by fine white paper, and on this
paper are drawn with a pen two fine black lines cross-
ing each other at right angles.   One of these lines is
vertical, and divides the field into two equal parts ; the
other, which is horizontal, is situated at the height of
two inches above the level of the upper surface of the
small table, which is formed by the bottom of the inverted box.

On this table are drawn (with the point of a pair of
compasses) two straight lines at right angles to each
other, and in such a manner as to divide the table into
four equal quadrangular parts.

This table is 7 inches in length and 5 inches in
width, and in the line which divides it in the direction
of its length are placed two vertical pillars or small

cylindrical columns, made of wood, each $\frac{1}{2}$ an inch in diameter and 2 inches in height.

The centres of the holes made in the table for receiving these columns are at the distance one inch and three quarters, the one on the right hand and the other on the left, from the horizontal line which crosses the table from the front to the back part of it. Consequently the cylinders are at the distance of three inches from each other, and the centre of each of them is three inches from the vertical line which is drawn in the middle of the field of the photometer.

The whole of this simple apparatus may be constructed of beech-wood; and it may be stained of a fine deep black colour by washing it several times with common writing ink. It must be made quite black, and it will be better to stain it than to paint it with oil colours.

The scale of this instrument is composed of long rulers, each one inch wide and above a quarter of an inch thick, with a circular hole of about half an inch in diameter within about half an inch of one of its ends. This hole is made to receive one of the cylindrical columns of the photometer, by means of which it is confined in its place when in use. These rulers serve to measure the distances of the lights which are the subject of an experiment, from the centre of the field of the photometer.

A few words will be sufficient to give such clear and distinct ideas of the nature of these experiments, and of the manner of performing the various operations they require, as will enable any intelligent person not only to construct the necessary apparatus, but also to use it with the greatest facility and success.

These experiments must be performed at night, or, if made by day, a room must be chosen from which daylight can be effectually excluded.

Three tables will be necessary in making these experiments : on one of them the photometer is to be placed, and on each of the others one of the lights that are to be compared. The heights of these tables should be such that the two flames of the lamps or candles that are to be compared and the centre of the field of the photometer may be at the same horizontal level, or nearly so; and, in order that the photometer may be at a proper height for observing with convenience the shadows projected on its field by its cylindrical columns, it may be placed on a small stand set down on the table, or on the flat bottom of a square wooden box of a proper height, turned upside down. The height of the photometer should be such that when the observer is seated in a chair before it his eye may be on a level with the upper extremities of the two columns by which the shadows are projected.

Suppose now that it were required to determine the relative intensities of the light emitted by two candles, the one made of wax, the other of tallow. The three tables are first to be placed at the distance of about eight feet from each other in the middle of the room, or as far as possible from its walls; the photometer, elevated to a proper height, being placed on one of these tables, and one of the candles on each of the two others.

The observer is now to seat himself before the table on which the photometer is placed, and with his back turned to the two other tables.

He will find two shadows in the field of the photometer, and by taking the photometer in both his hands he must turn it round till one of these shadows (that, for instance, which belongs to the cylindrical column on his left hand) comes into contact with the vertical line which divides the field of the photometer into two equal parts; the whole of the shadow being on that side of that line on which the column is placed, that is to say, to the left of it, if it be the shadow of the left-hand column, otherwise on the other side of it.

As soon as one of the shadows shall have been thus brought into its proper place by moving the photometer about its axis, the other light must be moved by an assistant to the right or to the left, till the second shadow be likewise brought into its proper situation, or till it comes into contact with the other shadow in the middle of the field of the photometer.

If the flames of the two candles happen to be at the same horizontal level, the shadows which belong to them will be at the same height in the field of the photometer; and, if they happen to be at the same elevation as the field of the photometer, these shadows will just touch the horizontal line which is drawn through the field of the photometer, at the level of the upper extremities of the two columns.

As this is the most favourable situation for the shadows, they should always be made to occupy it; and this may easily be done even without altering the elevation either of the candles or of the photometer, by means of the three wooden screws on the lower ends of which the photometer rests.

By elevating or depressing more or less one or both of the hindermost screws, 2 and 3, Fig. 6, the extremities of the cylinders, the flames of the two candles, and

the horizontal line drawn on the field of the photometer may be brought to be all in the same plane, which
is all that is necessary in order to the shadows being
brought to occupy their proper places.

When this operation is finished (which may be performed in a moment), the shadows must be brought to
be of the same density.   This may be done either by
removing the stronger light farther off, or by bringing
that which is the most feeble nearer to the photometer.

As the two shadows are reciprocally illuminated by
the two lights, it is perfectly evident that the shadow
which is least illuminated, or of the darkest shade,
must belong to the feeblest light, provided the light be
at the same distance from the field of the photometer;
but, as the intensity of the light emitted by luminous
bodies decreases as the distance from the source of
that light increases, on removing the stronger light to
a greater distance the intensity of its illumination at
the field of the photometer will be diminished, and
the two shadows may be brought to be of the same
density.

In that case it is quite certain that the intensity
of the light *at the field of the photometer* cannot be
greater on one side than on the other; and, in order to
ascertain the relative intensities of the light emitted by
the flames of these candles, we have only to compare
the distances of those flames from the centre of that
field; for those intensities must necessarily be as the
squares of those distances, which is a fact too well
known to require any elucidation.

Instead of the rods divided into inches and tenths
of inches which I formerly used for measuring these
distances, I now employ flat rulers divided into *degrees*,

which indicate directly and without any computation the relative intensities of these lights.

These two flat rods, which serve as a graduated scale to the photometer, are about one inch in width and near one quarter of an inch in thickness: they may be folded up by means of joints, like a joint rule, and the length of each of them may be about 10 or 12 feet. Their first division is marked 10°, and it is placed at the distance of 10 inches from the middle of the field of the photometer, when the apparatus is prepared for making an experiment.

The other divisions of this *scale of light* are determined in such a manner that the numbers which they bear, which I call *degrees*, are everywhere *as the squares of their distances from the middle of the field of the photometer*, where the two shadows are in contact whose densities are compared and equalized.

To fill the important office of a *standard light* with which all others are compared, I have chosen a wax candle of the first quality, just eight tenths of an English inch in diameter, and which when burning with a clear and steady flame has been found to consume very uniformly 108 grains Troy of wax per hour.

To this standard light I have assigned the value of 100 degrees, and it is always placed exactly opposite to that division of the scale of the photometer which is marked 100°. This division is of course at the distance of 31.62 inches from the middle of the field of the instrument, that marked 10° being at the distance of ten inches.

These two rods are supported in a horizontal position by means of light stands.

As this apparatus is much more simple and much

less expensive than that I formerly recommended, I have taken pains to describe it very particularly; and, to save others the trouble which I have had in making the calculations which were necessary in order to form the graduated scale of the instrument, I shall here give a table in which the measure of each of those divisions will be expressed in feet and inches: —

SCALE OF THE PHOTOMETER.							
Degrees.	Distance in inches.	Degrees.	Distance in inches.	Degrees.	Distance in inches	Degrees.	Distance in inches.
10	10	220	46.91	430	65.57	660	81.24
20	14.14	230	47.95	440	66.33	680	82.46
30	17.32	240	48.98	450	67.07	700	83.67
40	20	250	50	460	67 82	720	84.85
50	22.36	260	50.99	470	68.50	740	86.02
60	24.54	270	51.96	480	69.28	750	86.60
70	26.45	280	52.91	490	70	760	87.18
80	28.28	290	53.85	500	70.71	780	88.32
90	30	300	54.77	510	71 41	800	89.44
100	31.62	310	55.63	520	72.12	820	90.45
110	33.17	320	56.57	530	72.80	840	91.65
120	34.64	330	57.44	540	73.48	850	92.19
130	35.94	340	58.31	550	74.14	860	92.73
140	37.42	350	59 16	560	74.83	880	93.28
150	38.73	360	60	570	75 50	900	94.87
160	40	370	60.83	580	76.16	920	95.94
170	41.26	380	61.64	590	76.81	940	96.95
180	42.43	390	62.45	600	77.46	950	97.46
190	43.59	400	63.25	620	78 74	960	97.98
200	44.72	410	64.03	640	80	980	98.99
210	45.83	420	64.81	650	80.62	1000	100

By the help of this table the scale may be graduated without any difficulty, and the whole of the apparatus constructed and completely finished by any cabinet-maker or joiner of common talents.

As the improvement and simplification of the instruments which are necessary in scientific investigations have a powerful tendency to facilitate useful discoveries, too much pains cannot be taken in describing such new inventions as may be useful in prosecuting experimental inquiries.

If I have ventured to place *illumination* among the useful arts, if I have taken pains to investigate its scientific principles, and to contrive instruments for facilitating those inquiries which are still necessary in order to carry it nearer to perfection, I am very far indeed from supposing that it will be in my power to finish that great and important work.

I shall have done much if I succeed in turning the attention of ingenious men to this interesting subject; and I sincerely hope that the improvements resulting from their united efforts will soon cause all those I have proposed to be forgotten.

As all improvements in illuminators must depend in a great measure on the improvement of the methods employed in the dispersion of light, and the choice of the materials used for constructing luminous screens, it may be of use to enlarge a little on that particular subject.

By constructing screens of different substances, but of the same form and dimensions, and employing them in pairs to mask the flames of lamps, which are made to burn in such a manner as to emit equal quantities of light, the relative quantities of light diffused by those screens may easily be determined by means of the photometer, and consequently the precise amount of the loss of light which each of them occasions; and by a series of experiments of this kind, made with screens composed of various substances, every thing can be discovered that is necessary to be known, in order to contrive the most efficacious means of dispersing the too powerful light of the flames of lamps and candles in the most agreeable manner and with the least loss.

In order to determine with the greatest precision the quantity of light which is lost in passing through a screen, two Argand lamps, placed at equal distances before the photometer, and having been made to burn with precisely the same degree of intensity, the shadows projected in the field of the instrument will be of the same density.   If now a screen be interposed before one of these lamps, the shadow belonging to it will become a little less dark than the other shadow.   On moving the lamp, which is covered by a screen, a little nearer to the photometer, the equality of density of the shadows will be restored; and, when that has been done, the divisions of the scale of the photometer will indicate the intensities of the light, and the difference of the intensities indicated will show the quantity of light destroyed in passing through the screen.

As the object principally had in view in using a screen is to disperse the *direct rays* of a too powerful flame, it is evident that the less the flame is seen through the screen (the total quantity of light diffused remaining the same), the better it performs its office; but, as the flame is always seen more or less distinctly through a screen, it is certain that a considerable portion of the light diffused does not come from the screen, but directly through it from the flame in straight lines.   Now as it is very certain that two screens of the same form and dimensions, but composed of different substances, may moderate the intensity or brilliancy of the direct rays from a powerful flame in the same degree, and yet the total quantities of light sent off from the surfaces of these screens by which surrounding objects are illuminated may be very different, it is necessary to pay particular attention to that important circumstance in the choice of the sub-stances employed in constructing screens.

In comparing two screens in order to discover which of them is best calculated to answer the purposes for which they are designed, they must be examined first in respect to their powers of dispersing and softening the direct rays of the flame of a lamp, and in the next place in respect to the quantities of light which they emit from their surfaces.

It is not difficult to ascertain the first point with a considerable degree of precision by simple inspection; but, where greater precision is required, the following method may be employed: —

Having placed before the photometer, at equal dis-tances, two like lamps, burning with precisely the same degree of intensity, and having masked them with the two screens made of different substances which are to be compared, a sheet of thick pasteboard is to be inter-posed before each of these screens, and at the distance of about one inch from it. This sheet of pasteboard must be sufficiently large to mask the screen entirely from the photometer, and it must have a circular hole in its centre of about one inch in diameter, which must be so placed that the centre of this aperture, the centre of the flame of the lamp, and the middle of the field of the photometer may be in the same right line.

It is evident that in this situation of things little or no light will arrive at the field of the photometer but that which comes from the flames of the lamps directly, in straight lines, through the screens; and by measur-ing the relative intensities of those rays which arrive in this manner through the two screens, by means of the shadows and distances, it will be seen which of the screens ought to be preferred, and how much more one of them softens the direct rays from the flame than the other.

It will likewise be possible to determine in any given case, by means of experiments which are by no means difficult to perform, the relative quantities of the light which proceeding in straight lines from the flame pass directly through the sides of the screen into the room, and of that which coming from the surface of the screen in all directions illuminates the surrounding bodies.

These experiments, and many others of a similar nature which it is not necessary for me to describe particularly, will no doubt occur to those who may engage in these interesting investigations; and it is highly probable that many useful improvements will be derived from these researches.

CHAPTER V.

Of the relative Quantities of Light furnished by Lamps of different Sizes, with the Combustion of a given Quantity of Oil. — Of the relative Cost of Light furnished by Lamps and Candles under different Circumstances. — The Light furnished by a good Lamp does not cost half as much as that furnished by a Tallow Candle.

HAVING lately found, from the results of a course of experiments on the light manifested in the combustion of inflammable substances, of which an account was given in a paper read before the Royal Society the 23d of January, 1812, that the quantity of light thus produced is not in an invariable proportion to the quantity of inflammable matter consumed, but that it depends much on the form and dimensions of the flame, and that when the volume of the flame is given the quantity of light will be greatest when the form of the flame is such that the red-hot particles of which it is composed can retain their heat the longest time, I was led by this discovery to conclude that the great quantity of light which is emitted by an Argand lamp depends principally on the peculiar form of its flame, which is that of a hollow cylinder, and which is extremely well adapted for preserving its heat against the cooling influence of the surrounding cold bodies.

I saw likewise that lamps of different sizes, constructed on the same principles, must necessarily consume very different quantities of oil in producing equal quantities of light; for their flames being of different dimensions, and also of forms that are not exactly similar, they must necessarily be cooled with different degrees of celerity on being projected into a cold atmosphere.

As soon as the particles of which flame is composed have been so cooled as to be no longer red-hot, they cease to be luminous, and consequently to be visible; and they disappear entirely.

These facts appeared to me to be much too important to be neglected in establishing the principles of the art of illumination; and I contrived and executed a set of experiments for the sole purpose of giving them a thorough investigation.

I provided three lamps, all constructed on Argand's principles (with circular wicks), but which varied considerably in size.

The first, which I shall call No. 1, is a portable lamp with an Argand burner, which is so small that the circular wick of the lamp is only 0.28 of an inch in diameter, measured internally.

No. 2 is likewise a portable lamp with an Argand burner, but its burner is much larger. The diameter of the circular wick of this lamp is just 0.5 of an inch internally (half an inch).

No. 3 is an Argand lamp of the largest size commonly sold at Paris. The diameter of the wick of this lamp is 0.65 of an inch, measured internally.

These lamps being all in perfect order, each of them in their turns was exactly weighed, and was made to burn before the photometer just one hour, and was so managed as to be made to furnish constantly during that time the same given quantity of light; and on being removed from before the photometer was immediately extinguished and again weighed, in order to ascertain how much oil had been consumed in the experiment.

The results of these important experiments were as follows:—

When the lamps were made to furnish just 100° of light, which is the quantity furnished by a good wax candle, of such a size as to consume regularly 108 grains Troy of wax per hour (which quantity, for greater convenience, I shall call 100 parts of wax), the quantities of the best purified oil of colza consumed were found to be as follows:—

By the lamp No. 1 . . . . 137 parts.
By the lamp No. 2 . . . . 203 „
By the lamp No. 3 . . . . 228 „
Wax consumed by the standard wax candle in
furnishing constantly the same quantity of
light during the same time . . . . . . 100 „

When these lamps were made to furnish 200° of light during one hour, the quantities of oil consumed by them were as follows : —

By the lamp No. 1 . . . . 160 parts.
By the lamp No. 2 . . . . 226 „
By the lamp No. 3 . . . . 271 „
Quantity of wax necessary in order to furnish the
same quantity of light during the same time
by means of two wax candles . . . . . . 200 „

When 300° of light were furnished by each of these lamps during one hour, the quantities of oil consumed were found to be as follows : —

By the lamp No. 1 . . . . 201 parts.
By the lamp No. 2 . . . . 286 „
By the lamp No. 3 . . . . 305 „
Quantity of wax necessary to produce the same
quantity of light during the same time by
means of three wax candles . . . . . . 300 „

From these results it is perfectly evident that, where a small quantity of light is wanted, small lamps are much more economical than large ones, when both are constructed on the same principles. When Argand burners are used, the cause of this difference may easily be perceived and perfectly understood. A circular flame, which is at the same time low and wide, is much more exposed to being rapidly cooled by the air and by other surrounding cold bodies than a hollow flame, which is narrower and higher.

As the lamp No. 1 could not be made to furnish constantly for any considerable time much more than

300° of light, that lamp was now laid aside; and these researches were continued with the two more powerful lamps No. 2 and No. 3.

When these were made to furnish each 400° of light, the quantities of oil consumed in one hour were as follows: —

By the lamp No. 2 . . . . 320 parts.
By the lamp No. 3 . . . . 361 „
Wax required for producing the same quantity of
   light . . . . 400 „

Here again we find that the smaller light has still the advantage over the larger.

When 500° of light were furnished, the quantities of oil consumed were: —

By the lamp No. 2 . . . . 357 parts.
By the lamp No. 3 . . . . 405 „
Quantity of wax necessary to produce the same
   quantity of light . . . . 500 „

The smaller lamp still continues to maintain its superiority, but we shall soon find that the larger one will get before it.

When both lamps were so regulated as to produce each just 600° of light (equal to that of six wax candles), the quantities of oil consumed per hour were found to be as follows: —

By the lamp No. 2 . . . 474 parts = 512 grains Troy.
By the lamp No. 3 . . . 441 „   = 476 „   „
Quantity of wax necessary
   for producing the same
   light . . . . 600 „   = 648 „   „

As the smaller lamp could not be made to furnish much more than 600° of light, it could no longer be compared with the larger; but, in order to find out how much farther the economy of oil could be carried

in the production of light, the experiments were continued with the larger lamp, and it was found that
more light was produced by this lamp in the combustion of a given quantity of oil when the lamp was so
managed as to furnish 900° of light than when the
flame was either longer or shorter.

When the lamp was burning in such a manner
as to produce uniformly 900° of light, the oil
consumed in one hour was found to be . . . 560 parts.
The wax consumed by nine wax candles in furnishing the same quantity of light would
amount to . . . . 900 „
When this lamp furnished 800° of light, the oil
consumed per hour was . . . . 515 „
Wax required in producing the same quantity of
light by means of wax candles . . . . . 800 „

When the lamp was forced so as to make it give
1000° of light, its flame became very long, and it
emitted smoke at intervals, and more oil was employed
in producing a given quantity of light than when less
light was demanded.

When 1000° of light were furnished, the expense
of oil per hour was . . . . 669 parts.
Ten wax candles must have been employed to
produce this quantity of light, and they would
have consumed of wax . . . . 1000 „

When this lamp furnished 800° of light, 100 parts of
the oil gave as much light as could be furnished by
155 parts of wax.

When the lamp furnished 900° of light, 100 parts of
the oil then consumed furnished as much light as
could be produced in the combustion of 160 parts of
wax.

But when the lamp was made to give 1000° of light,
100 parts of the oil then burned or dissipated produced

no more light than that which could be produced in the combustion of 148 parts of wax.

Hence we may conclude that the maximum of effect with this lamp was obtained when it was made to furnish 900° of light.

The best effect produced with the lamp No. 1 was when it gave 300° of light.

And the maximum of the effect of the lamp No. 2 was that which was produced when it was so managed as to furnish 500° of light.

By comparing the quantities of oil which these lamps consumed in furnishing these quantities of light with the quantities of wax necessary for producing the same quantities of light by means of wax candles, we can ascertain how much cheaper any given quantity of light can be produced by one of these lamps than by the others, when they are all so managed as to produce their best effect.

300° of light were furnished by the lamp No. 1 with an expense of oil which amounted to 201 parts per hour.

To produce the same quantity of light, 300 parts of wax must have been burned. Consequently, if 201 parts of oil are equal in effect to 300 parts of wax, 100 parts of oil so employed must be equal in effect to 149 parts of wax.

Again, it was found that 500° of light were furnished by the lamp No. 2 with a regular consumption of oil, which amounted to 357 parts.

To have produced that quantity of light by means of wax candles, 500 parts of wax must have been consumed. Here 357 parts of oil were equal in effect to 500 parts of wax, consequently 100 parts of oil so employed were equal in effect to 140 parts of wax.

When the greatest effect was produced by the lamp No. 3, it was found that 100 parts of the oil consumed gave as much light as could have been furnished by 160 parts of wax, as we have just seen.

On comparing these results, we find that the maxima of the effects of these three lamps, in respect to the economy of the oil, were as follows: —

That of the lamp No. 1 149
      No. 2 140
      No. 3 160

The quantity of light which the lamp No. 3 usually furnished, when in good order, was seldom greater than 700°; and its ordinary consumption of oil, when furnishing that quantity of light, was at the rate of 470 parts per hour. This gives for the maximum of the effect of the lamp, *in the ordinary course of its service,* 100 parts of oil equal in effect to 149 parts of wax; and hence we might conclude that the light furnished by the smallest lamp did not cost more than that furnished by the largest.

From the results of all these experiments, I think we may safely conclude that 1 lb. of purified oil of colza burned in a good Argand lamp, well trimmed and properly managed, gives as much light as $1\frac{1}{2}$ lb. of beeswax, when good wax candles of the common size are used.

When tallow candles are used, the quantity of light produced will depend much on the attention that is paid to the management of them. If they are not frequently snuffed, a great deal of the tallow will be dissipated in vapour and lost, filling the air with a most insupportable stench.

I have found by the results of many experiments that a tallow candle which is suffered to burn with a long wick consumes more than twice as much tallow in producing any given quantity of light as when the same candle is kept well trimmed. I have even found that a tallow candle consumes faster when it burns dim and gives little light than when it burns well and furnishes a great deal of very pure light. This extraordinary fact was first announced in my paper on the Relative Intensities of the Light emitted by Luminous Bodies, which was read before the Royal Society the 6th February, 1794.

Many persons will no doubt be curious to know what are the relative quantities of light *usually furnished* in the combustion of tallow candles and wax candles.

After having made a considerable number of experiments, with a view to determining that point with as much precision as the nature of the subject will permit, I have found reason to conclude that when both the wax candles and the tallow candles are of the first quality, and when no more than the usual attention is paid to the latter in burning them, the quantity by weight of the tallow consumed in producing a given quantity of light is to the quantity of wax consumed in producing the same quantity of light as 130 to 100.

When a tallow candle is of such a size as to produce as much light as the wax candle, and when the greatest possible care is taken to keep it constantly well snuffed, equal quantities of light may be produced by 115 parts of tallow and 100 parts of wax; but when tallow candles are small and of ordinary quality, and when they are burned in the careless manner in which they are commonly used, we must reckon 150 parts of tallow to produce as much light as is usually produced in burning 100 parts of wax.

But where so much depends on the degree of attention that is paid to the subject, no estimate can be made with any considerable degree of certainty.

A chemical analysis has shown us that beeswax, tallow, and the fat oils are composed of nearly the same elements, and consequently contain nearly the same quantities of inflammable matter (*carbon* and *hydrogen*); and, as I have lately found that they furnish nearly the same quantities of heat in their combustion,* it might naturally have been supposed that they must likewise furnish equal quantities of light.

I have no doubt but they would do so, could they be managed in precisely the same manner ; but their difference of form at the ordinary temperature of the atmosphere, the difference of the temperature at which they become fluid and at which they are reduced to vapour, must necessarily produce a sensible difference in the arrangements employed in burning them, which cannot fail to occasion a sensible difference in the quantities of light produced in their combustion.

The intensity of the heat which accompanies the combustion of an inflammable substance is no doubt always the same ; but it does not follow that the quantity of light is always the same.

As the intensity of the light produced by lamps and candles may be ascertained with great certainty by means of the photometer, the *cost* of the light may in all cases be exactly determined.

Taking wax candles, tallow candles, and purified oil of colza at the prices these articles are now sold at

---

* An account of these experiments was given in a memoir on the Heat Manifested in the Combustion of Inflammable Substances, which was read before the First Class of the French National Institute, the 24th February, 1812. [See Vol. II, p. 80.]

Paris, we can estimate the cost of the light which is produced by each of them. We will begin by determining the cost of 100° of light furnished during one hour by a good wax candle.

A bundle of wax candles called a pound, but which weigh only 450 grammes (= 6954 grains Troy, or 53 grains less than a pound avoirdupois), is now sold at Paris for three francs, or two shillings and sixpence sterling, if we take the exchange at what it was formerly in time of peace.

One of these candles furnishes just 100° of light, and consumes just seven grammes of wax per hour. The five candles will burn 64 hours, 17 minutes, and 8 seconds, or $64\frac{3}{7}$ hours; and, as the five candles cost 2s. 6d. = 120 farthings, the 100° of light furnished by one of them costs $\frac{120}{64\frac{3}{7}}$ = 1.8666 of a farthing per hour.

Six tallow candles of the best quality usually sold in the shops of Paris, weighing together 476.4 grammes (= 7358.8 grains Troy, or $16\frac{82}{100}$ ounces avoirdupois), are now sold for sixteen sous, or eightpence sterling. And I find that one of these candles consumes 10.35 grammes (= 166 grains Troy) of tallow per hour, when the most scrupulous attention is paid in burning this candle to keep it constantly well snuffed.

Now as six of these candles weighing 476.4 grammes cost eightpence, or 32 farthings, the quantity of tallow consumed in one hour = 10.35 grammes must cost $\frac{10.35 \times 32}{476.4}$ = 0.69521 of a farthing.

If this tallow candle had furnished the same quantity of light as was furnished by the standard wax candle, viz. 100°, the cost of its light would have been to the cost of that furnished by the wax candle as

0.69521 to 1.86660; but the tallow candle furnishes 115° of light.

When a proper allowance is made for the difference between the quantities of light furnished by these two candles, it will appear that the cost of the light furnished by the tallow candle is to the cost of that furnished by the wax candle as 0.60454 to 1.86660, or as one to three nearly, when the quantities of light are equal.

But in the careless manner in which tallow candles are commonly used, the light they furnish is more expensive.

The candles usually burned in the workshops of tradesmen at Paris, such as joiners, cabinet-makers, etc., are such as are sold in bundles of eight to the pound. These candles cost two sous (= four farthings sterling) each; and they seldom burn longer than five hours. This gives 0.8 of a farthing for the cost of the light furnished by one of these small candles during one hour; but the quantity of light so furnished is far from being equal to that furnished by the standard wax candle. Instead of giving 100° of light, they seldom furnish 75° and frequently give less than 50°, that is to say, whenever they burn with a long wick and stand in need of being snuffed, which very often happens.

From the result of all my observations I have been induced to conclude that the light actually furnished by tallow candles amounts to little more than half what they ought to furnish, if well managed; and that the light they give costs nearly half as much as the light furnished by wax candles, which, as is well known, seldom stand in need of snuffing.

I shall now endeavour to estimate the cost of light which is produced in the combustion of purified oil of colza; and in doing this it will be indispensably necessary to have regard to the intensity of the light which is furnished, as also to the size of the lamp which is used in producing it. But the first thing to be ascertained is the price of the oil.

The best purified oil of colza is now selling at Paris for 20 sous the kilogramme, which is at the rate of two shillings and tenpence half penny sterling, the English wine gallon.

By an experiment made with my smallest Argand lamp (No. 1) I found that when it was arranged and managed in such a manner as to furnish constantly just 100° of light during one hour, the lamp consumed just 9.4 grammes of oil.

Now as 1000 grammes of this oil cost tenpence sterling, or 40 farthings, these 9.4 grammes must cost 0.3759 of a farthing, which is less than half what the same quantity of light costs when furnished by tallow candles.

But this lamp being so constructed as to produce its best effect when it furnishes 300° of light, the saving which will result from the use of it will be still greater when that quantity of light is produced.

In an experiment several times repeated, in which this lamp was made to furnish constantly 300° of light during one hour, it was found to consume, at a medium, 14.4 grammes of oil during that time.

	Farthings.
This quantity of oil, at the price it is now sold in Paris, would cost	0.57600
The same quantity of light furnished by the best tallow candles well managed would cost . . .	1.81362
Furnished by wax candles, it would cost . . .	5.59980

Hence it appears that where 300° of light are wanted it may be furnished by purified oil of colza, at less than *one third* part of the money it would cost when produced by means of the best tallow candles, and at a very little more than *one tenth* part of the sum it would cost if furnished by wax candles.

These computations may serve to give some idea of the immense importance to society of the subject I have endeavoured to investigate in this Essay.

ON ILLUMINATION

Observations on the Dispersion of the Light of Lamps by Means of Shades of unpolished Glass, Silk, &c.; with a Description of a new Lamp.

To Mr. NICHOLSON.

SIR,

I SEND you for your Journal, the following translation of a very ingenious paper of Count Rumford's, which was read at the Institute on Monday last. Count Rumford, at whose desire I send it, has taken the trouble to revise and correct the translation.

I am,

Paris,

27th March, 1806.

No: 17, Rue de Varenne.

Your very humble servant,

W. A. CADELL.

Amongst the necessaries of life may be reckoned *heat* and *light*; and each of them composes so considerable an article of expence, that every improvement that tends to facilitate their production, or to economise their consumption, is deserving of attention.

Having made, at different periods, a great number of

experiments on the production of light in the combustion of inflamable bodies, and on its distribution; and having lately contrived a lamp which, on trial, has been found to answer very well, I have resolved to submit to this learned assembly some of the results of my researches on this important subject.

The lamp, which I have the honour of presenting to the Institute, has nothing new in the essential part of it, that is, in the form of the wick; for, after the ingenious discovery of the circular wick by M. Argand, it does not appear to me probable that the economy of oil in the production of light can be carried much farther: When this lamp is in good order it gives no perceptible smoke, nor smell; and hence, I think, we may conclude that the combustion of the oil is complete, and, consequently, that the quantity of light is at its maximum. But there still remains much to be done to improve the general form of lamps, in regard to their elegance and convenience, and above all, to distribute their light in a more advantageous and agreeable manner.

If the facility with which the eye distinguishes objects depended solely on the intensity of the light by which they are illuminated, the scientific distribution of light would be less important; but that is far from being the case. We are able to see, very distinctly, with intensities of light which are extremely different; provided that the eye has had the time to conform itself to the quantity of light present, and that that quantity remains invariable.

It is well known that we can read printed characters of a moderate size, both by the light of the full moon, and by that of the sun at mid-day; the intensity, however, of the light, in the first case, is, to that in the second, as 1 to 300,000; but when the eye passes rapidly from a strong light, to one that is more feeble, or *vice versa*, we can distinguish nothing at first; and, when these changes succeed each other rapidly, they become extremely fatiguing to the eyes.

The facility with which we distinguish an enlightened object depends on its shadow. When shadows are simple, they are necessarily well defined, and we see distinctly; but when the light comes in several directions, several shadows are formed of the same object, which are so blended together as to render them confused and ill defined; and in that case we see indistinctly, even in the midst of a great glare of light. Hence we may conclude, that a considerable economy must result from a judicious distribution of the light employed in lighting a room. But this saving of expence, considerable as it would be, is however an object of much less importance than the advantage which must result in respect to the pleasantness of the light, and the preservation of the eyes.

If every sudden change in the intensity of the light that falls upon the eyes be hurtful to them, the direct rays coming from the flame of an Argand lamp must fatigue them very much, and even deprive them of the faculty of distinguishing easily objects which are placed near that dazzling source of brightness. It is impossible indeed to view the flame of one of these lamps near at hand without suffering excessive pain, and even at a distance it is always hurtful and unpleasant to the eye. It is well known how much we are dazzled and almost blinded on coming into a room lighted by several of these lamps, burning without shades, and placed so low that the eye cannot avoid them.

With a view to soften the light of these lamps, shades have been contrived, formed of materials whose transparency is more or less imperfect; for instance, large cylinders, or spheres of crape, gauze, or roughened glass. This contrivance is very useful, and deserves to be more generally adopted; it is even of so great importance that we cannot take too much pains to improve it, and recommend it to the public.

What has hindered these shades from being more generally employed is probably an opinion, that they must necessarily occasion a great loss of light. I hope to be able to shew that that opinion is not well founded.

The following simple experiment was made some years ago, with a view to determine nearly the quantity of light which is lost in passing through a roughened glass.

Two wax candles, of equal size, lighted, and burning with the same degree of intensity, were placed in two vertical cylinders of fine glass, pretty thin, six inches in diameter and six inches in height, the one of smooth and the other of roughened glass; these two cylinders being placed at the same height, on two tables, at the distance of eight feet from each other, in a room where there was no other light than that emitted by the candles, I presented to the two candles, placed in their cylinders, a sheet of white paper, at the distance of sixteen feet from each of them, and I interposed before the paper, at the distance of two inches from its surface, a small wooden cylinder in a vertical position, which projected two shadows on the paper.

I was much surprised to find these shadows very nearly of the same intensity. This result shewed me that the quantity of light lost in passing through a roughened glass is much less than I at first supposed; but, on reflection, I saw that there was nothing in the result of the experiment which did not admit of an easy explanation.

Although roughened glass appears opaque, it is by no means so. In the operation of roughening its surface, which from being smooth becomes furrowed, and broken in every direction, it at last presents an uninterrupted collection of asperities of every different form. Individually they are almost invisible to the naked eye, on account of their smallness; their sides are however smooth and shining, as is easy to perceive on examining them with a microscope. It is evident that the light which falls upon the smooth surface of one of these little prominent points must penetrate the glass with the same ease (when the angle of incidence is the same) as it would penetrate the plane surface of a large polished plate of the same sort of glass; and that having passed through the surface, the ray must pursue its course in the substance of the glass, and pass out on the other side in the same manner in one case as in the other.

When a pencil of parallel rays falls. perpendicularly upon a plate of well-polished glass, they pass through the glass without any perceptible change of direction; but when the pencil falls upon a plate of roughened glass, the rays of which it is composed are dispersed, and the cylindrical pencil is transformed into a cone. The ultimate course of each ray depends on the refractions that it has undergone in entering and issuing out of the glass, and these refractions are determined by the angles of incidence, and the respective inclinations of the refracting surfaces on each side of the glass at the point where the ray enters and at that where it goes out.

If the flame of a lamp be placed in the center of a globe of fine glass, well polished, the rays issuing from it will traverse the sides of the globe without undergoing any perceptible change, either in their intensity or their direction; and the flame will be seen so distinctly through the globe that this last might even escape observation. But if, instead of a globe of polished glass we employ a globe of roughened glass, in that case, the rays emitted by the flame will be dispersed by the glass in such a manner that each visible point of the surface of the globe will become a radiant cone, and consequently the globe will appear luminous, diffusing light from its surface in every direction.

From this explanation of the phenomena we see that a shade of fine glass roughened, when it is used with a view to disperse and soften the too vivid light of a lamp, does not occasion any considerable loss of light. This loss would even be imperceptible, or not greater with a shade of roughened glass than with one of the same kind of glass polished and transparent, notwithstanding the great dispersion of the light, were it not for the reflections which some of the rays suffer before they quit the shade.

It is well known that when a ray of light falls upon a polished surface of glass (or other substance), at a very small angle of incidence, it is necessarily reflected; and as the sides of the asperities of the roughened glass must present themselves to the rays which proceed from the lamp at angles of all possible magnitudes, there must necessarily be some whose inclination is sufficient to reflect some of the rays that fall upon them; and as that may occur at both surfaces of the shade, it is possible that a ray may be obliged to pass and repass in the glass from one side of the shade to the other several times before it be able to escape into the room.

If the glass were perfectly transparent, the light would be little, or perhaps not at all diminished by these repeated reflections and passages; but we know that even the finest glass is very far from being perfectly transparent.

When crape, gauze, or other substances are employed to make shades for the purpose of masking the flame of a lamp, the loss of light will be more or less considerable in proportion to the greater or less degree of transparency of the solid parts of the substance employed. But without engaging in the very delicate enquiry concerning the degree of transparence of the molecules or small solid particles of the substances to be employed in making shades, we may determine, by simple experiments, with ease and even precision, what are the substances to be preferred for that purpose. We have only to procure shades of the same form and size, made of the different substances to be examined, and to compare them, by pairs, by means of two argand lamps, made to burn with the same degree of vivacity, and of a simple photometer, which can be constructed at a very small expence.

The photometer which I used in my experiments on the comparative quantities of light produced in the combustion of wax, tallow, and different kinds of oil, and of the same kind of oil burned in an argand lamp and in a common lamp,* would serve perfectly well for the experiments in question; but as that instrument is somewhat complicated, I shall propose another more simple, which I have employed since with success. Its construction is as follows:—

In the middle of the upper surface of a wooden cube of 8 inches in diameter, composed of boards, covered with black paper, there is fixed vertically a small board, 4 inches in breadth, 6 inches in height, and half an inch in thickness, covered on one side with white paper. In the middle of this white side there is traced, with pen and

* See Phil. Transact. for 1794, and my Philosophical Papers, vol. i. page 270.

ink, a slender black line, from the top to the bottom, which divides the surface into two equal parts.

Before this white surface, at the distance of $2\frac{4}{10}$ inches, are placed two little pillars of wood, painted black, 4 inches in height and half an inch in diameter. These little pillars, which are cylindrical, are placed at the distance of $3\frac{2}{10}$ inches asunder, and they are firmly fixed in two holes formed to receive them in the upper surface of the cube. They are at equal distances from the black vertical line which marks the middle of the white surface of the photometer, that is to say, at the distance of 3 inches (English measure) from that vertical line.

This little instrument is employed in the following manner: Having placed, in a dark room, three little tables, at the distance of 7 or 8 feet from each other, so as to occupy the three angles of an equilateral triangle, the photometer is placed on one of these tables, and the two lamps upon the other two; taking care that the flames of the lamps and the middle of the white surface of the photometer are of the same height, or in the same horizontal plane.

The observer being seated before the photometer, with his back turned towards the lamps, he presents the photometer to the two lamps, in such a manner that the direct rays from their flames fall upon the white surface of that instrument at equal angles of incidence, or in such a direction that the two internal shadows formed by the two pillars may touch each other without being blended together, at the black vertical line in the middle of that face. As the two external shadows fall without the surface of the photometer, they are of course not seen.

When the photometer is placed, the distances of the lamps are verified, and brought to a perfect equality, and when that is done, the lamps are made to burn with the same degree of vivacity, which is easily done by elevating a little one of the wicks, or lowering the other: this must be performed by an assistant, whilst the observer keeps his eyes constantly fixed upon the shadows.

The equality of the quantities of light which the lamps emit is announced by the perfect equality in the densities of the two shadows which are formed in the middle of the white face of the photometer. This is evident, because each shadow being enlightened by the direct rays of the opposite lamp, if one of the lamps gives more light than the other, the shadow which it enlightens must of course be more enlightened, and consequently less dark than that enlightened by the weaker lamp.

If, instead of establishing an equality in the quantity of light emitted by the two lamps, we would ascertain the relative quantities of light that they emit when their flames are unequal, they must be placed on two tables before the photometer, and after having brought the shadows into contact with each other, we must remove the stronger lamp until the intensity of its light at the vertical field of the photometer be diminished by the increase of its distance, till a perfect equality is established between the densities of the two shadows; and then we measure exactly the distance of each lamp from the photometer.— The squares of the distances will be as the quantities of light emitted by the lamps.

In order to exclude the light reflected from the sides of the room and other surrounding bodies, with a view to render the shadows more distinct, and their comparison more easy, the photometer may be placed in a quadrangular box, open in the front, forming a kind of centry-box, 15 or 16 inches in height and 10 or 12 inches in width and depth, constructed of boards, or even of pasteboard, and lined within and without with black paper.

The experiments are simple and easy that may be made with this little apparatus for determining the different substances that may be employed in constructing shades to soften the light of lamps; and as this enquiry must lead to very important improvements, both with respect to economy and to elegance and comfort, I recommend these researches to all those who are occupied in the improvement of lamps. These experiments may be made in the following way:—

Having prepared two shades, of the same form and dimensions, that are to be compared together, we must begin by placing the two lamps at the same distance in front of the photometer, and causing them to burn with the same degree of brightness, and then masking the flames of the lamps by the two shades, we must examine anew the shadows. If these shadows are of equal densities, we may conclude that the two shades emit equal quantities of light; if the densities of the shadows are different, then the shade that enlightens the shadow which is the least dense is that which emits the most light; and in order to determine with precision the relative quantities of light emitted by the two shades, we must remove the lamp which bears the shade that emits the most light until the equality of the shadows be re-established, and then, measuring the distances of the lamps from the photometer, the quantities of light will be as the squares of these distances.

If we wish to know how much light is absorbed and lost in employing any given shade, we must operate in the following manner:—Having placed the two lamps, without their shades, at equal distances in front of the photometer,

and having equalised the flames of the lamps in the manner already described, we place the shade that is to be
tried upon one of the lamps, and the equality of the
shadows is instantly destroyed. In order to re-establish
this equality, we remove the lamp that is without a shade,
and when it re-established we measure the distances of the
two lamps from the photometer. The quantity of light
emitted by one of these lamps without a shade is to that
emitted by the same lamp with the shade, as the square
of the distance of the lamp that burns without a shade
is to the square of the distance of that masked by the
shade.

The object in view in using a shade being to disperse
the rays of a too dazzling flame, without destroying them,
it is evident that the less the flame of a lamp is apparent
through the sides of a shade, the quantity of light emitted
being the same, the better it will answer its purpose. But
as we always see, more or less distinctly, the brilliant
flame of an argand's lamp through the shade which masks
it, it is evident that a considerable part of the light emitted
by a lamp thus masked does not proceed from the shade,
but, passing directly through the sides of the shade, it
comes from the flame in straight lines.

It is light, coming from the flame to the eyes in straight
lines, which a shade is destined to disperse and to soften;
and as it is certain that two shades of different materials
may have an equal power in softening the direct rays of
the flame of a lamp, and that nevertheless the total
quantities of light that they emit may be very different,
it is necessary to pay attention to this remarkable circumstance in the choice of shades.

The shades to be compared should therefore be examined, first in regard to their power of masking and

softening the direct rays of the flame of a lamp, and afterwards in regard to the quantity of light that they distribute in a room. The first point seems susceptible of being pretty well determined by the simple inspection; but if we would employ more precision, we may make use of the following method:—

Having placed, at equal distance, two lamps burning with the same degree of vivacity, in front of the photometer, we mask them with the two shades (made of different materials), which are to be compared, and we place between each shade and the photometer, at the distance of about an inch from the shade, a disk of thick pasteboard, perforated in the middle by a circular hole, one inch in diameter. The diameter of this disk must be sufficiently large to mask completely the shade, and the center of the circular hole must be in a straight line drawn from the center of the flame to the center of the vertical face of the photometer.

We see that, in this state of things, it is almost solely the direct rays coming from the flames of the lamps in straight lines through the substance of the shades that fall upon the photometer; and that, on measuring the relative intensities of these rays on each side, by means of the shadows and the distances, we can determine not only which of the shades fulfils best its principal object, that of preserving the eyes, but likewise the proportion in which one of the flames is more softened than the other. We may also determine, by easy experiments and calculations, the proportion which exists, in any given case, between the quantity of light that passes directly from the flame in straight lines through the sides of the shade, and that which is dispersed by the shade and appears to issue from the shade itself. It would be too long to describe in this place all these experiments, and several others that might be made with the photometer, to complete the researches necessary for the improvement of lamps; but these details are the less necessary, as the experiments will not fail to present themselves to those who shall have made some progress in these enquiries.

I shall finish my observations upon shades for lamps by some remarks on the size that may be given to them. And first, it is evident that the diameter of a shade should be greater in proportion as the flame which it is intended to mask is greater and more bright; for if a shade be small, the light which it emits may be sufficiently strong to hurt the eyes, especially when viewed at a small distance.

The size and intensity of the flame being the same, the intensity of the light emitted by the surface of a shade that masks it will be as that surface, and consequently as the square of the diameter of the shade inversely.

If the intensity of the light emitted by a shade four inches in diameter be equal to four, it will be reduced to one on doubling the diameter of the shade, and that without any change in the total quantity of light which is diffused in the room. This shews the advantage to the eyes that will result from the use of shades of large dimensions.

The small spherical shades of roughened glass which are sometimes employed for lamps, have been found to emit a light too dazzling to the eyes. In order to remedy this inconvenience, all that is necessary is to make the shade larger. If these globes are more dazzling than globes of crape or gauze of the same dimensions, that circumstance proves no more than that roughened glass absorbs less light than these silk stuffs do; and from this we may conclude that the solid parts of silk are less transparent

than those of glass, and consequently that this substance
is less fit to be used in making shades for lamps than glass.

I will just mention here a circumstance respecting
roughened glass, which although not immediately connected with the subject of this paper, appears nevertheless
sufficiently important to deserve attention. It often
happens, in great towns, that a room has no other light
than what it receives by windows which look into a small
court, surrounded on all sides by high buildings: in these
cases the room would be more copiously and better lighted
by panes of roughened glass than by transparent panes.
The rays of day-light, which descend almost perpendicularly
from above into the court, fall upon the panes at so small
an angle of incidence that, when the exterior surface of
the glass is polished, they are in great part thrown off by
reflection, and do not get into the room; and even those
which, not being reflected, pass through the pane, as they
fall directly upon the floor, where they are almost all
absorbed, the objects in the room are very little enlightened; but when the pane is roughened, the asperities
of the glass presenting to the descending rays surfaces
less inclined, more of the rays enter the glass, and passing
through it afterwards in various directions, light is diffused
in all the parts of the room. And it is not solely for windows which look into small courts that it is useful to
employ roughened glass; it may be used with much advantage in all cases where windows look against a high
wall, at a small distance, and especially if the wall be of a
dark colour. But to return to my subject.

Without enlarging farther at this time on the construction of shades to be used for masking and softening the
too dazzling flame of lamps, I shall give an account of
the new lamp which I have lately caused to be constructed,

and which I have the honour of presenting to this learned society.

This lamp, which is destined to be suspended in the middle of a room, was particularly intended to light a dining-room, but it may likewise serve to light a drawing-room, or a billiard-table. The following are the details of its construction:—

A hollow hoop of tin, painted white, $12\frac{8}{10}$ English inches in diameter within, 16 inches in diameter without, and $\frac{8}{10}$ of an inch deep, suspended in a horizontal position, serves as a reservoir for the oil. In the centre of this circular reservoir there are three cylinders, or beaks, which inclose three circular wicks of the usual form and size. These three vertical cylinders, which touch each other, are soldered together, and connected with the reservoir by means of three oblique tubes $\frac{9}{20}$ of an inch square, through which the oil flows to the wicks from the reservoir.

In order to catch the oil which occasionally drops from these three cylinders, there is a cup, made of tin $4\frac{1}{2}$ inches in diameter above at its opening, and 1 inch in depth in the middle, which is placed at the distance of $\frac{3}{4}$ of an inch under the lower ends of the three cylinders.

Each of these cylinders is furnished with a chimney, or tube of glass, and they may be lighted either all three together, or two, or one only, according to the quantity of light that is wanted.

This lamp is suspended by means of a hoop of brass, gilt, $16\frac{2}{10}$ inches in diameter and $1\frac{1}{4}$ inch wide, having a little horizontal projection at its lower edge, internally, on which the circular reservoir of the lamp rests. To this brass hoop are fixed three arrows, of gilt brass, at equal distances from each other. These arrows, which are 6 inches in length and $\frac{4}{10}$ of an inch in diameter, are in a horizontal position, on the outer side of the hoop, and in the direction of three radii drawn from its centre.

To these three arrows, at the distance of 3 inches from the hoop, are fastened the ends of three chains of gilt copper, each of 28 inches in length, by which the hoop that receives the lamp is suspended.

These arrows serve the purpose of separating the chains from each other, in order that the lamp may be removed occasionally, and replaced, without deranging the chains.

For a lamp with four wicks, which serves to light a large drawing-room, the gilded hoop that receives the lamp has six arrows, to which are attached six chains; but in order to be able to remove and replace the lamp, there is one of the chains which, being attached to its arrow by a small hook, it is detached occasionally and laid aside, in order to allow a passage for the lamp.

The gilded hoop which receives the lamp is ornamented with pendants of cristal; and from the lower edge of the hoop, immediately behind the cristal ornaments, there descends a hoop of white crape, of the same diameter as the hoop of brass, and $4\frac{1}{2}$ inches in breadth, which serves to disperse and soften the direct rays of the flames of the lamp.

To reflect a part of the rays that mount towards the ceiling, in order to destroy the shadows that might be formed under the lamp, there is a conical reflector of white crape, which, resting on the three tubes that conduct the oil from the reservoir to the wicks, surrounds and conceals the tubes of glass that contain the flames.

This reflector is $12\frac{1}{2}$ inches in diameter below, $5\frac{1}{4}$ inches in diameter at its opening above, and 6 inches high.

The chief difficulty to be overcome in the construction of this lamp was to contain the oil in the reservoir in such a manner that it should not be in danger of being spilled in taking the lamp out of the hoop, in which it is suspended, in carrying it from one place to another, and in replacing it. Several attempts had already been made, by different persons, to construct suspended lamps with circular horizontal reservoirs, but none of them had been attended with success. That which I now propose is simple in its construction, and appears to me to answer perfectly well.

This reservoir is closed above, so as to form a hollow hoop, and it has three openings on its upper surface, equidistant from each other. These openings, which serve for pouring the oil into the reservoir, have each $\frac{7}{10}$ of an inch in diameter, and are hermetically closed by three stoppers of brass, ground with emery. In the axis of each of these stoppers there is a small hole, $\frac{3}{20}$ of an inch in diameter, which is occasionally closed by a small screw furnished with a collar of leather.

When the reservoir is filled with oil, the three stoppers are put in their places, and the small holes are then closed by means of the three screws. In this state of things, as the air cannot enter into the reservoir by the opening at its upper surface, the lamp may be transported, and even inclined considerably, without any danger of spilling the oil. As soon as the lamp is placed in its hoop (where care is taken to suspend it in a horizontal position), the communication must be opened between the air of the atmosphere and the upper surface of the oil in the reservoir, which is done by unscrewing a few turns the small screws which are in the axis of the stoppers. The oil then resumes its natural level, and afterwards passes freely into the cylinders that contain the wicks in order to feed the flames.

That it may not be necessary to take out the screw entirely when a passage for the air is opened by means of the vertical holes in the axis of the stoppers, these screws, which are half an inch in length, are not complete, being reduced on one side to the half of their diameters, in their whole length, except about $\frac{1}{10}$ of an inch at the top near the collar of leather.

When the screw is unscrewed two turns, the part of the screw that still remains in the hole not being entire, a free passage is necessarily opened into the interior of the reservoir.

It would be possible to fill the reservoir of this lamp by one opening only, which would require only one stopper and one screw; but I have found by experinece that it is inconvenient, and that it is much better to fill the reservoir by three holes, in the manner above described; for in that case the air gets out of the reservoir easily, and the oil enters without any obstacle.

When this lamp is filled with oil the reservoir must be firmly placed in a horizontal situation, upon a stand made on purpose to support it during the operation, and the three stoppers must be taken out; the reservoir being filled, care is taken to replace the stoppers, and to close the little holes by the screws before it is taken from its stand.

These little holes must not be opened till the lamp is suspended in its place in the gilt hoop, and at rest; and attention should always be paid to close them before lifting the lamp to take it from its hoop. These precautions are absolutely necessary in order to avoid the risk of spilling the oil.

When this lamp is suspended at a proper elevation above the middle of a round table, largee nough for placing

PLATE I.

Fig. 1.—Horizontal projection.

d. Hoop that serves for reservoir of oil.

e. Tubes that convey the oil from the reservoir to the cylinders.

f. Cylinders.

a. Brass stoppers, with their screws.

g. Brass hoop which serves to receive the lamp.

h. Arrows attached to the brass hoop: to these arrows the chains are fixed.

Fig. 2.—Vertical projection.

d. Hollow hoop that serves for reservoir of oil.

e. Tubes that convey the oil from the reservoir to the cylinders.

f. Cylinders, with their chimneys.

a. Brass stoppers, with their screws.

g. Brass hoop which serves to receive the lamp.

h. Arrows attached to the brass hoop.

i. Cup that receives the oil which may fall from the cylinders.

k. Cristal pendants attached to the brass hoop.

l. Hoop of white crape attached to the lower edge of the brass hoop immediately behind the pendants.

m. Reflector of white crape, which rests on the tubes *e.*

Fig. 3.—On a larger scale.

a. Section of the brass stopper with the small screw in its axis: the screw is represented as open to give admission to the air into the reservoir.

b. Collar of leather which, when the screw is closed, presses upon *c,* and excludes the air of the atmosphere from the reservoir.

d. Section of a part of the hollow hoop which serves as a reservoir for the oil.

PLATE I.

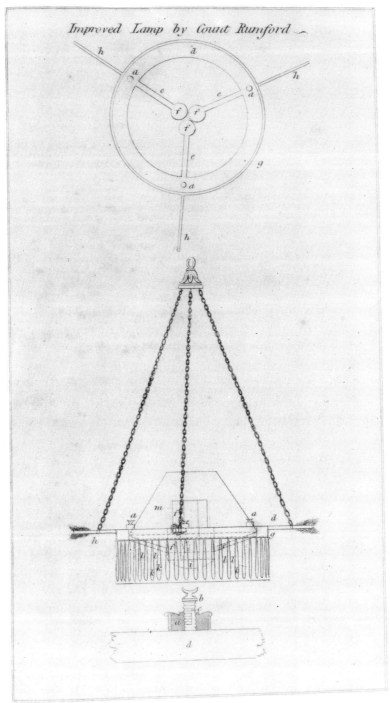

Improved Lamp by Count Rumford

conveniently ten or twelve persons, in a room 24 feet long, by 20 feet wide, and 15 high, not only the table, but likewise the whole room is completely lighted, without the least visible shadow being produced in any part, and without any person at table, or in the other parts of the room, being incommoded by the direct rays from the three flames which are united at the center of the lamp. The diameter of the hoop of crape which masks these flames is so great that the light which it emits from its surface is very soft, although it receives the direct rays of the three flames.

As the light which this lamp diffuses in a room proceeds from one single source, the shadows of the enlightened objects are of course simple, and well defined, a circumstance which certainly contributes much to the ease with which we distinguish objects, as well as to the pleasantness of the illumination, and the preservation of the eyes.

In order to light the table of a dining-room or study, of 5 or 6 feet in diameter, a small lamp with one wick will be sufficient, and instead of suspending it from the ceiling it may be placed on a pedestal, at the height of 12 or 15 inches above the table. For a lamp with one wick, intended to burn 8 or 10 hours, the circular reservoir for the oil may be made 6 inches in diameter within, 1 inch wide, and $\frac{6}{10}$ of an inch deep. The conical reflector of crape, or roughened glass, for this lamp should be 8 inches in diameter below, 2 inches in diameter at the top at its opening, and 5 inches in height. The hoop of crape which surrounds the lamp should be 8 inches in diameter and $3\frac{1}{2}$ inches in breadth. If it be desired to have more light upon the table, and less in the room, the conical reflector which covers the lamp above may be made of a thicker stuff, or even of tin, painted white within, and painted and varnished without.

To light a large drawing-room, or dining-room, a suspended lamp with six wicks may be used, with a reservoir of oil 18 inches in diameter within, $2\frac{1}{2}$ inches in breadth, and $\frac{8}{10}$ of an inch in depth, surrounded by a hoop of crape 6 inches broad.

Such a lamp, hung at the height of 8 or 9 feet in the middle of a large room, would be found to diffuse a very gentle and agreeable light.

It is almost superfluous to observe, that the general form of this lamp is simple and elegant; and that it is susceptible of being easily ornamented, a circumstance which is of real importance in this age of refinement, and even in every age in which the sentiment of beauty has any influence on the manners and happiness of mankind.

N.B. The openings of the tubes above, which contain the wicks, are situated one quarter of an inch above the level of the oil in the reservoir, when the reservoir is full.

AN INQUIRY

CONCERNING THE

SOURCE OF THE LIGHT WHICH IS MANIFESTED IN
THE COMBUSTION OF INFLAMMABLE BODIES.

OF THE LIGHT MANIFESTED IN COMBUSTION.

WHEN an inflammable substance, in a state of purity, such as wax, tallow, or purified oil, burns with a clear, bright flame, without smoke or smell and without leaving any residuum, the combustion is considered as being complete; and its chemical products, water in a state of vapour and carbonic acid gas, are always pure, and in quantities which are always in a constant ratio when the substance burned is the same.

Those who consider light as *a substance* emitted by luminous bodies have been obliged to search for the source of that which is manifested in the combustion of inflammable bodies among those substances which are known to concur in that process. Some have supposed that it is the inflammable substance which furnishes it; others, that it is derived from the air (oxygen gas) employed in the combustion, which gas is supposed to be decomposed; and of late the prevailing opinion among chemists appears to be that it is furnished in part by the inflammable substance and in part by the oxygen.

If the light manifested in the combustion of inflammable bodies were in fact one of the chemical products of that process, as has been supposed, it is most certain that it ought to be found pre-existing in some of the bodies that are decomposed in that operation ; and there is every reason to suppose, if that were really the case, that the quantity of light disengaged in the complete combustion of a given quantity of any given inflammable substance would be limited, and just as invariable as all the other chemical products of that process.

But if light be not a *substance emitted* by luminous bodies, but a vibration and undulation in an ethereal fluid, analogous to the vibration and undulation of the air which is the immediate cause of sound (as many distinguished philosophers have supposed), in that case we ought to search for the cause of the light which is diffused by the flame of a burning body in the very high temperature of the particles of matter which compose that flame. These particles must be considered as being luminous, in consequence of the action of the same cause which renders a cannon bullet luminous which has been heated red-hot in the fire. And as all known bodies cease to shine in the dark at a known given temperature (that of about 1000° of Fahrenheit's scale), the hot particles which compose a visible flame ought to disappear entirely the moment they become cooled down to that temperature.

If we adopt this hypothesis respecting light (which I confess has ever appeared to me to be the most probable), we must no longer expect to find the quantities of light excited in the process of combustion to be in any constant ratio to the quantities of inflammable matter burned : so far from it, we should be obliged to admit that the discovery of such an invariable relation ought to be considered as a demonstrative proof of the fallacy of that hypothesis.

Both the size and the form of a flame must necessarily have so much influence on the celerity of the cooling of the particles of which it is composed that, if it should be found that neither of these circumstances has any sensible influence on the quantity of light which it diffuses, this fact must be considered as a proof that the light does not depend entirely on the preservation of the heat of the flame, in the manner above described.

But if, on the other hand, it should be found from the results of decisive experiments that the light which accompanies the complete combustion of any given quantity of pure inflammable matter should be *variable*, it will be impossible, I imagine, not to perceive that that light *cannot be one of the chemical products of combustion;* and that the hypothesis which supposes light to be a *substance emitted* by luminous bodies must become more and more difficult to support.

If the question in dispute respecting the nature of light were merely speculative, and could never have any influence either on the progress of science or on the improvement of the useful arts, I should be the first to condemn this discussion, not only on account of its being useless, but also, and more especially, on account of the disagreeable consequences to society which always must result from disputes of that kind. But the subject under consideration is very far indeed from being uninteresting. To see the importance of it, we have only to consider for a moment the vast advantage to society that could not fail to result from the discovery of any fixed principle that could be employed with facility in improving the art of illumination and the instruments that are employed in it.

What vast sums are expended in dispelling the obscurity of the night in every part of the world; and yet in what a deplorable state is the science which ought to elucidate all the details of that important operation!

How is it possible to labour with any prospect of success to improve the methods employed in illuminating our dwellings, as long as we remain so perfectly ignorant respecting the nature of light as not even to know with any degree of certainty whence it proceeds or how it exists.

After having meditated a long time on this interesting subject, I have lately made a course of experiments which I thought might lead to some useful discoveries. But before I proceed to give an account of them it will be necessary to mention a few alterations and improvements which have been made in the apparatus (already known) which I employ for measuring the intensity of light.

Instead of the rods divided into inches and tenths of inches, which I formerly employed for measuring the distances of the lights which are compared from the middle of the field of the photometer, I now employ rods divided into degrees, which indicate directly and without any computation the relative intensities of those lights.

These two rods, which are twelve feet in length, are divided uniformly; and they serve as a graduated scale to the photometer. Their first division, which is at the extremity of the rod nearest the photometer, is marked 10°, and it is placed at the distance of ten inches from the middle of the field of the instrument, when the apparatus is prepared for making an experiment.

The other divisions of this *scale of light* are determined in such a manner that the numbers which they bear, which I call degrees, are everywhere *as the squares of their distances from the middle of the field of the photometer*, where the two shadows are in contact whose densities are to be compared and equalized.

To fill the important station of a standard light, with which all others are compared, I have chosen a wax candle of the first quality, just eight tenths of an English inch in diameter, and which burning with a clear and steady flame has been found to consume very regularly 108 grains Troy of wax per hour.

To this standard light I have assigned the value of 100 degrees; and it is always placed exactly opposite to that division of the scale of the photometer which is marked 100°. This division is, of course, at the distance of 31.62 inches from the middle of the vertical field of the instrument, that marked 10° being at the distance of 10 inches.

In order to express in a commodious manner the quantities of wax, tallow, oil, or other inflammable substance consumed in the experiments, I have supposed the 108 grains Troy of wax consumed by the standard light per hour to be divided into 100 equal parts (= 1.08 grains) to serve as a standard weight in all cases. The usefulness of this arrangement will be seen hereafter.

I have now to request the attention and the indulgence of the Royal Society while I use my best endeavours to give them a clear and distinct account of my experiments and their results.

The object I had particularly in view was to determine whether the quantity of light disengaged
in the combustion of inflammable bodies is or is not
in a constant invariable proportion to the quantity of
inflammable matter which is burned; and as the flame
of an Argand lamp, well arranged, is exceedingly
bright, and when purified oil is used gives neither
smoke nor smell, I endeavoured to find out whether
the quantities of light which that beautiful lamp diffuses are always as the quantities of oil which are
consumed.

First Experiment. — An excellent Argand lamp,
which had been most carefully cleaned and trimmed,
was weighed and lighted and immediately placed
before the photometer, where during 30 minutes it
was so regulated as to furnish constantly just 100° of
light (the same quantity that the standard wax candle
furnished).

At the end of this experiment the lamp was extinguished; and on weighing it carefully it was found
that 8 grammes of oil had been consumed, = 114
parts.   This gives 228 parts of oil per hour for 100° of
light, or for 100 parts of oil 48° of light, furnished
uniformly during one hour.

The standard light consumed 100 parts of wax per
hour, and furnished uniformly 100° of light.

Second Experiment. — The lamp having been most
carefully cleaned and trimmed was again weighed and
placed before the photometer, opposite to the division
of its scale marked 200°, when having been lighted
it was so managed during 30 minutes as to furnish
constantly just 200° of light, equal to that of two
wax candles.

In this experiment 10.3 grammes of oil were consumed. This is at the rate of 271 parts of oil per hour for 200° of light, or for 100 parts of oil 74° of light.

Third Experiment. — The lamp having been cleaned and properly arranged was again placed before the photometer. In this experiment it was made to furnish 300° of light during 30 minutes, and 10.7 grammes of oil were consumed. This is at the rate of 305 parts of oil per hour for 300° of light, or for 100 parts of oil 98° of light.

Fourth Experiment. — In this experiment the lamp, which had been arranged with the utmost care, furnished during 30 minutes 400° of light, and consumed 12.7 grammes of oil. This is at the rate of 361 parts of oil for 400° of light, or for 100 parts of oil 112° of light.

This is the first experiment in which a given quantity of oil was found to furnish more light than an equal quantity of wax. But without stopping here to make any particular remarks on that circumstance I shall hasten to give an account of still more interesting results.

In order to shorten my narrative as much as possible, I shall here place in a table the results of the four experiments of which I have just given the details, and shall add to them the results of five other similar experiments which complete this particular course. These nine experiments were all made on the same day, with the same lamp and the same standard light; and I will venture to say that no pains were spared to render them as complete and satisfactory as possible. Their results are so very striking that they hardly stand in need of any particular remarks or observations to recommend them to the attention of the Society.

Order of the Experiments.	Intensity of the light furnished by the lamp during 30 minutes.	Quantity of oil consumed per hour.	Light furnished per hour with the consumption of 100 parts of oil.
No. 1.	100°	228 parts.	48°
2.	200°	271	74°
3.	300°	305	98°
4.	400°	351	112°
5.	500°	405	121°
6.	600°	441	138°
7.	700°	470	149°
8.	800°	515	155°
9.	900°	560	160°

On comparing the results of these nine experiments, it appears that the quantities of light furnished were very far from being in a constant ratio to the quantities of oil consumed, as they would doubtless have been, were light one of the chemical products of combustion.

The intensity of the light answering to the consumption of 100 parts of oil per hour was near four times greater in the ninth experiment than in the first, though the flame was equally bright in these two experiments as well as in all the others, and was not accompanied either by smoke or smell.

Suspecting that a small flame of any given form must in all cases furnish less light in proportion to the oil consumed than a larger flame of the same form, to determine that fact I made the following experiments:—

I caused a lamp to be constructed with a wick composed of four flat ribbon wicks, each a quarter of an inch in diameter, sewed together on one of their sides, and placed vertically in such a manner as to compose a wick whose horizontal section forms a rectangular cross. And in the first experiment made with this new lamp its four united flat wicks were cut sloping upwards from without, in such a manner that the centre of the cross was about one tenth of an inch higher than its extremities. This was done, in order that it might be less difficult to cause the lamp to burn steadily with a very small flame.

This lamp is furnished with a small glass chimney, which serves as a blower, and renders the flame of the lamp very bright, clear, and vivid, and effectually prevents both smoke and smell.

Four experiments were made with this lamp, and their results were as follows: —

Order of the Experiments.	Intensity of the light furnished by the lamp during 30 minutes.	Quantity of oil consumed per hour.	Light furnished per hour with the consumption of 100 parts of oil.
No. 10.	25°	67 parts.	37°
11.	100°	143	70°
12.	225°	211	112°
13.	255°	214	118°

By comparing the results of these experiments, it appears that with the consumption of a given quantity of oil nearly *three times* as much light was produced in the thirteenth experiment as in the tenth, although the combustion appeared to be quite as perfect in the one as in the other.

Several other similar experiments were made with lamps of different forms and dimensions, and with similar results; but without stopping here to describe them particularly I shall proceed immediately to give an account of two or three subsequent experiments made with a more simple apparatus, whose results were extremely interesting.

Fourteenth Experiment. — As bleached beeswax is one of the purest of the inflammable substances used in producing artificial light, I was desirous of finding out whether the light furnished by wax candles of different sizes is always in proportion to the quantities of wax consumed. To ascertain this point, I began by placing a small wax taper, four tenths of an inch in diameter, before the photometer, where it continued to burn very steadily during 30 minutes.

As its wick was much thicker in proportion to its diameter than that of a common wax candle, it furnished very uniformly 64° of light, notwithstanding its diminutive size. During this time it consumed at the rate of 77 parts of wax per hour, consequently for 100 parts of wax it gave only at the rate of 83° of light, instead of 100° which the standard light constantly furnished. The result of the following experiment was much more striking : —

Fifteenth Experiment. — A small wax taper, with a very thin wick (called a *veilleuse* in France), six tenths of an inch in diameter and two inches in height, after having been carefully weighed, was placed upright and afloat in a small cylindrical vessel filled with water, where it was suffered to burn quietly during two hours and forty minutes : it was then extinguished, and, being taken out of the water and wiped till it was quite dry, it was again weighed, when it was found that just 4¾ grammes of wax had been consumed in the experiment. This is at the rate of 25 parts of wax per hour; and if this taper had given as much light, in proportion to the wax it consumed, as a wax candle of the common size furnishes, its light would have been that of 25°.

On measuring the intensity of the light of this taper by means of the photometer, it was found to be only 1.52°, or a little more than one degree and a half, instead of 25°!

Though I had been led, by the results of my former experiments and the conclusions I had drawn from them, to expect that the light of this little taper would be very feeble, yet I confess that the result of the experiment surprised me very much. I repeated the experiment several times with the utmost care, and though this taper sometimes gave a little more light during a few moments, yet it more frequently gave considerably less; and I am persuaded that in estimating its mean intensity at one degree and a half, that is quite as much as can be allowed.

Here, then, is a flame, and even the flame of a wax taper, which is 16 times more feeble than it ought to have been, were light really a substance emitted by inflammable bodies, and its quantity proportional to the quantity of the inflammable matter consumed.

This result can easily be explained, if we admit the hypothesis which supposes light to be analogous to sound. The flame of the taper was so small that the particles of which it was composed, though extremely hot, no doubt, at the moment of their formation, were nevertheless so rapidly cooled by the frigoric influence of the surrounding cold bodies that they had hardly time to shine an instant, before they became too cold to be any longer visible.

The extreme feebleness of the light in this experiment might easily have been mistaken for a proof that the combustion was likewise feeble, had we not known positively, from the great quantity of wax that was consumed, that this indication must necessarily have been fallacious.

But if we suppose the combustion to have been as vivid as it is commonly when wax candles are burned, what became of the heat which ought to have made its appearance in that process?

I sought for it, and had the extreme satisfaction to find it, and even to find it entire. I found that the little taper had never ceased a moment to furnish it, in full measure, from the beginning to the end of the experiment, notwithstanding the extreme feebleness of its light.

Suspecting that the ascending current of air above the taper was hotter than the diminutive size of the flame indicated, I presented the palm of my hand immediately over the flame, at the distance of two or three inches. The result was a most convincing proof that these suspicions were not unfounded.

My hand had not been in this situation two seconds before I found the heat to be quite intolerable.

I really do believe that nobody ever experienced more pleasure from a burn than I did on this occasion. I lost no time in arranging an experiment which I saw could not fail to clear up this mystery.

Sixteenth Experiment. — Very fortunately I had in my laboratory a little apparatus, which had been used in another research, which was perfectly well adapted for the experiment I now wished to make. It consists of a small conical tin boiler with a long cylindrical neck, fitted to receive one of my mercurial thermometers with long cylindrical bulbs. The diameter

of this boiler below is 8.3 inches, its depth about
4¾ inches, and its diameter above, where its neck
commences, is 6 inches. This boiler being placed
on a table, on its small wooden stand with four
feet, of about fifteen inches in height, having a circular hole in its centre of about three inches in
diameter, 2000 grammes in weight of cold water (about
four French pounds) were poured into it; and, its thermometer being in its place, this apparatus was suffered
to remain 24 hours in a quiet room, fronting to the
north, to acquire the mean temperature of the place.

At the end of that time the temperature of the
water in the boiler, and also of the air in the room,
being that of 65° F., one of my small wax tapers,
which had been carefully weighed, was placed afloat
in its small cylindrical vessel, and being lighted was
placed immediately under the centre of the boiler, at
such a distance below its bottom that the point of its
little flame was just on a level with the under side of
the perforated board on which the boiler was placed.

The taper having burned very quietly under the
boiler 52 minutes and 15 seconds, the thermometer indicating that the water had acquired 10° of heat, being
now at 75° F., the taper was blown out, and, after having been carefully wiped till it was quite dry, it was
weighed a second time, when it appeared that just
1.52 grammes (= 23.475 grains Troy) of wax had been
consumed in the experiment.

Seventeenth Experiment. — Having emptied the
boiler, it was filled a second time with 2000 grammes
of cold water; and, when the whole had acquired the
precise temperature of 65° F., a lighted wax candle
of the common size, and of a known weight, was placed

under it in such a manner that the point of its flame
was on a level with the under side of the wooden perforated stand on which the boiler reposed.

This candle had burned very equally and very quietly
just 12 minutes and 30 seconds, when I observed by
the thermometer that the water had acquired the temperature of 75° F.   The candle was immediately extinguished, and on weighing it I found that 1.62 grammes
(= 25.02 grains Troy) of wax had been consumed in
this experiment.

The difference between the quantities of wax consumed in these two experiments in communicating
the same quantity of heat to the same quantity of cold
water is very small, amounting to only about one grain
and a half Troy, and may easily be accounted for in
a satisfactory manner, without having recourse to the
very improbable supposition that the heat may perhaps be variable that accompanies the combustion of
the same inflammable substances.

The *light* which accompanies that process is most
certainly variable, and that to a very surprising
extent.

The results of these experiments are very interesting,
and the more attentively we examine the new facts with
which they make us acquainted, the more clearly we
shall perceive their importance.

They will make us better acquainted with light, and
also with heat, and will assist us in distinguishing and
appreciating their effects.

As long as the doctrine which supposes light to be
a substance emitted by luminous bodies continues to
be believed and universally taught, a great deal of
time will no doubt continue to be employed in useless

researches concerning its supposed affinities and combinations.

These investigations are connected with appearances so brilliant and fascinating that it is no wonder that they should often have engaged the attention of curious inquirers ; but experience has abundantly shown how fruitless these researches have hitherto been.

If light were in fact a substance, as has been supposed, it seems highly probable that means would long since have been found to discover where and how it exists ; but if it be nothing more than a blow given to the eye by the repercussion of an ethereal fluid which touches that organ, and at the same time every other body in the universe, it is evident that all attempts to discover it a state of combination must be vain.

Nobody, I imagine, ever thought of searching for sound in a fulminating powder. Is it more reasonable to search there for the light which accompanies the combustion of those substances? But, whatever may be the opinions of philosophers respecting the nature of light, no doubts can be entertained respecting the usefulness of discoveries which enable us to produce it with economy and to manage it with skill.

The methods and instruments hitherto employed in procuring and distributing light are certainly capable of considerable improvement. The subject is of very great importance to mankind, and on that account is highly deserving the attention of those who take pleasure in contributing to the progress of useful science. The investigation of this subject is likewise very entertaining on account of the many beautiful experiments that present themselves in the course of that research. It engaged my attention many years ago, and has for several months past employed nearly the whole of my leisure time.

In two memoirs of considerable length, written in the French language, the one published in the year 1807 in the Memoirs of the National Institute, the other about a month ago in the Bibliothèque Brittanique, I have proposed several improvements in lamps, which have been found by experience to be useful; but I cannot help flattering myself that the knowledge of the interesting fact discovered in my late experiments will lead to much more important improvements, and perhaps enable us to produce effects which we should not have supposed to be possible.

Many attempts have been made to increase the intensity of the light of lamps, in order to render them more useful in lighthouses, on the sea-coast, and for other purposes where a powerful light is wanted. The size of Argand's lamp has been increased in the expectation that it might perhaps be made to give more light, but none of these attempts have succeeded.

In the year 1804, I contrived a method for illuminating large rooms by means of a single luminous balloon of gauze, of about eighteen inches in diameter, suspended from the ceiling. In the centre of this balloon there are placed, as close together as possible, three, four, five, or six Argand lamps (according to the size of the room), which are supplied with oil from a large circular reservoir, which is concealed by the balloon. This invention has been found to answer very well, and many of the finest hotels in Paris are now lighted in this manner; but, if I am not much mistaken, this *illuminator* will soon give place to another much more simple in its construction, more economical, and which must produce a much finer effect.

Since I have become better acquainted with the light which accompanies the combustion of inflammable substances, I have found means by a very simple contrivance to increase its intensity in a centre of illumination, almost without limitation.

I lately caused a lamp to be constructed of a very simple form, which, with four flat or ribbon wicks, each one inch and six tenths English measure in width, placed vertically, one by the side of the other, at the distance of about two tenths of an inch, and so separated as to let the air come up between them, gives more light than six Argand lamps burning with their usual brilliancy.

I have often measured the intensity of its light, and have never found it to be less than 3800°; and in several experiments made in the presence of Professor Pictet and M. Micheli of Geneva, and of M. Charles and M. Gay-Lussac, members of the Institute, it was found to give 4000° of light, equal to that of 40 wax candles of the best kind, all burning together with their greatest brilliancy.

But in an experiment made at my country house at Auteuil, on the first of November, 1811, in the presence of M. Russell, Chargé d'Affaires of the United States (who takes this paper to England), the result was still more extraordinary.

Some little alterations having been made in the manner of trimming and arranging the lamp, it furnished no less than 5250° of light, more than that of

52 wax candles, and this without the least appearance of either smoke or smell.

On comparing the flame of an Argand lamp with the united flames of this new lamp, it appeared just as yellow and as dull as the flame of a common lamp appears when compared with that of an Argand lamp.

It is indeed quite impossible to form an adequate idea of the beautiful whiteness and transcendent brightness of this new illuminator without seeing it; and it never fails to excite the surprise and admiration of those who behold it for the first time.

The fundamental principle on which this lamp is constructed is so easy to be understood that it will be sufficient merely to mention it, in order to show clearly what must be done to put it in practice.

The object to be had in view in all cases is *to preserve the heat of the flame as long as possible.*

One of the most simple methods of doing this is, no doubt, the placing of several flat flames together, and as near as possible to each other without touching, in order that they may mutually cover and defend each other against the powerful cooling influence of the surrounding cold bodies.

It is evident that this principle may be employed with great facility in all cases where oil is burned to produce light, and that *polyflame* lamps of the smallest size, or of any given power of illumination, must necessarily be superior in effect and be more economical than any of the lamps now in use.

As a clear flame is perfectly transparent to the light of another flame which passes through it, as I have shown in another place,* there is no danger of any loss

* See my paper on Light, published in the Philosophical Transactions in the year 1794 [this volume, page 93].

of light on account of these flames covering each other.

I caused the light of one flame to pass successively through eight other like flames, without being able to perceive the smallest diminution of its intensity.

A considerable advantage attending these new poly-flame lamps is that they do not require a narrow glass chimney as a blower to animate the combustion: it will be sufficient to cover their flames at a distance by a wide cylindrical glass tube placed upright on a disk of glass or metal having apertures in the middle of it for the admission of the air, which must always be made to come up from below, between the flat tin tubes which contain the wicks.

This wide glass must be four or five inches higher than the level of the tops of the flames, and no air must be permitted to come up through it but that which passes between the wicks, otherwise the draught of air between the wicks will not be sufficiently strong.

The flat tin tubes which contain the wicks must be all enclosed together in a larger tube (which may be either square or cylindrical), in order that the air that comes up between these flat tubes may be confined in its passage and brought properly into the fire.

Care must be taken that the outside wicks, as well as those placed between, receive air *on both their sides*, and this air must be made to rise up perpendicularly from below; but no other currents of air should ever be permitted to come near them or to enter the glass tube which covers and defends them.

It is highly probable that it will be found to be very useful to be able to regulate the quantity of air admitted; but this may easily be done by a variety of simple contrivances.

If more air be permitted to mix with the flame than is necessary to the complete combustion of oil, it must necessarily cool the flame, and consequently must diminish the quantity of light.

The lamp which I have in my possession being the only one of this kind that has yet been made, it is still in a rude and unfinished state; but, as it has answered far beyond my most sanguine expectation, I lose no time in giving an account of the principles on which it is constructed, in hopes that others may be induced to assist in improving it.

So far from being jealous of their success, I shall rejoice in it, and shall ever be most ready to contribute to it by all the means in my power.

EXPERIMENTS

ON THE

PRODUCTION OF AIR FROM WATER,

EXPOSED WITH VARIOUS SUBSTANCES TO THE ACTION OF LIGHT.

VARIOUS opinions having been entertained with respect to the origin of the air produced by exposing healthy vegetables in water to the action of the sun's rays, according to the method of Dr. Ingen-Housz, and not being myself thoroughly satisfied with any of the theories proposed for explaining the phænomena, I made the following experiments with a view to throwing some new light upon that subject.

Having found by accident that raw silk possesses a power of attracting and separating air from water in great abundance when exposed in it to the action of light, it occurred to me to examine the properties of this air, and to consider more attentively the circumstances attending its production, thinking that this might possibly lead to some further discoveries, relative to the production of the air yielded by water, under other circumstances ; and though my success in these inquiries has not been equal to my wishes, yet, as in the course of my researches I have discovered some facts which I take to be new, and as I have confirmed others already known by a variety of new experiments, I flatter myself that an account of my labours upon this subject will not be thought altogether uninteresting.

Before I enter upon the detail of my experiments, it will be necessary to premise that I shall in general confine myself merely to the facts as they present themselves, without applying them to the confirmation or refutation of the theories of others, and without entering into any speculative inquiries relative to their remote causes; and in describing the different appearances I shall make use of the most familiar terms. Thus, in speaking of the air produced upon exposing raw silk in water to the action of light, I shall sometimes mention it as being yielded by the silk; and I shall sometimes speak of the air furnished by exposing water, which has previously turned green in the sun's rays, as being immediately produced by the water, though it is probable that the *green matter* acts a very important part in the production of this air in the one case and perhaps in the other. But how it acts is not well ascertained; and I had in general much rather confine myself to a simple and even an unlearned description of facts, than, by endeavouring to give more precise definitions, at first, to involve myself in all the difficulties which would attend an attempt to account for phænomena whose causes are but very imperfectly known.

Experiment No. 1.

My first object was to collect a sufficient quantity of the air, separated from water by silk, to determine its goodness by the test of nitrous air; and to this end having filled with clear spring-water a globe of thin, white, and very transparent glass, $4\frac{1}{2}$ inches in diameter, with a cylindrical neck $\frac{3}{4}$ of an inch in diameter, and about 12 inches long, I introduced into it 30 grains of raw silk, which had been previously washed in water in order to free it of air ; and inverting the globe under water, and placing its neck in a glass jar containing a quantity of the same water with which the globe was filled, I exposed it in my window to the action of the sun's rays, and prepared myself to examine the progress of the generation or production of the air.

The globe had not been exposed ten minutes to the action of the sun's rays, when I discovered an infinite number of exceedingly small air-bubbles, which began to make their appearance upon the surface of the silk ; and, these bubbles continuing to increase in number and in size, at the end of about two hours, the silk, appearing to be entirely covered with them, rose to the upper part of the globe.

These bubbles going on to increase in size, and running into each other, at length began to detach themselves from the silk, and to form a collection of air in the upper part of the globe ; but, the measure of my eudiometer being rather large, it was not till after the globe had been exposed in the sun near four days, that a sufficient quantity of air was collected to make the experiment with nitrous air, in order to ascertain its goodness by that test.

Having at length collected a sufficient quantity of this air for that purpose, I carefully removed it from the globe, and mixing with 1 measure of it 3 measures of nitrous air, they were reduced to 1.24 measures ; which shews that it was actually *dephlogisticated air*,[*] and of a considerable degree of purity.

Common air, tried at the same time, 1 measure of it with 1 measure of nitrous air were reduced to 1.08 measure.

---

[*] It must be remembered that this was written in the year 1786, at which period this elastic fluid was generally denominated *dephlogisticated air*.

Having again exposed the globe, with the same water and silk, in my window, where the sun shone the greatest part of the day, at the end of three days I had collected $3\frac{3}{4}$ cubic inches of air, which, proved with nitrous air, gave $1\,a + 3\,n = 1.18$; that is to say, 1 measure of this air *added to* 3 measures of nitrous air were reduced to 1.18 measure.

A wax taper, which had been just blown out, a small part only of the wick remaining *red-hot*, upon being plunged into a phial filled with this air immediately took fire, and burnt with a very bright and enlarged flame.

The water in the globe appeared to have lost something of its transparency, and had changed its color to a very faint greenish cast, having at the same time acquired the odour or fragrance proper to raw silk.

This experiment I repeated several times with fresh water (retaining the same silk), and always with nearly the same result; with this difference, however, that when the sun shone very bright, the quantity of air produced was not only greater, but its quality likewise was much superior to that yielded when the sun's rays were more feeble, or when they were frequently intercepted by flying clouds. The air, however, was always not only much better than common air, but better than the air in general produced by the fresh leaves of plants exposed in water to the sun's rays, in the experiments of Dr. Ingen-Housz; and under the circumstances the most favourable, it was so good that 1 measure of it required 4 measures of nitrous air to saturate it, and 3.65 measures of the two airs were destroyed; or, proved with nitrous air, it gave $1\,a + 4\,n = 1.35$, which, I believe, is better than any air that has yet been produced in the experiments with vegetables.

The method I have here adopted of using algebraic characters in noting the result of the experiments made to determine the goodness of air, though not strictly mathematical, is very convenient; and for that reason I shall continue to make use of it. a represents the air which is proved; n nitrous air; and the numbers which are joined to these letters shew the quantities or the number of measures of the different airs made use of in the experiment. The other number, which stands alone, or without any letter attached to it, on the other side of the equation, shews the volume, or the number of measures and parts of a measure to which the two airs are reduced after they are mixed. I shall sometimes add a fourth number, shewing the quantities of the two airs destroyed, as this more immediately shews the goodness of the air which is proved.

Thus, in the experiment last mentioned, 1 measure of the air proved, mixed with 4 measures of nitrous air, were reduced to 1.35 measure; consequently, 3.65 measures of the two airs were destroyed, for it is $1 + 4 = 5 - 1.35 = 3.65$; and the result of this trial I should write thus, $1 a + 4 n = 1.35$ or 3.65.

Or, for still greater convenience in practice, as this last number 3.65, or $3\frac{65}{100}$, shews more immediately the goodness of the air in question, as I have just observed, by supposing with Dr. Ingen-Housz the measure of the eudiometer to be divided into 100 equal parts, it will be $100 a + 400 n = 135$; and 365, expressing the volume of the two airs destroyed, will become a whole number.

But, instead of writing $100 a + 400 n = 135$, &c., I shall continue to write $1 a + 4 n = 1.35$, and shall express the last number (3.65) as a whole number notwithstanding; and I shall sometimes (following the example of Dr. Ingen-Housz) write this number *only*, in noting the goodness of any air in question.

I would just observe, with respect to the process of proving the goodness of any kind of air by the test of nitrous air, that I mix the two airs in a phial about 1 inch in diameter, and 4 inches long, putting the air to be proved into the phial first, and then introducing the nitrous air, one measure after another, till the volume of the two airs, after the diminution has taken place, amounts to more than *one* measure and is less than *two* measures.

Immediately after the introduction of each measure of nitrous air, I give the phial a couple of shakes; after which I suffer it to stand at rest, while I prepare another measure of nitrous air, which commonly takes up about 20 seconds.

The measure of the eudiometer being filled with air, I suffer it to remain quiet under water 15 seconds, or while I can leisurely count 30, in order that the air may have time to acquire the temperature of the water in the trough, and that the water in the measure may have time to run down from the sides of the glass tube; and in shutting the slide of the eudiometer, I take care to bring it out to be exactly even with the surface of the water in the trough. Similar precautions are likewise made use of in measuring the volume of the two airs in the tube of the eudiometer, after they have been mixed and diminished in the phial.

In order that I may know when I have added nitrous air enough to the air in the phial, so that the volume of the two airs may amount to 1 measure, and may not be greater than 2 measures, there are two marks upon the

phial, made with the point of a diamond, the one shewing 1 measure of my eudiometer, the other shewing 2
measures.

The tube of my eudiometer is half an inch in diame-
ter internally, and 1 measure occupies $3\frac{1}{4}$ inches in length
upon it, and the measure itself is made of a piece of the
same tube. Both the one and the other are ground with
fine emery on the inside, in order to take off the polish
of the glass, and by that means facilitate the running
down of the water, which might otherwise hang in drops
upon the inside of the tube upon the introduction of air.

The nitrous air was always fresh made, and of the
same materials, *viz.* fine copper wire dissolved in smok-
ing spirits of nitre, diluted with 5 times its volume of
water ; and all possible attention was paid to every other
circumstance that could contribute to the accuracy of the
experiments.

I have thought it necessary to mention these particu-
lars, on account of the great difference in the apparent
goodness of any kind of air, proved by the test of nitrous air, which arises from the difference of the circumstances under which the experiments are made.

But to return to my experiments upon the air produced upon exposing silk in water to the action of the
sun's rays.

Experiment No. 2.

Finding that the quantity and the quality of the air
produced depended in a great measure upon the intensity of the light by which the water and the silk were
illuminated, I was desirous of seeing whether, by depriv-
ing them entirely of all light, they would not at the same
time be deprived of the power of furnishing air. To

ascertain this fact, I took a globe A, similar to that made use of in the foregoing experiment, and having filled it with fresh spring-water, I introduced into it 30 grains of raw silk, and placing it with its cylindrical neck inverted in a jar filled with the same water, I covered the whole with a large, inverted earthen vessel, and exposed it, so covered up, for several days, in my window, by the side of another globe B, containing a like quantity of water and silk, which I left naked, and consequently exposed to the direct rays of the sun.

The result of this experiment was, that the water and silk in the globe exposed to the sun's rays furnished air in great abundance, as in the experiment before mentioned ; while that in the globe covered up in darkness produced only a few very inconsiderable air-bubbles which remained attached to the silk.

Experiment No. 3.

To see if heat would not facilitate the production of air in the globe sheltered from the light, I now removed it from the window, and placed it near a German stove, where I kept it warmed to about 90° of Fahrenheit's thermometer for more than 24 hours ; but this was all to no purpose. The air produced was so exceedingly small in quantity that it could neither be proved nor measured, there being only a few detached air-bubbles which had collected themselves near the top of the globe.

The mean heat of the water in the globe exposed in the sun's rays, at the time when it furnished air in the greatest abundance, was about 90° Fahrenheit. It was sometimes as high as 96° ; but air was frequently produced in considerable quantities when the heat did not exceed 65° and 70°.

Experiment No. 4.

Finding by the last experiment (No. 3) that heat alone, without light, was not sufficient to enable silk in water to produce air, I was desirous of seeing the effect of light without heat upon them. To this end, I took the globe B, with its contents, and, plunging it into a mixture of ice and water, brought it to the temperature of about 50° F. and taking it out of this mixture, and exposing it immediately in the sun's rays (which were very piercing at the time), I entertained it in this temperature above two hours by the occasional application of cloths, wet in ice-water, to the lower part of the globe.

Notwithstanding this degree of cold, a considerable quantity of air was produced ; though it was not furnished in so great abundance as when the globe was suffered to become hot in the sun's rays.

Having thus ascertained the great effect of the sun's rays in the production of the air furnished upon exposing silk in water to their influence, my next attempt was to determine whether this arose from any peculiar quality in the sun's light ; or whether *other light* would not produce the same effect. With a view to ascertain this point, which I conceived to be of very great importance, I made the following interesting experiment.

Experiment No. 5.

Having removed all the air from the globe B, and having supplied its place with a quantity of fresh water, so as to render it quite full, I replaced it, inverted, in its jar, and, removing it into a dark room, surrounded it with 6 lamps, with reflectors, and 6 wax-candles, placed at different distances, from 3 to 6 inches from it, and so disposed as to throw the greatest quantity of light possible upon the silk in the water, taking care at the same time that the water should not acquire a greater heat than that of about 90° F. Things had not remained in this situation above 10 minutes, when I plainly discovered the air-bubbles beginning to make their appearance upon the surface of the silk, and at the end of 6 hours there was collected at the upper part of the globe a quantity of air sufficient to make a proof of its goodness with nitrous air; and, upon trial, I had the pleasure to find that it was *dephlogisticated*, and of such a degree of purity that 1 measure of it with 3 measures of nitrous air occupied no more than 1.68 measure.

I afterwards exposed to the same light, in small inverted glass jars, filled with water, a fresh-gathered healthy leaf of the peach-tree, and a stem of the pea-plant, with three leaves upon it; and both these vegetables furnished air in the same manner as they are known to furnish it when exposed, under similar circumstances, to the action of the sun's direct rays, but in less quantities, which I attribute to the greater intensity of the sun's light above that of my lamps.

The experiment with the silk and water I repeated several times, always with nearly the same result. The quantity of air furnished was sometimes a little greater and sometimes a little less, but it was always in much greater abundance than that furnished by an equal quantity of water and silk exposed to the same heat, but excluded from the light; and I have reason to think it was of a much superior quality, though the quantity of that produced in the dark was too small to be submitted to any proof.

These experiments appear to me to be of so much importance, that I could wish they might be repeated and varied in such a manner as thoroughly to establish the facts relative to the subject in question. For my part I would most readily undertake the investigation of the matter; but, being employed in another pursuit (the continuation of my Experiments upon Heat), and, besides this, much of my time being taken up by the duties of my military employment, I have not leisure at present for such an undertaking.

Perhaps it may be proved by future experiment that the matter of light is a constituent part of what is called pure or dephlogisticated air; if so, may we not venture to conclude with M. Scheele, that the *light*, as well as the heat, produced by flame, and in general all burning bodies, arises *solely* from the decomposition of this air, and not from the phlogiston or inflammable principle of the body which is burnt? There are many phænomena which would seem to justify this opinion.

But to proceed in the account of my experiments. The operation of inverting the globes under water, and placing them in the jars, and of displacing and replacing them upon removing the air produced, being attended with some inconveniences, I had recourse to another method of disposing of the apparatus, much more simple and more convenient. The globes, being filled, were laid upon a small piece of deal board, with their necks inclined at an angle of about 20° above the plane of the horizon, and supported in this position by a perpendicular fork of wood fixed to the end of the board, as represented by the following figure. The part of the board upon which the under part of the globe reposed was hollowed a little, to prevent the globe from rolling; or, what I found more safe and convenient, a small ring

or hoop of soft wood was nailed down upon the board in that part.

By this arrangement the jars were spared, and the end of the neck of the globe being easy to be come at, by introducing a wire, or, what I commonly made use of in preference, a small glass tube, into the globe, the air hanging attached to the silk can at all times be separated from it; which is often necessary, in order to determine with greater precision the quantity of air furnished in any given time.

The air produced naturally rises to that part of the globe which is uppermost, where it collects in a body, driving out an equal volume of water; which, to prevent its running about, may be collected by placing a proper vessel under the mouth, or end of the neck of the globe, to receive it.

The method of removing the air from the globe is too well known to require a description. I would, however, observe that, in doing it, care should be taken that the water in which the globe is immersed be quite clean, and of the same kind with that in the globe, otherwise that which enters the globe, to replace the air removed, might derange the experiment.

Having provided myself with a number of globes of different sizes, all fitted with boards or stands to support them in the manner above described, I proceeded in the course of my experiments as follows.

Finding that raw silk, exposed in water to the action of light, causes the water to yield pure air in so great abundance, I was desirous of finding out whether this arose from any peculiar quality possessed by the silk ; or whether other bodies might not be made to produce the same effect : to this end, having provided 6 globes, each about $4\frac{1}{2}$ inches in diameter, and having filled them with fresh spring-water, I introduced into them the following substances, and exposed them all at the same time to the action of the sun's rays.

In the globe No. 1. I put 15 grains of sheep's wool,

No. 2. —— 15 grains of eider-down,

No. 3. —— 15 grains of the fine fur of a Russian hare,

No. 4. —— 15 grains of cotton-wool,

No. 5. —— 15 grains of lint or the ravelings of fine linen,

No. 6. —— 15 grains of human hair ;

these substances being all well washed, and being thoroughly freed of air by being wetted before they were put into the globes.

The results of these experiments were as follows.

Experiment No. 6.

The globe No. 1, which contained the sheep's wool, did not begin to furnish air in any considerable quantity till the third day of its being exposed to the action of the sun's rays ; and, several days of cloudy weather intervening, I did not remove the air till the eighth day, when I collected $1\frac{3}{4}$ cubic inch, which, proved with nitrous air, gave $1\,a + 3\,n = 1.28$, or 272 degrees.

The wool at no time furnished more than one-third part of the air which an equal quantity of silk would have furnished under the same circumstances.

The water was very faintly tinged of a greenish hue.

Experiment No. 7.

The water in the globe No. 2, with the eider-down, began almost immediately to furnish air, and continued to yield it during the whole time of the experiment nearly in as large quantities as the water with silk had done in the former experiments, and nearly of the same quality. $1\frac{3}{4}$ cubic inches of this air, furnished the eighth day from the beginning of the experiment, or the third of sunshine, proved with nitrous air, gave $1\,a + 3\,n = 1.34$, or 266 degrees of purity.

The water was faintly tinged of a greenish, yellowish cast; and the eider-down, when examined attentively, appeared to be covered with a greenish slime.

Experiment No. 8.

The globe No. 3, with the hare's fur (which was white), furnished more air than the sheep's wool, but not so much as the eider-down. After four days of sunshine, I collected 2 cubic inches of this air, which, proved with nitrous air, gave $1\,a + 3\,n = 1.44$, or 256.

The water had acquired a very faint yellowish hue; but it did not appear to have lost much of its transparency, or to be disposed to deposit any sediment.

The air produced in this experiment made its appearance in a different manner from that furnished in those preceding it, the air-bubbles which appeared upon the surface of the fur being at considerable distances from each other, and growing to an uncommon size before they detached themselves to rise to the surface of the water.

Experiment No. 9.

The globe No. 4, with cotton-wool, furnished a considerable quantity of air, which appeared to be better than that furnished by any of the five other globes. Proved with nitrous air, it turned out $1\,a + 3\,n = 1.07$, or 293, and, what was particular, the water did not appear to have altered its colour in the least, or to have lost anything of its transparency.

Experiment No. 10.

The globe No. 5, with ravelings of linen, was very tardy in furnishing air, and produced but a small quantity; at the end of a fortnight, however, I collected about 2 cubic inches, which, proved with nitrous air, gave $1\,a + 3\,n = 1.51$, or 249.

The air appeared to have very little disposition to fix itself to the surface of this substance. It was very seldom that there were air-bubbles enough attracted to it to cause it to rise to the surface of the water, and the few bubbles which occasionally made their appearance very soon disappeared upon the diminution of the light and heat of the sun. In short, it appeared that there is but a very feeble attraction between this substance and the particles of air, at least when they are dissolved in water. Whether this arises from the superior affinity of the substance to water or not, I will not pretend to decide; but it appears to be probable, as there is so strong an attraction between water and linen, or flax, which is apparent from the avidity with which a piece of dry linen drinks up that fluid, and becomes wet even to a considerable distance when one end of it only is placed in water.

It must be remembered that I here consider the separation of the air from water as a simple operation ; and that I do not take into the account the purification, or rather the generation, of this air.　Though there is great reason to conclude that these two operations are very nearly connected, yet, to simplify my inquiries, I shall, in the first place, consider the appearances as they presented themselves to my senses.　It will be easy afterwards to draw any conclusions from the results of the experiments which a careful examination and comparison of the various phænomena will justify.

Experiment No. 11.

The globe No. 6, with human hair, furnished still less air than that with ravelings of linen in the last-mentioned experiment ; but notwithstanding the smallness of the quantity, it was considerably superior in quality to atmospheric air, for, proved with nitrous air, it gave $1\,a + 2\,n = 1.45$, or 155, whereas common air proved at the time gave $1\,a + 1\,n = 1.08$, or 92.

Experiment No. 12.

To ascertain the relative goodness of the air furnished by the water in these experiments, and of that produced by exposing fresh healthy vegetables, in water, to the action of the sun's light, according to the method of Dr. Ingen-Housz, I collected a small quantity of air from a stem of a pea-plant, which had four healthy leaves upon it, exposed in water to the sun's light, and found it to be much inferior to that furnished in the experiments with silk and the various other substances I made use of. Proved with nitrous air, it gave $1\,a + 2\,n = 1.05$, or 195.

An entire plant of housewort, of a moderate size, exposed in 12 ounces of water 7 hours to the action of the sun's rays, at a time when the weather was remarkably fine and very hot, furnished about $\frac{3}{4}$ of a cubic inch of air, which was so much worse than common air, that 1 measure of it with 1 measure of nitrous air occupied 1.36 measures; or it was $1\,a + 1\,n = 1.36$, or 64. But I lay no kind of stress upon the result of this experiment, as it is more than probable that the badness of the air arose from the roots of the plants; for from the leaves alone I have frequently since obtained air which appeared to be considerably better than common air.

From the leaves of the peach-tree I obtained an air, which, proved with nitrous air, gave $1\,a + 2\,n = 1.32$, or 168; but I did not think it necessary to multiply these experiments, particularly as Dr. Ingen-Housz and Mr. Sennebier have given us the results of so many of theirs upon the same subject, of the accuracy of which there is no room left to doubt. I shall, therefore, content myself with referring to the results of their experiments.

With a view to determining, with greater precision, the quantity and quality of the air produced by a given quantity of water and of silk, exposed for a given time to the action of the sun's rays, I made the following experiment.

Experiment No. 13.

A globe of fine, clear, white glass, about $8\frac{3}{10}$ inches in diameter, and containing 296 cubic inches, being filled with fresh spring-water and 30 grains of raw silk, was exposed in my window three days, *viz.* 12th, 13th, and 14th of May last (1786), these days being for the most part cold and cloudy, with short intervals of sunshine.

Air produced, $9\frac{1}{2}$ cubic inches ; quality, $1\,a + 3\,n = 1.61$, or 239.

May 15. This air being removed, and its place supplied with fresh water, the globe exposed in the sun this day, from nine o'clock in the morning till five o'clock in the afternoon, the weather being very fine, yielded $8\frac{46}{100}$ cubic inches of air, which, proved with nitrous air, gave $1\,a + 4\,n = 1.74$, or 326. The heat of the water in the globe, during the experiment, was from 70° to 98° F. The water had now lost considerably of its transparency, and had assumed a light greenish hue.

May 16. The air furnished yesterday being removed, the globe furnished this day, during six hours of sunshine, 9 cubic inches of air, which, proved with nitrous air, gave $1\,a + 4\,n = 1.44$, or 356.

May 17. The globe furnished this day, during $3\frac{1}{2}$ hours of sunshine, 6 cubic inches of air, of a very eminent quality ; for, proved with nitrous air, it gave $1\,a + 4\,n = 1.35$, or 365.

May 18. This day cold and cloudy ; not more than $1\frac{1}{2}$ hours sunshine; air produced $\frac{3}{4}$ of a cubic inch ; quality $1\,a + 4\,n = 1.56$, or 344.

May 19. The globe appearing now to be quite exhausted of air, shewing no signs of furnishing any additional quantity, though exposed to the action of a very bright sun, I removed the globe from the window, and placed it by the side of a German stove, where it was kept warm to 100° F. from 10 o'clock in the morning till 5 o'clock in the afternoon. By this means, I obtained $\frac{1}{4}$ of a cubic inch of air, which, proved with nitrous air, gave $1\,a + 4\,n = 1.74$, or 326.

Not being able to obtain any more air from the globe, I now put an end to the experiment.

The quantities and qualities of the airs furnished upon the different days were as follows : —

	Quantity.			Quality.	
Upon the 12th, 13th, and 14th of May	$9\frac{1}{2}$ cubic inches			$1\,a + 3\,n =$ 1.61,	or 239
15th . . .	$8\frac{46}{100}$	. . .		$1\,a + 4\,n =$ 1.74,	or 326
16th . . .	9	. . .		$1\,a + 4\,n =$ 1.44,	or 356
17th . . .	6	. . .		$1\,a + 4\,n =$ 1.35,	or 365
18th . . .	$\frac{3}{4}$	. . .		$1\,a + 4\,n =$ 1.56,	or 344
19th . . .	$\frac{1}{4}$	. . .		$1\,a + 4\,n =$ 1.74,	or 326
Total quantity	$33\frac{96}{100}$	mean qual.		$1\,a + 4\,n =$ 1.84,	or 316

As in this experiment the air furnished each day was removed at night, and the place it occupied in the globe supplied with fresh water, I was desirous of seeing what variation it would occasion in the result of the experiment, if, instead of removing the air from time to time, I suffered it to remain in the globe till the end of the experiment; to this end I made

Experiment No. 14.

In which the globe being filled with fresh water, and the silk used in the last experiment (being first well washed), the whole was exposed four days to the action of the sun's rays, the weather being remarkably fine and very hot. Upon removing the air produced, I found it amounted to $30\frac{1}{10}$ cubic inches ; and its quality, proved with nitrous air, was $1\,a + 3\,n =$ 1.02, or 298.

I should have continued the experiment for some days longer, as the globe did not appear to be exhausted; but the quantity of air already collected in the globe was so great that it became very difficult to remove it, without running the risk of losing a part of it, or of letting the air of the atmosphere enter the globe, either of which events would, of course, have spoiled the experiment.

For safety, therefore, and that I might not by an accident lose the trouble I had already had with it, I put an end to the experiment at the end of the fourth day.

The water had lost of its transparency, and had acquired a greenish cast, as in the last experiment; and in both these experiments I observed that a considerable quantity of whitish yellowish earth was precipitated from the water, which, falling to the bottom of the globe, attached itself to the glass in such a manner that it was with difficulty that it could be removed. These were general appearances, and took place in all cases, in a greater or less degree, where a considerable quantity of pure air was separated from water by the influence of light.

Experiment No. 15.

The silk made use of in the last experiment having been frequently used in the foregoing experiments, I was desirous of seeing the effect of making use of fresh silk; and also of varying the proportion between the quantity of silk, the quantity of water, and the size of the globe; accordingly at 6 o'clock, P. M., upon the 13th of June, I filled a small globe, about three inches in diameter, or (to ascertain its size more exactly), which contained just 20 cubic inches, with fresh spring-water, and 17 grains of raw silk, wound in a single thread, which had never been put into water, or otherwise used, since it came out of the hands of the silk-winder.

At the end of four days, *viz.* the 14th, 15th, 16th, and 17th of June, this globe had only furnished $\frac{1}{4}$ of a cubic inch of air, which, proved with nitrous air, gave $1\,a + 1\,n = 1.32$, or 68; consequently, was much worse than common air.

Upon the 18th it began to produce good air, and during six hours of sunshine it furnished $1\frac{15}{100}$ cubic inches, which, proved with nitrous air, gave $1\,a + 3\,n = 1.15$, or 285.

The two following days (*viz.* the 19th and 20th of June), it furnished $1\frac{27}{100}$ cubic inch of air, which, proved with nitrous air, gave $1\,a + 3\,n = 1.37$, or 263; after which it totally ceased to yield air, though exposed for several days in the sun's rays.

Total quantity of air produced, $2\frac{67}{100}$ cubic inches; mean quality, $1\,a + 3\,n = 1.46$, or 254.

By this experiment it appears that raw silk, when used for the first time, does not immediately dispose the water to yield pure air ; on the contrary, that it phlogisticates the air yielded by water to a very considerable degree; and this I afterwards found to be the case with several other substances.

Though the quality, at a medium, of the air furnished in this experiment was not quite so good as that furnished in the two experiments last mentioned (*viz.* No. 13 and No. 14), yet its quantity, in proportion to the quantity of water made use of, was greater than in either of them ; it amounted to something more than *one eighth* of the volume of the water.

Of all the substances I had hitherto made use of in these experiments, raw silk had furnished the greatest quantity of pure air, or, to express myself more properly, had caused the water to furnish the greatest quantity ; but it appeared to me very probable that some other body might be found that possessed this property in a still greater degree. Turning this matter in my mind, it occurred to me to make the experiment with the silky, or rather cotton-like, substance produced by a certain species of the poplar-tree, *Populus nigra*, very common in this country (Bavaria), and which, I believe, grows in England. I recollected that, examining it some time before, with a different view (that of seeing if it might not be made use of with advantage as a substitute for eider-down), and endeavouring to render it very dry by exposing it in a china plate over a chafing-dish of hot embers, when it had acquired a certain degree of heat, small parcels of it quitted the plate of their own accord, and mounted up to the top of the room.

This convinced me at the time, not only of its extreme fineness, but also of the strong attraction which subsists between it and the particles of air; and it now occurred to me that these qualities not only render it peculiarly proper as a substitute for eider-down, for confining heat, but likewise are properties of all others the most necessary to its supplying the place of silk in the production of air, by exposing it in water to the action of the sun's rays. I, therefore, lost no time in making the following experiments.

Experiment No. 16.

The large globe (contents, 296 cubic inches) being filled with fresh spring-water, and 120 grains of poplar-cotton, upon the evening of the 9th of June, and being the next day, the 10th of June, exposed to the sun about four hours, upon the morning of the 11th the air produced was removed, and its quantity was found to be $1\frac{3}{4}$ cubic inch. Its quality was very bad, *viz.* $1\,a + 1\,n = 1.65$, or 35 degrees only better than thoroughly phlogisticated air (azote).

Upon the 11th, 12th, and 13th, 1 cubic inch of air only was produced, and this appeared to be as bad as possible; for, proved with nitrous air, it gave $1\,a + 1\,n = 2$, or 0.

Upon the 14th, a few air-bubbles only were furnished; but, notwithstanding these unfavourable appearances, I still continued the experiment, and my patience was amply rewarded; for the next day, the 15th, the sun being very powerful, and the weather very hot, the water, changing suddenly to a greenish colour, began all at once to give good air in great abundance. In the course of the day, $10\frac{42}{100}$ cubic inches were produced, which, proved with nitrous air, gave $1\,a + 3\,n = 1.43$, or 257.

June 16th, a very warm, clear day. The globe, exposed in the sun from 8 o'clock in the morning till 5 o'clock in the afternoon, furnished $14\frac{34}{100}$ cubic inches of air, which, proved with nitrous air, gave $1\,a + 3\,n = 1.34$, or 266.

June 17th, cloudy, with intervals of sunshine. The globe, with about four hours sun, gave $7\frac{34}{100}$ cubic inches of air, of a very eminent quality, *viz.* $1\,a + 4\,n = 1.40$, or 360.

The water having by degrees lost its transparency, and having acquired a deep green colour, it broke up this day, and deposited a green sediment; after which it recovered its transparency, and became almost colourless. It continued, notwithstanding, to furnish air in considerable quantities.

June 18th, being exposed in the sun's rays from 8 o'clock in the morning till 2 o'clock in the afternoon, (when the heavens became overcast,) the globe yielded $6\frac{27}{100}$ cubic inches of air, which, proved with nitrous air, gave $1\,a + 4\,n = 1.44$, or 356.

June the 19th and 20th. These two days the globe furnished no more than $3\frac{13}{100}$ cubic inches of air, which, proved with nitrous air, gave $1\,a + 3\,n = 1.06$, or 294; after which it ceased totally to furnish air, and the colour of the water changed to a dead yellowish cast, and the cotton assumed the same hue.

The following are the quantities and qualities of the different parcels of air furnished in the course of this experiment.

	Quantity.		Quality.
Upon the 10th of June	$1\frac{3}{4}$ cubic inches		$1\,a + 1\,n = 1.65,$ or 35
11th, 12th, and 13th	1 . . .		$1\,a + 1\,n = 2.00,$ or 0
14th	0		—————— ——
15th	$10\frac{42}{100}$ . . .		$1\,a + 3\,n = 1.43,$ or 257
16th	$14\frac{34}{100}$ . . .		$1\,a + 3\,n = 1.34,$ or 266
17th	$7\frac{34}{100}$ . . .		$1\,a + 4\,n = 1.40,$ or 360
18th	$6\frac{27}{100}$ . . .		$1\,a + 4\,n = 1.44,$ or 356
19th and 20th	$3\frac{13}{100}$ . . .		$1\,a + 3\,n = 1.06,$ or 294
Total quantity	$44\frac{1}{4}$	Mean qual.	$1\,a + 3\,n = 1.23,$ or 277

This experiment was repeated, and with nearly the same result; the total quantity of air produced being $41\frac{1}{3}$ cubic inches, and its quality, at a medium, $1\,a + 3\,n = 1.26$, or 274.

To ascertain the relative fineness of this poplar cotton and the thread of raw silk as spun by the worm, in order to make an estimate of the surface of the former, I examined them both at the same time under an excellent microscope, when the diameter of the cotton, that is to say, of a single thread or fibre of it, appeared to be not more than half as great as the diameter of the silk, consequently its diameter was not more than $\frac{1}{3648}$ part of an inch; for I have found by experiment that the diameter of a thread of silk, as spun by the worm, is only $\frac{1}{1824}$ of an inch.

The specific gravity of the cotton I found to be very nearly equal to that of water, consequently it is to that of silk as 1000 to 1734; its surface, therefore, is to the surface of an equal weight of raw silk in the compound proportion of 2 to 1, and of 1734 to 1000; that is to say, as 3468 to 1000.

Now, as the surface of 30 grains of raw silk amounts to 476 square inches, the surface of 30 grains of poplar cotton must amount to 1651 square inches, which gives 55 square inches of surface for each grain in weight; consequently, the surface of the cotton made use of in the foregoing experiment (No. 16) did not amount to less than 6600 square inches (for 120 grains, the weight of the cotton, multiplied by 55, gives 6600), — an enormous surface indeed for a body whose *solid contents* did not amount to quite half a cubic inch.

From hence it appears evidently, that the quantities of air furnished by water, in the experiments with raw silk and with poplar cotton, were neither in proportion to the quantities of these substances made use of, nor to the quantities of their surfaces. It appears, likewise, from the two last experiments, that the air which is furnished in the beginning of the experiment, or when the water is first exposed to the action of the sun's rays, is neither so good, nor in so great abundance, as afterwards, at a more advanced period; and that it totally ceases to be produced after a certain time.

To ascertain, with greater precision, the qualities of the air furnished at different periods of the experiment, or rather the period when the water begins to give good air; and also to determine the relative quantities and qualities of the airs produced in the experiments with raw silk and in those with poplar cotton, I made the following experiments.

Experiment No. 17.

A globe, about $4\frac{1}{2}$ inches in diameter, containing just

46 cubic inches, being filled in the evening with fresh spring-water, and 30 grains of raw silk, which had been previously washed thoroughly to free it of air and the remains of former experiments, and being exposed the next day in my window, the weather being cold and cloudy, with not more than one hour of sunshine, $\frac{1}{4}$ of a cubic inch of air was produced, which, proved with nitrous air, gave $1\,a + 2\,n = 1.86$, or 114.

The two following days, the weather being clear and moderately warm, $3\frac{1}{4}$ cubic inches of air were produced, which, proved with nitrous air, gave $1\,a + 3\,n = 1.14$, or 296.

Experiment No. 18.

The globe having been again filled with fresh spring-water, and the same silk which had served in the last experiment, after 2 nights and 1 day of about 4 hours sun, it had furnished $1\frac{1}{8}$ cubic inch of air, whose quality was $1\,a + 2\,n = 1.13$, or 197.

The two following days, the weather being very fine, it furnished $3\frac{8}{10}$ cubic inches of air, which, proved with nitrous air, gave $1\,a + 4\,n = 1.58$, or 342.

Experiment No. 19.

The globe being again filled with fresh water, and the same silk well washed, and being exposed two days in the sun, it gave $2\frac{2}{10}$ cubic inches of air, which, proved with nitrous air, gave $1\,a + 3\,n = 1.67$, or 233.

Experiment No. 20.

A like globe with fresh water, and an equal quantity of poplar cotton which had been used in former experiments, being exposed at the same time (*viz.* when the last experiment was made), gave $2\frac{53}{100}$ cubic inches of air, whose quality was $1\,a + 3\,n = 1.20$, or 280.

Experiment No. 21.

A small globe (contents, 20 cubic inches), with 17 grains of raw silk, exposed at the same time, give 1 cubic inch of air, which turned out $1\,a + 3\,n = 1.37$, or 263.

Experiment No. 22.

A large globe, containing 296 cubic inches, being filled with fresh water and a small quantity of *conferva rivularis*, and exposed at the same time with the three globes above mentioned, gave $1\frac{1}{2}$ cubic inch of air, which, proved with nitrous air, gave $1\,a + 2\,n = 1.76$, or 124.

The water, in this experiment, was changed to a brown colour, owing, as I conceived, to the too great heat the *conferva* acquired in the sun.

These experiments were made between the 2d and the 5th of July (1786).

Experiment No. 23.

Surprised at the smallness of the quantity, and the inferior quality, of the air produced in the last experiment, I was induced to repeat it; accordingly, the globe being again filled with water and a quantity of fresh *conferva rivularis* (a small handful), and being exposed to the action of the sun's rays during 3 fine days, $13\frac{34}{100}$ cubic inches of air were produced, which, proved with nitrous air, gave $1\,a + 3\,n = 1.54$, or 246.

At the end of the experiment, the water appeared to be very faintly tinged of a greenish cast.

The two following experiments were made upon the 20th and 21st of August.

Experiment No. 24.

A globe about $4\frac{1}{2}$ inches in diameter (contents, 46 cubic inches) being filled with fresh spring-water, and 30 grains of raw silk, which had been used in many preceding experiments, and being exposed to the action of the sun's rays two days, in all about 8 hours of sunshine, the weather being cloudy great part of the time, $1\frac{6}{100}$ cubic inch of air was produced, which, proved with nitrous air, gave $1\,a + 3\,n = 1.96$, or 204.

Experiment No. 25.

At the same time an equal globe, containing fresh spring-water, and about 15 grains of poplar cotton (which had likewise been used in former experiments), produced $1\frac{28}{100}$ cubic inch of air, which, proved with nitrous air, gave $1\,a + 3\,n = 1.40$, or 260.

The water in both these experiments had acquired a faint greenish cast ; but the colour of that with the cotton was rather the deepest.

Upon examining this water under a microscope, I found it contained a great number of animalcules exceedingly small, and of nearly a round figure. That with the silk contained them likewise, and of the same kind, but not in so great abundance. I never failed to find them in every case in which the water used in an experiment had acquired a greenish hue ; and from their presence alone, I think it more than probable that the colour of the water, *in the first instance*, arose in all cases. I have spent a great deal of time in observing them, and have made many experiments upon their production ; but as I have not yet been able to satisfy my own mind, with respect to the part they act in the operation of purifying the air in water, or generating pure air from it, I shall not add to the length of this paper, by giving an account of my inquiries and observations respecting them.

I was yet by no means satisfied with respect to the part which the silk and other bodies, exposed in water in the foregoing experiments, acted in the generation of the air produced.

Dr. Priestley has long since discovered that many animal and vegetable substances, putrefying, or rather dissolving, in water in the sun, cause the water to yield large quantities of dephlogisticated air; but I could hardly conceive that the small quantity of silk which was used in my experiments, and which had been constantly in water for more than three months, and had so often been washed, and even boiled in water, should yet retain a power of communicating anything to the large quantities of fresh water in which it was successively placed, — at least, *anything* in sufficient quantities to impregnate those bodies of water, and to cause them to yield the great abundance of air which they produced.

It was still more difficult to account for the pure air produced in the experiments with wool and fur and human hair; especially, as in some of these experiments the water had not sensibly changed colour, nor did it appear to have lost anything of its transparency. It is true, in these cases, the quantities of air produced were very small; but yet its quality was better than that of common air, and considerably superior to that of the air commonly existing in the water, previous to its being exposed to the action of the sun's light. In short, it was dephlogisticated in the experiment; but the *manner* in which this was done is very difficult to ascertain.

With a view to throwing some new light upon this intricate subject, I made the following experiments.

Experiment No. 26.

Concluding that if silk and other bodies, used in the foregoing experiments, actually did not contribute any-thing *considered as chemical substances*, in the process of the production of pure air yielded by water; but if, on the contrary, they acted merely as a mechanical aid, in the *separation* of the air from the water, by affording a con-venient surface for the air to attach itself to, — in this case, any other body having a large surface, and attract-ing air in water, might be made use of instead of silk in the experiment, and pure air would be furnished, though the body so made use of should be totally incapable of communicating *anything whatever* to the water.

To ascertain this fact, washing the great globe (con-taining 296 cubic inches) perfectly clean, and filling it with fresh spring-water, I introduced into it a quantity of the fine flexible thread of glass, commonly called *spun glass*, such as is used for making brushes for clean-ing jewels, and for making a kind of artificial feather frequently sold by the Jew pedlars. This spun glass is no other than common glass drawn out, when hot, into an exceeding fine thread; which thread, in consequence of its extreme fineness, retains its flexibility after it has grown cold.

I made choice of this substance, not only on account of its great surface, but also on account of the strong attraction which is known to subsist between glass and air, and the impossibility of its communicating anything to the water.

The result of the experiment was, that, the globe being exposed in the sun, air-bubbles began almost im-mediately to make their appearance upon the surface of the spun glass, and in four hours $\frac{7.7}{100}$ of a cubic inch of air was collected, which, proved with nitrous air, gave $1 a + 1 n = 1.12$, or 88 ; after which, not a single air-bubble more was produced, though the globe was exposed a whole week in the window, during which time there were several very warm, fine, sunshiny days.

This experiment shews evidently that something more is wanting to the production of pure air by water, exposed in the sun, than merely a surface to which the air dissolved in the water can attach itself in order to its making its escape.

The air furnished in this experiment was doubtless merely that with which the water, issuing from the earth, was overcharged, and which would have made its escape from the water, had the water, instead of being exposed with the spun glass in the sun, been simply left for some time exposed to the free air of the atmosphere.

It appears that this air, naturally existing in spring-water, instead of being dephlogisticated, is something worse than common air ; and this agrees with the observations of Dr. Priestley, and seems to justify his opinion with respect to the cause of the fertility of lands washed by waters issuing from the earth.

If the above experiment shews that something is wanting to be mixed with water in order to enable it to yield pure air, when exposed to the action of the sun's light, the following shew that this *something*, whatever it may be, is frequently to be found in the water itself in its natural state.

Experiment No. 27.

A large jar of clear white glass containing 455 cubic inches, being washed very clean, was filled with fresh spring-water, and inverted in a glass bason of the same, and placed in the middle of the garden of the Elector's palace at Munich, where it was left exposed to the weather 28 days.

At the same time another like jar was filled with water taken from a pond in the garden, in which many aquatic plants were growing, and was exposed in the same place, and during the same period. This water had a very faint greenish cast. The pond from which it was taken is fed by a large river (the Isar) which runs by the town.

The second day after these waters had been exposed in the sun, I observed that a small quantity of air had collected itself at the upper part of each of the jars.

The third, fourth, and fifth days, the pond-water furnished air in pretty large quantities; and it went on to yield it without intermission, when the sun shone upon it, till the fourteenth day, when it seemed to be nearly exhausted. I continued the experiment, however, till the twenty-eighth day, though, during the last fortnight, the quantity of air in the jar did not appear to be sensibly increased.

The spring-water, during the first five or six days, furnished very little air; and it was not till the fourteenth day that it began to yield it in any considerable quantities. From this time it went on to furnish it, though but very slowly, till about the twenty-second day, when it ceased, appearing to be quite exhausted.

Upon the twenty-eighth day I removed the airs from the jars, when I found their quantities and qualities to be as follows : —

	Quantity.	Quality.
Air furnished by the spring-water	14 cubic in.	$1a + 2n = 1.62$, or 138
" " " " pond "	$31\frac{1}{2}$ "	$1a + 3n = 1.48$, or 252

Neither the colour of the spring-water, nor that of the pond-water, appeared to be sensibly changed ; but both the one and the other of these waters had deposited a considerable quantity of earth, which was found adhering to the surfaces of the glass basons in which the jars were inverted.

As these basons were rather deep, and as they were very thick in glass, and consequently not very transparent, their bottoms, where the sediment of the water was collected, were, in a great measure, obscured, or deprived of the direct rays of the sun. Suspecting that this circumstance might have had some effect, so as to have hindered the water from furnishing so much air as otherwise it might have yielded, — to satisfy myself respecting this matter, I repeated the experiment, disposing the apparatus in such a manner that the sediment of the water which attached itself to the bottom of the vessel in which the jar was inverted had the advantage of being perfectly illuminated.

Experiment No. 28.

In a large cylindrical jar, of very fine transparent glass, 10 inches in diameter, and 12 inches high, filled with spring-water, I inverted a conical glass jar, $9\frac{3}{4}$ inches in diameter at the bottom, and containing 344 cubic inches, filled with the same water ; and exposed the whole 21 days in a window fronting the south.

The quantity of air produced amounted to 40 cubic inches ; and its quality, proved by the test of nitrous air, gave $1\,a + 3\,n = 1.87$, or 213.

The water, in this experiment, furnished very little air till the seventh day ; but after that time, having assumed a faint greenish cast, and a fine greenish slimy sediment (the *green matter* of Dr. Priestley) beginning to be found upon the bottom of the jar, it began to yield air in abundance, and continued to furnish it in pretty large quantities till about the eighteenth day, when it appeared to be exhausted.

Why the water should turn green in this experiment, and not in the last, I know not ; unless it was in conse-quence of the large surface of water in the cylindrical jar which was exposed to the air in this experiment ; or in consequence of the sun's shining directly upon the bottom of the vessel where the sediment was formed.

In the former experiment, the bason in which the jar was inverted was but just big enough to admit the jar ; and as the jar was cylindrical, the surface of the water exposed to the atmosphere in the bason was but very small ; and the bason being very thick, and formed of glass which, though of the white kind, was of an inferior quality, and very imperfectly transparent, as I have al-ready observed, the bottom of the bason where the sed-iment was formed was but very imperfectly illuminated.

Having never been thoroughly satisfied with respect to the origin of the dephlogisticated air produced upon ex-posing fresh vegetables in water to the action of the sun's rays, according to the method of Dr. Ingen-Housz, my doubts with respect to the opinion generally entertained, of its being *elaborated* in the vessels of the plant, instead of being removed, were rather confirmed by the result of these experiments ; and however disposed I was to adopt the beautiful theory of the purification of the at-mosphere by the vegetable kingdom, I was not willing to admit a fact which has been brought in support of it, till it should appear to me to have been proved by the most decisive experiments.

That the fresh leaves of certain vegetables, exposed in water to the action of the sun's rays, cause a certain quantity of pure air to be produced, is a fact which has been put beyond all doubt; but it does not appear to me to be by any means so clearly proved, that this air is "*elaborated* in the plant by the powers of vegetation"; — "phlogisticated or fixed air being first absorbed, or imbibed by the plant as food, and the dephlogisticated air being rejected as an excrement": for, besides that many other substances, and in which no elaboration, or circulation, can possibly be suspected to take place, cause the water in which they are exposed to the action of light to yield dephlogisticated air as well as plants, and even in much greater quantities, and of a more eminent quality, the circumstances of the leaves of a vegetable which, accustomed to grow in air, are separated from its stem, and confined in water, are so unnatural that I cannot conceive that they can perform the same functions in such different situations.

Among many facts which have been brought in support of the received opinion of the *elaboration* of the air in the vessels of the plants in the experiments in question, there is one upon which great stress has been laid, which, I think, requires further examination.

The fresh, healthy leaves of vegetables, separated from the plant, and exposed in water to the action of the sun's rays, appear, by all the experiments which have hitherto been made, to furnish air *only for a short time*; after a day or two, the leaves, changing colour, cease to yield air; and this has been conceived to arise from the powers of vegetation being destroyed; or, in other words, *the death of the plant*; and from hence it has been inferred, with some degree of plausibility, not only that the leaves actually retained their vegetative powers for some time after they were separated from their stock, but also that it was in consequence of the exertion of these powers that the air yielded in the experiment was produced.

But I have found, that though the leaves, exposed in water to the action of light, actually do cease to furnish air after a certain time, yet that they *regain* this power after a short interval, when they furnish (or rather cause the water to furnish) more and better air than at first, which can hardly be accounted for upon the supposition that the air is *elaborated* in the vessels of the plant.

Experiment No. 29.

A globe containing 46 cubic inches, filled with fresh spring-water and two peach-leaves, was exposed in the window to the action of the sun's rays 10 days successively (the weather being in general fine), when the following appearances took place : —

The 1st and 2d day a certain quantity of air was produced, about as much as in former like experiments. The 3d day very little was produced ; and the 4th day none at all, the globe to all appearance being quite exhausted.   Continuing the experiment, however, upon the 5th day, the water having acquired a faint greenish hue, air was again produced pretty plentifully, *making its appearance upon the surface of the leaves in the form of air-bubbles, as at the beginning of the experiment ;* at the end of the 6th day the air was removed, and it was found to amount to $\frac{54}{100}$ of a cubic inch, its quality being 232 degrees, or $1\ a + 3\ n = 1.68$.

Upon the 7th day $\frac{9}{10}$ of a cubic inch of air was produced of 297 degrees, or $1\ a + 3\ n = 1.03$; and,

During the 8th, 9th, and 10th days, $1\frac{3}{4}$ cubic inch of

air, of 307 degrees (or $1a + 4n = 1.93$), was furnished ; after which an end was put to the experiment.

Total quantity of air produced, $3\frac{19}{100}$ cubic inches;
mean quality, 291 degrees, or $1a + 3n = 1.09$.

Finding that *leaves which were dead*, or in which all the
powers of vegetation were evidently destroyed, continued,
notwithstanding, to separate air from water, and that in
so great abundance, I was desirous of seeing the effect
of exposing fresh, healthy leaves in water which I knew
to be previously saturated with, and disposed to yield,
dephlogisticated air. I conceived that if the plants exposed in water actually imbibed fixed or phlogisticated
air as food, and after digesting it, " discharged the dephlogisticated air as an excrement"; in that case, as there
is no instance of any plant or animal being able to
nourish itself with its own excrement, the leaves exposed
in water saturated with dephlogisticated air, instead of
imbibing and elaborating it, would immediately die.

The experiments which I made to ascertain this fact, and
which, without any comment, I shall submit to the consideration of the reader, were as follows.

Experiment No. 30.

Having provided a quantity of water, which, by being
exposed with a few green leaves in the sun, had acquired
a greenish cast, and which I found was disposed to yield
dephlogisticated air in great abundance, I filled a globe,
containing 46 cubic inches, with this water, and putting
to it two healthy peach-leaves, exposed the globe in the
sun upon the 7th of September, from 11 o'clock in the
morning till 2 o'clock in the afternoon (3 hours), when
$\frac{7}{10}$ of a cubic inch of air was produced, which, proved
with nitrous air, gave $1a + 3n = 1.52$, or 248 degrees.

A like globe, with fresh spring-water and two peach-leaves, exposed at the same time, furnished only $\frac{1}{9}$ of a cubic inch of air, which, on account of the smallness of its quantity, I did not submit to the test of nitrous air.

Experiment No. 31.

September 8. Very fine clear weather, but rather cold for the season. Three equal globes, A, B, and C, containing each 46 cubic inches, were filled as follows, and exposed in the sun from 9 o'clock in the morning till half an hour past 4 in the afternoon, when they were found to have produced air as under mentioned.

The globe A, filled with water, which, by being previously exposed in the sun for several days, with potatoes cut in thin slices, had turned green, furnished $\frac{9}{10}$ of a cubic inch of air of 299 degrees, or $1\,a + 3\,n = 1.01$. N. B. This water, before it was put into the globe, was strained through two thicknesses of very fine Irish linen.

The globe B, filled with the same green potatoe-water (strained as before), to which were added four middling-sized peach-leaves, furnished $2\frac{1}{2}$ cubic inches of air of 320 degrees, or $1\,a + 4\,n = 1.80$.

The globe C, filled with *fresh spring-water*, with four peach-leaves, furnished $\frac{52}{100}$ of a cubic inch of air of 151 degrees, or which, proved with nitrous air, gave $1\,a + 2\,n = 1.49$.

To ascertain the quantities and qualities of the airs remaining in the different waters used in this experiment, putting the globes separately over a chafing-dish of live coals, and making the water boil, taking care to hold the globe in such an inclined position as that the air separated from the water might be collected in the upper part of the globe, the airs produced were as follows : —

	Quantity.	Quality.
By the green water in the globe A,	$\frac{85}{100}$ of a cubic inch	280 degrees
" " " " " B,	$\frac{31}{100}$ " "	241 "
By the spring-water in the globe C,	$\frac{11}{100}$ " "	68 "

The waters in these experiments were made to boil but for a moment ; otherwise it is probable more air might have been separated from them.

Finding that fresh leaves, exposed to the action of the sun's rays, in water which had already turned green, caused pure air to be separated from the water in so great abundance, I repeated the experiment, — only, instead of leaves, I now made use of a small quantity of *conferva rivularis;* when I had nearly the same result as with the leaves.

To ascertain the relative quantities and qualities of the airs yielded by the green water, when exposed with fresh leaves, and when exposed with raw silk ; and also to ascertain, at the same time, how long, leaves, exposed in green water, retain their power of separating air from it, I made

Experiment No. 32.

Two equal globes, A and B (containing each 46 cubic inches), the former (A) filled with green potatoe-water, strained through linen, and four peach-leaves ; the latter (B) filled with the same potatoe-water, strained in like manner, and 17 grains of raw silk, — were exposed from Sunday noon, September 10th, till Monday evening ; the weather being cold, with many flying clouds, in all about 6 or 7 hours sun.

The airs produced were as follows : —

	Quantity.	Quality.
By the globe A, with green water and 4 peach-leaves	$2\frac{7}{10}$ cubic inches	292 degrees.
By the globe B, with green water and 17 grs. of raw silk . . .	$2\frac{7}{10}$ " "	307 "

Another globe (C), filled with green water *alone*, was exposed at the same time; but it was broken by an accident before the experiment was completed.

The two globes (A and B), with their contents, being again exposed from Tuesday noon till Thursday evening, yielded air as follows : —

	Quantity.		Quality.
The globe A, with the peach-leaves	$4\frac{47}{100}$ cubic inches		344 degrees.
The globe B, with raw silk . . .	$4\frac{3}{10}$ "	"	350 "

N. B.   The weather on Tuesday and Wednesday was cold, with very little sunshine; but Thursday was a very fine, warm day, when the greatest part of the air was produced.   This air was removed, and proved on Friday morning, the 15th September.

Perhaps all the appearances above described might be satisfactorily accounted for, by supposing the air produced in the different experiments to have been generated in the mass of water by the *green matter*, and that the leaves, the silk, &c. did no more than *assist it in making its escape* by affording it a convenient surface, to which it could attach itself, in order to its collecting itself together, and taking upon itself its elastic form.

The phænomena might likewise be accounted for, by supposing the *green matter* to be a vegetable substance agreeable to the hypothesis of Dr. Priestley, and that attaching itself to the surfaces of the bodies exposed in the water, as a plant is attached to its soil, it grows; and in consequence of the exertion of its vegetative powers, the air yielded in the experiment is produced.

I should most readily have adopted this opinion, had not a careful and attentive examination of the green water, under a most excellent microscope, at the time when it appeared to be most disposed to yield pure air in abundance, convinced me that, *at that period*, it contains nothing that can possibly be supposed to be of a vegetable nature. The colouring matter of the water is evidently of an animal nature, being nothing more than the assemblage of an infinite number of very small, active, oval-formed animalcules, without anything resembling *tremella*, or that kind of *green matter*, or water moss, which grows upon the bottom and sides of the vessel when this water is suffered to remain in it for a considerable time, and into which Dr. Ingen-Housz supposes the animalcules above mentioned to be actually transformed.

But having finished the account of my experiments, I shall finish this paper, not daring to venture conjectures upon a subject so intricate in itself and so new, and upon which the ablest philosophers of the age seem to be so much divided in opinion.

AN ACCOUNT

OF

SOME EXPERIMENTS UPON GUNPOWDER,

With occasional Observations and practical Inferences, to which are added an Account of a new Method of determining the Velocities of all Kinds of Military Projectiles, and the Description of a very accurate Eprouvette for Gunpowder.

THESE experiments were undertaken principally with a view to determine the most advantageous situation for the vent in fire-arms, and to measure the velocities of bullets, and the recoil under various circumstances. I had hopes, also, of being able to find out the velocity of the inflammation of gunpowder, and to measure its force more accurately than had hitherto been done. They were begun in the month of July, in the year 1778, at Stoneland Lodge, a country seat belonging to Lord George Germain ; and I was assisted by the Reverend Mr. Bale, rector of Withyham, who lives in the neighbourhood.

The weather proved remarkably favourable for our experiments, being settled and serene, so that the course of them was never interrupted for a whole day by rain or by any accident. The mercury in the barometer stood, in general, pretty high, and the temperature of the atmosphere was very equal and

moderately warm for the season. In order that each
experiment might, as nearly as possible, be made under
similar circumstances, they were all made between the
hours of ten in the morning and five in the afternoon ;
and after each experiment the piece was wiped out with
tow till the inside of its bore was perfectly clean, and as
bright as if it had just come out of the hands of the
maker ; and great care was taken to allow as much
time to elapse between the firings as was necessary to
render the heat of the barrel nearly the same in every
experiment.

A Description of the Apparatus.

The barrel principally used in these experiments
was made by Wogdon, one of the most famous gunsmiths in London ; and nothing can exceed the accuracy with which it is bored, or the fineness of the
polish on the inside. It is made of the very best iron,
and, agreeably to Mr. Robins's advice, I took care to
have it well fortified in every part, that there might be
no danger of its bursting. Its weight and dimensions
may be seen in the table of the weight and dimensions
of the apparatus, p. 307.

Fig. 1 represents a longitudinal section of a part
of the barrel, with the apparatus first made use of for
shifting the vent from one part of the chamber to
another, or rather for moving the bottom of the chamber further from, or bringing it nearer to, the vent,
in order that the fire might be communicated to the
powder in different parts of the charge.

a, b, represent the lower part of the barrel. *c* is the
breech-pin, which is perforated with a hole four tenths

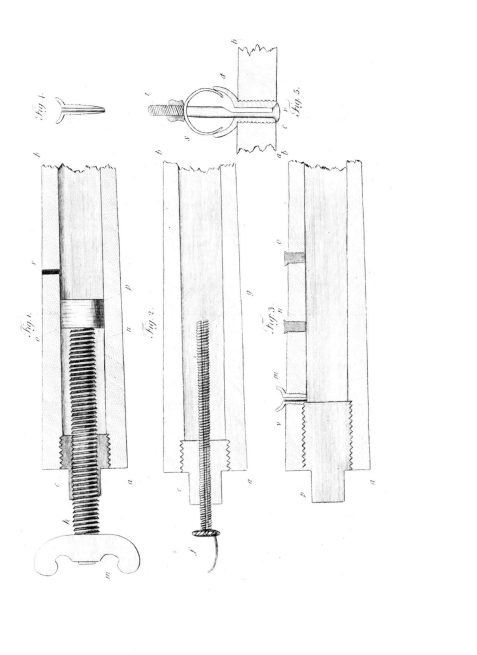

Fig. 1.

Fig. 5.

Fig. 1.

Fig. 2.

Fig. 3.

of an inch in diameter, the axis of which perforation coincides with the axis of the bore.

Into this hole the screw *h*, *n*, about four inches in length, is fitted; to the end of which, *n*, that passes up into the bore, is fixed a piston, *o*, *p*, which, by means of collars of oiled leather, is made to fit the bore of the piece very exactly. The end of the piston *p*, nearest the muzzle, is of brass, and forms a moveable bottom to the bore, which by turning the screw *h*, *n*, by means of the handle *m*, is brought nearer to, or removed further from, the fixed vent *v*, by which means the powder is lighted at any assignable distance from the bottom of the charge.

But the length of the bore being altered by moving the piston, which occasioned a small inaccuracy, and some inconvenience attending the apparatus, it was laid aside, and another, represented by Fig. 2, was substituted in the room of it.

a, *b*, is a section of part of the barrel as before, and *c* is the breech-pin, which, being perforated with a small hole through its center, receives the screw *f*, *g*, which is about two tenths of an inch in diameter, and four inches long. This screw, being perforated with a very small hole, serves to convey the fire into the chamber of the piece, and by screwing it further up into the bore, or drawing it backwards, the fire is communicated to different parts of the charge.

But, this method being found to be not entirely free from inaccuracies and inconveniences, a third was substituted in the room of it, which was found to answer much better than either of the preceding.

The end of the bore was now firmly closed by a solid breech-pin, *p*, Fig. 3, and three vent-holes, *m*, *n*, and *o*, were made in the barrel ; one of them, *m*, even with the bottom of the bore, and the other two at different distances from it. Any two of these vent-holes, as *n* and *o*, for instance, being closed up by solid screws, a perforated screw, or vent-tube, *v*, was screwed into the third, which served to contain the priming, and to convey the fire to the powder lodged in the bore of the piece.

Sometimes a longer vent-tube, represented by Fig. 4, was made use of, which, passing through the powder in the chamber of the piece, communicated the fire immediately to that part of the charge that lay in the axis of the bore.

Another vent-tube, also, was used occasionally, which differs in many respects from both those that have been described. It is so constructed as to convey the fire to the charge ; but as soon as the powder in the chamber of the piece begins to kindle, and the elastic fluid to be generated, the vent is firmly closed by a valve, and no part of the generated fluid is permitted to escape. This I shall call the *valve-vent*, and it is represented by Fig. 5, upon an enlarged scale, that the parts of it may appear more distinct.

a, *b*, is a longitudinal section of a small portion of the solid side of the barrel.

c, *d*, is the vent-tube, which is in all respects like the short vent-tube commonly made use of, except only that in this the end of the vent-hole (*c*), which goes into the chamber, is enlarged in the form of the wide end of a trumpet or funnel.

To this enlarged aperture the valve, *v*, is accurately fitted, and by means of the small stem or tail, *t*, which is fixed to the valve, and which passes up through the vent-hole, and is connected with the spring, *s*, the valve is pressed, or rather drawn into its place, and the vent is closed. The stem of the valve was at first made cylindrical; but in order to make way for the priming to pass down to the valve, one half of its substance was taken away, as is represented in the figure.

When this vent is primed, the space between the vent-hole and the stem of the valve is filled with fine-grained powder, and the valve is gently opened, by pressing upon the end of the stem till one or more grains of powder lodge themselves between the valve and the aperture; which preventing the valve from closing again, a small opening is left for the passage of the flame into the chamber of the piece; when the priming is lighted, the fire passing down the vent, and entering the chamber, inflames the charge, and the small grains of powder that were lodged between the valve and the aperture being destroyed by the flame in its passage through the vent, the valve immediately closes, and prevents the escape of any part of the elastic fluid generated by the inflammation of the powder in the chamber of the piece. The pressure of this fluid upon the valve assists the action of the spring, by which means the valve is more expeditiously and more effectually closed.

The valve was very accurately fitted to the aperture by grinding them together with powdered emery and afterwards polishing them one upon the other. And it is very certain that no part of the elastic fluid made its escape by this vent; for, upon firing the piece, there was only a simple flash from the explosion of the priming, and no stream of fire was to be seen issuing from the vent, as is always to be observed when a common vent is made use of, and in all other cases where this fluid finds a passage.

In order that every part of the apparatus employed in these experiments might be as perfect as possible, all the more delicate parts of it were executed by Mr. Frazer, mathematical instrument maker in Duke's Court, St. Martin's Lane, and, among the rest, all the contrivances just described relative to the vent.

The velocities of the bullets were determined by means of a pendulum, according to the method invented by Mr. Robins.

The pendulum I made use of (Fig. 6) is composed of a circular plate of hammered iron (*a*) 13 inches in diameter and 0.65 of an inch thick, to which is firmly fastened a bar of iron (*b*, *c*,) 56.5 inches in length, 2.6 inches broad, and half an inch in thickness, by which it is suspended, by means of two pivots (*d*, *e*), at the end of the bar (*c*) and at right angles to its length. These pivots being very accurately finished, and moving on polished grooves, which were kept constantly oiled to lessen the friction, the vibration of the pendulum was very free, as appeared by the great length of time its vibrations continued after it had been put in motion, and was left to itself. To the circular plate of the pendulum, targets of circular pieces of wood of different thicknesses were fixed, which in the course of the experiments were often spoiled and replaced; and in order to mark the weight and dimensions of the pendulum in each experiment, the pendulums are numbered according to the different targets that were made use of; and the weight and dimensions of each pendulum are set down in a table at the end of the description of the apparatus.

The target of the pendulum No. 1 was made of a circular piece of elm-plank, $3\frac{1}{2}$ inches thick, and equal in diameter to the iron plate of the pendulum to which

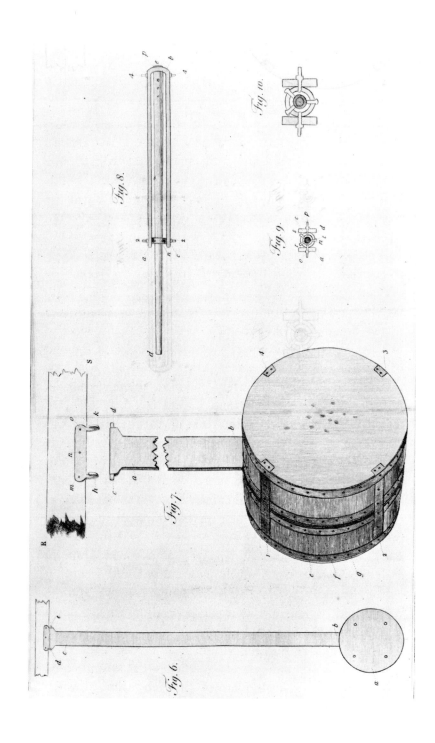

Fig. 8.

Fig. 10.

Fig. 9.

Fig. 7.

Fig. 6.

it was fixed ; but this target, being too thin, was very soon ruined.

The pendulum No. 2 was furnished with two targets, which were circular pieces of very tough oak-plank, near five inches thick, placed on opposite sides of the plate of the pendulum, and firmly fixed to it by screws, and to each other by iron straps. When one of these targets was ruined the pendulum was turned about and the other was made use of. This pendulum lasted from experiment No. 9 to experiment No. 39, when it was so much shattered as to be rendered unfit for further service.

The pendulum No. 3 was like No. 2 ; only, instead of oak, elm-plank, near seven inches in thickness, was made use of for the targets. This pendulum served from experiment No. 40 to experiment No. 101, inclusively.

But finding that targets made of planks of the toughest wood were very soon shattered to pieces by the bullets, I composed the pendulum No. 4 in a different manner. Instead of circular pieces of plank, solid cylinders of elm-timber were made use of for the targets, so that the bullets now entered the wood in the direction of its fibres. These cylinders are 13 inches in diameter, and about $5\frac{1}{2}$ inches in length, hooped with iron at both their ends, to prevent their splitting, and they are firmly fastened to the plate of the pendulum and to each other by four iron straps. This pendulum lasted till the experiments were finished. It is still in being, and appears to be very little the worse for the service it has undergone.

Fig. 7 shows the two ends of the pendulum upon a large scale, together with the hooks by which it was suspended.

a, b, is the bar of the pendulum which is seen broken off, as there is not room to shew the whole of its length.

c, d, are the pivots by which it was suspended. *e* is the circular plate of the pendulum, to which *f, g,* two circular targets, are fastened by screws, and by means of the iron straps 1, 2, 3, 4, which are nailed to the edges of the targets. *h, k,* are the hooks which served to receive the pivots *c, d,* of the pendulum.

The hooks were firmly fixed to the horizontal beam R, S, which supported the whole apparatus by means of three screws, *m, n, o,* which passed through three holes in the plate that connects the two hooks. When the hooks are fastened to the beam, the middle screw, *n,* was first put into its place, and the pendulum was allowed to settle itself in a position truly vertical, after which the hooks were immoveably fixed by means of the screws *m, o.*

The chord of the arc through which the pendulum ascended in each experiment was measured by a ribbon, according to the method invented and described by Mr. Robins.

The recoil was measured in the following manner : The barrel was suspended in an horizontal position (and nearly in a line with the center of the target) by two small pendulous rods 64 inches in length, and 25.6 inches asunder ; which, being parallel to each other, and moving freely upon polished pivots, about the axes of their suspension, and upon two pair of trunnions that were fixed to the barrel, formed, together with the barrel, a compound pendulum ; and from the lengths of the vibrations of this pendulum, the velocity with which the barrel began to recoil, or rather its greatest velocity, was determined.

But in order that the velocity of the recoil might not be too great, so as to endanger the apparatus, when large charges were made use of, it was found necessary to load the barrel with an additional weight of more than 40 lbs. of iron.

This additional weight of iron, which I shall call the *gun-carriage*, as it was so constructed as to serve as a carriage to the barrel, is composed of a bar of hammered iron 28 inches in length, 2.6 inches broad, and half an inch in thickness, which is bent in the middle of its length, in such a manner that its two flat sides or ends are parallel to each other, and distant asunder two inches. In the middle of this bar, where it is bent, is a hole in the form of an oblong square, which, receiving the end of the breech-pin, supports the lower end or breech of the barrel. The other end of the barrel is supported and confined in the following manner : A ring or hoop of iron, near half an inch thick, and two inches in diameter, is placed in a vertical position between the parallel sides of the bar and near its two ends, and firmly fixed to them by screws. The barrel, passing through the middle of this ring, is supported upon the ends of three screws, which, passing through the ring in different parts of its circumference, all point towards its center.

The carriage, together with the barrel, was suspended by the pendulous rods by means of two pair of polished trunnions, that are fixed to the outside of the carriage. They are placed in an horizontal line perpendicular to, and passing through, the axis of the bore.

Fig. 8 represents the barrel fixed to the carriage. *a, b, c,* is the bar of iron seen edgeways which forms the carriage.

2, 2, 4, 4, are the trunnions by which it was suspended.

d, e, is the barrel in its proper place.

p is the breech-pin, which, passing through a hole in
the middle of the bar, *a, b, c,* supports the end *e* of the
barrel ; and

n is the ring that supports the end *d* of the barrel.

Fig. 9 represents a perpendicular section through the
line 2, 2, Fig. 8, and in a line perpendicular to the length
of the barrel.

This figure is designed to shew the manner in which
the muzzle of the piece was supported and confined in
the ring *n,* Fig. 8.

a, c, are the two ends of the bar that are seen cut off.

n is the ring, and

o, p, are the screws by which it is fastened to the two
parallel sides of the bar, the ends of which screws form
the trunnions 2, 2, Fig. 8.

d is a transverse section of the barrel, and

r, s, t, are the three screws by which the barrel is supported and confined in the center of the ring.

Fig. 10 is the same as Fig. 9, but upon a larger scale,
and without the letters of reference.

Fig. 11 represents the two ends of one of the pendulous rods by which the barrel was suspended ; and Fig.
13 shews the same seen sideways.

a, b, is the rod which is seen broken off.

c, d, are the pivots by which it was suspended by a
pair of hooks that were fastened to an horizontal beam,
in the same manner as the pendulum for measuring the
velocities of the bullets was suspended.

e, f, are the hooks which receive the trunnions that
are fixed to the carriage.

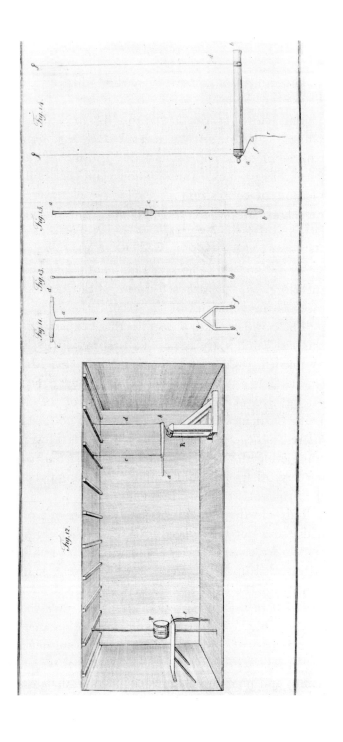

Fig. 14.

Fig. 15.

Fig. 13.

Fig. 11.

Fig. 12.

The dimensions of every part of this apparatus may be seen in the table, page 309.

The chord of the arc through which the barrel ascended in its recoil was measured by a ribbon, and the lengths of those chords, expressed in inches and decimal parts of an inch, are set down in the tables. The method of computing the velocity of the recoil from the chord of the arc through which the barrel ascended is too well known to require an explanation; and it is also well known that the velocities are to each other as the chords of those arcs. The lengths of those chords, therefore, as they are set down in the tables, are in all cases as the velocities of the recoil.

The powder made use of in these experiments was of the best kind, such as is used in proving great guns at Woolwich. A cartridge containing 12 lbs. of this powder was given to me by the late General Desaguliers, of the Royal Artillery, and Inspector of Brass and Iron Ordnance; who also, in the politest manner, offered me every other assistance in his power, towards completing the experiments I had projected, or in making any others I should propose, that might be useful in the prosecution of my inquiries.

This powder was immediately taken out of the cartridge and put into glass bottles, which were previously made very clean and dry; and in these it was kept carefully sealed up till it was opened for use. When it was wanted for the experiments, it was weighed out in a very exact balance, with so much attention, that there could not possibly be an error in any instance greater than one quarter part of a grain. The bottles were never opened but in fine weather, and in a room that was free from damp, and no more charges of powder than were necessary for the experiments of the day were weighed out at a time. Each charge was carefully put up in a cartridge of very fine paper, and these filled cartridges were kept in a turned wooden box, that was varnished on the inside as well as the outside, to prevent its imbibing moisture from the air.

The paper of which these cartridges were made was so fine and thin, that 1,280 sheets of it made no more than an inch in thickness, and a cartridge capable of containing half an ounce of powder weighed but three quarters of a grain.

The cartridges were formed upon a wooden cylinder, and accurately fitted to the bore of the piece, and the edges of the paper were fastened together with paste made of flour and water.

When a cartridge was filled, the powder was gently shaken together, and its mouth was tied up and secured with a piece of fine thread ; and when it was made use of, it was put intire into the piece, and gently pushed down into its place with the ram-rod, and afterwards it was pricked with a priming-wire thrust through the vent, and the piece was primed ; so that no part of the powder of the charge was lost in the act of loading, as is always the case when the powder is put loose into the barrel ; nor was any part of it expended in priming ; but the whole quantity was safely lodged in the bottom of the bore or chamber of the piece, and the bullet was put down immediately upon it, without any wadding either between the cartridge and the bullet, or over the bullet.

The bullets were all cast in the same mould, and, consequently, could not vary in their weights above two or three grains at most, especially as I took care to bring the mould to a proper temperature as to heat, before I began casting; and when leather was put about them, or other bullets than those of lead were made use of, the weight was determined very exactly before they were put into the piece.

The diameter of the bullet was determined by measurement, and also by computation, from its weight, and the specific gravity of the metal of which it was formed; and both these methods gave the same dimensions very nearly.

The apparatus was put up for making the experiments in a coach-house, which was found very convenient for the purpose, as the joists upon which the floor overhead was laid afforded a firm and commodious support for suspending the pendulum and the barrel, and the walls and roofs of the building served to screen the apparatus, which otherwise might have been disturbed by the wind, and injured by the rain and dews. A pair of very large doors, which formed the whole of one end of the room, were kept constantly open during the time the experiments were making, in order to preserve the purity of the air within the house, which otherwise would have been much injured by the smoke of the gunpowder, which might, possibly, have had some effect in lessening the force of the powder, and vitiating the experiments. In order still further to guard against this evil, the barrel was placed as near as possible to the door, and the pendulum was hung up at the bottom of the room.

Fig. 12 represents the apparatus as it was put up for making the experiments.

a, *b*, is the barrel with its carriage, suspended by the pendulous rods *c*, *d*, and

R is the ribbon which served to measure the ascending arc of its recoil.

P is the pendulum, and

r the ribbon that measured the arc of its vibration.

The distance from the mouth of the piece to the pendulum was just 12 feet.

A TABLE SHEWING THE WEIGHTS AND DIMENSIONS OF ALL THE PRINCIPAL PARTS OF THE APPARATUS.

Of the Barrel.

Inches.

Length 44.7

Length of the bore from the muzzle to the
    breech-pin 43.45

Diameter of the bore 0.78

Thickness of metal at the lower vent . . 0.36

Thickness of metal at the muzzle . . . 0.1

Weight of the barrel, together with the solid breech-pin
    and the vent-screws and vent-tube, 6 lbs. 6 oz.

Of the Gun-Carriage.

Inches.

Length 28.4

Distance between the two pair of trunnions . 25.6

Diameter of each trunnion 0.25

Weight, 40 lbs. 14 oz.

Of the Rods by which the Carriage was suspended.

Length from the axis of suspension or center of
    the pivots, to the center of the trunnions   Inches.
    of the gun-carriage 64

Weight of each rod, 1 lb. 4 oz.

Total weight of the barrel and its carriage, together with the allowance that was made for the weight of the rods by which it was suspended, 48 lbs.

N. B. — This was its weight from experiment No. 3 to experiment No. 123, inclusive.

Of the Bullet.

Diameter, 0.75 of an inch.
Weight in lead, 580 grains.

Of the Pendulum.

Inches.

Total length of the pendulum from the axis of
suspension to the bottom of the circular
plate 69.5
Diameter of the circular plate to which the tar-
gets were fastened   .   .   .   .   13.
Distance between the shoulders of the pivots .   3.8
Diameter of the pivots 27
Weight of the iron part of the pendulum, 47 lbs. 4 oz.

*Of the Pendulum with the Targets fixed to it, as it was
prepared for making the Experiments.*

	Total Length to the Ribbon.	Distance from the Axis of Suspension.		Total Weight of Iron and Wood.	
		To the Center of Gravity.	To the Center of Oscillation.		
	Inches.	Inches.	Inches.	lbs.	oz.
Pendulum No. 1	69.25	50.25	58.45	57	0
" No. 2	69.5	54.4	59.15	82	4
" No. 3	. . . .	55.62	60.23	100	12
" No. 4	. . . .	54.6	59.18	88	4

N. B. — The measure is English feet and inches, and
the weight is avoirdupois.

Having now gone through with the description of all
the principal parts of the apparatus, I shall proceed to
give an account of the experiments; and as it may be
satisfactory to see the method of conducting these en-

quiries as well as the result of them, I shall first give a table of the experiments in the exact order in which they were made, together with my original remarks ; I shall then make such general observations as may occur ; and afterwards I shall select, combine, and compare them, in the manner which may best answer the different purposes to which I shall apply them.

General Table of the Experiments.

In the two first experiments the barrel was fixed to a carriage (that has not been described), which, together with the barrel and rods by which it was suspended, weighed only $23\frac{1}{2}$ lbs.

Length of the bore of the piece, 43.5 inches.

Weight of the bullet, 580 grains.

The Pendulum No. 1.

Order of Experiments.	The Charge of Powder.		Vent from the Bottom of the Charge.	Chord of the ascending Arc of the Pendulum.	The Bullet struck the Target below the Axis of the Pendulum.	Chord of the Arc of the Recoil.	Velocity of the Bullet.	Remarks.
	Weight.	Height.						
No.	Grains.	Inches.	Inches.	Inches.	Inches.	Inches.	Feet in Seconds.	
								First day.
1	208	1.8	0.	13.2	64.5	33.5	1267	
2	...	...	.5	14.5	...	36.5	1399	

This gun-carriage being found to be too light, the other, described above, and represented Fig. 8, was substituted in the room of it.

Order of Experiments.	The Charge of Powder.		Vent from the Bottom of the Charge.	Chord of the ascending Arc of the Pendulum.	The Bullet struck the Target below the Axis of the Pendulum.	Chord of the Arc of the Recoil.	Velocity of the Bullet.	Remarks.
	Weight.	Height.						
No.	Grains.	Inches.	Inches.	Inches.	Inches.	Inches.	Feet in Seconds.	
								Second day.
3	208	1.8	0.0	12.6	65.0	17.8	1213	{ The pendulum gave
4	...	..	0.5	..	..	18.5	...	{ way.
5	...	..	0.0	..	..	38.68	...	{ 4 bullets were fired
6	...	..	0.5	..	..	38.48	...	{ at once. Ditto.
7	...	..	0.0	..	..	6.1	...	Without any bullet.
8	416	3.6	..	..	..	16.5	...	Ditto.
9	208	1.8	0.0	8.5	65.0	17.69	1281	{ Pendulum No. 2 { very fair third day.
10	104	0.9	..	5.2	65.25	10.18	782	
11	310	2.7	0.0	9.6	64.6	24.69	1459	}
12	...	..	1.22	10.1	65.0	24.95	1527	
13	...	..	2.65	11.85	64.75	24.9	1801	} The powder was lighted by the long
14	...	..	..	10.9	65.25	..	1646	vent-tube (Fig. 4).
15	330	2.9	2.65	10.9	61.5	26.2	1748	
16	...	..	..	13.25	63.5	..	2060	}
17	330	2.7	2.65	..	..	12.7	...	{ The barrel very { much heated.
18	...	2.9	0.0	10.4	63.5	26.3	1619	
19	...	..	..	..	63.0	26.4	1633	
20	165	1.45	0.0	6.8	62.2	14.73	1084	
21	...	..	..	6.85	..	14.2	1093	
22	...	..	1.32	6.7	..	14.8	1071	
23	...	..	..	6.3	60.6	14.58	1035	{ The short vent- { tube (*v*, Fig. 3) was
24	...	..	..	7.5	61.5	14.68	1142	{ made use of.

In order to determine how much of the force of the powder was lost by *windage*, and by the *vent*, oiled leather was fastened round the bullet, so that it now accurately fitted the bore of the piece ; and in the five experiments, from No. 35 to No. 39, inclusive, the valve-vent was made use of.

Weight of the bullet, together with the leather in which it was enveloped, 603 grains.

Order of Experiments.	The Charge of Powder.		Vent from the Bottom of the Charge.	Chord of the ascending Arc of the Pendulum.	The Bullet struck the Target below the Axis of the Pendulum.	Chord of the Arc of the Recoil.	Velocity of the Bullet.	Remarks.
	Weight.	Height.						
No.	Grains.	Inches.	Inches.	Inches.	Inches.	Inches.	Feet in Seconds.	
								Fourth day.
25	165	1.45	0.0	6.8	65.0	14.95	1004	
26	. . .	. .	. .	7.8	. .	15.6	1153	
27	. . .	. .	. .	8.05	. .	16.15	1192	
28	330	2.9	. .	10.2	63.0	26.0	1559	
29	. . .	. .	2.6	. .	64.0	28.1	1536	
30	165	3.2	. .	5.9	62.4	13.2	914	
31	. . .	1.45	1.3	6.65	62.6	15.15	1027	

Finding that the blast of the powder always reached as far as the pendulum, when large charges were used, and suspecting that this circumstance, together with the impulse of the unfired grains, might, in a great measure, occasion the apparent irregularity in the velocities of the bullets; to remedy these inconveniences, a large sheet of paper of a moderate thickness was stretched upon a square frame of wood, and interposed as a screen before the pendulum, at the distance of two feet from the surface of the target.

Two reasons conspired to induce me to prefer this method of preventing the impulse of the flame upon the pendulum, to the obvious one of removing the pendulum further from the mouth of the piece; the first was, that I was unwilling to increase the distance between the barrel and the pendulum, lest the resistance of the air might affect the velocities of the bullets; and the second, which I confess did not operate less strongly than the first, was that the length of the house did not admit of a greater distance, and I was unwilling to expose any part of the apparatus in the open air.

But the screen was found to answer perfectly well the purpose for which it was designed, and it was continued during the remainder of the experiments; the paper being replaced every third or fourth experiment.

The Experiments continued.

Order of Experiments.	The Charge of Powder.		Vent from the Bottom of the Charge.	Chord of the ascending Arc of the Pendulum.	The Bullet struck the Target below the Axis of the Pendulum.	Chord of the Arc of the Recoil.	Velocity of the Bullet.	Remarks.
	Weight.	Height.						
No.	Grains.	Inches.	Inches.	Inches.	Inches.	Inches.	Feet in Seconds.	
32	165	1.45	0	5.45	63.	15.45	839	Not leathered; weight of the bullet and wad 603 grs. In exp. No. 32 no less than 40 grains of unfired powder were driven through the screen.
33	..	..	..	...	...	12.65	839	
34	..	..	..	7.9	...	15.45	1217	In these 6 experiments the bullets were leathered and the powder was lighted by the valve-vent.
35	..	..	..	7.	60.25	15.25	1129	
36	..	..	..	7.4	62.	16.3	1161	
37	..	..	1.3	8.	61.	17.9	1277	
38	290	2.6	2.6	9.	58.6	23.5	1497	The pendulum No. 2 ruined.
39	..	..	..	...	...	24.8	...	

The bullets were now put naked into the piece, and the powder was lighted by the short vent-tube (*v*, Fig. 3), and some little improvement was made in the steel edges between which the ribbons passed that served to measure the ascending arcs of the pendulum and of the recoil, by which means the friction was lessened, and the ribbon was prevented from twisting or entangling itself as it was drawn out.

Apparatus.

The barrel with its carriage as before. The pendulum No. 3, and leaden bullets weighing 580 grains each.

Order of Experiments.	The Charge of Powder.		Vent from the Bottom of the Charge.	Chord of the ascending Arc of the Pendulum.	The Bullet struck the Target below the Axis of the Pendulum.	Chord of the Arc of the Recoil.	Velocity of the Bullet.	Remarks.
	Weight.	Height.						
No.	Grains.	Inches.	Inches.	Inches.	Inches.	Inches.	Feet in Seconds.	
								Fifth Day.
40	218	1.9	o	6.45	64.6	18.	1236	Mean velocity in these experiments and No. 47, 1225.
41	..	..	..	6.31	65.3	17.71	1197	
42	..	..	..	6.45	65.	17.91	1230	
43	..	..	1.3	6.5	64.6	18.3	1248	Mean velocity 1276.
44	..	..	..	6.75	64.5	18.35	1299	
45	..	..	..	6.6	64.9	. . .	1265	
46	..	..	..	6.4	61.6	. . .	1293	
47	..	..	o	6.3	62.	18.1	1266	
48	290	2.6	o	7.2	63.5	22.58	1414	Mean velocity 1427.
49	..	..	..	7.4	. . .	22.92	1455	
50	..	..	..	7.3	64.6	22.38	1412	
51	290	2.6	1.3	7.4	63.	23.21	1476	Mean velocity 1493.
52	..	..	..	7.6	64.	23.76	1520	
53	..	..	..	7.25	61.	23.6	1483	
54	..	..	2.6	7.5	62.3	. . .	1502	Mean velocity 1460.
55	..	..	..	7.4	64.	23.26	1450	
56	..	..	..	7.1	62.2	. . .	1433	
57	..	..	..	7.4	64.	23.56	1454	In these 4 experiments the piece was fired with powder alone, and the screen was taken away from before the pend.
58	..	..	..	1.31		11.12	—	
59	..	..	..	1.2		11.62	—	
60	..	..	o	1.16		9.62	—	
61	..	..	1.3	0.6		11.33	—	
62	330	2.9	1.3	8.	63.	26.4	1599	*Sixth Day.* Mean velocity 1625.
63	..	..	..	8.5	65.	. . .	1652	
64	..	..	2.6	7.2	59.5	25.3	1562	Mean velocity 1528.
65	..	..	..	7.7	65.	. . .	1495	
66	..	..	o	8.4	. . .	26.35	1633	Mean velocity 1594.
67	..	..	..	8.	. . .	25.8	1556	
68	218	1.9	o	6.82	64.	19.56	1349	Powder was ram'd very hard.
69	..	..	..	6.6	64.6	18.2	1294	Ditto much harder.
70	..	..	..	6.85	. . .	19.12	1345	Ditto as hard as in No. 68.
71	..	..	1.3	5.5	. . .	16.33	1080	Ditto, Ditto.
72	..	..	o	—	—	8.72	—	Gov. pow. no bullet.
73	..	..	..	—	—	8.44	—	Best double battle powder.
74	..	..	1.3	—	—	8.47	—	Government powder.
75	..	..	..	—	—	9.3	—	Double battle pow.

The following experiments, Nos. 78, 79, 80, and 81, were made in hopes of being able to discover a method of adding to the force of gunpowder. *Twenty grains* of the substances mentioned in the remarks upon each experiment were intimately mixed with the powder of the charge. In the experiment No. 82 a large wad of tow, well soaked in ethereal spirit of turpentine, was put into the piece immediately upon the bullet; and in the experiment No. 83 a wad, soaked in alcohol, was put into the piece in like manner.

Order of Experiments.	The Charge of Powder.		Vent from the Bottom of the Charge.	Chord of the ascending Arc of the Pendulum.	The Bullet struck the Target below the Axis of the Pendulum.	Chord of the Arc of the Recoil.	Velocity of the Bullet.	Remarks.
	Weight.	Height.						
No.	Grains.	Inches.	Inches.	Inches.	Inches.	Inches.	Feet in Seconds.	
								Seventh Day.
76	145	1.3	0	5.3	65.	13.25	1037	} Medium vel. 1040.
77	. .	. .	. .	. . .	64.6	13.25	1044	
78	. .	. .	. .	3.2	. . .	8.92		{ 20 grs. best alkaline salt of tartar.
79	. .	. .	. .	4.35	. . .	11.68		{ 20 grains æthiops mineral.
80	. .	. .	. .	3.3	63.6	9.83		20 grs. sal. ammon.
81	. .	. .	. .	4.2	63.4	11.45		{ 20 grs. fine brass dust.
82	. .	. .	. .	—	—	15.25	—	{ The screws which held the hooks by which the pendulum was suspended gave way, and the pendulum came down.
83	. .	. .	. .	—	—	14.35	—	

In the nine following experiments, *viz.* from No. 84 to No. 92, inclusive, the valve-vent was made use of, and the bullets were made to fit the bore of the piece very exactly by means of oiled leather, which was so firmly fastened about them that in each experiment it entered the target with the bullet.

The bullet made use of in experiment No. 85 was of wood.

Those used in the experiments No. 86 and No. 87 were formed in the following manner: a small bullet was cast of plaister of Paris, which, being thoroughly dried and well heated at the fire, was fixed in the center of the mould that served for casting all the leaden bullets used in these experiments; and melted lead being poured into this mould, the cavity that surrounded the small plaister bullet was intirely filled up, and a bullet was produced, which to the eye had every appearance of solidity, but was as much lighter than a solid leaden bullet of the same diameter as the small plaister bullet was lighter than a leaden bullet of the same size.

In the experiments No. 88 and No. 89 solid leaden bullets were made use of. In the experiment No. 90 *two* bullets were discharged at once; in the experiment No. 91 *three*, and in the experiment No. 92 *four* were used.

In each of these experiments a fresh sheet of paper was made use of as a screen to the pendulum, in order that the velocities of the bullets might be measured more accurately; and also that the quantity of unfired powder might be estimated with greater precision.

Order of Experiments.	The Charge of Powder.		Vent from the Bottom of the Charge.	Weight of the Bullet.	Chord of the ascending Arc of the Pendulum.	The Bullet struck the Target below the Axis of the Pendulum.	Chord of the Arc of the Recoil.	Velocity of the Bullet.	Remarks.
	Weight.	Height.							
No.	Grs.	Inches.	Inches.	Grains.	Inches.	Inches.	Inches.	Feet in Seconds.	
									Eighth Day.
84	145	1.3	0	—	—	—	4.5	—	In each of these 4 experiments from 50 to 70 granulæ or particles of unfired powder were driven through the screen.
85	..	..	..	90	1.33	62.2	7.16	1763	
86	..	..	..	251	2.82	63.2	9.62	1317	
87	..	..	..	354	3.32	61.2	11.3	1136	
88	..	..	..	600	6.5	65.4	15.22	1229	Very few unfired grains of powder struck the screen.
89	..	..	..	603	6.3	64.6	15.13	1229	
90	..	..	..	1184	10.12	65.	21.92	978	There were no marks of any unfired powder having reached the screen.
91	..	..	..	1754	13.65	63.4	27.18	916	
92	..	..	..	2352	16.55	63.3	32.25	833	

In the seven following experiments the piece was fired with powder only.

Order of Experiments.	The Charge of Powder.		Vent from the Bottom of the Charge.	Chord of the ascending Arc of the Pendulum.	Chord of the Arc of the Recoil.	Remarks.
	Weight.	Height.				
No.	Grains.	Inches.	Inches.	Inches.	Inches.	
93	145	1.3	0	—	4.3	
94	165	1.45	..	—	5.5	
95	..	..	..	—	5.6	
96	290	2.6	..	—	11.70	
97	437½	3.9	..	1.68	17.5	The screen was taken away.
98	..	..	..	6.7	15.88	The whole surface of the target was bespattered with unfired grs. of powder.
99	..	..	..	—	17.9	The pendulum was not observed.

In the following experiments, No. 100 and No. 101, the bullets were not put down into the bore, but were supported by three wires, which being fastened to the end of the barrel projected beyond it, and confined the bullet in such a situation that its center was in a line with the axis of the bore, and its hinder-part was one twentieth of an inch without or beyond the mouth of the piece.

In experiment No. 102 the bullet was just stuck into the barrel in such a manner that near one half of it was without the bore.

Order of Experiments.	The Charge of Powder.		Vent from the Bottom of the Charge	Chord of the ascending Arc of the Pendulum.	The Bullet struck the Target below the Axis of the Pendulum.	Chord of the Arc of the Recoil.	Velocity of the Bullet.	Remarks.
	Weight.	Height.						
No.	Grains.	Inches.	Inches.	Inches.	Inches.	Inches.	Feet in Seconds.	
100	165	1.45	o	.65	60.5	4.9	138	In each of these experiments near one-tenth part of the substance of the bullet was melted and blown away by the impulse of the flame.
101	..	..	..	.43	Uncertain.	4.8	92	
102				.86	63.	5.6	180	

All that part of the bullet which lay towards the bore of the piece appeared to be quite flat from the loss of substance it had sustained; and its surface was full of small indents, which, probably, were occasioned by the unfired grains of powder that impinged against it.

The following experiments were made with the pendulum No. 4. The rest of the apparatus as before.

Order of Experiments.	The Charge of Powder.		Vent from the Bottom of the Charge.	Chord of the ascending Arc of the Pendulum.	The Bullet struck the Target below the Axis of the Pendulum.	Chord of the Arc of the Recoil.	Velocity of the Bullet.	Remarks.
	Weight.	Height.						
No.	Grains.	Inches.	Inches.	Inches.	Inches.	Inches.	Feet in Seconds.	*Ninth Day.*
103	104	.9	0	4.51	65.	10.6	732	About 40 grains of powder were driven through the screen.
104	145	1.3	..	5.4	...	12.92	877	About 40 unfired grains of powder.
105	..	..	..	5.6	...	13.28	910	Mean velocity 894. 40 unfired grains.
106	..	1.14	..	6.18	65.8	14.3	990	Double proof battle powder; no unfired grains.
107	218	1.8	..	8.48	65.	19.68	1380	Ditto, Ditto.
108	290	2.6	..	9.45	65.6	23.9	1526	Government powder, bullet leathered; weight 602 grains.
109	..	..	..	8.73	65.2	22.8	1419	Bullet naked; very few unfired gr.
110	..	..	..	9.3	65.6	23.4	1460	Mean velocity 1444.
111	..	..	..	..	...	...	1462	
112	..	..	..	8.85	65.5	22.94	1436	
113	..	..	2.6	8.65	64.	23.7	1438	
114	..	..	..	8.5	63.6	24.1	1423	Medium veloc. 1413.
115	..	..	..	8.4	65.	23.8	1378	
116	..	2.28	..	9.15	64.	24.6	1525	Double proof battle powder.
117	437½	3.9	..	10.56	64.9	33.	1738	Gov. pow. No unfired grs. through the screen.
118	..	..	..	11.	64.5	33.3	1824	Mean vel. 1764.
119	..	..	..	10.5	65.	33.6	1729	
120	..	..	2.6	10.35	...	32.5	1706	
121	..	..	..	10.65	...	33.2	1757	Mean velocity 1751.
122	..	..	..	10.6	63.6	32.9	1789	
123	..	..	0	—	—	17.9	—	Without any bullet.

Of the Method made Use of for computing the Velocities of the Bullets.

As the method of computing the velocity of a bullet from the arc of the vibration of a pendulum into which it is fired is so well known, I shall not enlarge upon it in this place, but shall just give the theorems that have been proposed by different authors, and shall refer those who wish to see more on the subject to Mr. Robins's New Principles of Gunnery; to Professor Euler's Observations upon Mr. Robins's Book; and lastly, to Dr. Hutton's Paper on the initial Velocities of Cannon Balls, published in the Transactions of the Royal Society, for the year 1778.

If a denote the length from the axis of the pendulum to the ribbon which measures the chord of the arc of its vibration;

g the distance of the center of gravity below the axis of the pendulum;

f the distance of the center of oscillation; and

h the distance of the point struck by the bullet from that axis;

c the chord of the ascending arc of the pendulum;

P the weight of the pendulum;

b the weight of the bullet, and

v the original velocity of the bullet;

$$v = \frac{c}{a} \times \overline{\frac{Pg}{bh} + \frac{h}{f}} \times \frac{f}{\sqrt{2h}},$$

is a theorem for finding the velocity upon Mr. Robins's principles.

$$* \quad v = \frac{c}{a} \times \frac{Pg}{bh} + \frac{f+h}{2f} \times \sqrt{\frac{f}{2}},$$

is the theorem proposed by Professor Euler, who has corrected a small error in Mr. Robins's method; and

$$v = 5.672 \; cg \; \sqrt{f} \times \frac{P+b}{bha},$$

* Put the rational part $\frac{c}{a} \times \overline{\frac{Pg}{bh} + \frac{f+h}{2f}} = n$ and express f in thousandth parts of a Rhynland foot; then the velocity with which the ball strikes the pendulum will be $= \frac{n}{4} \sqrt{\frac{f}{2}}$ Rhynland feet in a second.

is Dr. Hutton's theorem, which is sufficiently accurate, and far more simple and expeditious than either of the preceding. It is to be remembered that g, h, and c may be expressed in any measure; but f must be English feet, and v will be the velocity of the bullet in English feet in a second.

The velocities of the bullets in most of the foregoing experiments were first computed by Euler's method, as I had not then seen Dr. Hutton's paper; but in going over the calculations a second time, I made use of Dr. Hutton's theorem. Both these methods gave the same velocity very nearly, but the Doctor's method is by much the easiest in practice.

In these computations care was taken to make a proper allowance for the bullets that were lodged in the pendulum, and also for the velocity lost by the bullet in passing through the screen.

The corrections necessary on account of the bullets lodged in the pendulum were made in the following manner : —

b was continually added to the value of P,

$\dfrac{h-g}{P} \times b$ "   "   "   to the value of g, and

$\dfrac{f-h}{P} \times b$ "   "   "   to the value of f.

Of the Spaces occupied by the different Charges of Powder.

The heights of the charges of powder, or the lengths of the spaces which they occupied in the bore, were determined by measurement; and in order that this might be done with greater accuracy, inches and tenths of inches were marked upon the ramrod, and the charge was gently forced down till it occupied the same space in each experiment.

The following table shews the heights of the charges as they were determined by measurement, and also their heights computed from the diameter of the bore of the piece, and the specific gravity of the powder that was used.

N. B. — By an experiment, of which I shall give an account hereafter, I found the specific gravity of this powder, shaken well together, to be to that of rain-water as 0.937 is to 1.000.

Weight of the Powder.	Height of the Charge.	
	Measured.	Computed.
Grains.	Inches.	Inches.
104	.9	0.8957
145	1.3	1.2490
165	1.45	1.4211
208	1.8	1.7914
218	1.9	1.8775
290	2.6	2.4980
310	2.7	2.6700
330	2.9	2.8422
416	3.6	3.5828
437½	3.9	3.7680

In the experiment No. 30 the powder was put into a cartridge so much smaller than the bore of the piece that the charge, instead of occupying 1.45 inches, extended 3.2 inches. By this disposition of the powder, its action upon the bullet appears to have been very much diminished.

Of the Effect that the Heat which Pieces acquire in being fired produces upon the Force of Powder.

It is very probable that the excess of the velocity of the bullet in the second experiment over that of the first was occasioned more by the heat which the barrel had acquired in the first experiment than by the position of the vent, or any other circumstance; for I have since found, upon repeated trials, that the force of any given charge of powder is considerably greater when it is fired in a piece that has been previously heated by firing, or by any other means, than when the piece has not been heated. Everybody that is acquainted with artillery knows that the recoil of great guns is much more violent after the second or third discharge than it is at first; and on shipboard, where it is necessary to attend to the recoil of the guns, in order to prevent very dangerous accidents that might be occasioned by it, the constant practice has been in our navy, and I believe on board the ships of all other nations, to lessen the quantity of powder after the first four or five rounds; our 32 pounders, for instance, are commonly fired with 14 lbs. of powder at the beginning of an action, but the charge is very soon reduced to 11 lbs., and afterwards to 9 lbs., and the filled cartridges are prepared accordingly.

By the recoil, it should seem that the powder exerted a greater force also in the fourth experiment, being the second upon the second day, than it did upon the third, or the first upon that day; but, the pendulum giving way, it was not possible to compare the velocities of the bullets in the manner we did in the two experiments mentioned above.

This augmentation of the force of powder, when it is fired in a piece that is warm, may be accounted for in the following manner. There is no substance we are acquainted with that does not require to be heated before it will burn; even gunpowder is not inflammable when it is cold. Great numbers of sparks, or red-hot particles from the flint and steel are frequently seen to light upon the priming of a musket, without setting fire to the powder, and grains of powder may be made to pass through the flame of a candle without taking fire ; and what is still more extraordinary, if large grains of powder are let fall from the height of two or three feet upon a red-hot plate of iron, laid at an angle of about 45° with the plane of the horizon, they will rebound intire, without being burnt, or in the least altered by the experiment. In all these cases the fire is too feeble, or the duration of its action is not sufficiently long to heat the powder to that degree which is necessary in order to its being rendered inflammable.

Now as gunpowder, as well as all other bodies, acquires heat by degrees, and as some space of time is taken up in this, as well as in all other operations, it follows that powder which has been warmed by being put into a piece made hot by repeated firing is much nearer that state in which it will burn, or, I may say, is more inflammable, than powder which is cold; consequently, more of it will take fire in a given short space of time, and its action upon the bullet and upon the gun will, of course, be greater.

The heat of the piece will also serve to dry the air in the bore, and to clear the inside of the gun of the moisture that collects there when it has not been fired for some time; and these circumstances doubtless contribute something to the quickness of the inflammation of the powder, and consequently to its force.

As it takes a longer time to heat a large body than a small one, it follows that meal-powder is more inflammable than that which is grained ; and the smaller the particles are, the quicker they will take fire. Sailors bruise the priming after they have put it to their guns, as they find it very difficult, without this precaution, to fire them off with a match; and if those who are fond of sporting would make use of a similar artifice, and prime their pieces with meal-powder, they would miss fire less often, — the springs of the lock might be made more tender, and its size considerably reduced without any risque, and, the violence of the blow of the flint and steel in striking fire being lessened, the piece might be fired with greater precision.

Concluding from the results of the four experiments mentioned above, as well as from the reasons just cited, that the temperature of the piece has a considerable effect upon the force of the powder, I afterwards took care to bring the barrel to a proper degree of heat by firing it once or oftener with powder, each time I recommenced the experiments after the piece had been left to cool.

Of the Manner in which Pieces acquire Heat in firing.

I was much surprised upon taking hold of the barrel immediately after the experiment No. 17, when it was fired with 330 grains of powder without any bullet, to find it so very hot that I could scarcely bear it in my hand, evidently much hotter than I had ever observed it before, notwithstanding the same charge of powder had been made use of in the two preceding experiments, and in both these experiments the piece was loaded with a bullet, which, one would naturally imagine, by confining the flame and prolonging the time of its action, would heat the barrel much more than when it was fired with powder alone.

I was convinced that I could not be mistaken in the fact, for it had been my constant practice to take hold of the piece to wipe it out as soon as an experiment was finished, and I never before had found any inconvenience from the heat in holding it. But in order to put the matter beyond all doubt, after letting the barrel cool down to the proper temperature, I repeated the experiment twice, with the same charge of powder and a bullet; and in both these trials (experiments No. 18 and No. 19), the heat of the piece was evidently much less than what it was in the experiment above mentioned (No. 17).

I now regretted exceedingly the loss of a small pocket thermometer, which I had provided on purpose to measure the heat of the barrel, but it was accidentally broken by a fall the day before I began my experiments; and, being so far from London, I had it not in my power to procure another; I was, therefore, obliged to content myself with determining the heat of the barrel as well as I could by the touch.

Being much struck with this accidental discovery of the great degree of heat that pieces acquire when they are fired with powder without any bullet, and being desirous of finding out whether it is a circumstance that obtains universally, I was very attentive to the heat of the barrel after each of the succeeding experiments; and I constantly found the heat sensibly greater when the piece was fired with powder only than when the same charge was made to impel one or more bullets.

Though the result of these experiments was totally unexpected, and even contrary to what I should have foretold, if I had been asked an opinion upon the subject previous to making them, yet, after mature consideration, I am now convinced that it is what ought to happen, and that it may be accounted for very well, upon principles that are clearly admissible.

It is certain that a very small part only of the heat that a piece of ordnance acquires in being fired is communicated to it by the flame of the powder, for the time of its action is so short (not being, perhaps, in general, longer than about $\frac{1}{200}$th or $\frac{1}{150}$th part of a second) that if its heat, instead of being 4 times, as Mr. Robins supposes, was 400 times hotter than red-hot iron, it could not sensibly warm so great a mass of metal as goes to form one of our large pieces of cannon. And besides, if the heat of the flame were sufficiently intense to produce so great an effect in so short a time, it would certainly be sufficient, not only to burn up all inflammable bodies that it came near, but also to melt the shot that it surrounded and impelled, especially when they were small, and composed of lead, or any other fusible metal ; but so far from this being the case, we frequently see the finest paper come out of the mouth of a piece uninflamed, after it has sustained the action of the fire through the whole of the bore, and the smallest lead shot is discharged without being melted.

But it may be objected here, that the bullets are always found to be very hot, if they are taken up immediately after they come out of a gun ; and that this circumstance is a proof of the intensity of the heat of the flame of powder, and of its great power of communicating heat to the densest bodies. But to this I answer, I have always observed the same thing of bullets discharged from wind-guns and cross-bows, especially when they have impinged against any hard body, and are much flattened; and bullets from muskets are always found to be hotter in proportion to the hardness of the body against which they are fired. If a musket-ball be fired into a very soft body, as (for instance) into water, it will not be found to be sensibly warmed; but if it is fired against a thick plate of iron, or any other body that it cannot penetrate, the bullet will be demolished by the blow, and the pieces of it that are dispersed about will be found to be in a state very little short of fusion, as I have often found by experience. It is not by *the flame*, therefore, that bullets are heated, but by percussion. They may indeed receive some small degree of warmth from the flame, and still more perhaps by friction against the sides of the bore, but it is in striking against hard bodies, and from the resistance they meet with in penetrating those that are softer, that they acquire by far the greater part of the heat we find in them as soon as they come to be at rest, after having been discharged from a gun.

There is another circumstance that may possibly be brought as an objection to this opinion, and that is, the running of the metal in brass guns upon repeatedly firing them, by which means the vent is often so far enlarged as to render the piece intirely useless. But this, I think, proves nothing but that brass is very easily corroded and destroyed by the flame of the gunpowder; for it cannot be supposed that in these cases the metal is ever fairly melted. The vent of a musket is very soon enlarged by firing, and after a long course of service, it is found necessary to stop it up with a solid screw, through the center of which a new vent is made of the proper dimensions. This operation is called bushing, or rather bouching, the piece; but in

all the better kind of fowling-pieces the vent is lined
or bouched with gold, and they are found to stand fire
for any length of time without receiving the least injury.
But everybody knows that gold will run with a less heat
than is required to melt iron; but gold is not liable to
be corroded by anything that can be produced in the
combustion of gunpowder; but this is not the case with
iron, and that I take to be the only reason why a vent
that is lined with gold is so much more durable than
one that is made in iron.   But it seems that iron is
more durable than brass; and perhaps steel or some
other cheap metal may be found that will supply the
place of gold, and by that means the great expence
that attends bouching pieces with that precious metal
may be spared, and this improvement may be introduced into common use.

This leads us to a very easy and effectual remedy for
that defect so long complained of in all kinds of brass
ordnance, *the running of the vent;* for if these pieces
were bouched with iron, there is no doubt but they
would stand fire as well as iron guns; and if steel, or
any other metal, either simple or compounded, should,
upon trial, be found to answer for that purpose better
than iron, it might be used instead of it; and even if
gold were made use of for lining the vent, I imagine it
might be done in such a manner as that the expence
would not be very considerable, at the same time that
the thickness of the gold should be sufficient to withstand the force of the flame for a very great length of
time.

But to return to the heat acquired by guns in firing.
It being pretty evident that it is not *all* communicated
by the flame, there is but one other cause to which it

can be attributed, and that is the *motion* and *friction* of the internal parts of the metal among themselves, occasioned by the sudden and violent effort of the powder upon the inside of the bore, and to this cause I imagine the heat is principally, if not almost intirely, owing. It is well known that a very great degree of heat may be generated in any hard and dense body in a short time by friction, and in a still shorter time by collision. " For if two dense, hard, elastic bodies be struck against each other with great force and velocity, all the parts of such bodies will every moment be closely compressed, and, being rigid, will react with equal force. Hence, a quick and powerful contraction and expansion will arise in every part, resembling that swift kind of vibration observed in stretched strings; how great these vibrations are may be learnt from the instance of a bell when struck with a single blow, by which the whole bulk, however vast, will for a long time expand and contract itself in infinite ellipses. And when the attrition above described is produced, with what force and velocity are all the particles of the rubbed body compressed, shaken, and loosened to their very intimate substance ! " * And in proportion to the swiftness of this vibration, and the violence of the attrition and friction, will be the heat that is produced.

A piece of iron that would sustain the pressure of any weight, however large, without being warmed, may be made quite hot by the blow of a hammer; and even soft and un-elastic bodies may be warmed by percussion, provided the velocity with which their parts are made to give way to the blow is sufficiently rapid. If a leaden bullet be laid upon an anvil, or on any other hard body,

* Vide Shaw's Translation of Boerhave's Chemistry, vol. i. p. 249.

and in that situation be struck with a smart blow of the hammer, it will be found to be much heated; but the same bullet, in the same situation, may be much more flattened by pressure, or by the stroke of a very heavy body moving with a small velocity, without being sensibly warmed.

To generate heat, therefore, the action of the powder on the inside of the piece must not only be sufficient to *strain the metal,* and produce a motion in its parts, but this effect must be *extremely rapid;* and the heat will be much augmented if the exertion of the force and the duration of its action are momentaneous; for in that case the fibres of the metal (if I may use the expression) that are violently stretched will return with their full force and velocity, and the swift, vibratory motion and attrition before described will be produced.

The heat generated in a piece by firing is, therefore, as the force by which the particles of the metal are strained and compressed, the suddenness with which this force is exerted, and the shortness of the time of its action; that is to say, as the strength of the powder and the quantity of the charge, the quickness of its inflammation, and the velocity with which the generated fluid makes its escape.

Now the effort of any given charge of powder upon the gun is very nearly the same, whether it be fired with a bullet or without a bullet; but the velocity with which the generated elastic fluid makes its escape is much greater when the powder is fired alone than when it is made to impel one or more bullets; the *heat* ought, therefore, to be greater in the former case than in the latter, as I found it to be by experiment.

But to make this matter still plainer, we will suppose

any given quantity of powder to be confined in a space that is just capable of containing it, and that, in this situation, it is by any means set on fire. Let us suppose this space to be the chamber of a piece of ordnance of any kind, and that a bullet or any other solid body is so firmly fixed in the bore, immediately upon the charge, that the whole effort of the powder shall not be able to remove it. As the powder goes on to be inflamed, and the elastic fluid is generated, the pressure upon the inside of the chamber will be increased, till at length, all the powder being burnt, the strain upon the metal will be at its greatest height, and in this situation things will remain, the cohesion or elasticity of the particles of metal counterbalancing the pressure of the fluid.

Under these circumstances very little heat would be generated; for the continued effort of the elastic fluid would approach to the nature of the pressure of a weight; and that *concussion, vibration,* and *friction* among the particles of the metal, which in the collision of elastic bodies is the cause of the heat that is produced, would scarcely take effect.

But, instead of being firmly fixed in its place, let the bullet now be moveable, but let it give way with great difficulty, and by slow degrees. In this case the elastic fluid will be generated as before, and will exert its whole force upon the chamber of the piece; but as the bullet gives way to the pressure, and moves on in the bore, the fluid will expand itself and grow weaker, and the particles of the metal will gradually return to their former situations; but the velocity with which the metal restores itself being but small, the *vibration* that remains in the metal, after the elastic fluid has made its escape, will be very languid, as will be the *heat* that is generated by it.

But if, instead of giving way with so much difficulty, the bullet be much lighter, so as to afford but little resistance to the elastic fluid in making its escape, or if the powder be fired without any bullet at all, then, there being little or nothing to oppose the flame in its passage through the bore, it will expand itself with an amazing velocity, and its action upon the gun will cease almost in an instant, the strained metal will restore itself with a very rapid motion, and a sharp vibration will ensue, by which the piece will be *much heated*.

Of the Effect of ramming the Powder in the Chamber of the Piece.

The charge, consisting of 218 grains of powder, being put gently into the bore of the piece in a cartridge of very fine paper without being rammed, the velocity of the bullets at a mean of the 40th, 41st, 42d, and 47th experiments was at the rate of 1225 feet in a second; but in the 68th, 69th, and 70th experiments, when the same quantity of powder was rammed down with five or six hard strokes of the ramrod, the mean velocity was 1329 feet in a second. Now the total force or pressure exerted by the charge upon the bullet is as the square of its velocity, and $\overline{1329}^2$ is to $\overline{1225}^2$ as 1.1776 is to 1, or nearly as 6 is to 5; and in that proportion was the force of the given charge of powder increased by being rammed.

In the 71st experiment the powder was also rammed, but the vent, instead of being at the bottom of the bore, was at 1.3, and the velocity of the bullet was very considerably diminished, being only at the rate of 1080 feet in a second, instead of 1276 feet in a second, which was the mean velocity with this charge and with the vent in this situation when the powder was rammed. See the experiments No. 43, 44, 45, and 46.

When, instead of ramming the powder or pressing it gently together in the bore, it is put into a space larger than it is capable of filling, the force of the charge is thereby very sensibly lessened, as Mr. Robins and others have found by repeated trials. In my 30th experiment the charge, consisting of no more than 165 grains of powder, was made to occupy 3.2 inches of the bore, instead of 1.45 inches, which space it just filled when it was gently pushed into its place without being rammed; the consequence was, the velocity of the bullet, instead of being 1100 feet in a second, or upwards, was only at the rate of 914 feet in a second, and the recoil was lessened in nearly the same proportion.

And from hence we may draw this practical inference, that the powder with which a piece of ordnance or a fire arm is charged ought always to be pressed together in the bore; and if it be rammed to a certain degree, the velocity of the bullet will be still farther increased. It is well known that the recoil of a musket is greater when its charge is rammed than when it is not; and there cannot be a stronger proof that ramming increases the force of the powder.

Of the Relation of the Velocities of Bullets to the Charges of Powder by which they are impelled.

It appears by all the experiments that have hitherto been made upon the initial velocities of bullets, that when the weights and dimensions of the bullets are the same, and they are discharged from the same piece by different quantities of powder, the velocities are nearly in the sub-duplicate ratio of the weights of the charges.

The following table will shew how accurately this law obtained in the foregoing experiments : —

Charges.	Velocities.		Difference.	No. of Exp.
	Computed.	Actual.		
$437\frac{1}{2}$	1764	1764	0	3
330	1533	1594	+ 61	2
310	1486	1459	— 27	1
290	1436	1436	0	7
218	1232	1225	— 7	4
208	1216	1256	+ 40	3
165	1083	1087	+ 4	2
145	1018	1040	+ 22	2
104	860	757	—103	2

The computed velocities as they are set down in this table were determined from the ratio of the square root of $437\frac{1}{2}$ — the weight, in grains, of the largest charge of powder — to the mean velocity of the bullet with that charge and the vent at o, *viz.*, 1764 feet in a second, and the square root of the other charges expressed in grains. And the *actual* velocities are means of all experiments that were made under similar circumstances with the given charges.

The fourth column shews the difference of the computed and actual velocities, or the number of feet in a second by which the actual velocity exceeds or falls short of the computed; and in the fifth column is set down the number of experiments with each charge from the mean of which the actual velocity was determined.

The agreement of the computed and actual velocities will appear more striking if we take the sum and difference of those velocities with all the charges except the first, thus : —

Sum of the Velocities — 1764.

Computed.	Actual.	Difference.	No. of Exp.
9864	9854	— 10	23

So that it appears that the difference or the actual velocity was smaller than the computed by $\frac{1}{985}$ part only, at a mean of 23 experiments.

But as by far the greater number of the experiments were made with the following charges, *viz.*, 290, 218, 208, 165, and 145 grains of powder, let us take the sum and difference of the computed and actual velocities of those charges, thus : —

Sum of the Velocities.

Computed.	Actual.	Difference.	No. of Exp.
5985	6044	+ 59	18

Here the agreement of the theory with the experiments is so very remarkable that we must suppose it was in some measure accidental; for the difference of the velocities in repeating the same experiment is, in general, much greater than the difference of the computed and actual velocities in this instance; but I think we may fairly conclude, from the result of all these trials, that the velocities of like *musket*-bullets, when they are discharged from the same piece by different quantities of the same kind of powder, are very nearly in the sub-duplicate ratio of the weights of the charges. Whether this law will hold good when applied to cannon-balls, and bomb-shells of large dimensions, I dare not at present take upon me to decide; but for several reasons that might be mentioned, I am rather of opinion that it will not; at least not with that degree of accuracy which obtained in these experiments.

Of the Effect of placing the Vent in different Parts of the Charge.

There have been two opinions with respect to the manner in which gunpowder takes fire. Mr. Robins supposes that the progress of its inflammation is so extremely rapid " that all the powder of the charge is fired and converted into an elastic fluid before the bullet is sensibly moved from its place "; while others have been of opinion that the progress of the inflammation is much slower, and that the charge is seldom or never completely inflamed before the bullet is out of the gun.

The large quantities of powder that are frequently blown out of fire-arms uninflamed seem to favour the opinion of the advocates for the gradual inflammation ; but Mr. Robins endeavors to account for that circumstance upon different principles ; and supports his opinion by shewing that every increase of the charge, within the limits of practice, produces a proportional increase of the velocity of the bullet ; and that when the powder is confined by a great additional weight, by firing two or more bullets at a time, instead of one, the velocity is not sensibly greater than it ought to be, according to his theory.

If this were a question merely speculative, it might not be worth while to spend much time in the discussion of it; but as it is a matter upon the knowledge of which depends the determination of many important points respecting artillery, and from which many useful improvements may be derived, too much pains cannot be taken to come at the truth. Till the manner in which powder takes fire and the velocity with which the inflammation is propagated are known, nothing can with

certainty be determined with respect to the best form
for the chambers of pieces of ordnance, or the most advantageous situation for the vent ; nor can the force of
powder, or the strength that is required in different
parts of the gun, be ascertained with any degree of
precision.

As it would be easy to determine the best situation
for the vent from the velocity of the inflammation of
powder being known, so, on the other hand, I had hopes
of being able to come at that velocity by determining
the effect of placing the vent in different parts of the
charge ; for which purpose the following experiments
were made : —

A Table of Experiments shewing the Effect of placing the
Vent in different Parts of the Charge.

Weight of the Charge of Powder.	Space occupied by the Powder.	Vent from the Bottom of the Bore.	Velocity of the Bullet at a Medium.	Recoil measured upon the Ribbon at a Medium.	No. of Exp.
Grains.	Inches.	Inches.	Feet in a Sec.	Inches.	
165	1.45	0	1087	14.465	2
. . .	. . .	1.32	1082	14.31	3
218	1.9	0	1225	17.93	4
. . .	. . .	1.3	1276	18.34	4
290	2.6	0	1427	22.626	3
. . .	. . .	1.3	1493	23.34	3
. . .	. . .	2.6	1460	23.286	4
. . .	. . .	0	1444	23.135	4
. . .	. . .	2.6	1413	24.5	3
310	2.7	0	—	24.69	1
. . .	. . .	1.32	—	24.95	1
. . .	. . .	2.65	—	24.9	1
330	2.9	0	1594	26.075	2
. . .	. . .	1.3	1625	26.4	2
. . .	. . .	2.6	1525	25.3	2
437½	3.9	0	1764	33.3	3
. . .	. . .	2.6	1751	32.866	3

By the foregoing experiments it appears that the
difference in the force of any given charge of powder

which arises from the particular situation of the vent is extremely small.

With 165 grains of powder, and the vent at o, the velocity of the bullet, at a mean of two experiments (*viz.* the 20th and 21st), was 1087 feet in a second ; and with the same charge, and the vent at 1.32 inches, the velocity, at a mean of the 22d, 23d, and 24th experiments, was 1082 feet in a second ; the difference (equal to five feet in a second) is less than what frequently occurred in a repetition of the same experiment.

With 218 grains of powder, and the vent at o, the velocity, at a mean in the 40th, 41st, 42d, and 47th experiments, was at the rate of 1225 feet in a second ; and with the same charge, and the vent at 1.3, the velocity was 1276 feet in a second, at a mean of four experiments, *viz.* the 43d, 44th, 45th, and 46th.

In the first set of experiments, with 290 grains of powder, the velocities were,

	Vent at o.	Vent at 1.3.	Vent at 2.6.
	1414	1476	1502
	1455	1520	1450
	1412	1483	1433
			1454
	3)4281	3)4479	4)5839
Means,	1427	1493	1460

See the experiments from No. 48 to No. 57, inclusive. In the second set the velocities were,

	Vent at o.	Vent at 2.6.
	1419	1438
	1460	1423
	1462	1378
	1436	
	4)5777	3)4239
Means,	1444	1413

See the experiments from No. 109 to No. 115, inclusive.

And taking the means of all the velocities in both
sets in each position of the vent, it will be,

	Vent at o	Vent at 1.3.	Vent at 2.6.
Mean Velocity,	1436	1493	1437

The mean recoils in these experiments were,

Vent at o.	Vent at 1.3.	Vent at 2.6.
22.88	23.34	23.61

In the experiments with 310 grains of powder, the
velocities of the bullets were not determined with sufficient accuracy to be depended on ; but the recoils, which
were measured with great nicety, were as follows, *viz.*

Vent at o.	Vent at 1.3.	Vent at 2.6.
24.69	24.95	24.9

With 330 grains of powder, the mean velocities and
recoils were,

	Vent at o.	Vent at 1.3.	Vent at 2.6.
Velocities,	1594	1625	1525
Recoils,	26.075	26.4	25.3

In the experiments with $437\frac{1}{2}$ grains (an ounce avoirdupois) of powder, the velocities and recoils were,

	Vent at o.		Vent at 2.6.	
	Velocity.	Recoil.	Velocity.	Recoil.
	1738	33.	1707	32.5
	1824	33.3	1757	33.2
	1728	33.6	1789	32.9
	3)5291	3)99.9	3)5253	3)98.6
Means,	1764	33.3	1751	32.866

From the result of these experiments it appears that
the effect of placing the vent in different positions with
respect to the bottom of the chamber is different in
different charges ; thus, with 165 grains of powder, the

velocity of the bullet was rather diminished by removing the vent from o, or the bottom of the bore, to 1.32;
but with 218 grains of powder, the velocity was a little
increased, as was also the recoil. With 290 grains
of powder, the velocity was greatest when the powder
was lighted at the vent 1.3, which was near the middle
of the charge, and rather greater when it was lighted at
the top, or immediately behind the bullet, than when it
was lighted at the bottom. And by the recoil it would
seem that the velocities of the bullets varied nearly in
the same manner when the charge consisted of 310
grains of powder.

With 330 grains of powder, both the velocity and
the recoil were greater when the powder was lighted at
the middle of the charge than when it was lighted at
the bottom ; but they were least of all when it was
lighted near the top. And when *an ounce* of powder
was made use of for the charge, its force was greatest
when it was lighted at the bottom. But the difference
in the force exerted by the powder, which arose from
the particular position of the vent, was in all cases so
inconsiderable (being, as I have before observed, less
than what frequently occurred in repeating the same
experiment) that no conclusion can be drawn from the
experiments except only this, that any given charge of
powder exerts nearly the same force, whatever is the
position of the vent.

And hence the following practical inference naturally
occurs, *viz.* that in the construction of fire-arms no
regard need be had to any supposed advantages that
gunsmiths and others have hitherto imagined were to be
derived from particular situations for the vent, such as
diminishing the recoil, increasing the force of the charge,

&c.; but the vent may be indifferently in any part of the chamber where it will best answer upon other accounts; and there is little doubt but the same thing will hold good in great guns, and all kinds of heavy artillery.

Almost every workman who is at all curious in fire-arms has a particular fancy with regard to the best form for the bottom of the chamber, and the proper position of the vent. They, in general, agree that the vent should be as low or far back as possible, in order, as they pretend, to lessen the recoil; but no two of them make it exactly in the same manner. Some make the bottom of the chamber flat, and bring the vent out even with the end of the breech-pin. Others make the vent slanting through the breech-pin, in such a manner as to enter the bore just in its axis. Others again make the bottom of the chamber conical; and there are those who make a little cylindric cavity in the breech-pin of about two tenths of an inch in diameter, and near half an inch in length, coinciding with the axis of the bore, and bring out the vent even with the bottom of this little cavity.

The objection to the first method is, the vent is apt to be stopped up by the foul matter that adheres to the piece after firing, and which is apt to accumulate, especially in damp weather. The same inconvenience, in a still greater degree, attends the other methods, with the addition of another, arising from the increased length of the vent; for, the vent being longer, it is not only more liable to be obstructed, but it takes a longer time for the flame to pass through it into the chamber, in consequence of which the piece is slower in going off, or, as sportsmen term it, is apt to hang fire.

The form I would recommend for the bottom of the bore is that of a hemisphere, and the vent should be brought out directly through the side of the barrel, in a line perpendicular to its axis, and pointing to the center of the hemispheric concavity of the chamber. In this case the vent would be the shortest possible; it would be the least liable to be obstructed, and the piece would be more easily cleaned than if the bottom of the bore was of any other form. All these advantages, and several others not less important, would probably be gained by making the bottom of the bore and vent of great guns in the same manner.

A new Method of determining the Velocities of Bullets.

From the equality of *action* and *reaction*, it appears that the *momentum* of a gun must be precisely equal to the momentum of its charge; or that the weight of the gun, multiplied into the velocity of its recoil, must be in all cases just equal to the weights of the bullet and of the powder (or the elastic fluid that is generated from it), multiplied into their respective velocities: for every particle of matter, whether solid or fluid, that issues out of the mouth of a piece must be impelled by the action of some power, which power must *react* with equal force against the bottom of the bore.

Even the fine, invisible, elastic fluid that is generated from the powder in its inflammation cannot put itself in motion without reacting against the gun at the same time. Thus we see pieces, when they are fired with powder alone, recoil, as well as when their charges are made to impel a weight of shot, though the recoil is not in the same degree in both cases.

It is easy to determine the velocity of the recoil in

any given case by suspending the gun in an horizontal position by two pendulous rods, and measuring the arc of its ascent by means of a ribbon, according to the method already described; and this will give the momentum of the gun (its weight being known), and consequently the momentum of its charge. But in order to determine the velocity of the bullet from the recoil, it will be necessary to find out how much the weight and velocity of the elastic fluid contributes to produce that recoil.

That part of the recoil which arises from the expansion of this fluid is always very nearly the same, whether the powder is fired alone, or whether the charge is made to impel one or more bullets, as I have found by a great variety of experiments.

If therefore a gun, suspended according to the method prescribed, be fired with any given charge of powder, but without any bullet or wad, and the recoil be observed, and if the same piece be afterwards fired with the same quantity of powder and a bullet of a known weight, the excess of the velocity of the recoil in the latter case over that in the former will be proportional to the velocity of the bullet; for the difference of these velocities, multiplied into the weight of the gun, will be equal to the weight of the bullet multiplied into its velocity.

Thus, if W be put equal to the weight of the gun,

U = the velocity of its recoil, when it is fired with any given charge of powder, without any bullet,

V = the velocity of the recoil, when the same charge is made to impel a bullet,

B = the weight of the bullet, and

v = its velocity,

It will be $$v = \frac{\overline{V - U} + W}{B}.$$

Let us see how this method of determining the velocities of bullets will answer in practice.

In the 94th experiment, the recoil, with 165 grains of powder without a bullet, was 5.5 inches, and in the 95th experiment, with the same charge, the recoil was 5.6 inches. The mean is 5.55 inches, and the length of the rods by which the barrel was suspended being 64 inches, the velocity of the recoil ($= U$), answering to 5.55 inches measured upon the ribbon, is that of 1.1358 feet in a second.

In five experiments with the same charge of powder, and a bullet weighing 580 grains, the recoil was as follows, *viz.* : —

The 20th experiment 14.73 inches.
21st	"	14.2
22d	"	14.8
23d	"	14.58
24th	"	14.68

5)73. ($= 14.6$ inches at a mean.

And the velocity of the recoil ($= V$) answering to this length (14.6 inches) is that of 2.9880 feet in a second ; consequently $V - U$, or $2.9880 - 1.1358$ is equal to 1.8522 feet in a second.

But as the velocities of the recoil are known to be as the chords of the arcs through which the barrel ascends, it is not necessary, in order to determine the velocity of the bullet, to compute the velocities V and U ; but the quantity $V - U$, or the difference of the velocities of the recoil when the given charge is fired with and without a bullet, may be computed from the value of the difference of the chords by one operation. Thus the velocity answering to the chord $9.05 = 14.6 - 5.55$ is that of 1.8522 feet in a second, which is just equal to $V - U$, as was before found.

The weight of the barrel, together with its carriage, was $47\frac{1}{4}$ pounds, to which three quarters of a pound is to be added on account of the weight of the rods by which it was suspended, which makes W = 48 pounds, or 336,000 grains; and the weight of the bullet was 580 grains. B is, therefore, to W as 580 is to 336,000, that is, as 1 is 579.31 very nearly; and $v \left(= \dfrac{\overline{V - U} \times W}{B}\right)$ is equal to $\overline{V - U} + 579.31$.

The value of $\overline{V - U}$ answering to the experiments before mentioned was found to be 1.8522, consequently the velocity of the bullets ($= v$) was $1.8522 \times 579.31 = 1073$ feet in a second, which is extremely near 1083 feet in a second, the mean of the velocities, as they were determined by the pendulum.

But the computation for determining the velocity of a bullet upon these principles may be rendered still more simple and easy in practice; for the velocities of the recoil being as the chords measured upon the ribbon, if

c be put equal to the end of the chord of the recoil, expressed in English inches, when the piece is fired with powder only,

and C = the chord when a bullet is discharged by the same charge,

then $C - c$ will be as $V - U$, and consequently as $\dfrac{V - U \times W}{B}$, which measures the velocity of the bullet; the ratio of W to B remaining the same.

If, therefore, we suppose a case in which $C - c$ is equal to one inch, and the velocity of the bullet be computed from that chord, the velocity in any other case in which $C - c$ is greater or less than one inch, will be found by multiplying the difference of the chords C and c by the velocity that answers to a difference of one inch.

The length of the parallel rods by which the barrel was suspended being 64 inches, the velocity of the recoil answering to $C - c = 1$ inch, measured upon the ribbon, is 0.204655 parts of a foot in a second; and this is also, in this case, the value of $V - U$; the velocity of the bullet is therefore $v = 0.204655 \times 579.31 = 118.35$ feet in a second.

Consequently the velocity of the bullet, expressed in feet *per* second, may, in all cases, be found by multiplying the difference of the chords C and c by 118.35, the weight of the barrel, the length of the rods by which it is suspended, and the weight of the bullet remaining the same; and this, whatever the charge of powder may be that is made use of, and however it may differ in strength or goodness.

According to this rule, the velocities of the bullets in the following experiments have been computed from the recoil; and by comparing them with the velocities shewn by the pendulum, we shall be enabled to judge of the accuracy of this new method of determining the velocities of bullets.

In the 76th and 77th experiments, when the piece was fired with 145 grains of powder and a bullet, the recoil was 13.25 and 13.15, or 13.2 at a mean; and with the same charge of powder, without a bullet, the recoil was 4.5 and 4.3, or 4.4 at a mean (see the 84th and 93d experiments).

$C - c$ is therefore $13.2 - 4.4 = 8.8$ inches, and the velocity of the bullets $= 8.8 \times 118.35 = 1045$ feet in a second. The mean of the velocities as they were determined by the pendulum is that of 1040 feet in a second. In the 104th and 105th experiments, the recoil was 12.92 and 13.28, and the velocity computed from the mean of those chords is 1030 feet in a second ; but the velocity shewn by the pendulum was no more than about 900 feet in a second. As the recoil was so nearly equal to what it was in the 76th and 77th experiments before mentioned, when the velocities shewn by the recoil and by the pendulum were almost exactly the same, I am inclined to believe that there must have been some mistake in determining the velocities by the pendulum in these last experiments, and that the velocity shewn by the recoil is most to be depended on.

With 290 grains, or half the weight of the bullet in powder, in the 48th, 49th, and 50th experiments, the recoil was 22.58, 22.92, and 22.38 ; and the recoil with the same charge of powder, without a bullet, at a mean of the 60th and 96th experiments, was 10.66. The mean of the velocities of the bullets computed from the recoil is therefore 1416 feet in a second, and the velocity shewn by the pendulum was 1427 feet in a second ; the difference is not considerable. The mean of the velocities in the 109th, 110th, 111th, 112th experiments is by the recoil 1464, and by the pendulum 1444 feet in a second.

With 330 grains of powder the velocities of the bullets appear to have been as follows, *viz.* : —

	Vent at 0.	Vent at 1.3.	Vent at 2.6.
By the Recoil,	1543	1620	1610
By the Pendulum,	1594	1625	1528

See the 62d, 63d, 64th, 65th, 66th, 67th, and 17th experiments.

The *uniformity of the recoil* was in all cases very remarkable. Thus, in the first set of experiments with

290 grains of powder (from the 48th to the 57th experiment inclusive), the recoil was,

Vent at 0.	Vent at 1.3	Vent at 2.6.
22.58	23.21	23.06
22.92	23.76	23.26
22.38	23.06	23.26
		23.56
3)67.88	3)70.03	4)93.14
Means = 22.626	23.343 and	23.285

If now we take a mean of the 60th and 96th experiments, and call the recoil, without a bullet, 10.66, as before, the velocities will turn out,

	Vent at 0.	Vent at 1.3.	Vent at 2.6.
By the recoil,	1416	1501	1494
And by the pendulum they were	1427	1493	1460
The difference is only	— 11	+ 8	+ 34

The recoil was equally regular in the 117th and five succeeding experiments, when the charge was no less than $437\frac{1}{2}$ grs. = 1 ounce avoirdupois in powder; and the velocities of the bullets determined from the recoil are very nearly the same as they were shewn by the pendulum. Thus, in the 117th, 118th, and 119th experiments the mean recoil was 33.3 : and in the 120th, 121st, and 122d experiments it was 32.866. And if the recoil without a bullet be called 17.9, as it was determined by the 123d experiment, which was made immediately after the experiments before mentioned, then will the velocities be,

	Vent at 0.	Vent at 2.6.
By the recoil,	1822	1771
And by the pendulum they were	1764	1751
The difference is only	+ 58 and	+ 20 feet

in a second, which is less than what frequently occurs in repeating the same experiment.

In the 11th, 12th, 13th, and 14th experiments, when the piece was fired with 310 grains of powder and a bullet, the recoil was 24.69, 24.95, 24.9, and 24.9 : and in the 15th, 16th, 18th, and 19th experiments, with 330 grains of powder, the recoil was 26.2, 26.2, 26.3, and 26.4. The regularity of these numbers is very striking; and though we cannot compare the velocities of the bullets determined by the two methods, as we have done in other cases (as there are reasons to believe that the velocities, as they are set down in the tables, are not much to be depended on, and as the recoil, with the given charge of 310 grains of powder, without a bullet, is not known), yet the regularity of the recoil in these experiments affords good grounds to conclude that the method of determining the velocities of bullets founded upon it must be very accurate.

But of all the experiments those numbered from 84 to 92, inclusive, afford the strongest proof of the accuracy of this method. In those, every possible precaution was taken to prevent errors arising from adventitious circumstances; and the weights of the bullets and their velocities were so various that the uniform agreement of the two methods of determining the velocities, in those trials, amounts almost to a demonstration of the truth of the principles upon which this new method is founded.

By the following table the result of these experiments may be seen at one view.

The Experiments.	Weight of the Bullets.	The Barrel heavier than the Bullet.	The Recoil.	Velocity of the Bullet.		Difference.
				By the Recoil.	By the Pendulum.	
	Grs.	$\dfrac{W}{B} =$	$C =$	$v =$	$v =$	
84th and 93d	——	——	$(c = 4.4)$	———	——	——
85th	90	3733.3	7.16	2109	1763	$+346$
86th	251	1338.6	9.62	1430	1317	$+113$
87th	354	949.15	11.03	1288	1136	$+152$
88th	600	560.	15.22	1240	1229	$+ 11$
89th	603	557.22	15.13	1224	1229	$- 5$
90th	1184	283.78	21.92	1017	978	$+ 39$
91st	1754	191.56	27.18	893	916	$- 23$
92d	2352	141.86	32.25	812	833	$- 21$

The charge of powder consisted of 145 grains in weight in each experiment.

In order to shew in a more striking manner the result of these experiments and the comparison of the two methods of ascertaining the velocities of bullets, I have drawn the Fig. 16 where the numbers that are marked upon the line AB are taken from A towards B, in proportion to the weights of the bullets; while the lines drawn from those numbers, perpendicular from AB (as w, v, for instance at the number 2352) and ending at the curve c, d, express their velocities as shown by the pendulum. The continuations of those lines on the opposite side of the line A B shew the recoil, and also the velocities of the bullets as determined from it: thus w, r, and the (dotted) lines parallel to it, which end at the line g, f, express the recoil; and the portion of each of those lines that is comprehended between the line A B and the curve m, n, (as w, u,) is as the velocity of the bullet in the several experiments. The line A, e, denotes the weight of the charge of powder; and the line A, m, the velocity with which the elastic fluid escapes out of the piece, when the powder is fired without any bullet.

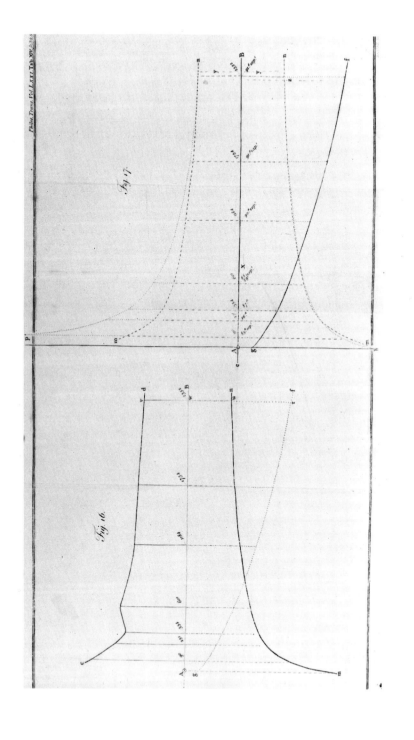

Fig. 17.

Fig. 16.

Upon an inspection of this figure, as well as from an examination of the foregoing table, it appears that the velocities determined by the two methods agree with great nicety in all the experiments after the 87th; but in the 87th experiment and also in the 86th, but particularly in the 85th, the difference in the result of these different methods is very considerable : and it is remarkable that in those experiments, where they disagree most, the velocities of the bullets, as determined by the pendulum, are extremely irregular; while, on the other hand, the gradual increase of the recoil as the bullets were heavier, and the great regularity of the corresponding velocities, afford good grounds to conclude that this disagreement is not owing to any inaccuracy in the new method of ascertaining the velocities, but to some other cause, which remains to be investigated.

But before we proceed in this inquiry, let us separate the five last experiments in the foregoing table; and summing up the velocities determined by the two methods, we shall see by their difference how those methods agreed, upon the whole, in this instance.

		Velocity.		
Experiments.	Weight of the Bullets.	By the Recoil.	By the Pendulum.	Difference.
	Grs.			
88th	600	1240	1229	+ 11
89th	603	1224	1229	— 5
90th	1184	1017	978	+ 39
91st	1754	893	916	— 23
92d	2352	812	833	— 21
Sums & diff. of the Velocities,		5186	5185	+ 1

Here the difference in the result of the two methods does not amount to $\frac{1}{5000}$th part of the whole velocity; but I lay no stress upon this extraordinary argument. I am sensible that it must in some degree have been accidental; but as the difference in the velocities, computed by these different methods, was in no instance considerable, not being in any case so great as what frequently occurred in the most careful repetition of the same experiment, and as the velocities, as determined by the recoil, were much more regular than those shewn by the pendulum, as appears by comparing the curves, *g*, *f*, and *m*, *n*, (Fig. 16) with the crooked line *c*, *d*, I think we may fairly conclude that this new method may with safety be relied on in practice.

The greatest difference in the velocities, as ascertained by the two methods, appears in the instance of the 85th experiment, where the velocity, determined from the recoil, exceeds that shewn by the pendulum, by 346 feet in a second, the former velocity being that of 2109 feet in a second, the latter only 1763 feet in a second; and in the two succeeding experiments, the velocities shewn by the pendulum are likewise deficient, though not in so great a degree.

This apparent deficiency remains now to be accounted for; and first, it cannot be supposed that it arose from any imperfection in Mr. Robins's method of determining the velocities of bullets, for that method is founded upon such principles as leave no room to doubt of its accuracy ; and the practical errors that occur in making the experiments, and which cannot be entirely prevented, or exactly compensated, are in general so small that the difference of the velocities in question cannot be attributed to them. It is true the effect of those errors is more likely to appear in experiments made under such circumstances as those under which the experiments we are now speaking of were made, than in any other case; for the bullets being very light, the arc of the ascent of the pendulum was but small, and a small mistake in measuring the chord upon the ribbon would have produced a very considerable error in computing the velocity of the bullet; thus, a difference of one tenth of an inch, more or less, upon the ribbon in the 85th experiment would have made a difference in the velocity of more than 120 feet in a second. But independent of the pains that were taken to prevent mistakes, the striking agreement of the velocities determined by the two methods in the experiments which immediately follow, as also in all other cases where they could be compared, affords abundant reason to conclude that the errors arising from those causes were in no instance very considerable.

But if both methods of ascertaining the velocities of bullets are to be relied on, then the difference of the velocities, as determined by them, in these experiments, can only be accounted for by supposing that it arose from their having been diminished by the resistance of the air in the passage of the bullets from the mouth of the piece to the pendulum; and this suspicion will be much strengthened when we consider how great the resistance is that the air opposes to bodies that move very swiftly in it, and that the bullets in these experiments were not only projected with great velocities, but were also very light, and consequently more liable to be retarded by the resistance on that account.

To put the matter beyond all doubt, let us see what the resistance was that these bullets met with, and how much their velocities were diminished by it. The weight of the bullet (in the 85th experiment) was 90 grains; its diameter was 0.78 of an inch, and it was projected with a velocity of 2109 feet in a second.

If now a computation be made according to the method laid down by Sir Isaac Newton for compressed fluids, it will be found that the resistance to this bullet was not less than $8\frac{1}{2}$ lbs. avoirdupois, which is something more than 660 times its weight. But Mr. Robins has shewn, by experiment, that the resistance of the air to bodies moving in it with very great velocity is near three times greater than Sir Isaac has determined it, and as the velocity with which this bullet was impelled is considerably greater than any in Mr. Robins's experiments, it is highly probable that the resistance in this instance was at least 2000 times greater than the weight of the bullet.

The distance from the mouth of the piece to the pendulum, as we have before observed, was 12 feet; but, as there is reason to think that the blast of the powder, which always follows the bullet, continues to act upon it for some sensible portion of time after it is out of the bore, and by urging it on counterbalances, or at least counteracts, in a great measure the resistance of the air, we will suppose that the resistance does not begin, or rather that the motion of the bullet does not begin to be retarded, till it has got to the distance of two feet from the muzzle. The distance, therefore, between the barrel and the pendulum, instead of 12 feet, is to be estimated at 10 feet; and as the bullet took up about $\frac{1}{192}$ part of a second in running over that space, it must, in that time, have lost a velocity of about 335 feet in a second, as will appear upon making the computation, and this will very exactly account for the apparent diminution of the velocity in the experiment; for the difference of the velocities, as determined by the recoil and by the pendulum, $= 2109 - 1763 = 346$ feet in a second, is extremely near 335 feet in a second, — the diminution of the velocity by the resistance as here determined.

If the diminution of the velocities of the bullets in the two subsequent experiments be computed in like manner, it will turn out in the 86th experiment $= 65$ feet in a second, and in the 87th experiment $= 33$ feet in a second; and making these corrections, the comparison of the two methods of ascertaining the velocities will stand thus : —

	85th Exp.	86th Exp.	87th Exp.
Velocities shown by the pendulum,	1763	1317	1136
Add the diminution of the velocity by the resistance of the air,	335	65	33
Making together	2098	1382	1169
Velocity by the recoil,	2109	1430	1288
The difference =	+11	+48	+119

So that it appears, notwithstanding these corrections, that the velocities in the 86th and 87th experiments, and particularly in the last, as they were determined by the pendulum, are still considerably deficient.   But the manifest irregularity of the velocities in those instances affords abundant reason to conclude that it must have arisen from some extraordinary accidental cause, and, therefore, that little dependence is to be put upon the result of those experiments.   I cannot take upon me to determine positively what the cause was which produced this irregularity; but I strongly suspect that it arose from the breaking of the bullets in the barrel by the force of the explosion; for these bullets, as has already been mentioned, were formed of lead, inclosing lesser bullets of plaster of Paris; and I well remember to have observed at the time several small fragments of the plaster, which had fallen down by the side of the

pendulum. I confess I did not then pay much attention to this circumstance, as I naturally concluded that
it arose from the breaking of the bullet in penetrating
the target of the pendulum, and that the small pieces of
plaster I saw upon the ground had fallen out of the
hole by which the bullet entered. But if the bullets
were not absolutely broken in pieces in the firing, yet if
they were considerably bruised, and the plaster, or a
part of it, were separated from the lead, such a change
in their form might produce a great increase of the resistance, and even their initial velocities might be affected
by it; for their form being changed from that of a globe
to some other figure, they might not fit the bore, and
a part of the force of the charge might be lost by the
windage.

That this actually happened in the 87th experiment
seems very probable, as the velocity with which the bullet was projected, even as it was determined by the recoil,
is considerably less, in proportion, in that experiment,
than in either of those that precede it in that set, or in
those which follow it, as will appear upon inspecting the
curvature of the line m, n, Fig. 16. But I forbear to
insist further upon this matter.

As I have made an allowance for the resistance of the
air in these experiments, it may be expected that I
should do it in all other cases; but I think it will appear, upon inquiry, that the diminution of the velocities
of the bullets on that account was, in general, so inconsiderable that it might safely be neglected; thus, for
instance, in the experiments with an ounce of powder,
when the velocity of the bullet was more than 1750
feet in a second, the diminution turns out no more
than about 25 or 30 feet in a second, though we sup-

pose the full resistance to have begun so near as two feet from the mouth of the piece; and in all cases where the velocities were less, the effect of the resistance was less in a much greater proportion; and even in this instance there is reason to think that the diminution of the velocity, as we have determined it, is too great; for the flame of gunpowder expands with such an amazing rapidity that it is scarcely to be supposed but that it follows the bullet and continues to act upon it more than two feet, or even four feet, from the gun, and when the velocity of the bullet is less, its action upon it must be sensible at a still greater distance.

With 218 grains of powder, the recoil appears to have been very uniform; but if the velocities of the bullets are determined from the recoil in the 40th and seven following experiments, when this charge was made use of, and from the recoil without a bullet in the 72d and 73d experiments, the velocities will turn out considerably too small, as we shall see by making the computation.

		Vent at o.	Vent at 1.3.
	40th exp. was 18.	and in the 43d exp. it was 18.3
The recoil	41st	17.71	44th 18.35
in the	42d	17.91	45th 18.35
	47th	18.1	46th 18.35
		4)71.72	4)73.35
Means =		17.93	and 18.34

And in the 72d and 73d experiments the recoil, with the same charge without a bullet, was 8.72 and 8.47 = 8.595 at a medium; the velocities therefore turn out,

	Vent at o.	Vent at 1.3.
By the recoil	1105	1153
instead of	1225	and 1276 as they were shown by the pend.

The diff. 120 and 123 feet in a second amounts to near one twelfth part of the whole velocity.

This difference is undoubtedly owing to the recoil without a bullet being taken too great, for it is not only greater than it ought to be, in order that the velocities of the bullets may come out right, but it is considerably greater in proportion than the recoil with any other charge.

Thus, with 145 grains of powder the recoil was 4.4
with 165 grains   it was   5.55
      290 grains   10.66
      330 grains   12.7
and with $437\frac{1}{2}$ grains   it was 17.9

And if the recoil with 218 grains is determined from these numbers by interpolation, it comes out 7.5; and with that value for C, the velocities of the bullets in the before-mentioned experiments appear to be,

	Vent at o.		Vent at 1.3.	
	1243	and	1283	by the recoil
which is extremely near	1225	and	1276	the velocities
shown by the pendulum.				

It is to be remembered, that the 72d and 73d experiments, from which we before determined the recoil with the given charge of powder without a bullet, were not made upon the same day with the experiments before mentioned; and it is well known that the force of powder is different upon different days. And it is worthy of remark, that in those two experiments the strength of government powder appeared to be considerably the greatest. I mention these circumstances to shew the probability there is that the recoil in those experiments, from some unknown cause, was greater than it ought to have been, or rather than it would have been had the experiments been made at the same time when the experiments with the bullets were made, or at any other time under the same circumstances.

As this method of determining the velocities of the bullets did not occur to me till after I had finished the course of my experiments, and had taken down my apparatus, I have not had an opportunity of ascertaining the recoil with and without a bullet with that degree of precision that I could wish. If I had thought of it sooner, or if I had recollected that passage in Mr. Robins's new Principles of Gunnery where he says, "The part of the recoil arising from the expansion of the powder alone is found to be no greater when it impels a leaden bullet before it than when the same quantity is fired without any wad to confine it,"— I say, if that passage had occurred to me before it had been too late, I certainly should have taken some pains to have ascertained the fact; but as it is, I think enough has been done to shew that there is the greatest probability that the velocities of bullets may, in all cases, be determined by the recoil with great accuracy; and I hope soon to have it in my power to put the matter out of all doubt, and to verify this new method by a course of conclusive experiments, which I am preparing for that purpose.

In the mean time I would just observe, that if this method should be found to answer when applied to musket bullets, it cannot fail to answer equally well when it is applied to cannon balls and bomb shells of the largest dimensions; and it is apprehended that it will be much preferable to any method hitherto made public; not only as it may be applied indifferently to all kinds of military projectiles, and that with very little trouble and expence in making the experiment; but also, because by it the velocities with which bullets are *actually projected* are determined; whereas by the pendulum their velocities can only be ascertained at some distance from the gun, and after they have lost a part of their initial velocities by the resistance of the air through which they are obliged to pass to arrive at the pendulum.

At the trifling expence of ten or fifteen pounds, an apparatus might be constructed that would answer for making the experiments with all the different kinds of ordnance in the British service. The advantages that might be derived from such a set of experiments are too obvious to require being mentioned.

Of a very accurate Method of proving Gunpowder.

All the *éprouvettes*, or powder-triers, in common use are defective in many respects. Neither the absolute force of gunpowder can be determined by means of them, nor the comparative force of different kinds of it, but under circumstances very different from those in which the powder is made use of in service.

As the force of powder arises from the action of an elastic fluid that is generated from it in its inflammation, the quicker the charge takes fire, the more of this fluid will be generated in any given short space of time, and the greater of course will be its effect upon the bullet. But in the common method of proving gunpowder, the weight by which the powder is confined is so great in proportion to the quantity of the charge, that there is time quite sufficient for the charge to be all inflamed, even when the powder is of the slowest composition, before the body to be put in motion can be sensibly removed from its place. The experiment, therefore, may shew which of two kinds of powder is the strongest when equal quantities of both are confined in equal spaces, and *completely inflamed;* but the degree of inflammability, which is a property essential to the goodness of the powder, cannot by these means be ascertained.

Hence it appears how powder may answer to the proof, such as is commonly required, and may nevertheless turn out very indifferent when it comes to be used in service. And this, I believe, frequently happens; at least I know that complaints from officers of the badness of our powder are very common; and I would suppose that no powder is ever received by the Board of Ordnance but such as has gone through the established examination, and has answered to the usual test of its being of the standard degree of strength.

But though the common powder-triers may shew powder to be better than it really is, they never can make it appear to be worse than it is. It will therefore always be the interest of those who manufacture that commodity to adhere to the old method of proving it; but the purchaser will find his account in having it examined in a manner by which its goodness may be ascertained with greater precision.

The method I would recommend is as follows. A quantity of powder being provided, which from any previous examination or trial is known to be of a proper degree of strength to serve as a standard for the proof of other powder, a given charge of it is to be fired, with a fit bullet, in a barrel suspended by two pendulous rods, according to the method before described, and the recoil is to be carefully measured upon the ribbon; and this experiment being repeated three or four times, or oftener, if there should be any considerable difference in the recoil, the mean and the extremes of the chords may be marked upon the ribbon, by black lines drawn across it, and the word *proof* may be written upon the middle line; or if the recoil be uniform (which it will be, to a sufficient degree of accuracy, if care is taken to make the experiments under the same circumstances), then the *proof mark* is to be made in that part of the ribbon to which it was constantly drawn out by the recoil in the different trials.

The recoil with a known charge of standard powder being thus ascertained, and marked upon the ribbon, let an equal quantity of any other powder (that is to be proved) be fired in the same barrel, with a bullet of the same weight, and every other circumstance alike, and if the ribbon is drawn out as far or farther than the proof mark, the powder is as good or better than the standard; but if it falls short of that distance, it is worse than the standard, and is to be rejected.

For the greater the velocity is with which the bullet is impelled, the greater will be the recoil; and when the recoil is the same, the velocities of the bullets are equal, and the powder is of the same degree of strength if the quantity of the charge is the same. And if care is taken in proportioning the charge to the weight of the bullet, to come as near as possible to the medium proportion that obtains in practice, the determination of the goodness of gunpowder from the result of this experiment cannot fail to hold good in actual service.

Fig. 14 represents the proposed apparatus drawn to a scale of one foot to the inch. *a, b,* is the barrel suspended by the pendulous rods *c, d;* and *r* is the ribbon for measuring the recoil.

The length of the bore is 30 inches, and its diameter is one inch, consequently it is just 30 calibres in length, and will carry a leaden bullet of about 3 ounces.

The barrel may be made of gun-metal, or of cast-iron, as that is a cheaper commodity; but great care must be taken, in boring it, to make the cylinder perfectly straight and smooth, as well as to preserve the proper dimensions. Of whatever metal the barrel is made, it ought to weigh at least 50 lbs., in order that the velocity of the recoil may not be too great; and the rods by which it is suspended should be five feet in length. The vent may be about one twentieth of an inch in diameter; and it should be *bouched* or lined with gold, in the same manner as the touchhole is made in the better kind of fowling-pieces, in order that its dimensions may not be increased by repeated firing.

The bullets should be made to fit the bore with very little windage; and it would be better if they were all cast in the same mould and of the same parcel of lead, as in that case their weights and dimensions would be more accurately the same, and the experiments would of course be more conclusive.

The stated charge of powder may be half an ounce, and it should always be put up in a cartridge of very fine paper; and after the piece is loaded it should be primed with other powder, first taking care to prick the cartridge by thrusting a priming-wire down the vent.

As it appears, from several experiments made on purpose to ascertain the fact, that ramming the powder more or less has a very sensible effect to increase or diminish the force of the charge, to prevent any inaccuracies that might arise from that cause, a ramrod such as is represented Fig. 15 may be made use of. It is to be made of a cylindrical piece of wood in the same manner as ramrods in general are made, but with the addition of a ring, C, about one inch and a half or two inches in diameter, which, being placed at a proper distance from the end (*a*) of the ramrod that goes up into the bore, will prevent its being thrust up too far. This ring may be made of wood or of any kind of metal, as shall be found most convenient. The other end of the ramrod (*b*) may be 31 or 32 inches in length from the ring, and the extremity of it being covered with a proper substance, it may be made use of for wiping out the barrel after each experiment.

The machine (*f*) for the tape to slide through may be the same as that described by Dr. Hutton in his account of his experiments on the initial velocities of cannon balls, as his method is much better calculated to answer the purpose than that proposed and made use of by Mr. Robins. It will also be better for the axis of each of the pendulous rods to rest upon level pieces of wood or iron, than for them to move in circular grooves ; care must however be taken to confine them by staples, or by some other contrivance, to prevent their slipping out of their places.

The trunnions, by means of which the barrel is connected with the pendulous rods and upon which it is supported, should be as small as possible, in order to lessen the friction ; and for the same reason they should be well polished, as well as the grooves which receive them. They need not be cast upon the barrel, but may be screwed into it after it is finished.

In making the experiments, regard must be had to the heat of the barrel as well as to the temperature and state of the atmosphere ; for heat and cold, dryness and moisture, have very sensible effects upon gunpowder, to increase or diminish its force. If therefore a very great degree of accuracy is at any time required, it will be best to begin by firing the piece two or three times, merely to warm it; after which three or four experiments may be made with standard powder, to determine anew the proof mark (for the strength of the same powder is different upon different days); and when this is done, the experiments with the powder that is to be proved are to be made, taking care to preserve the same interval of time between the firings, that the heat of the piece may be the same in each trial.

If all these precautions are taken, and if the bullets are of the same weight and dimensions, powder may be proved by this method with much greater accuracy than has hitherto been done by any of the methods hitherto used for that purpose.

Of the comparative Goodness, or Value, of Powder of different Degrees of Strength.

Let V denote the velocity of the bullet with the stronger powder, and put v equal to the velocity with the weaker, when the charges are equal, and the weight and dimensions of the bullets are the same, and when they are discharged from the same piece. If the charge is augmented when the weaker powder is made use of, till the velocity of the bullet is increased from v to V, or till it becomes equal to the velocity with the given charge of the stronger powder, the *value* of the charges may then be said to be equal; and consequently the weaker powder is as much worse than the stronger — or is of less value — in proportion as the quantity of it, by the pound, required to produce the given effect is greater.

But we have seen that the velocities, with different quantities of the same kind of powder, are in the *subduplicate ratio* of the weights of the charges. The

charges, therefore, must be as the squares of the velocities, and consequently the charge of the weaker powder
must be to that of the stronger, when the velocities are
equal, as VV is to *vv*. The weaker powder is therefore
as much worse than the stronger as VV is greater than
vv; or the comparative goodness of powder of different degrees of strength is as the squares of the velocities of the bullets, when the charges are equal.

The mean velocity of the bullets, as shewn by the
pendulum, in the 104th and 105th experiments, when
the piece was fired with 145 grains of government powder, was 894 feet in a second; and with the same quantity of *double proof** battle powder (experiment No. 106),
the velocity was 990 feet in a second. Now the squares
of these velocities (which, as we just observed, measure
the goodness of the powder) are to each other as 1 is to
1.2263, or nearly as 5 is to 6.

With 218 grains of government powder, the mean
velocity in four experiments (*viz.* the 40th, 41st, 42d,
and 43d) was 1225 feet in a second; and in the experiment No. 107, when the same quantity of *double proof*
battle powder was made use of, the velocity was 1380
feet in a second; and $\overline{1225}^2$ is to $\overline{1380}^2$ as 1 is to 1.2691.

With 290 grains, or half the weight of the bullet in
government powder in the 109th, 110th, 111th, and 112th
experiments, the mean velocity of the bullet was 1444
feet in a second; but with the same quantity of the battle powder (experiment No. 116), the velocity was 1525
feet in a second; $\overline{1444}^2$ is to $\overline{1525}^2$ as 1 is to 1.1153.

By taking a medium of these trials it appears that
double proof battle powder is better than government

* This is called *battle* powder, not because it is used in battle or in war, but from
Battle, the name of a village in Kent, where that kind of powder is made.

powder, in proportion as 1.2036 is to 1, or nearly as 6 is to 5.

But if, instead of weighing the powder, we estimate the quantity of the charge by measurement, or the space it occupies in the bore of the piece, the comparative strength of battle powder will appear to be considerably greater, or its strength will be to that of government powder nearly as 4 is to 3 ; for the grains of this better kind of powder being more compact, and nearly of a spherical form, a greater weight of it will lie in any given space than of government powder, which is formed more loosely, and of various and of very irregular figures.

Now the common price of double proof battle powder, as it is sold by the wholesale dealers in that commodity, is at the rate of £ 10 *per* cwt. net, which is just two shillings by the pound ; while government is sold at £ 5 5s. *per* hundred, or one shilling and $\frac{6}{10}$th of a penny *per* pound ; but battle powder is better than government powder only in the proportion of 1.2036 to 1, or of one shilling and two pence to one shilling and $\frac{6}{10}$th of a penny ; battle powder is therefore sold at the rate of ten pence by the pound, or 41⅔ *per cent.* dearer than it ought to be ; or those who make use of it in preference to government powder do it at a certain loss of 41⅔ *per cent.* of the money that the powder costs them.

Of the Relation of the Velocities of Bullets to their Weights.

According to Mr. Robins's theory, when bullets of the same diameter but different weights are discharged from the same piece, by the same quantity of powder, their *velocities* should be in the *reciprocal sub-duplicate ratio of their weights;* but as this theory is founded upon a supposition that the action of the elastic fluid generated from the powder, is always the same in any and every given part of the bore, when the charge is the same, whatever may be the weight of the bullet, and as no allowance is made for the expenditure of force required to put the fluid itself in motion or for the loss of it by the vent, it is plain that the theory is defective. It is true, Dr. Hutton in his experiments found this law to obtain without any great error, and possibly it may hold good with sufficient accuracy in many cases ; for it sometimes happens that a number of errors, or actions, whose operations have contrary tendencies, so compensate each other that their effects, when united, are not sensible. But when this is the case, if any one of the causes of error be removed, those which remain will be detected.

When any given charge is loaded with a heavy bullet, more of the powder is inflamed in any very short space of time than when the bullet is lighter, and the action of the powder ought, of course, to be greater on that account ; but then, a heavy bullet takes up more time in passing through the bore than a light one, and consequently more of the elastic fluid generated from the powder escapes by the vent and by windage. It may happen that the augmentation of the force on account of one of these circumstances may exactly counterbalance the diminution of it arising from the other ; and if it should be found upon trial that this is the case in general, in pieces as they are now constructed, and with all the variety of shot that are made use of in practice, it would be of great use to know the fact: and possibly it might answer as well, as far as it relates to the art of gunnery, as if we were perfectly acquainted with, and were able to appreciate, the effect of each varying circumstance, under which an experiment can be made. But when, concluding too hastily from the result of a partial experiment, we suppose, with Mr. Robins, that, because the sum total of the action or pressure of the elastic fluid upon the bullet, during the time of its passage through the bore, happens to be the same when bullets of different weights are made use of (which collective pressure is in all cases proportional to, and is accurately measured by, the velocity, or rather motion, communicated to the bullet), that, *therefore,* the pressure in any given part is always exactly the same when the quantity of powder is the same with which the piece is fired; and from thence endeavour to prove that the inflammation of gunpowder is instantaneous, or that the whole charge is, in all cases, inflamed and "converted into an elastic fluid before the bullet is sensibly moved from its place," — such reasonings and conclusions may lead to very dangerous errors.

It is undoubtedly true, that if the principles assumed by Mr. Robins, with respect to the manner in which gunpowder takes fire, and the relation of the elasticity of the generated fluid to its density, or the intensity of its pressure upon the bullet, as it expands in the barrel, were just, and if the loss of force by the vent and by windage were in all cases inconsiderable, or if it were prevented, the deductions from the theory respecting the velocities of bullets of different weights would always hold good. But if, on the contrary, it should be found upon making the experiments carefully, and in such a manner as entirely to prevent inaccuracies arising from adventitious circumstances, that the velocities observe a law different from that which the theory supposes, we may fairly conclude that the principles upon which the theory is founded are erroneous.

Let us now see how far these experiments differ from the theory. Those numbered from 84 to 92 inclusive were made in such a manner that no part of the force of the powder was lost by the vent or by windage, as has already been mentioned, and all possible attention was paid to every circumstance that could contribute to render them perfect and conclusive.

A particular account has already been given of them, and notice has been taken of the means that were used for forming the bullets and making them fit the bore, and of the contrivance for preventing the escape of the elastic fluid by the vent. The following table shews the results of them.

N. B. The charge of powder was the same in each experiment, and consisted of 145 grains in weight.

Experiment.	Weight of the Bullet. Grs.	Velocity of the Bullet.		Difference.
		Actual.	Computed.	
85	90	2109	2109	————
86	251	1430	1262	+168
87	354	1288	1063	+225
88	600	1240	817	+423
89	603	1224	815	+409
90	1184	1017	581	+436
91	1754	893	478	+415
92	2352	812	413	+399

The computed velocities, as they are set down in this table, were determined from the actual velocity of the bullet, as determined by the recoil, in the 85th experiment, and the reciprocal sub-duplicate ratio of its weight to the weight of the bullet in each subsequent experiment; and in the last column is marked the difference between the experiment and the theory, or the number of feet in a second by which the actual velocity exceeded the computed.

But in order that we may see this matter in different points of view, let the order of the experiments be now inverted, and let the computed velocities be determined from the actual velocity in the 92d experiment; and assuming the total or collective pressure exerted by the power upon the bullet in that experiment equal to unity, let the collective pressure in the other experiments be computed from the ratio of the actual to the computed velocities, and the table will stand thus : —

Experiment.	Weight of the Bullet. Grs.	Velocity of the Bullet.		Difference.	Collective Pressure.
		Actual.	Computed.		
92	2352	812	812	——	1.0000
91	1754	893	940	— 47	0.9020
90	1184	1017	1145	— 128	0.7897
89	603	1224	1604	— 380	0.5825
88	600	1240	1608	— 368	0.5949
87	354	1288	2093	— 805	0.3778
86	251	1430	2486	—1056	0.3310
85	90	2109	4151	—2042	0.2581

In the following figure let A B represent the axis of the piece, and A P the length of the space filled with powder ; and at the point P let the perpendicular P H be erected, upon which let P L and P M be taken from P towards H of such magnitudes that while P L expounds the uniform force of gravity, or the weight of the bullet, P M shall be as the force exerted by the powder upon the bullet, at the moment of the explosion. If now we suppose that while the bullet moves on from P towards B, the line P M or *p m* goes along with it, and that the point *m* is always taken in such a manner that the line pm shall be to pl or P L as the force acting upon the bullet in the point p is to its weight, till pm co-

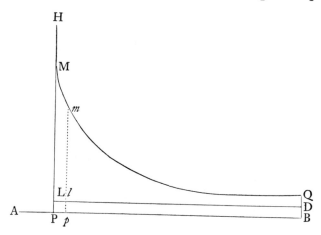

incides with Q B, then will the area P M Q B be to the area P L D B in the duplicate proportion of the velocities which the bullet would acquire when acted on by its own gravity through the space P B, and when impelled through the same space by the force of the powder, as may be seen demonstrated by Sir Isaac Newton in his Mathematical Principles of Natural Philosophy, Book I., prop. 39.

Now what I call the collective pressure, or sum total of the action of the powder upon the bullet, is the measure of the area P M Q B; and it is plain, from what has been said above, that its measure may in all cases be accurately determined, when the weight and velocity of the bullet are known.

If all the powder of the charge were inflamed at once, or before the bullet sensibly moved from its place, and if the pressure of the generated fluid were always as its density, or inversely as the space it occupies, then would the line M Q be an hyperbola, the area P M Q B would always be the same when the charge was the same, and consequently the velocities of the bullets would be as the square roots of their weights inversely.   But it appears, from the before-mentioned experiments, that when the weight of the bullet was increased four times, the action of the powder, or area P M Q B, was nearly doubled; for in the 92d experiment, when four bullets were discharged at once, the collective pressure was as 1; but in the 89th experiment, when a single bullet was made use of, the collective pressure was only as 0.5825; and in the 85th, 86th, and 87th experiments, when the bullets were much lighter, the action of the charge on them was still less.

But though we can determine with great certainty, from these experiments, *the ratio in which the action of the powder upon the bullet was increased or diminished,* by making use of bullets of greater or less weight, yet we cannot from thence ascertain the relation of the elasticity of the generated fluid to its density, nor the quantity of powder that is inflamed at different periods before and after the bullet begins to move in the bore.

But assuming Mr. Robins's principles, as far as relates to the elasticity of the fluid, and supposing that in all the experiments except the 92d, a part only of the charge took fire, and that that part was inflamed and converted into an elastic fluid before the bullet began to move, upon that supposition we can determine the quantity of powder that took fire in each experiment, for the quantity of powder in that case would be as the collective pressure.

Thus if the whole charge, = 145 grains in weight, is supposed to have been inflamed in the 92d experiment, the quantity inflamed in each of the other experiments will appear to have been as follows, viz. : —

Experiment.	Weight of the Bullet. Grs.	Velocity of the Bullet.	Collective Pressure.	Powder Inflamed. Grs.
85	90	2109	0.2581	37
86	251	1430	0.3310	48
87	354	1288	0.3778	55
88	600	1240	0.5949	86
89	603	1224	0.5825	84
90	1184	1017	0.7897	114
91	1754	893	0.9020	131

But there are many reasons to suppose that the diminution of the action of the powder upon the bullet when it is lighter is not so much owing to the smallness of the quantity of powder that takes fire in that case, as to the *vis inertiæ* of the generated fluid. It is true that a greater portion of the charge takes fire and burns when the bullet is heavy than when it is light, as I found in the very experiments of which I am now speaking; but then, the quantity of unfired powder in any case was much too small to account for the apparent diminution of the force when light bullets were made use of.

If the elastic fluid, in the action of which the force of powder consists, were infinitely rare, or if its weight bore no proportion to that of the powder that generated it, and if the gross matter, or *caput mortuum* of the powder, remained in the bottom of the bore after the explosion, then, and upon no other supposition, would the pressure upon the bullet be inversely as the space occupied by the fluid; but it is evident that this can never be the case.

A curious subject for speculation here occurs: How

far would it be advantageous, were it possible, to diminish the specific gravity of gunpowder, and the fluid generated from it, without lessening its elastic force? It
would certainly act upon very light bullets with greater
force; but when heavy ones came to be made use of,
there is reason to think that, except extraordinary precaution was taken to prevent it, the greatest part of the
force would be lost by the vent and by windage.

The velocity with which elastic fluids rush into a void
space is as the elasticity of the fluid directly, and inversely as its density; if, therefore, the density of the
fluid generated from powder were four times less than it
is, its elasticity remaining the same, it would issue out
at the vent, and escape by the side of the bullet in the
bore, with nearly four times as great a velocity as it does
at present; but we know from experiment that the loss
of force on those accounts is now very considerable.

In the experiments Nos. 76 and 77, when the piece
was fired with 145 grains of powder, the velocity of the
bullets at a medium was 1040 feet in a second; but in
the 88th and 89th experiments, when the bullets were
even heavier, and the piece was fired with the same quantity of powder, the mean velocity was 1232 feet in a second. The difference, = 192 feet in a second, answers to
a difference of force, greater in the last experiments than
in the first in the proportion of 14 to 10.

I know of no way to account for this difference but
by supposing that it was owing entirely to the escape of
the elastic fluid by the vent and by windage, in those
experiments where the vent was open, and the bullets
were put naked into the piece.

An elastic bow, made of very light wood, will throw
an arrow, and especially a light one, with greater velocity

than a bow of steel of the same degree of stiffness ; but for practice I think it is plain that gunpowder may *be supposed* to be so light as to be rendered entirely useless, and for some purposes it seems probable that it would not be the worse for being even heavier than it is now made. Vents are absolutely necessary in fire-arms, and in large pieces of ordnance the windage must be considerable, in order that the bullets, which are not always so round as they should be, may not stick in the bore ; and those who have been present at the firing of heavy artillery and large mortars with shot and shells must have observed that there is a sensible space of time elapses between the lighting of the prime and the explosion ; and that during that interval, the flame is continually issuing out at the vent with a hissing noise, and with a prodigious velocity, as appears by the height to which the stream of fire mounts up in the air. It is plain that this loss must be greater in proportion as the shot that is discharged is heavier ; and I have often fancied that I perceived a sensible difference in the time that elapsed between the firing of the prime and the explosion when bullets were discharged, and when the piece has been fired with powder only ; the time being apparently longer in the former case than the latter.

Almost all the writers upon gunpowder, and particularly those of the last century, gave different *recipes* for powder that is designed for different uses. Thus the French authors mention *poudre a mousquet, poudre ordinaire de guerre, poudre de chasse,* and *poudre d'artifice ;* all of which are composed of nitre, sulphur, and charcoal, taken in different proportions. Is it not probable that this variety in the composition of powder was originally introduced, in consequence of observation that one kind of powder was better adapted for particular purposes than another, or from experiments made on purpose to ascertain the fact? There is one circumstance that would lead us to suppose that that was the case. That kind of powder which was designed for great guns and mortars was weaker than those which were intended to be used in smaller pieces; for if there is any foundation for these conjectures, it is certain that the weakest powder, or the heaviest in proportion to its elastic force, ought to be used to impel the heaviest bullets, and particularly in guns that are imperfectly formed, where the vent is large and the windage very great.

I am perfectly aware that an objection may here be made, viz. that the elastic fluid which is generated from gunpowder must be supposed to have the same properties very nearly, whatever may be the proportion of the several ingredients, and that therefore the only difference there can be in powder is, that one kind may generate more of this fluid and another less; and that when it is generated, it acts in the same manner, and will alike escape, and with the same velocity, by any passage it can find. But to this I answer, though the fluid may be the same, as undoubtedly it is, and though its density and elasticity may be the same in all cases, at the instant of its generation, yet, in the explosion, the elastic and unelastic parts are so mixed and blended, that I imagine the fluid cannot expand without taking the gross matter along with it, and the velocity with which the flame issues out at the vent is to be computed from the elasticity of the fluid and the density or weight of the fluid and the gross matter taken together, and not simply from the elasticity and density of the fluid. If antimony in an impalpable powder, or any other heavy body, were intimately mixed with water in a vessel of any kind, and kept in suspension by shaking or stirring them about; and if a hole were opened in the side or bottom of the vessel, the water would not run out without taking the particles of the solid body along with it. And in the same manner I conceive the solid particles that remain after the explosion of gunpowder to be carried forward with the generated elastic fluid, and, being carried forward, to retard its motion. But to return from this digression.

As it appears from these experiments that the relation of the velocities of bullets to their weights is different from that which Mr. Robins's theory supposes, it remains to inquire *what the law is which actually obtains.* And first, as the velocities bear a greater proportion to each other than the reciprocal sub-duplicate ratio of the weights of the bullets, let us see how near they come to the reciprocal sub-triplicate ratio of their weights.

| | | Velocity of the Bullet. | | | | |
| | | Computed. | | Actual. | | Computed. |
Experiment.	Weight of the Bullet.	Recip. sub- dup. ratio.	Error of the Theory.		Error of the Theory.	Recip. sub- trip. ratio.
92	2352	812	——	812	——	812
91	1754	940	+ 47	893	+ 2	895
90	1184	1145	+ 128	1017	+ 4	1021
89	603	1604	+ 380	1224	+ 54	1278
88	600	1608	+ 368	1240	+ 40	1280
87	354	2093	+ 805	1288	+239	1527
86	251	2486	+1056	1430	+282	1712
85	90	4151	+2042	2109	+301	2410

Here the velocities computed upon the last supposition appear to agree much better with the experiments than those computed upon Mr. Robins's principles; but still there is a considerable difference between the actual and the computed velocities in the three last experiments in the table.

As the powder itself is heavy, it may be considered as a weight that is put in motion along with the bullet; and if we suppose the density of the generated fluid is always uniform from the bullet to the breech, the velocity of the center of gravity of the powder, or (which amounts to the same thing) of the elastic fluid, and the gross matter generated from it will be just half as great as the velocity of the bullet. If therefore we put P to denote the weight of the powder, B the weight of the bullet, and v its initial velocity: then $B\,v + \frac{1}{2}\,P\,v = \overline{B + \frac{1}{2}\,P} \times v$ will express the *momentum* of the charge at the instant when the bullet quits the bore.

If now, instead of ascertaining the relation of the velocities to the weights of the bullets, we add half the weight of the powder to the weight of the bullet and compute the velocities from the reciprocal sub-triplicate ratio of the quantity $\overline{B + \frac{1}{2}\,P}$ in each experiment, the table will stand thus : —

.Experiment.	Weight of the Bullet and half the Powder. $B + \frac{1}{2}\,P =$	Velocity of the Bullet.		Error of the Theory.
		Actual.	Computed.	
92	$2352 + 72\frac{1}{2}$	812	812	——
91	$1754 + 72\frac{1}{2}$	893	892	— 1
90	$1184 + 72\frac{1}{2}$	1017	1011	— 6
89	$603 + 72\frac{1}{2}$	1224	1243	+ 19
88	$600 + 72\frac{1}{2}$	1240	1245	+ 5
87	$354 + 72\frac{1}{2}$	1288	1449	+161
86	$251 + 72\frac{1}{2}$	1430	1589	+159
85	$90 + 72\frac{1}{2}$	2109	1999	—110

The agreement between the actual and computed velocities is here very remarkable, and particularly in the five first experiments, which are certainly those upon which the greatest dependence may be placed.

And hence we are enabled to determine the natures of the curves *m n* and *gf* (Fig. 16); for since B (which expresses the weight of the bullet) is as the length taken from A towards B in the several experiments, and as the velocities are as the lines drawn perpendicular to the line A B from the places where those lengths terminate, as *w*, *u*, &c. ending at the curve *m*, *n*; if we put $a = \frac{1}{2}$ P, $x =$ B, and $y = w u$, then will the relation of *x* and *y* be defined by this equation $\dfrac{1}{\sqrt{a + x^3}} = y$. And if *z* be put to denote the line *w r*, and *b* the recoil when the given charge is fired without any bullet, it will be $\dfrac{x}{\sqrt{a + x^3}} + b = z$ in the curve *g f*, *x* being the abscissa, and *z* the corresponding ordinate to the curve.

In the 92d experiment half the weight of the powder $(= a)$ was $72\frac{1}{2}$ grains; the weight of the bullet was 2352 grains $(= x)$; the recoil $(= z)$ was 32.25 inches, and with the given charge without any bullet the recoil $(= b)$ was 4.4 inches; if now from these *data*, and the known weight of the bullet in each of the other experiments in this set, the recoil be computed by means of the theorem $\dfrac{x}{\sqrt{a + x^3}} + b = z$ we shall see how the result of those experiments agrees with this theory, thus:

| | | Recoil. | | |
Experiment.	Weight of the Bullet.	Actual.	Computed.	Difference.
92	2352	32.25	32.25	——
91	1754	27.18	27.22	+0.04
90	1184	21.92	21.85	—0.07
89	603	15.13	15.33	+0.20
88	600	15.22	15.29	+0.07
87	354	11.03	11.87	+0.84
86	251	9.62	10.21	+0.59
85	90	7.16	7.02	—0.14
84 and 93	0	4.40	4.40	——

Here the agreement of the actual and computed recoils is as remarkable as that of the actual and computed velocities in the foregoing table.

By the Figure 17 may be seen at one view the result
of all these experiments and computations. The numbers upon the line A B (as in the Fig. 16) represent the
weights of the bullets, while the lines drawn from those
numbers perpendicular to A B on each side, and ending
at the curves *m, n,* are as the velocities of the bullets in
the several experiments ; the line A B being the axis of
the curves, the lengths taken from A to the different
numbers towards B ($= x$) the abscissas, and the perpen-
diculars ($= y$) the corresponding ordinates. The ordinates to the curve *h n* are as the velocities computed
from the theorem, $\dfrac{1}{\sqrt{a + x^3}} = y$, and the ordinates to
the curve *p, n* (which is the logarithmic curve, as it is
$\dfrac{1}{\sqrt{x}} = y$) shew the velocities computed upon Mr.
Robins's principles. The curve *gf* is drawn from the
theorem $\dfrac{x}{\sqrt{a + x^3}} + b = z$; and the actual recoil is
marked upon the ordinates to this curve by large round
dots, which in all the experiments except the 86th and
87th very nearly coincide with the curve.

In the Fig. 18, the numbers upon the line A B, taken
from A, denote the different charges of powder used in
the course of the experiments, while the ordinates to the
curve *c d* express the velocities of the bullets with the
vent at o. The lines drawn perpendicular from the line
A B to the line *e f* represent the recoil with the several
charges of powder and a leaden bullet, and the portion
of those lines that is comprehended between the line
A B and the line *g h* denotes the recoil when the given
charge was fired without any bullet.

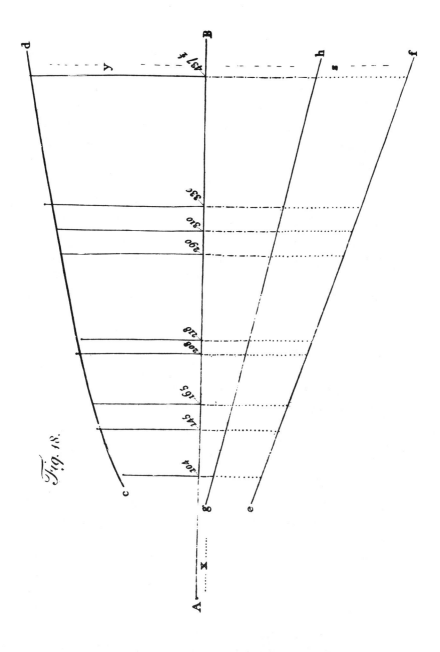

Fig. 18.

Having now shewn by experiment the relation of the velocities of bullets to their weights when care is taken to prevent entirely the loss of force by the escape of the elastic fluid through the vent, and by the windage, I shall leave it to mathematicians to determine from these *data* the properties of that fluid, or the relation of its elasticity to its density.

But before I take my leave of this subject, I would just observe that Mr. Robins is not only mistaken in the principle he assumes, respecting the relation of the elasticity of the fluid generated from gunpowder to its density, or rather the law of its action upon the bullet as it expands in the bore, but his determination of the force of gunpowder is also erroneous, even upon his own principles ; for he determines its force to be 1000 times greater than the mean pressure of the atmosphere ; whereas it appears, from the result of the 92d experiment, that its force is at least 1308 times greater than the mean pressure of the atmosphere, as will be evident to those who will take the trouble to make the computation.

Of an Attempt to determine the explosive Force of Aurum Fulminans, *or a Comparison between its Force and that of Gunpowder.*

Having provided myself with a small quantity of this wonderful powder, upon the goodness of which I could depend, I endeavored to ascertain its explosive force, by making use of it, instead of gunpowder, for discharging a bullet, and measuring, by means of the pendulum, the velocity which the bullet acquired ; and concluding, from the tremendous report with which this substance explodes, that its elastic force was vastly greater than that of gunpowder, I took care to have a barrel provided of uncommon strength, on purpose for the experiment. Its length in the bore is 13.25 inches, the diameter of the bore is 0.55 of an inch, and its weight 7 lbs. 2 oz. It is of the best iron, and was made by Wogdon; and the accuracy with which it is finished does credit to the workman.

This barrel being charged with one sixteenth of an ounce (= 27.34 grains) of *aurum fulminans*, and two leaden bullets, which, together with the leather that was put about them to make them fit the bore without windage, weighed 427 grains, it was laid upon a chaffing-dish of live coals, at the distance of about 10 feet from the pendulum, and against the center of the target of the pendulum the piece was directed.

Having secured the barrel in such a manner that its direction should not alter, I retired to a little distance, in order to be out of danger in case of an accident, where I waited, in anxious expectation, the event of the explosion.

I had remained in this situation some minutes, and almost despaired of the experiment's succeeding, when the powder exploded, but with a report infinitely less than what I expected; the noise not greatly exceeding the report of a well-charged wind-gun; and it was not till I saw the pendulum in motion, that I could be persuaded that the bullets had been discharged. I found, however, upon examination, that nothing was left in the barrel, and from the great number of small particles of revived metal that were dispersed about, I had reason to think that all the powder had exploded.

The bullets struck the pendulum nearly in the center of the target, and both of them remained in the wood; and I found, upon making the calculation, that they had impinged against it with a velocity of 428 feet in a second.

If we now suppose that the force of *aurum fulminans* arises from the action of an elastic fluid, that is generated from it in the moment of its explosion, and that the elasticity of this fluid, or rather the force it exerts upon the bullet as it goes on to expand, is always as its density, or inversely as the space it occupies ; then from the known dimensions of the barrel, — the length of the space occupied by the charge (which in this experiment was 0.47 of an inch), — and the weight and velocity of the bullets, the elastic force of this fluid, at the instant of its generation, may be determined : and I find, upon making the calculation upon these principles, that its force turns out 307 times greater than the mean elastic force of common air.

According to Mr. Robins's theory, the elastic force of the fluid generated from gunpowder in its combustion is 1000 times greater than the mean pressure of the atmosphere ; the force of *aurum fulminans*, therefore, appears to be to that of gunpowder as 307 is to 1000, or as 4 is to 13 very nearly.

Of the Specific Gravity of Gunpowder.

To determine the specific gravity of gunpowder, I made use of the following method. A large glass bucket with a narrow mouth being suspended to one of the arms of a very nice balance, and counterpoised by weights put in the opposite scale, it was filled first with government powder poured in lightly, then with the same powder shaken well together, afterwards with powder and water together, and lastly with water alone, and in each case the contents of the bucket were very exactly weighed.

The specific gravity of gunpowder, as determined from these experiments, is as follows : —

Specific gravity of rain water 1.000
Government powder as it lies in a heap mixed with air . 0.836
Government powder well shaken together 0.937
The solid substance of the powder 1.745

Hence it appears that a cubic inch of government powder shaken well together weighs just 243 grains ; that a cubic inch of solid powder would weigh 422 grains ; and consequently, that the interstices between the particles of the powder, as it is grained for use, are nearly as great as the spaces which those particles occupy.

MISCELLANEOUS EXPERIMENTS.

Of some unsuccessful Attempts to increase the Force of Gunpowder.

It has been supposed by many, that the force of steam is even greater than that of gunpowder ; and that if a quantity of water, confined in the chamber of a gun, could at once be rarefied into steam, it would impel a bullet with prodigious velocity. Several attempts have been made to shoot bullets in this manner ; but I know of none that have succeeded ; at least so far as to render it probable that water can ever be substituted in the room of gunpowder, for military purposes, as some have imagined.

The great difficulty that attends making these experiments lies in finding out a method by which the water can at once be rarefied and converted into elastic steam ; and it occurred to me that possibly that might be effect-

ed by means of gunpowder, by confining a small quantity of water in some very thin substance, and surrounding and inclosing it with powder, and afterwards setting
fire to the charge. The method I took to do this was as
follows. Having procured a number of air-bladders of
very small fishes, I put different quantities of water into
them, from the size of a small pea to that of a small
pistol bullet, and tying them up close, with some very
fine thread, I hung up these little globules in the open
air till they were quite dry on the outside. I then
provided a number of cartridges, made of fine paper,
and filled them with a known quantity of powder, equal
to the customary charge for a common horseman's pistol, and having loaded such a pistol with one of them,
and a fit bullet, I laid it down upon the ground, and di-
recting it against an oaken plank, that was placed about
six feet from the muzzle, I fired it off by a train, and
carefully observed the recoil, and also the penetration of
the bullet. I then took several of the filled cartridges
that remained, and pouring out part of the powder, I put
one or more of the little bladders filled with water in the
center of the cartridge, and afterwards, pouring back the
remaining part of the charge, confined the water in the
midst of the powder.

With these cartridges and a fit bullet, the pistol was
successively loaded, and being placed on the ground as
before, and fired by a train, the recoil and the penetration of the bullets were observed, and I constantly found
that the force of the charge was very sensibly diminished
by the addition of the globule of water, and the larger the
quantity of water was that was thus confined, the less
was the effect of the charge ; neither the recoil of the
pistol, nor the penetration of the bullet, being near

equal to what they were when the given quantity of powder was fired without the water; and the report of the explosion appeared to be lessened in a still greater proportion than the recoil or penetration.

Concluding that this diminution of the force of the charge arose from the bursting of the little bladder, and the dispersion of the water among the powder before it was all inflamed, by which a great part of it was prevented from taking fire, I repeated the experiments with highly rectified spirits of wine, instead of water; but the result was nearly the same as before; the force of the charge was constantly and very sensibly diminished. I afterwards made use of ethereal oil of turpentine, and then of small quantities of quicksilver; but still with no better success. Everything I mixed with the powder, instead of increasing, served to lessen the force of the charge.

These trials were all made several months before I began the course of my experiments upon gunpowder, of which I have here given an account, and though they were altogether unsuccessful, yet I resumed the inquiry at that time, and made several new experiments, with a view to find out something that should be stronger than gunpowder, or which, when mixed with it, should increase its force.

It is well known that the elastic force of quicksilver converted into vapour is very great; this substance I made use of in my former trials, as I have just observed, but without success. I thought, however, that the failure of that attempt might possibly be owing to the quicksilver being too much in a body, by which means the fire could not act upon it to the greatest advantage; but that if it could be divided into exceeding small particles, and so ordered that each particle might be completely surrounded by, and exposed to, the action of the flame of the powder, it would be very soon heated, and possibly might be converted into an elastic steam, or vapour, before the bullet could be sensibly removed from its place. To determine this point, I mixed 20 grains of æthiops mineral very intimately with 145 grains of powder, and charging the piece with this compound, it was loaded with a fit bullet and fired: but the force of the charge was less than that which the powder alone would have exerted, as appears by comparing the 76th and 77th experiments with the 79th.

Common *pulvis fulminans* is made of one part of sulphur, two parts of salt of tartar, and three parts of nitre; and if we may judge by the report of the explosion, the elastic force of this compound is considerably greater than that of gunpowder. I was willing to see the effect of mixing salt of tartar with gunpowder, and accordingly, having provided some of this alkaline salt in its purest state, thoroughly dry, and in a fine powder, I mixed 20 grains of it with 145 grains of gunpowder; and upon discharging the bullet with the mixture, I found that the alkaline salt had considerably lessened the force of the powder. See experiment No. 78.

I next made use of *sal ammoniacum*. That salt has been found to produce a very large quantity of gas, or elastic vapour, when exposed to heat under certain circumstances; but when 20 grains of it were mixed with a charge of gunpowder, instead of adding to its force, it diminished it very sensibly. See the 80th experiment.

Most, if not all, the metals, when they are dissolved in proper *menstrua*, cause large quantities of gas to be produced, or set at liberty; and particularly brass, when it is dissolved in nitrous acid. Desirous of seeing if this could be done by the flame, or acid vapour of fired gunpowder, I mixed 20 grains of brass, in a very fine powder, commonly called brass dust (being the small particles of this metal that fly off from the wheel in sharpening pins), with 145 grains of powder, and with this compound and a fit bullet I loaded my barrel, and discharged it; but the experiment (No. 81) shewed that the force of the powder was not increased by the addition of the brass dust, but the contrary.

It seems probable, however, that neither brass dust nor æthiops mineral are of themselves capable of diminishing the force of gunpowder in any considerable degree, otherwise than by filling up the interstices between the grains, and obstructing the passage of the flame, and so impeding the progress of the inflammation. And hence it appears how earthy particles and impurities of all kinds are so very detrimental to gunpowder. It is not that they destroy or alter the properties of any of the bodies of which the powder is composed, but simply by obstructing the progress of the inflammation, that they lessen its force, and render it of little or no value. Too much care, therefore, cannot be taken in manufacturing gunpowder, to free the materials from all heterogeneous matter.

Of an Attempt to shoot Flame instead of Bullets.

Having often observed paper and other light bodies to come out of great guns and small-arms inflamed, I was led to try if other inflammable bodies might not be set on fire in like manner, and particularly inflammable fluids; and I thought, if this could be effected, it might be possible to project such ignited bodies by the force of the explosion, and by that means communicate the fire to other bodies at some considerable distance; but in this attempt I failed totally. I never could set dry tow on fire at the distance of five yards from the muzzle of my barrel. I repeatedly discharged large wads of tow and paper, thoroughly soaked in the most inflammable fluids, such as *alkohol, ethereal spirit of turpentine, balsam of sulphur*, &c., but none of them were ever set on fire by the explosion. Sometimes I discharged three or four spoonfuls of the inflammable fluid, by interposing a very thin wad of cork over the powder, and another over the fluid, but still with no better success. The fluid was projected against the wall as before, and left a mark where it hit it, but it never could be made to take fire; so I gave up the attempt.

EXPERIMENTS

THE FORCE OF FIRED GUNPOWDER.

NO human invention of which we have any authentic
records, except, perhaps, the art of printing, has
produced such important changes in civil society as the invention of *gunpowder*. Yet, notwithstanding the uses to
which this wonderful agent is applied are so extensive,
and though its operations are as surprising as they are
important, it seems not to have hitherto been examined
with that care and perseverance which it deserves. The
explosion of gunpowder is certainly one of the most
surprising phænomena we are acquainted with, and I
am persuaded it would much oftener have been the subject of the investigations of speculative philosophers, as
well as of professional men, in this age of inquiry, were
it not for the danger attending the experiments ; but
the force of gunpowder· is so great, and its effects so
sudden and so terrible, that, notwithstanding all the precautions possible, there is ever a considerable degree of
danger attending the management of it, as I have more
than once found to my cost.

Several eminent philosophers and mathematicians, it
is true, have, from time to time, employed their attention upon this curious subject; and the modern improvements in chemistry have given us a considerable
insight into the cause and the nature of the explosion

which takes place in the inflammation of gunpowder, and the nature and properties of the elastic fluids generated in its combustion. But the great desideratum, — the real measure of the initial expansive force of inflamed gunpowder, — so far from being known, has hitherto been rather guessed at than determined ; and no argument can be more convincing to shew our total ignorance upon that subject, than the difference in the opinions of the greatest mathematicians of the age, who have undertaken its investigation.

The ingenious Mr. Robins, who made a great number of very curious experiments upon gunpowder, and who, I believe, has done more towards perfecting the art of gunnery than any other individual, concluded, as the result of all his inquiries and computations, that the force of the elastic fluid generated in the combustion of gunpowder is 1000 times greater than the mean pressure of the atmosphere. But the celebrated mathematician Daniel Bernouilli determines its force to be not less than 10,000 times that pressure, or ten times greater than Mr. Robins made it.

Struck with this great difference in the results of the computations of these two able mathematicians, as well as with the subject itself, which appeared to me to be both curious and important, I many years ago set about making experiments upon gunpowder, with a view principally of determining the point in question, namely, *its initial expansive force* when fired ; and I have ever since occasionally, from time to time, as I have found leisure and convenient opportunities, continued these inquiries.

In a paper printed in the year 1781, in the LXXI. Volume of the Philosophical Transactions, I gave an account of an experiment (No. 92), by which it appeared that, calculating even upon Mr. Robins's own principles, the force of gunpowder, instead of being 1000 times, must at least be 1308 times greater than the mean pressure of the atmosphere. However, not only that experiment, but many others, mentioned in the same paper, had given me abundant reason to conclude that the principles assumed by Mr. Robins, in his treatise upon gunnery, were erroneous, and I saw no possibility of ever being able to determine the initial force of gunpowder by the methods he had proposed, and which I had till then followed in my experiments. Unwilling to abandon a pursuit which had already cost me much pains, I came to a resolution to strike out a new road, and to endeavour to ascertain the force of gunpowder by *actual measurement*, in a direct and decisive experiment.

I shall not here give a detail of the numerous difficulties and disappointments I met with in the course of these dangerous pursuits; it will be sufficient briefly to mention the plan of operations I formed, in order to obtain the end I proposed, and to give a cursory view of the train of unsuccessful experiments by which I was at length led to the discovery of the truly astonishing force of gunpowder, — a force at least *fifty thousand* times greater than the mean pressure of the atmosphere!

My first attempts were to fire gunpowder in a confined space, thinking, that when I had accomplished this, I should find means, without much difficulty, to measure its elastic force. To this end, I caused a short gun-barrel to be made, of the best wrought iron, and of uncommon strength; the diameter of its bore was $\frac{3}{4}$ of an inch, its length 5 inches, and the thickness of the metal was equal to the diameter of the bore, so that its external diameter was $2\frac{1}{4}$ inches. It was closed at both ends by two long screws, like the breech-pin of a musket; each of which entered two inches into the bore, leaving only a vacuity of 1 inch in length for the charge.

The powder was introduced into this cavity by taking out one of the screws or breech-pins; which being afterwards screwed into its place again, and both ends of the barrel closed up, fire was communicated to the powder by a very narrow vent, made in the axis of one of the breech-pins for that purpose. The chamber, which was 1 inch in length, and $\frac{3}{4}$ of an inch in diameter, being about half filled with powder, I expected that when the powder should be fired, the generated elastic fluid being obliged to issue out at so small an opening as the vent, which was no more than $\frac{1}{20}$ of an inch in diameter, instead of giving a smart report, would come out with something like a hissing noise; and I intended, in a future experiment, to confine the generated elastic fluid entirely by adding a valve to the vent, as I had done in some of my experiments mentioned in the preceding paper. But when I set fire to the charge (which I took the precaution to do by means of a train), instead of a hissing noise, I was surprised by a very sharp and a very loud report; and, upon examining the barrel, I found the vent augmented to at least four times its former dimensions, and both the screws loosened.

Finding, by the result of this experiment, that I had to do with an agent much more troublesome to manage than I had imagined, I redoubled my precautions.

As the barrel was not essentially injured, its ends were now closed up by two new screws, which were firmly fixed in their places by solder, and a new vent was opened in the barrel itself. As both ends of the barrel

were now closed up, it was necessary, in order to introduce the powder into the chamber, to make it pass
through the vent, or to convey it through some other
aperture made for that purpose. The method I employed was as follows: a hole being made in the barrel,
about $\frac{2}{10}$ of an inch in diameter, a plug of steel was
screwed into this hole ; and it was in the center or axis
of the plug that the vent was made. To introduce the
powder into the chamber the plug was taken away.
The vent was made conical, its largest diameter being
inwards, or opening into the chamber ; and a conical pin
of hardened steel was fitted into it, which pin was intended to serve as a valve for closing up the vent, as
soon as the powder in the chamber should be inflamed.
To give a passage to the fire through the vent in entering the chamber, this pin was pushed a little inwards, so
as to leave a small vacuity between its surface and the
concave surface of the bore of the vent.

But notwithstanding all possible care was taken in the
construction of this instrument to render it perfect in all
its parts, the experiment was as unsuccessful as the former:
upon firing the powder in the chamber (though it did
not fill more than half its cavity), the generated elastic
fluid not only forced its way through the vent, notwithstanding the valve (which appeared not to have had time
to close), but it issued with such an astonishing velocity
from this small aperture, that instead of coming out
with a hissing noise, it gave a report nearly as sharp and
as loud as a common musket. Upon examining the
vent-plug and the pin, they were both found to be much
corroded and damaged ; though I had taken the precaution to harden them both before I made the experiment.

I afterwards repeated the experiment with a simple vent, made very narrow, and lined with gold to prevent its being corroded by the acid vapour generated in the combustion of the gunpowder; but this vent was found, upon trial, to be as little able to withstand the amazing force of the inflamed gunpowder as the others. It was so much and so irregularly corroded by the explosion, in the first experiment, as to be rendered quite unserviceable; and, what is still more extraordinary, the barrel itself, notwithstanding its amazing strength, was blown out into the form of a cask; and though it was cracked, it was not burst quite asunder, nor did it appear that any of the generated elastic fluid had escaped through the crack. The barrel in the state it was found after this experiment is still in my possession.

These unsuccessful attempts, and many others of a similar nature, of which it is not necessary to give a particular account, as they all tended to shew that the force of fired gunpowder is in fact much greater than has generally been imagined, instead of discouraging me from pursuing these inquiries, served only to excite my curiosity still more, and to stimulate me to further exertions.

These researches did not by any means appear to me as being merely speculative; on the contrary, I considered the determination of the real force of the elastic fluid generated in the combustion of gunpowder as a matter of great importance.

The use of gunpowder is become so extensive that very important mechanical improvements can hardly fail to result from any new discoveries relative to its force and the law of its action. Most of the computations that have hitherto been made relative to the action of gunpowder have been founded upon the supposition that the elasticity of the generated fluid is, in all cases, as its density; but if this supposition should prove false, all those computations, with all the practical rules founded on them, must necessarily be erroneous; and the influence of these errors must be as extensive as the uses to which gunpowder is applied.

Having found by experience how difficult it is to confine the elastic vapour generated in the combustion of gunpowder, when the smallest opening is left by which any part of it can escape, it occurred to me that I might perhaps succeed better by closing up the powder entirely, in such a manner as to leave no opening whatever, by which it could communicate with the external air; and by setting the powder on fire, by causing the heat employed for that purpose to pass through the solid substance of the iron barrel used for confining it.

In order to make this experiment, I caused a new barrel to be constructed for that purpose; its length was 3.45 inches, and the diameter of its bore $\frac{7}{10}$ of an inch; its ends were closed up by two screws, each 1 inch in length, which were firmly and immoveably fixed in their places by solder; a vacuity being left between them in the barrel 1.45 inch in length, which constituted the chamber of the piece, and whose capacity was nearly $\frac{6}{10}$ of a cubic inch. An hole 0.37 of an inch in diameter being bored through both sides of the barrel, through the center of the chamber, and at right angles to its axis, two tubes of iron, 0.37 of an inch in diameter, the diameter of whose bore was $\frac{1}{10}$ of an inch, were firmly fixed in this hole with solder, in such a manner that while their internal openings were exactly opposite to each other, and on opposite sides of the chamber, the axes of their bores were in the same right line.

The shortest of these tubes, which projected 1.3 inch beyond the external surface of the barrel, was closed at its projecting end, or rather it was not bored quite through its whole length, $\frac{3}{10}$ of an inch of solid metal being left at its end, which was rounded off in the form of a blunt point. The longer tube, which projected 2.7 inches beyond the surface of the barrel, on the other side, and which served for introducing the powder into the chamber, was open; but it could occasionally be closed by a strong screw, furnished with a collar of oiled leather, which was provided for that purpose. The method of making use of this instrument was as follows. The barrel being laid down, or held, in an horizontal position, with the long tube upwards, the charge, which was of the very best fine-grained glazed powder, was poured through this tube into the chamber.

In doing this, care must be taken that the cavity of the short tube be completely filled with powder, and this can best be done by pouring in only a small quantity of powder at first, and then, by striking the barrel with a hammer, cause the powder to descend into the short tube. When, by introducing a priming wire, through the long tube, it is found that the short tube is full, it ought to be gently pressed together, or rammed down, by means of the priming wire, in order to prevent its falling back into the chamber upon moving the barrel out of the horizontal position. The short tube being properly filled, the rest of the charge may be introduced into the chamber, and the end of the long tube closed up by its screw.

More effectually to prevent the elastic fluid generated in the combustion of the charge from finding a passage to escape by this opening, after the charge was introduced into the chamber, the cavity of the long tube was filled up with cold tallow, and the screw that closed up its end (which was $\frac{1}{2}$ an inch long, and but a little more than $\frac{1}{10}$ of an inch in diameter) was pressed down against its leather collar with the utmost force.

The manner of setting fire to the charge was as follows: a block of wrought iron about $1\frac{1}{2}$ inch square, with a hole in it, capable of receiving nearly the whole of that part of the *short tube* which projects beyond the barrel, being heated red-hot, the end of the short tube was introduced into this hole, where it was suffered to remain till the heat, having penetrated the tube, set fire to the powder it contained, and the inflammation was *from thence* communicated to the powder in the chamber.

The result of this experiment fully answered my expectations. The generated elastic fluid was so completely confined that no part of it could make its escape. The report of the explosion was so very feeble as hardly to be audible; indeed, it did not by any means deserve the name of a report, and certainly could not have been heard at the distance of twenty paces; it resembled the noise which is occasioned by the breaking of a very small glass tube.

I imagined at first that the powder had not all taken fire, but the heat of the barrel soon convinced me that the explosion must have taken place, and after waiting near half an hour, upon loosening the screw which closed the end of the long vent-tube, the confined elastic vapours rushed out with considerable force, and with a noise like that attending the discharge of an air-gun. The quantity of powder made use of in the experiment was indeed very small, not amounting to more than $\frac{1}{8}$ part of what the chamber was capable of contain-

ing; but having so often had my machinery destroyed
in experiments of this sort, I began now to be more
cautious.

Having found means to confine the elastic vapour
generated in the combustion of gunpowder, my next attempts were to measure its force; but here again I met
with new and almost insurmountable difficulties.

To measure the expansive force of the vapour, it was
necessary to bring it to act upon a moveable body of
known dimensions, and whose resistance to the efforts
of the fluid could be accurately determined; but this
was found to be extremely difficult. I attempted it in
various ways, but without success. I caused a hole to
be bored in the axis of one of the screws, or breech-pins,
which closed up the ends of the barrel just described,
and fitting a piston of hardened steel into this hole
(which was $\frac{2}{10}$ of an inch in diameter), and causing the
end of the piston which projected beyond the end of the
barrel to act upon a heavy weight, suspended as a pendulum to a long iron rod, I hoped, by knowing the
velocity acquired by the weight, from the length of the
arc described by it in its ascent, to be able to calculate
the pressure of the elastic vapour by which it was put in
motion; but this contrivance was not found to answer,
nor did any of the various alterations and improvements
I afterwards made in the machinery render the results of
the experiment at all satisfactory.

It was not only found almost impossible to prevent
the escape of the elastic fluid by the sides of the piston,
but the results of apparently similar experiments were so
very different, and so uncertain, that I was often totally
at a loss to account for these extraordinary variations.
I was, however, at length led to suspect, what I after-

wards found abundant reason to conclude, was the real cause of these variations, and of all the principal difficulties which attended the ascertaining the force of fired gunpowder by the methods I had hitherto pursued.

It has generally been believed, after Mr. Robins, that the force of fired gunpowder consists in the action of a permanently elastic fluid, similar in many respects to common atmospheric air; which, being generated from the powder in combustion, in great abundance, and being moreover in a very compressed state, and its elasticity being much augmented by the heat (which is likewise generated in the combustion), it escapes with great violence by every avenue, and produces that loud report, and all those terrible effects, which attend the explosion of gunpowder.

But though this theory is very plausible, and seems upon a cursory view of the subject to account in a satisfactory manner for all the phænomena, yet a more careful examination will shew it to be defective. There is no doubt but the permanently elastic fluids, generated in the combustion of gunpowder, *assist* in producing those effects which result from its explosion; but it will be found, I believe, upon ascertaining the real expansive force of fired gunpowder, that this cause alone is quite inadequate to the effects actually produced; and that, therefore, the agency of some other power must necessarily be called in to its assistance.

Mr. Robins has shewn that if all the permanently elastic fluid generated in the combustion of gunpowder be compressed in the space originally occupied by the powder, and if this fluid, so compressed, be supposed to be heated to the intense heat of red-hot iron, its elastic force *in that case* will be 1000 times greater than the mean pressure of the atmosphere; and this, according to his theory, is the real measure of the force of gunpowder *fired in a cavity which it exactly fills.*

But what will become of this theory, and of all the suppositions upon which it is founded, if I shall be able to prove, as I hope to do in the most satisfactory manner, that the force of fired gunpowder, instead of being 1000 times, is at least 50,000 greater than the mean pressure of the atmosphere?

For my part, I know of no way of accounting for this enormous force, but by supposing it to arise principally from the elasticity of the *aqueous vapour* generated from the powder in its combustion. The brilliant discoveries of modern chemists have taught us, that both the constituent parts of which water is composed, and even water itself, exist in the materials which are combined to make gunpowder; and there is much reason to believe that aqueous vapour, or steam, is actually formed in its combustion. M. Lavoisier, I know, imagined that the force of fired gunpowder depends in a great measure upon the expansive force of uncombined *caloric* supposed to be let loose in great abundance during the combustion or deflagration of the powder; but it is not only dangerous to admit the action of an agent whose *existence* is not yet clearly demonstrated, but it appears to me that this supposition is quite unnecessary, the elastic force of the heated aqueous vapour, whose existence can hardly be doubted, being quite sufficient to account for all the phænomena.

It is well known that the elasticity of aqueous vapour is considerably more augmented by any given augmentation of temperature, than that of any permanently elastic fluid whatever; and those who are acquainted with the amazing force of steam, when heated only to a few degrees above the boiling point, can easily perceive that its elasticity must be almost infinite, when greatly condensed and heated to the temperature of red-hot iron; and this heat it must certainly acquire in the explosion of gunpowder. But if the force of fired gunpowder arises *principally* from the elastic force of heated aqueous vapour, a cannon is nothing more than a *steam-engine* upon a peculiar construction; and upon determining the ratio of the elasticity of this vapour to its density, and to its temperature, a law will be found to obtain, very different from that assumed by Mr. Robins, in his Treatise on Gunnery. What this law really is, I do not pretend to have determined with that degree of precision which I wished; but the experiments of which I am about to give an account will, I think, demonstrate in the most satisfactory manner, not only that the force of fired gunpowder is in fact much greater than has been imagined, but also that its force consists principally in the temporary action of a fluid not permanently elastic, and consequently that all the theories hitherto proposed for the elucidation of this subject must be essentially erroneous.

The first step towards acquiring knowledge is undoubtedly that which leads us to a discovery of the falsehood of received opinions. To a diligent inquirer every common operation, performed in the usual course of practice, is an experiment, from which he endeavours to discover some new fact, or to confirm the result of former inquiries.

Having been engaged many years in the investigation of the force of gunpowder, I occasionally found many opportunities of observing, under a variety of circum-

stances, the various effects produced by its explosion;
and as a long habit of meditating upon this subject
rendered everything relating to it highly interesting to
me, I seized these opportunities with avidity, and examined all the various phænomena with steady and in-
defatigable attention.

During a cruise which I made, as a volunteer, in the
Victory, with the British fleet, under the command of
my late worthy friend Sir Charles Hardy, in the year
1779, I had many opportunities of attending to the firing of heavy cannon; for though we were not fortunate
enough to come to a general action with the enemy, as is
well known, yet, as the men were frequently exercised at
the great guns and in firing at marks, and as some of
my friends in the fleet, then captains, (since made
admirals,) as the Honourable Keith Stewart, who
commanded the Berwick of 74 guns, — Sir Charles
Douglas, who commanded the Duke of 98 guns, — and
Admiral Macbride, who was then captain of the Bien-
faisant of 64 guns, were kind enough, at my request, to
make a number of experiments, and particularly by firing a greater number of bullets at once from their heavy
guns than ever had been done before, and observing the
distances at which they fell in the sea; I had opportunities of making several very interesting observations,
which gave me much new light relative to the action of
fired gunpowder. And afterwards, when I went out to
America, to command a regiment of cavalry which I
had raised in that country for the King's service, his
Majesty having been graciously pleased to permit me to
take out with me from England four pieces of light
artillery, constructed under the direction of the late
Lieutenant-General Desaguliers, with a large propor-

tion of ammunition, I made a great number of interesting experiments with these guns, and also with the ship
guns on board the ships of war in which I made my
passage to and from America.

It would take up too much time, and draw out this
paper to too great a length, to give an account in detail
of all these experiments, and of the various observations I have had opportunities of making from time to
time, relative to this subject. I shall, therefore, only
observe, at present, that the result of all my inquiries
tended to confirm me more and more in the opinion,
that the theory generally adopted relative to the explosion of gunpowder was extremely erroneous, and
that its force is in fact much greater than is generally
imagined. That the position of Mr. Robins, which
supposes the inflammation and combustion of gunpowder to be so instantaneous "that the whole of the
charge of a piece of ordnance is actually inflamed and
converted into an elastic vapour before the bullet is
sensibly moved from its place," is very far from being
true; and that the ratio of the elasticity of the generated
fluid to its density, or to the space it occupies as it
expands, is very different from that assumed by Mr.
Robins.

The rules laid down by Mr. Robins for computing
the velocities of bullets from their weight, the known
dimensions of the gun, and the quantities of powder
made use of for the charge, may, and certainly do, very
often give the velocities very near the truth; but this is
no proof that the principles upon which these computations are made are just; for it may easily happen that
a complication of erroneous suppositions may be so
balanced that the result of a calculation founded on

them may, nevertheless, be very near the truth ; and this is never so likely to happen as when, from known effects, the action of the powers which produce them are computed.   For it is not in general very difficult to assume such principles as, when taken together, may in the most common known cases answer completely all the conditions required.   But in such cases, if the truth be discovered with regard to any one of the assumed principles, and it be substituted in the place of the erroneous supposition, the fallacy of the whole hypothesis will immediately become evident.

As I have mentioned the experiments made with heavy artillery, as having been led by their results to form important conjectures relative to the nature of the expansion of the fluid generated in the combustion of gunpowder; it may perhaps be asked, and indeed with some appearance of reason, what the circumstances were which attended the experiments in question, which could justify so important a conclusion as that of the fallacy of the commonly received theory relative to that subject. To this I answer briefly, that in regard to the supposed instantaneous inflammation of the powder, upon which the whole fabric of this theory is built, or rather of all the computations which are grounded upon it, a careful attention to the phænomena which take place upon firing off cannon led me to suspect, or rather confirmed me in my former suspicions, that, however rapid the inflammation of gunpowder may be, its *total combustion* is by no means so sudden as this theory supposes.   When a heavy cannon is fired in the common way, that is, when the vent is filled with loose powder, and the piece is fired off with a match, the time employed in the passage of the inflammation through the vent into the chamber of the piece is perfectly sensible, and this time is evidently shorter after the piece has been heated by repeated firing. With the same charge, the recoil of a gun (and consequently the velocity of its bullet) is greater after the gun has been heated by repeated firing than when it is cold. The velocity of the bullet is considerably greater when the cannon is fired off with a vent tube, or by firing a pistol charged with powder into the open vent, than when the vent is filled with loose powder. The velocity of two, three, or more fit bullets discharged at once from a piece of ordnance, compared to the velocity of one single bullet discharged by the same quantity of powder from the same cannon, is greater than it ought to be according to the theory. Considerable quantities of powder are frequently driven out of cannon and other fire-arms *unconsumed*. The manner in which the smoke of gunpowder rises in the air, and is gradually dissolved and rendered invisible, shews it to partake of the nature of steam. But not to take up too much time with these general observations, I shall proceed to give an account of experiments, the results of which will be considered as more conclusive.

Having found it impossible to measure the elastic force of fired gunpowder with any degree of precision by any of the methods before mentioned, I totally changed my plan of operations, and instead of endeavouring to determine its force by causing the generated elastic fluid to act upon a moveable body through a determined space, I set about contriving an apparatus in which this fluid should be made to act, by a determined surface, against a weight, which, by being increased at pleasure, should at last be such as would just be able to confine it, and which in that case would just counterbalance, and consequently *measure*, its elastic force.

The idea of this method of determining the force of fired gunpowder occurred to me many years ago ; but a very expensive and troublesome apparatus being neces- sary in order to put it in execution, it was not till the year 1792, when, being charged with the arrangement of the army of his most Serene Highness the ELECTOR PALATINE, reigning Duke of Bavaria, and having all the resources of the military arsenal, and a number of very ingenious workmen at my command, with the permis- sion and approbation of his most Serene Electoral Highness, I set about making the experiments which I shall now describe ; and as they are not only important in themselves and in their results, but as they are, I believe, the first of the kind that have been made, I shall be very particular in my account of them, and also of the apparatus used in making them.

One difficulty being got over, that of setting fire to the powder without any communication with the external air, by causing the heat employed for that purpose to pass through the solid substance of the barrel, it only remained to apply such a weight to an opening made in the barrel as the whole force of the generated elastic fluid should not be able to lift or displace ; but in doing this many precautions were necessary. For, first, as the force of gunpowder is so very great, it was necessary to employ an enormous weight to confine it ; for although by diminishing the size of the opening the weight would be lessened in the same proportion, yet it was necessary to make this opening of a certain size, otherwise the experiments would not have been satisfactory ; and it was necessary to make the support or base upon which the barrel was placed very massy and solid, to prevent the errors which would unavoidably have arisen from its want of solidity or from its elasticity.

The annexed drawings will give a complete idea of the whole apparatus made use of in these experiments. A (Fig. 1) is a solid block of very hard stone, 4 feet 4 inches square, placed upon a bed of solid masonry, which descended 6 feet below the surface of the earth. Upon this block of stone, which served as a base to the whole machinery, was placed the barrel B of hammered iron, upon its support C, which is of cast brass, or rather of gun-metal; which support was again placed upon a circular plate of hammered iron D, 8 inches in diameter, and $\frac{3}{4}$ of an inch thick, which last rested upon the block of stone. The opening of the bore of the barrel (which was placed in a vertical position, and which was just $\frac{1}{4}$ of an inch in diameter) was closed by a solid hemisphere E of hardened steel, whose diameter was 1.16 inch; and upon this hemisphere the weight F, made use of for confining the elastic fluid generated from the powder in its combustion, reposed. This weight (which in some of the most interesting experiments was a brass cannon, a heavy twenty-four pounder, placed vertically upon its cascabel), being fixed to the timbers G G which formed a kind of carriage for it, was moveable up and down; the ends of these timbers being moveable in grooves cut in the vertical timbers K K, which being fixed below in holes made to receive them in the block of stone, and above by a cross-piece L, were supported by braces and iron clamps made fast to the thick walls of the building of the arsenal.

This weight was occasionally raised and lowered in the course of the experiments (in placing and removing the barrel), by means of a very strong lever, which is omitted in the drawing to make it less complicated. The barrel, a section of which is represented in Fig. 2 of its natural size, is 2.78 inches long, and 2.82 inches in diameter at its lower extremity, where it reposes upon its supporter, but something less above, being somewhat diminished and rounded off at its upper extremity. Its bore, which, as I have already observed, is $\frac{1}{4}$ of an inch in diameter, is 2.13 inches long, and it ends in a very narrow opening below, not more than 0.07 of an inch in diameter, and 1.715 inch long, which forms the vent (if I may be permitted to apply that name to a passage which is not open at both ends), by which the fire is communicated to the charge. From the center of the bottom of the barrel there is a projection of about 0.45 of an inch in diameter, and 1.3 inch long, which forms the vent tube V. Fig. 3 is a view of an iron ball W, which, being heated red-hot, and being applied to the vent tube by means of an hole O, made in it for that purpose, fire is communicated through the solid substance of the vent tube to the powder it contains, and from thence to the charge.

Fig. 4, which is drawn on a scale of two inches to the inch, or half the real size of the machinery, shews how the barrel B was placed upon its support C, how this last was placed upon its circular plate of iron D, and how the red-hot iron ball W was applied to the vent tube V. This ball is managed by means of a long handle *h*, of iron, and being introduced through a circular opening *g*, in the support, and applied to the vent tube V, is kept in its place by means of a wedge, or rather lever *l*, whose external end is represented in the drawing as being broken off, to save room. The circular opening in front of the support is seen in front, and consequently more distinctly, in the drawing, Fig. 1. In this drawing the end of the vent tube may be likewise discovered through

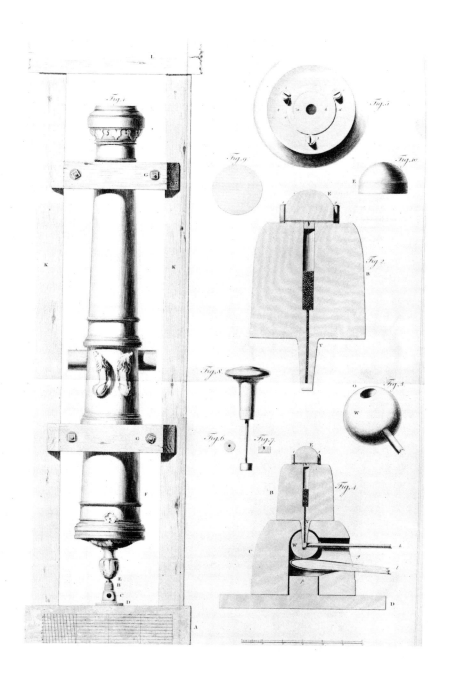

Fig. 1

Fig. 5

Fig. 9

Fig. 10

Fig. 2

Fig. 8

Fig. 3

Fig. 6   Fig. 7

Fig. 4

this opening; but as it was necessary, in order to introduce all the parts of this machinery, to make the drawing upon a very small scale, it was not possible to express all the smaller parts with that distinctness which I
wished. The other figures which are added, in which
the parts are expressed separately, and upon a larger
scale, will, it is hoped, supply this defect.

The stand, or support, as I have called it, upon
which the barrel was placed, is circular, and in order that
it might be united more firmly to the plate of iron upon
which it reposes, this plate is furnished with a cylindrical projection p, 1 inch long and $1\frac{1}{2}$ in diameter, which
enters a hole made in the bottom of the stand to receive it.

Fig. 5 is a view of the barrel from above, in which
the projecting screws, or rather cylinders, are seen, by
which the hemisphere E, Fig. 2, which closed the end of
the barrel, was kept in its place. Two of these screws
1, 2, are seen in the figures 2 and 4. The smaller
circle $a\,b$, Fig. 5, shews the diameter of a circular plate
of gold, which was let into the end of the barrel, being
firmly fixed to the iron with solder; and the larger
circle $c\,d$ represents a circular piece of oiled leather,
which was placed between the end of the barrel and the
hemisphere which rested upon it.

The end of the barrel was covered with gold, in order
to prevent, as much as possible, its being corroded by
the elastic vapour, which, when the weight is not heavy
enough to confine it, escapes between the end of the
barrel and the flat surface of the hemisphere; but even
this precaution was not found to be sufficient to defend
the apparatus from injury. The sharp edge of the barrel, at the mouth of the bore, was worn away almost

immediately, and even the flat surface of the hemisphere, notwithstanding it was of hardened steel and very highly polished, was sensibly corroded. This corrosion of the mouth of the bore, by which the dimensions of the surface upon which the generated elastic fluid acted were rendered very uncertain, would alone have been sufficient to have rendered all my attempts to determine the force of fired gunpowder abortive, had I not found means to remedy the evil. The method I employed for this purpose was as follows. Having provided some pieces of very good compact sole-leather, I caused them to be beaten upon an anvil with a heavy hammer to render them still more compact; and then, by means of a machine made for that purpose, cylindric stoppers, of the same diameter precisely as the bore of the barrel, and 0.13 of an inch in length (that is to say, equal in length to the thickness of the leather), were formed of it; and one of these stoppers, which had previously been greased with tallow, being put into the mouth of the piece after the powder had been introduced, and being forced into the bore till its upper end coincided with the end of the barrel, upon the explosion taking place, this stopper (being pressed on the one side by the generated elastic fluid, and on the other by the hemisphere, loaded with the whole weight employed to confine the powder) so completely closed the bore that when the force of the powder was not sufficient to raise the weight to such a height that the stopper was actually blown out of the piece, not a particle of the elastic fluid could make its escape. And in those cases in which the weight was actually raised, and the generated elastic fluid made its escape, as it did not corrode the barrel in any other part but just *at the very extremity of the bore*, the experiment by which the weight was ascertained, which was just able to counterbalance the pressure of the generated elastic fluid, was in no wise vitiated, either by the increased diameter of the bore at its extremity or by any corrosion of the hemisphère itself; for as long as the bore retained its form and its dimensions in that part to which the efforts of the elastic fluid were confined, that is, in that part of the bore immediately in contact with the lower part of the stopper, the experiment could not be affected by any imperfection of the bore either above or below.

In the figures 2 and 4 this stopper is represented in its place, and Fig. 6 shews the plan, and Fig. 7 the profile of one of these stoppers of its full size. Fig. 8 shews a small, but very useful instrument, employed in introducing these stoppers into the bore, and more especially in occasionally extracting them ; it resembles a common cork-screw, only it is much smaller.

In the figure (where it is shewn in its full size) it is represented screwed into a stopper. Fig. 9 shews the plan, and Fig. 10 a side view, of the full size, of the hemisphere of hardened steel, by which the end of the barrel was closed. In the figures 2 and 4 the barrel is represented as being about half filled with powder.

Presuming that what has been already said, together with the assistance of the annexed drawings, will be sufficient to give a perfect idea of all the different parts of this apparatus, I shall now proceed to give an account of the experiments, which, from time to time, have been made with it. And in order to render these details as intelligible as possible, and to shew the results of all these inquiries in a clear and satisfactory manner, I shall first give a brief account of the manner in

which the experiments were made; of the various precautions used; and the particular appearances which
were observed in the prosecution of them.

The powder made use of in these experiments was of
the best quality, being that kind called *poudre de chasse*
by the French, and very fine grained; and it was all
taken from the same parcel. Care was taken to dry it
very thoroughly, and the air of the room in which it
was weighed out for use was very dry. The weights
employed for weighing the powder were German apothecary's grains, 104.8 of which make 100 grains Troy. I
have reduced the weights employed to confine the elastic
vapour generated in the combustion of the powder from
Bavarian pounds, in which they were originally expressed,
to pounds avoirdupois. The measures of length were
all taken in English feet and inches. The experiments
were all made in the open air, in the court-yard of the
arsenal at Munich; and they were all made in fair
weather, and between the hours of nine and twelve in
the forenoon, and two and five in the afternoon; but the
barrel was always charged, and the extremity of the bore
closed by its leather stopper, in the room where the
powder was weighed. In placing the barrel upon the
block of stone, great care was taken to put it exactly
under the center of gravity of the weight employed
to confine the generated elastic vapour. Upon applying
the red-hot ball to the vent tube, and fixing it in its
place by its lever which supported it, the explosion
very soon followed.

When the force of the generated elastic vapour was
sufficient to raise the weight, the explosion was attended
by a very sharp and surprisingly loud report; but when
the weight was not raised, as also when it was only a

little moved, but not sufficiently to permit the leather stopper to be driven quite out of the bore, and the elastic fluid to make its escape, the report was scarcely audible at the distance of a few paces, and did not at all resemble the report which commonly attends the explosion of gunpowder. It was more like the noise which attends the breaking of a small glass tube than anything else to which I can compare it.

In many of the experiments in which the elastic vapour was confined, this feeble report attending the explosion of the powder was immediately followed by another noise, totally different from it, which appeared to be occasioned by the falling back of the weight upon the end of the barrel, after it had been a little raised, but not sufficiently to permit the leather stopper to be driven quite out of the bore. In some of these experiments, a very small part only of the generated elastic fluid made its escape; in these cases the report was of a peculiar kind, and though perfectly audible at some considerable distance, yet not at all resembling the report of a musket. It was rather a very strong, sudden hissing, than a clear, distinct, and sharp report.

Though it could be determined with the utmost certainty, by the report of the explosion, whether any part of the generated elastic fluid had made its escape, yet for still greater precaution a light collar of very clean cotton wool was placed around the edge of the steel hemisphere, where it reposed upon the end of the barrel, which could not fail to indicate, by the black color it acquired, the escape of the elastic fluid, whenever it was strong enough to raise the weight by which it was confined sufficiently to force its way out of the barrel.

Though the end of the barrel, at the mouth of the

bore, was covered with a circular plate of gold, in order the better to defend the mouth of the bore against the effects of the corrosive vapour, yet this plate being damaged in the course of the experiments (a piece of it being blown away), the remainder of it was removed; and it was never after thought necessary to replace it by another.

When this plate of gold was taken away, the length of the barrel was of course diminished as much as the thickness of this plate amounted to, which was about $\frac{1}{400}$ part of an inch; but in order that even this small diminution of the length of the barrel might have no effect on the result of the experiments, its bore was deepened $\frac{1}{400}$ of an inch when this plate was removed, so that the capacity of the bore remained the same as before.

After making use of a great variety of expedients, the best and most convenient method of closing the end of the bore, and defending the flat surface of the steel hemisphere from the corroding vapours, was found to be this: first, to cover the end of the bore with a circular plate of thin oiled leather, then to lay upon this a very thin circular plate of hammered brass, and upon this brass plate the flat surface of the hemisphere. When the elastic fluid made its escape, a part of the leather was constantly found to have been torn away, but never in more places than one, that is to say, always on one side only.

What was very remarkable in all those experiments in which the generated elastic vapour was completely confined, was the small degree of expansive force which this vapour appeared to possess after it had been suffered to remain a few minutes, or even only a few seconds, confined in the barrel; for, upon raising the weight by means of its lever, and suffering this vapour to escape, instead of escaping with a loud report, it rushed out with a hissing noise hardly so loud or so sharp as the report of a common air gun; and its efforts against the leathern stopper, by which it assisted in raising the weight, were so very feeble as not to be sensible. Upon examining the barrel, however, this diminution of the force of the generated elastic fluid was easily explained; for what was undoubtedly in the moment of the explosion in the form of an elastic fluid was now found transformed into a *solid body* as hard as a stone! It may easily be imagined how much this unexpected appearance excited my curiosity; but, intent on the prosecution of the main design of these experiments, the ascertaining the force of fired gunpowder, I was determined not to permit myself to be enticed away from it by any extraordinary or unexpected appearances, or accidental discoveries, however alluring they might be; and, faithful to this resolution, I postponed the examination of this curious phænomenon to a future period; and since that time I have not found leisure to engage in it. I think it right, however, to mention in this place such cursory observations as I was able, in the midst of my other pursuits, to make upon this subject; and it will afford me sincere pleasure, if what I have to offer should so far excite the curiosity of philosophers as to induce some one who has leisure, and the means of pursuing such inquiries with effect, to precede me in the investigation of this interesting phænomenon; and as the subject is certainly not only extremely curious in itself, but bids fair to lead to other and very important discoveries, I cannot help flattering myself that some attention will be paid to it.

I have said that the solid substance into which the
elastic vapour generated in the combustion of gunpowder was transformed was *as hard as a stone.* This I
am sensible is but a vague expression; but the fact is,
that it was very hard, and so firmly attached to the inside of the barrel, and particularly to the inside of the
upper part of the vent tube, that it was always necessary, in order to remove it, to make use of a drill, and
frequently to apply a considerable degree of force. This
substance, which was of a black colour, or rather of a
dirty grey, which changed to black upon being exposed
to the air, had a pungent, acrid, alkaline taste, and smelt
like liver of sulphur. It attracted moisture from the
air with great avidity. Being moistened with water, and
spirit of nitre being poured upon it, a strong effervescence ensued, attended by a very offensive and penetrating smell. Nearly the whole quantity of matter of which
the powder was composed seemed to have been transformed into this substance; for the quantity of elastic
fluid which escaped upon removing the weight was very
inconsiderable; but this substance was *no longer gunpowder;* it was not even inflammable. What change
had it undergone? what could it have lost? It is very
certain that the barrel was considerably heated in these
experiments. Was this occasioned by the *caloric,* disengaged from the powder in its combustion, making its
escape through the iron? And is this a proof of the
existence of *caloric,* considered as a fluid *sui generis;* and
that it actually enters into the composition of inflammable bodies, or of pure air, and is necessary to their
combustion? I dare not take upon me to decide upon
such important questions. I once thought that the heat
acquired by a piece of ordnance in being fired arose

from the vibration or friction of its parts, occasioned
by the violent blow it received in the explosion of the
powder ; but I acknowledge fairly, that it does not
seem to be possible to account in a satisfactory manner
for the very considerable degree of heat which the barrel acquired in these experiments, merely on that supposition.

That this hard substance, found in the barrel after an
experiment in which the generated elastic vapour had
been completely confined, was actually in a fluid or
elastic state in the moment of the explosion, is evident
from hence, that in all those cases in which the weight
was raised, and the stopper blown out of the bore,
nothing was found remaining in the barrel. It was
very remarkable that this hard substance was not found
distributed about in all parts of the barrel indifferently,
but there was always found to be more of it near the
middle of the length of the bore, than at either of its
extremities ; and the upper part of the vent tube in
particular was always found quite filled with it.   It
should seem from hence, that it attached itself to those
parts of the barrel which were soonest cooled; and hence
the reason, most probably, why none of it was ever
found in the lower part of the vent tube, where it was
kept hot by the red-hot ball by which the powder was
set on fire.

I found by a particular experiment, that the gunpowder made use of, when it was well shaken together,
occupied rather less space in any given measure than the
same weight of water ; consequently, when gunpowder is
fired in a confined space which it fills, the density of the
generated elastic fluid must be at least equal to the
density of water.   The real specific gravity of the solid

grains of gunpowder, determined by weighing them in air, and in water, is to the specific gravity of water as 1.868 to 1.000. But if a measure whose capacity is one cubic foot hold 1000 ounces of water, the same measure will hold just 1077 ounces of fine grained gunpowder, such as I made use of in my experiments; that is to say, when it is well shaken together. When it was moderately shaken together, I found its weight to be exactly equal to that of an equal volume, or rather measure, of water. But it is evident that the weight of any given measure of gunpowder must depend much upon the forms and sizes of its grains.

I shall add only one observation more, relative to the particular appearances which attended the experiments in which the elastic vapour generated in the combustion of gunpowder was confined, and that is with regard to a curious effect produced upon the inferior flat surface of the leathern stopper, where it was in contact with the generated elastic vapour. Upon removing the stopper, its lower flat surface appeared entirely covered with an extremely white powder, resembling very light white ashes, but which almost instantaneously changed to the most perfect black colour upon being exposed to the air.

The sudden change of colour in this substance, upon its being exposed to the air, has led me to suspect that the solid matter found in the barrel was not originally black, but that it became black merely in consequence of its being exposed to the air. The dirty gray colour it appeared to have immediately on its being drilled out of the cavity of the bore, where it had fixed itself, seems to confirm this suspicion. An experiment made with a very strong glass barrel would not only decide this question, but would most probably render the experiment peculiarly beautiful and interesting on other accounts; and I have no doubt but a barrel of glass might be made sufficiently strong to withstand the force of the explosion. Whether it would be able to withstand the sudden effects of the heat, I own I am more doubtful; but as the subject is so very interesting, I think it would be worth while to try the experiment. Perhaps the apparatus might be so contrived as to set fire to the powder by the solar rays, by means of a common burning glass; but even if that method should fail, there are others equally unexceptionable, which might certainly be employed with success; and it is hardly possible to imagine anything more curious than an experiment of this kind would be if it were successful.

But to proceed to the experiments by which I endeavoured to ascertain the force of fired gunpowder. All the parts of the apparatus being ready, it was in the autumn of the year 1792 that the first experiment was made.

The barrel being charged with 10 grains of powder (its contents when quite full amounting to about 28 grains), and the end of the barrel being covered by a circular piece of oiled leather, and the flat side of the hemisphere being laid down upon this leather, and a heavy cannon, a twenty-four pounder, weighing 8081 lbs. avoirdupois, being placed upon its cascabel in a vertical position, upon this hemisphere, in order to confine by its weight the generated elastic fluid, the heated iron ball was applied to the end of the vent tube; and I had waited but a very few moments in anxious expectation of the event, when I had the satisfaction of observing that the experiment had succeeded.

The report of the explosion was extremely feeble, and so little resembling the usual report of the explosion of gunpowder, that the by-standers could not be persuaded that it was anything more than the cracking of the barrel, occasioned merely by its being heated by the red-hot ball ; yet, as I had been taught by the result of former experiments not to expect any other report, and as I found upon putting my hand upon the barrel that it began to be sensibly warm, I was soon convinced that the powder must have taken fire ; and after waiting four or five minutes, upon causing the weight which rested upon the hemisphere to be raised, the confined elastic vapour rushed out of the barrel. Upon removing the barrel and examining it, its bore was found to be choaked up by the solid substance which I have already described, and from which it was with some difficulty that it was freed, and rendered fit for another experiment.

The extreme feebleness of the report of the explosion, and the small degree of force with which the generated elastic fluid rushed out of the barrel upon removing the weight which had confined it, had inspired my assistants with no very favourable idea of the importance of these experiments. I had seen, indeed, from the beginning, by their looks, that they thought the precautions I took to confine so inconsiderable a quantity of gunpowder as the barrel could contain perfectly ridiculous ; but the result of the following experiment taught them more respect for an agent, of whose real force they had conceived so very inadequate an idea.

In this second experiment, instead of 10 grains of powder, the former charge, the barrel was now quite filled with powder, and the steel hemisphere, with its oiled leather under it, was pressed down upon the end of the barrel by the same weight which was employed for that purpose in the first experiment, namely, a cannon, weighing 8081 lbs.

In order to give a more perfect idea of the result of this important experiment, it may not be amiss to describe more particularly one of the principal parts of the apparatus employed in it, I mean the barrel. This barrel (which though similar to it in all respects, was not the same that has already been described) was made of the best hammered iron, and was of uncommon strength. Its length was $2\frac{3}{4}$ inches ; and though its diameter was also $2\frac{3}{4}$ inches, the diameter of its bore was no more than $\frac{1}{4}$ of an inch, or less than the diameter of a common goose quill. The length of its bore was 2..5 inches. Its diameter being $2\frac{3}{4}$ inches, and the diameter of its bore only $\frac{1}{4}$ of an inch, the thickness of the metal was $1\frac{1}{4}$ inch ; or it was 5 times as thick as the diameter of its bore.

The charge of powder was extremely small, amounting to but little more than $\frac{1}{10}$ of a cubic inch ; not so much as would be required to load a small pocket pistol, and not *one-tenth part* of the quantity frequently made use of for the charge of a common musket.

I should be afraid to relate the result of this experiment, had I not the most indisputable evidence to produce in support of the facts. This inconsiderable quantity of gunpowder, when it was set on fire by the application of the red-hot ball to the vent tube, exploded with such inconceivable force as to *burst the barrel asunder* in which it was confined, notwithstanding its enormous strength ; and with such a loud report as to alarm the whole neighbourhood.

It is impossible to describe the surprise of those who were spectators of this phænomenon. — They literally turned pale with affright and astonishment, and it was some time before they could recover themselves.

The barrel was not only completely burst asunder, but the two halves of it were thrown upon the ground in different directions : one of them fell close by my feet, as I was standing near the machinery to observe more accurately the result of the experiment. Though I thought it possible that the weight might be raised, and that the generated elastic vapour would make its escape, yet the bursting of the barrel was totally unexpected by me. It was a new lesson to teach me caution in these dangerous pursuits.

It affords me peculiar satisfaction in laying these accounts before the Public to be able to produce the most respectable testimony of their authenticity.

My friend, Sir Charles Blagden, formerly Secretary of the Royal Society, visited Munich in the summer of the year 1793, in his return from Italy ; and though I was then absent (travelling for the recovery of my health), yet, by my directions, he was not only shewn every part of the apparatus made use of in these experiments, but several experiments were actually repeated in his presence ; and he was kind enough to take with him to England one half of the barrel which was burst in the experiment just mentioned, which, at my request, he has deposited in the Museum of the Society, and which, I flatter myself, will be looked upon as an unequivocal proof of my discoveries relative to the amazing force of the elastic vapour generated in the combustion of gunpowder.

When the amazing strength of this barrel is considered, and the smallness of the capacity of its bore, it appears almost incredible, that so small a quantity of powder as that which was employed in the experiment could burst it asunder.

But without insisting on the testimony of several persons of respectable character, who were eye witnesses of the fact, and from whom Sir Charles Blagden received a verbal account, in detail, of all the circumstances attending the experiment, I fancy I may very safely rest my reputation upon the silent testimony which this broken instrument will bear in my favour; much doubting whether it be in the power of art to burst asunder such a mass of solid iron by any other means than those I employed.

Before I proceed to give an account of my subsequent experiments upon this subject, I shall stop here, for a moment, to make an estimate — from the known strength of *iron*, and the area of the fracture of the barrel — of the real force employed by the elastic vapour to burst it.

In a course of experiments upon the strength of various bodies, which I began many years ago, and an account of which I intend at some future period to lay before the Public,* I found, by taking the mean of the results of several experiments, that a cylinder of good

---

* Since writing the above, I have met with a misfortune which has put it out of my power to fulfil this promise.   On my return to England from Germany in October, 1795, after an absence of eleven years, I was stopped in my post-chaise, in St. Paul's church-yard, in London, at six o'clock in the evening, and robbed of a trunk which was behind my carriage, containing all my private papers, and my original notes and observations on philosophical subjects.   By this cruel robbery I have been deprived of the fruits of the labours of my whole life; and have lost all that I held most valuable.   This most severe blow has left an impression on my mind, which I feel that nothing will ever be able entirely to remove.

It is the more painful to me, as it has clouded my mind with suspicions that never can be cleared up.

tough hammered iron, the area of whose transverse section was only $\frac{3}{1600}$ of an inch, was able to sustain a weight of 119 lbs. avoirdupois without breaking. This gives 63,466 lbs. for the weight which a cylinder of the same iron whose transverse section is one inch would be able to sustain without being broken.

The area of the fracture of the barrel before mentioned was measured with the greatest care, and was found to measure very exactly $6\frac{1}{2}$ superficial inches. If now we suppose the iron of which this barrel was formed to be as strong as that whose strength I determined (and I have no reason to suspect it to be of an inferior quality), in that case the force actually employed in bursting the barrel must have been equal to the pressure of a weight of 412,529 lbs. For the resistance or cohesion of one inch is to 63,466 lbs. as that of $6\frac{1}{2}$ inches to 412,529 lbs.; and this force, so astonishingly great, was exerted by a body which weighed less than 26 grains Troy, and which acted in a space that hardly amounted to $\frac{1}{10}$ of a cubic inch.

To compare this force exerted by the elastic vapour generated in the combustion of gunpowder, and by which the barrel was burst, to the pressure of the atmosphere, it is necessary to determine the area of a longitudinal section of the bore of the piece. Now the diameter of the bore being $\frac{1}{4}$ of an inch, and its length (after deducting 0.15 of an inch for the length of the leathern stoppers) 2 inches, the area of its longitudinal section turns out to have been $\frac{1}{2}$ an inch. And if now we assume the mean pressure of the atmosphere $= 15$ lbs. avoirdupois for each superficial inch, this will give $7\frac{1}{2}$ lbs. for that upon a surface $= \frac{1}{2}$ inch, equal to the area of a longitudinal section of the bore of the barrel.

But we have just found that the force actually exerted by the elastic vapour in bursting the barrel, amounted to 412,529 lbs.; this force was therefore 55,004 times greater than the mean pressure of the atmosphere. For it is as $7\frac{1}{2}$ lbs. to 1 atmosphere, so 412,529 lbs. to 55,004 atmospheres.

Thinking it might perhaps be more satisfactory to know the *real strength* of the identical iron of which the barrel used in the before-mentioned experiment was constructed, rather than to rest the determination of the strength of the barrel upon the decision of the strength of iron taken from another parcel, and which very possibly might be of a different quality, since writing the above, I have taken the trouble to ascertain the strength of the iron of which the barrel was made, which was done in the following manner. Having the one half of the barrel still in my possession, I caused small pieces, 2 inches long, and about $\frac{1}{8}$ of an inch square, to be cut out of the solid block of metal, in the direction of its length, with a fine saw; and these pieces being first made round in their middle by filing, and then by turning in a lathe with a very sharp instrument, were reduced to such a size as was necessary, in order to their being pulled asunder in my machine for measuring the strength of bodies. In this machine the body to be pulled asunder is held fast by two strong vices, the one fastened to the floor, and the other suspended to the short arm of a Roman balance, or common steel-yard; and, in order that the bodies so suspended may not be injured by the jaws of the vices, so as to be weakened and to vitiate the experiments, they are not made cylindrical, but they are made larger at their two ends where they are held by the vices, and from thence their diameters were gradually diminished toward the middle of their lengths, where their measures were taken, and where they never failed to break.

As I had found by the results of many experiments, which I had before made upon the strength of the various metals, that iron, as well as all other metals, is rendered much stronger by hammering, I caused those pieces of the barrel which were prepared for these experiments to be separated from the solid block of metal, and reduced to their proper sizes, by sawing, filing, and turning, and without ever receiving a single blow of a hammer ; so that there is every reason to believe that the strength of the iron, as determined by the experiments, may safely be depended on. The results of the experiments were as follows : —

Exp.	Diameter of the Cylinder at the Fracture.	Area of a transverse section of the Cylinder at the Fracture.	Weight required to break it.	Weight required to break 1 inch of this Iron.
	Inch.	Inch.	Lbs. avoirdupois.	Lbs. avoirdupois.
I	$\frac{50}{1000}$	$\frac{1}{509.29}$	123.18	62,737
2	$\frac{60}{1000}$	$\frac{1}{353.68}$	182.00	64,366
3	$\frac{66}{1000}$	$\frac{1}{292.03}$	220.75	64,526
4	$\frac{76}{1000}$	$\frac{1}{220.07}$	277.01	61,063
(Number of Experiments = 4.)				252,692
			Mean	63,173

If now we take the strength of the iron of which the barrel was composed, as here determined by actual experiments, and compute the force required to burst the barrel, it will be found equal to the pressure of a weight of $410,624\frac{1}{2}$ lbs. instead of 436,800 lbs. as before determined. For it is the resistance or force of cohesion of 1 inch of this iron to 63,173 lbs., as that of $6\frac{1}{2}$ inches (the area of the fracture of the barrel) to $410,624\frac{1}{2}$ lbs.

And this weight turned into atmospheres, in the manner above described, gives 54,750 atmospheres for the measure of the force which must have been exerted by the elastic fluid in bursting the barrel.   But this force, enormous as it may appear, must still fall short of the real initial force of the elastic fluid generated in the combustion of gunpowder, before it has begun to expand; for it is more than probable that the barrel was in fact burst before the generated elastic fluid had exerted all its force, or that this fluid would have been able to have burst a barrel still stronger than that used in the experiment.   But I wave these speculations in order to hasten to more interesting and more satisfactory investigations.

Passing over in silence a considerable number of promiscuous experiments, which, having nothing particularly remarkable in their results, could throw no new light upon the subject, I shall proceed immediately to give an account of a regular set of experiments, undertaken with a view to the discovery of certain determined facts, and prosecuted with unremitting perseverance.

These experiments were made by my directions, under the immediate care of Mr. Reichenbach, commandant of the corps of artificers in the Elector's military service, and of Count Spreti, first lieutenant in the regiment of artillery.

Though I was prevented, by ill-health, from being actually present at all these experiments, yet being at hand, and having every day, and almost every hour, regular reports of the progress that was made in them, and of everything extraordinary that happened, the experiments may be said, with great truth, to have been made under my immediate direction; and as the two gentlemen by whom I was assisted were not only every way qualified for such an undertaking, but had been present, and had assisted me in a number of similar experiments, which I had myself made, they had acquired all that readiness and dexterity in the various manipulations which are so useful and necessary in experimental inquiries; and I think I can safely venture to say that the experiments may be depended on.

It would have afforded me great satisfaction to have been able to say that the experiments were all made by myself; and I had resolved to repeat them before I made them public, particularly as there appear to have been some very extraordinary and quite unaccountable differences in the results of those made in different seasons of the year; but having hitherto been prevented by ill-health, and by various avocations, from engaging in these laborious researches, I have thought it right not to delay any longer the publication of facts which appear to me to be both new and interesting, as their being known may perhaps excite others to engage in their farther investigation.

The principal objects I had in view in the following set of experiments were, first, to determine the expansive force of the elastic vapour generated in the combustion of gunpowder, in its various states of condensation, and to ascertain the ratio of its elasticity to its density: and secondly, to measure, by one decisive experiment, the utmost force of this fluid in its most dense state; that is to say, when the powder completely fills the space in which it is fired, and in which the generated fluid is confined. As these experiments were very numerous, and as it will be more satisfactory to be able to see all their results at one cursory view, I have brought them into the form of a general table.

In this table, which does not stand in need of any particular explanation, may be seen the results of all these investigations.

The dimensions of the barrel made use of in the experiments mentioned in this table were as follows : —

Diameter of the bore at its muzzle = 0.25 of an inch.

Joint capacities of the bore, and of its vent tube, exclusive of the space occupied by the leathern stopper = 0.08974 of a cubic inch.

Quantity of powder contained by the barrel and its vent tube when both were quite full (exclusive of the space occupied by the leathern stopper), 25.641 German apothecary's grains, $= 24\frac{1}{2}$ grains Troy.

The capacities of the barrel and of its vent tube were determined by filling them with mercury, and then weighing in the air, and in water, the quantity of mercury required to fill them ; and the quantity of powder required to fill the barrel and its vent tube was determined by computation, from the known joint capacities of the barrel and its vent tube in parts of a cubic inch, and from the known specific gravity of the powder used in the experiments.

Thus the contents of the barrel and its vent tube having been found to amount to 0.08974 of a cubic inch, and it having been found that 1 cubic inch of the gunpowder in question, well shaken together, weighed just 272.68 grains Troy, this gives 24.47 grains Troy ($= 25.641$ grains German apothecary's weight) for the contents of the barrel and its vent tube.

The numbers expressing the charges of powder in *thousandth parts* of the joint capacities of the barrel and of its vent tube were determined from the known quantities of powder used in the different experiments, ex-

pressed in German apothecary's grains, and the relation
of these quantities to the quantity required to fill the
barrel and its vent tube completely.

Thus, as the barrel and its vent tube were capable of
containing 25.641 apothecary's grains of powder, if we
suppose this quantity to be divided into 1000 equal
parts, this will give 39 of those parts for 1 grain; 78
parts for 2 grains; 390 for 10 grains, &c. For it is
25.641 to 1000, as 1 to 39, very nearly.

As this method of expressing the quantities of powder
shows at the same time the relative density of the generated elastic fluid, it is the more satisfactory on that
account: it will also considerably facilitate the computations necessary, in order to ascertain the ratio of the
elasticity of this fluid to its density.

The elastic force of the fluid generated in the combustion of the charge of powder is measured by the
weight by which it was confined, or rather by that which
it was just able to move, but which it could not raise
sufficiently to blow the leathern stopper quite out of the
mouth of the bore of the barrel.

This weight, in all the experiments, except those
which were made with very small charges of powder,
was a piece of ordnance of greater or less dimensions
or greater or less weight, according to the force of the
charge, placed vertically upon its cascabel, upon the steel
hemisphere which closed the end of the barrel; and the
same piece of ordnance, by having its bore filled with a
greater or smaller number of bullets, as the occasion required, was made to serve for several experiments.

The weight employed for confining the generated
elastic fluid is expressed in the following table in *pounds
avoirdupois;* but in order that a clearer and more perfect

idea may be formed of the real force of this elastic fluid, I have added a column in which its force, answering to each charge of powder, is expressed in *atmospheres*.

The numbers in this column were computed in the following manner. The diameter of the bore of the barrel at its muzzle being just $\frac{1}{4}$ of an inch, the area of its transverse section is 0.049088 of a superficial inch; and, assuming the mean pressure of the atmosphere upon 1 superficial inch equal to 15 lbs. avoirdupois, this will give 0.73631 of a pound avoirdupois, for that pressure upon 0.049088 of a superficial inch, or upon a surface equal to the area by which the generated elastic fluid acted on the weight employed to confine it; consequently the weight expressed in *pounds avoirdupois* which measured the force of the generated elastic fluid in any given experiment, being divided by 0.73631, will show how many times the pressure exerted by the fluid was greater than the mean pressure of the atmosphere. Thus in the experiment No. 6, where the weight which measured the elastic force of the generated fluid was = 504.8 lbs. avoirdupois, it is $\frac{504.8}{0.73631} = 685.6$ atmospheres. And so of the rest.

I have said that the diameter of the bore of the barrel made use of in the following experiments was just $\frac{1}{4}$ of an inch *at its muzzle*, and this is strictly true, as I found upon measuring it with the greatest care; but its diameter is not perfectly the same throughout its whole length, being rather narrower towards its lower end; yet the *capacity* of the barrel being known, and also *the diameter of the bore of its muzzle*, any small inequalities of the bore in any other part can in no wise affect the results of the experiments, as will be evident to those who will take the trouble to consider the matter for a moment with attention. I should not indeed have thought it necessary to mention this circumstance, had I not been afraid that some one who should calculate the joint capacities of the bore and of the vent tube from their lengths and diameters, finding their calculation not to agree with my determination of those capacities, as ascertained by filling them with mercury, might suspect me of having committed an error. The *mean* diameter of the bore of barrel, as determined from its length and its capacity, turns out to be just 0.2281 of an inch; the diameter of the vent tube being taken equal to 0.07 of an inch, and its length 1.715 inch.

TABLE I.

Experiments on the Force of Fired Gunpowder.

Number of the Experiment.	Time when the Experiment was made.	State of the Atmosphere.		The Charge of Powder.		Weight employed to confine the Elastic Fluid.		General Remarks.
		Thermometer.	Barometer.	In Apothecary's Gr.	In 1000 parts of the capacity of the Bore.	In lbs. avoirdupois.	In Atmospheres.	
	1793. h. m.	F.°	Eng. In.	Gr.	Parts.	Lbs.		
1	23d Feb. 9 0	31	28.58	1	39	504.80	—	{ The generated elastic fluid was completely confined, the weight not being raised.
2	9 30	–	—	2	78	—	—	
3	25th· 9 0	37	28.56	3	117	—	—	Ditto.
4	10 15	–	—	4	156	—	—	Ditto, weight not raised.
5	10 30	–	—	5	195	—	—	Ditto, ditto.
6	11 0	–	—	6	234	—	685.60	Weight just moved.
7	P. M. 3 0	57	28.37	1	39	14.16	—	{ In these three experiments the weight was raised with a report as loud as that of a pistol.
8	3 15	–	—	–	—	26.50	—	
9	3 30	–	—	–	—	38.90	—	
10	3 45	–	—	–	—	51.30	—	{ Just raised, report much weaker.
11	4 0	–	——	–	—	57.40	77.86	Weight hardly moved.
12	26th 9 0	34	28.10	2	78	163.50	—	Not raised.
13	9 15	–	—	–	—	124.00	—	Raised with a loud report.
14	9 30	–	—	–	—	130.50	—	Ditto, the report weaker.
15	9 45	–	—	–	—	133.00	—	Ditto, the report still weaker.

Experiments to determine

TABLE I.— *Continued.*

Number of the Experiment.	Time when the Experiment was made.	State of the Atmosphere.		The Charge of Powder.		Weight employed to confine the Elastic Fluid.		General Remarks.
		Thermometer.	Barometer.	In Apothecary's Gr.	In 1000 parts of the capacity of the Bore.	In lbs. avoirdupois.	In Atmospheres.	
	1793. h. m.	F.°	Eng. In.	Gr.	Parts.	Lbs.		
16	26th Feb.10 0	34	28.10	2	78	134.20	182.30	Weight but just moved.
17	3 0	48	28.31	3	117	186.30	—	Raised with a loud report.
18	3 15	—	—	—	—	198.70	—	Ditto, ditto.
19	3 30	—	—	—	—	204.80	—	Ditto, report weaker.
20	3 45	—	—	—	—	208.50	—	Raised, report weaker.
21	4 0	—	—	—	—	212.24	288.20	{ The weight hardly moved, no report.
22	27th 3 0	50	28.36	4	156	269.20	—	Raised with a loud report.
23	3 15	—	—	—	—	274.13	—	Ditto, ditto.
24	3 30	—	—	—	—	277.90	—	Ditto, report less loud.
25	3 45	—	—	—	—	281.57	382.40	{ Weight hardly moved and no report.
26	28th 9 0	34	28.32	5	195	319.68	—	Raised, loud report.
27	9 15	—	—	—	—	351.37	—	Ditto, ditto.
28	9 30	—	—	—	—	400.90	—	Ditto, ditto.
29	10 0	—	—	—	—	475.20	—	Not raised.
30	3 0	48	28.35	—	—	443.50	—	Not raised.
31	3 15	—	—	—	—	425.65	—	Not raised.
32	3 30	—	—	—	—	419.46	—	Not raised.
33	3 45	—	—	—	—	413.27	561.20	Weight but just moved.
34	1st Mar. 9 0	34	28.35	7	273	535.79	—	Raised with a loud report.
35	9 15	—	—	—	—	548.14	—	Ditto, ditto.
36	9 30	—	—	—	—	560.52	—	Ditto, ditto.
37	3 0	59	28.34	—	—	572.90	—	Ditto, ditto.
38	3 15	—	—	—	—	585.28	—	Ditto, report weaker.
39	3 30	—	—	—	—	597.66	811.70	{ Weight but just moved, no report.
40	3 45	—	—	8	312	690.52	—	Raised, report very loud.
41	4 0	—	—	—	—	752.42	—	Ditto, ditto.
42	4 15	—	—	—	—	783.37	—	Ditto, ditto.
43	2d 9 0	50	28.32	—	—	876.22	—	Not raised.
44	9 15	—	—	—	—	845.19	—	But just raised, report weak
45	9 30	—	—	—	—	857.64	1164.8	{ Weight but just moved and no report.
46	9 45	—	—	9	351	961.65	—	Raised with a loud report.
47	10 0	—	—	—	—	1209.4	—	Not raised.
48	10 30	—	—	—	—	1142.3	1551.3	Weight just moved, no report.
49	3 0	52	28.33	10	390	1456.8	—	Not raised.
50	3 30	—	—	—	—	1329.9	—	Raised, loud report.
51	5th 9 0	32	28.20	—	—	1387.5	1884.3	{ Weight but just moved and no report.
52	9 15	—	—	11	429	1708.2	—	Not raised.

TABLE I.—*Continued.*

Number of the Experiment.	Time when the Experiment was made.	State of the Atmosphere.		The Charge of Powder.		Weight employed to confine the Elastic Fluid.		General Remarks.
		Thermometer.	Barometer.	In Apothecary's Gr.	In 1000 parts of the capacity of the Bore.	In lbs. avoirdupois.	In Atmospheres.	
	1793. h. m.	F.	Eng. In.	Gr.	Parts.	Lbs.		
53	5th Mar. 9 45	32°	28.20	11	429	1646.2	1884.3	Not raised.
54	10 15	-	—	-	—	1615.2	—	Raised with a weak report.
55	10 45	-	—	-	—	1634.0	2219.0	{ Weight but just moved and no report.
56	6th 9 0	36	28.34	1	468	1943.3	—	Not raised.
57	9 30	-	—	-	—	1932.2	—	Not raised.
58	10 30	-	—	-	—	1907.4	—	Weight not raised.
59	11 0	-	—	-	—	1878.4	—	Raised with a loud report.
60	11 30	-	—	-	—	1895.1	2573.7	{ Weight but just moved and no report.
61	3 0	42	28.30	13	507	2142.7	—	Raised with a loud report.
62	3 15	-	—	-	—	2204.6	—	Ditto, ditto.
63	3 30	-	—	-	—	2266.5	—	Raised with a loud report.
64	3 45	-	—	-	—	2390.3	—	Raised, report weaker.
65	4 0	-	—	-	—	2422.0	3288.3	Weight just moved, no report.
66	9th 9 0	43	28.31	14	546	3213.0	—	Not raised.
67	9 30	-	—	-	—	3093.0	—	Not raised.
68	10 0	-	—	-	—	2968.0	—	Not raised.
69	10 30	-	—	-	—	2846.0	—	Raised with a loud report.
70	10 45	-	—	-	—	2908.0	—	Raised, report weaker.
71	11 0	-	—	-	—	2939.0	—	Ditto, report still weaker.
72	11 15	-	—	-	—	2951.0	4008.0	{ Weight but just moved, no report.
73	11 30	-	—	15	585	3750.0	—	Not raised.
74	11 45	-	—	-	—	3508.0	—	Not raised.
75	12 15	-	—	-	—	3477.0	4722.5	{ Weight but just moved and no report.
76	11th 9 0	43	28.30	16	624	4037.0	—	{ The weight was raised with a loud report.
77	9 15	-	—	-	—	4284.0	—	Raised, loud report.
78	9 30	-	—	-	—	4532.0	—	Ditto, ditto.
79	4th Apr. 3 0	70	28.20	-	—	5027.0	—	Ditto, ditto.
80	3 15	-	—	-	—	5138.0	—	Raised, report weaker.
81	3 30	-	—	-	—	5262.0	—	Not raised.
82	3 45	-	—	-	—	5220.0	7090.0	{ Weight just moved, but no report.
83	5th 3 0	68	28.30	17	663	8081.0	—	Not raised.
84	3 30	-	—	18	702	8081.0	10977.	{ The weight was raised with a very sharp report, louder than that of a well-loaded musket.
85	4 0	-	—	-	—	8700.0	—	{ The vent tube of the barrel was burst, the explosion being attended with a very loud report.

The barrel being rendered unfit for further service by the bursting of its vent tube, an end was put to this set of experiments.

In order that a clear and satisfactory idea may be formed of the results of these experiments I have drawn the figure in Plate VI., in which the given densities of the generated elastic fluid, or (which amounts to the same thing) the quantities of powder used for the charge, being taken on the line A B, from A towards B, the corresponding elasticities, as found by the experiments, are represented by lines perpendicular to the line A B at the points where the measures of the densities end.

As the irregularities of the dotted line A C are owing, no doubt, merely to the errors committed in making the experiments, these irregularities being removed, by drawing the line A D in such a manner as to balance the errors of the experiments, this line A D, which must necessarily be regular, will, by bare inspection, give us a considerable degree of insight into the nature of the equation which must be formed to express the relation of the densities to the elasticities; the discovery of which was one principal object of these experimental enquiries.

Putting the density $= x$ and the elasticity $= y$, the line A D will be the locus of the equation expressing the relation of x to y; and had Mr. Robins's supposition that the elasticity is as the density been true, x would have been found to be to y in a constant (simple) ratio, — A D would have been a straight line, — and A E would have been the position of this line, had Mr. Robins's determination of the force of fired gunpowder been accurate.

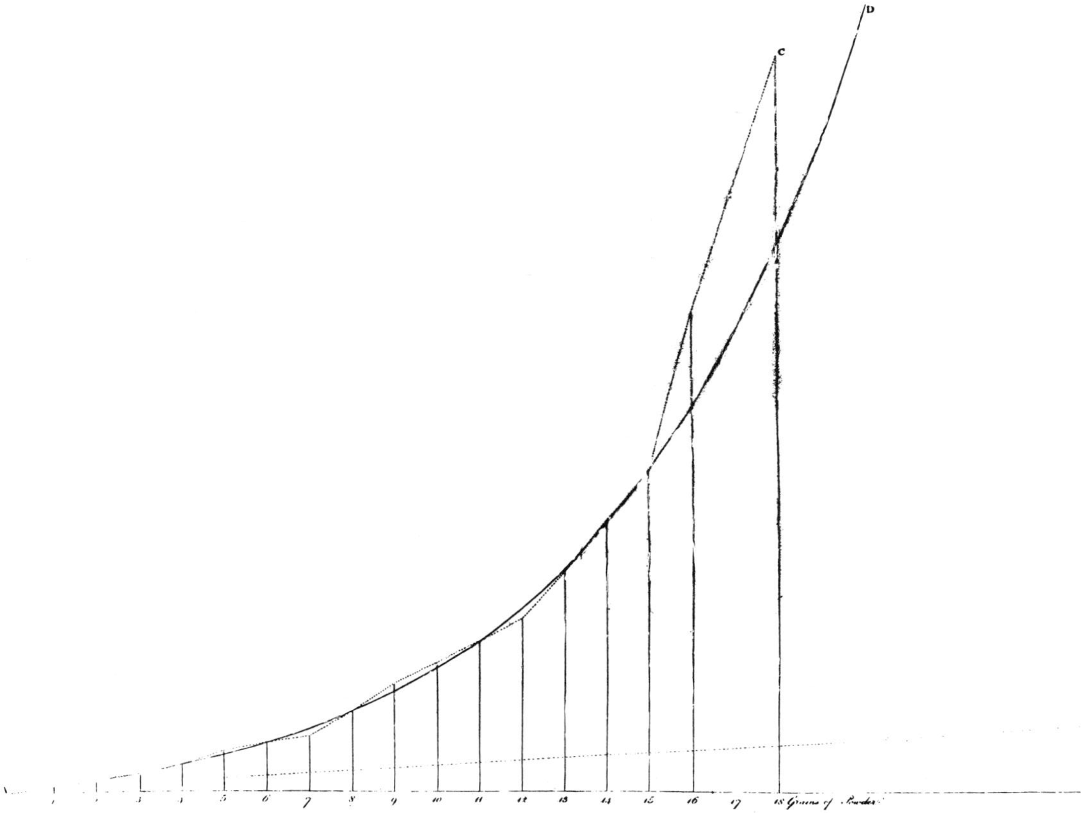

PLATE VI.

But A D is a curve, and this shows that the ratio of x to y is variable; and moreover it is a curve *convex towards the line* A B, on which x is taken, and this circumstance proves that the ratio of y to x is continually increasing.

Though these experiments all tend to show that the ratio of y to x increases as x is increased, yet when we consider the subject with attention, we shall, I think, find reason to conclude that the exponent of that ratio can never be less than *unity;* and farther, that it must of necessity have *that value precisely*, when, the density being taken infinitely small, or $= 0$, x and y vanish together.

Supposing this to be the case, namely, that the exponent of the ultimate ratio of y to x is $= 1$, let the densities or successive values of x be expressed by a series of natural numbers,

$$0, 1, 2, 3, 4, \text{ &c. to } 1000,$$

the last term $= 1000$ answering to the greatest density; or when the powder completely fills the space in which it is confined; then, by putting $z =$ the variable part of the exponent of the ratio of y to x,

To each of the successive values of

$$x = 0, 1, 2, 3, 4, \text{ &c.}$$

The corresponding value of y will be accurately expressed by the equations

$$0^{1+z}, 1^{1+z}, 2^{1+z}, 3^{1+z}, 4^{1+z}, \text{ &c.}$$

For as the variable part (z) of this exponent may be taken of *any dimensions*, it may be so taken at each given term of the series (or for each particular value of x), that the equation $x^{1+z} = y$ may always correspond with the result of the experiments; and when this is done, the value of z, and the law of its increase as x increases, will be known ; and this will show the relation of x to y, or of the elasticities of the generated fluid to their corresponding densities, in a clear and satisfactory manner.

Without increasing the length of this paper still more (it being perhaps already too voluminous), by giving an account in detail of all the various computations I made, in order, from the results of the experiments in the foregoing table, to ascertain the real value of z, and the rate at which it increases as x is increased, I shall content myself with merely giving the general results of these investigations, and referring for farther information to the following Table II., where the agreement of the law founded on them, with the results of the foregoing experiments, may be seen.

Having, from the results of the experiments in Table I., computed the different values of z, corresponding to all the different densities, or different charges of powder, from 1 grain, or 39 *thousandth parts*, to 18 grains, or 702 *thousandth parts* of the capacity of the barrel, I found, that while the density of the elastic fluid $= x$, expressed in *thousandth parts*, is increased from 0 to 1000 (or till the powder completely fills the space in which it is confined), the variable part z of the exponent of x, $(1 + z)$, is increased from 0 to $\frac{4}{10}$. And though some of the experiments, and particularly those which were made with large charges of powder, seemed to indicate that while x is increased with an equable or uniform motion, z increases with a motion continually accelerated ; *yet*, as the results of by far the greatest number of the other experiments showed the velocity of the increase of z to be *equable*, this circumstance, added to some other reasons, drawn from the nature of the subject, have induced me to assume the ratio of the increase of z to the increase of x as constant.

But if, while x increases with an equable velocity from 0 to 1000, z is increased with an *equable velocity* from 0 to $\frac{4}{10}$, then it is everywhere z to x as $\frac{4}{10}$ to 1000; or 1000 $z = \frac{4}{10}$, and consequently $z = \frac{4x}{10000}$; and when x is $= 1$, it is $z = \frac{4}{10000} = 0.0004$; and when x is greater or less than 1, it is $z = 0.0004\,x$; and z being expunged, the general equation expressing the relation of x to y becomes $x^{1 + 0.0004x} = y$; and this is the equation which was made use of in computing the values of y, expressed in the following Table.

In order that the elasticities might be expressed in atmospheres, the values of y, as determined by this equation, were multiplied by 1.841.

If it be required to express the elasticity in *pounds avoirdupois*, then the value of y, as determined by the foregoing equation, being multiplied by 27.615, will show how many pounds avoirdupois, pressing upon a superficial inch, will be equal to the pressure exerted by the elastic fluid in the case in question.

TABLE II.

General Results of the Experiments in Table I. on the Force of Fired Gunpowder.

The Charge of Powder.		Value of the Exponent	Computed Elasticity of the Generated Fluid, or value of y according to the Theorem, $x^{1\,+\,0.0004x} = y.$		Actual Elasticity as shewn by the Experiments.	Difference of the Computed and the Actual Elasticities.
In Grains.	In Equal Parts.	$1+0.0004x.$	In Equal Parts.	In Atmospheres.	In Atmospheres.	In Atmospheres.
1.	39	1.0156	41.294	76.822	77.86	+ 1.838
2.	78	1.0312	89.357	164.506	182.30	+ 17.794
3.	117	1.0468	146.210	269.173	228.20	— 40.973
4.	156	1.0624	213.784	393.577	382.40	— 11.177
5.	195	1.0780	294.209	541.640	561.20	+ 19.560
6.	234	1.0936	389.919	717.841	685.60	— 32.241
7.	273	1.1092	503.723	927.353	811.70	— 115.653
8.	312	1.1248	638.889	1176.190	1164.80	— 12.390
9.	351	1.1404	799.223	1471.370	1551.30	+ 79.930
10.	390	1.1560	989.169	1821.060	1884.30	+ 63.240
11.	429	1.1716	1213.910	2234.810	2219.00	— 15.810
12.	468	1.1872	1479.500	2723.770	2573.70	— 150.070
13.	507	1.2028	1793.000	3300.910	3283.30	— 17.610
14.	546	1.2184	2162.690	3980.520	4008.00	+ 27.480
15.	585	1.2340	2598.180	4783.260	4722.50	— 60.760
16.	624	1.2496	3110.730	5726.830	7090.00	+1363.170
17.	663	1.2652	3713.460	6836.460		
18.	702	1.2808	4421.690	8140.340	10977.00	+2836.660
19.	741	1.2964	5253.300	9671.330		
20.	780	1.3120	6229.140	11467.800		
25.641	1000	1.4000	15848.900	29177.900		

The agreement of the elasticities computed from the theorem $x^{1\,+\,0.0004x} = y$, with the actual elasticities as they were measured in the experiments, may be seen in the foregoing table ; but this agreement may be seen in a much more striking manner by a bare inspection of the figure in Plate VI.; for the line A D in this figure, having been drawn from the computed elasticities, its general coincidence with the line A C shews how nearly the computed and the actual elasticities approach each other. And when the irregularities of the line A C (which, as has already been observed, must be attributed to the unavoidable errors of the experiments) are corrected, these two curves will be found to coincide with much precision, throughout a considerable part of the range of the experiments ; but towards the end of the set of experiments, when the charges of powder were considerably increased, the elasticities seem to have increased faster than, according to the assumed law, they ought to have done.

From this circumstance, and from the immense force the charge must have exerted in the experiment when the barrel was burst, I was led to suspect that the elastic force of the fluid generated in the combustion of gunpowder, when its density is great, is still much greater than these experiments seem to indicate; and a farther investigation of the subject served to confirm me in this opinion.

It has been shewn that the force exerted by the charge in the experiment in which the barrel was burst could not have been less than the pressure of 54,752 atmospheres ; but the greatest force of the generated elastic fluid, when, the powder filling the space in which it is confined, its density is $= 1000$, on computing its elasticity by the theorem $x^{1 + 0.0004x} = y$, turns out to be only equal to 29,178 atmospheres.

In this computation the mean of the results of all the experiments in the foregoing set is taken as a standard to ascertain the value, expressed in atmospheres, of y, and it is $y \times 1.841 = 29,178$.

But if, instead of taking the mean of the whole set of experiments as a standard, we select that experiment in which the force exerted by the powder appears to have been the greatest, yet, in this case, even the initial force of fired gunpowder computed by the above rule would be much too small.

In the experiment **No. 84**, when the charge consisted of 18 grains of powder, and the lensity, or value of x was 702, a weight equal to the pressure of 10,977 atmospheres was raised. Here the value of y ($= x^{1 + 0.0004 x}$) is found to be ($702^{1.2808}$), $= 4421.7$; and to express this value of y in atmospheres, and at the same time to accommodate it to the actual result of the experiment, it must be multiplied by 2.4826; for it is 4421.7 (the value of y expressed in equal parts) to 10,977 (its value in atmospheres, as shewn by the experiment), as 1 to 2.4826, and consequently $4421.7 \times 2.4826 = 10,977$.

If now the value of y be computed on the same principles, when x is put $= 1000$, it will turn out to be $y = 1000^{1 + 0.4} = 15,849$; and this number expressed in atmospheres, by multiplying it by 2.4826, gives the value of $y = 39,346$ atmospheres.

This, however, falls still far short of 54,752 atmospheres, the force the powder was actually found to exert when the charge filled the space in which it was confined. But in the 84th experiment, when 18 grains of powder were used, as the weight (8081 lbs. avoirdupois) was raised with *a very loud report*, it is more than probable that the force of the generated elastic fluid was in fact considerably greater than that at which it was estimated, namely, greater than the pressure of 10,977 atmospheres.

But, without wasting time in fruitless endeavours to reconcile anomalous experiments, which, probably, never can be made to agree, I shall hasten to give an account of another set of experiments; the results of which, it must be confessed, were still more various, extraordinary, and inexplicable.

The machinery having been repaired and put in order, the experiments were recommenced in July, 1793, the weather at that time being very hot.

The principal part of the apparatus, *the barrel,* had undergone a trifling alteration : upon refitting and cleaning it, the diameter of its bore at the muzzle was found to be a little increased, so that a weight equal to 8081 lbs. avoirdupois,. instead of being equal to 10,977 atmospheres (as was the case in the former experiments), was now just equal to the pressure of 9431 atmospheres.

Though I was not at Munich when this last set of experiments was made, they, however, were undertaken at my request, and under my direction, and I have no reason to doubt of their having been executed with all possible care. They were all made by the same persons who were employed in making the first set; and as these experimenters may be supposed to have grown expert in practice, and as they could not possibly have had any interest in deceiving me, I cannot suspect the accuracy of their reports.

TABLE III.

Experiments on the Force of Fired Gunpowder.

Number of the Experiment.	Time when the Experiment was made.	State of the Atmosphere.		The Charge of Powder.		Weight employed to confine the Elastic Fluid.		General Remarks.
		Thermometer.	Barometer.	In Apothecary's Gr.	In 1000 parts of the capacity of the Bore.	In lbs. avoirdupois.	In Atmospheres.	
	1793. h. m.	F. °	Eng. In.	Gr.	Parts.	Lbs.		
86	1st July 4 0	88	28.37	17	663	8081	9431	{ The weight was raised with an astonishing loud report.
87	4 30	–	–	–	–	–	–	
88	4 45	–	—	16	624	—	—	{ In these three experiments the weight was raised with a very loud report.
89	5 0	–	—	15	585	—	—	
90	5 30	–	—	12	468	—	—	Weight not raised.
91	6 0	–	—	13	507	—	9431	{ Weight but just raised, report very weak.
92	2d 9 0	71	28.38	–	—	—	—	Raised, loud report.
93	9 30	–	—	12	468	—	—	Raised, feeble report.
94	10 0	–	—	–	—	—	9431	Raised, report very feeble.
95	10 30	80	—	11⅞	—	—	—	*Just moved*, no report.
96	3d 10 0	70	28.55	12	468	—	—	Not raised.
97	10 30	–	—	13	507	—	—	Not raised.
98	11 0	75	—	14	546	—	9431	Just raised, feeble report.
99	4th 9 0	70	28.56	14	546	—	—	Not raised.
100	9 30	–	—	–	—	—	—	Not raised.
101	10 0	72	—	15	585	—	—	{ The weight was raised, the report not very loud.
102	10 30	–	—	15½	—	—	—	Nearly as above.
103	8th 9 0	74	28.42	–	—	—	—	{ Raised, and with an uncommonly loud report.
104	9 30	–	—	13	507	—	—	Raised, report very loud.
105	10 45	85	—	12	468	—	9431	{ But just raised, the report very feeble.
106	17th 9 0	75	28.40	–	—	—	—	Nearly as above.
107	9 45	–	—	–	—	—	—	Ditto.
108	10 30	–	—	11¼	—	—	—	*Just moved*, no report.
109	11 0	–	—	–	—	—	—	The same as above.

It appears, from the foregoing table, that, in the afternoon of the 1st of July, the weight (which was a heavy brass cannon, a 24 pounder, weighing 8081 lbs. avoirdupois) was not raised by 12 grains of powder, but that 13 grains raised it with an audible though weak report. That, the next morning, July 2d, at 10 o'clock, it was raised twice by charges of 12 grains. That, in the morning of the 3d of July, it was not raised by 12 grains nor by 13 grains; but that 14 grains just raised it. That, in the afternoon of the same day, two experiments were made with 14 grains of powder, in neither of which the weight was raised; but that in another experiment, in which 15 grains of powder were used, it was raised with a moderate report. That, in the morning of the 8th of July, in two experiments, one with $15\frac{1}{2}$ grains, and the other with 13 grains of powder, the weight was raised with a *loud report;* and in an experiment with 12 grains, it was raised with a *feeble report.* And lastly, that in two successive experiments, made in the morning of the 17th of July, the weight was raised by charges of 12 grains.

Hence it appears that, under circumstances the most favourable to the development of the force of gunpowder, a charge (= 12 grains) filling $\frac{468}{1000}$ of the cavity in which it is confined, on being fired, exerts a force against the sides of the containing vessel, equal to the pressure of 9431 atmospheres; which pressure amounts to 141,465 lbs. avoirdupois on each superficial inch.

Mr. Robins makes the initial, or greatest force of the fluid generated in the combustion of gunpowder (namely, when the charge completely fills the space in which it is confined) to be only equal to the pressure of 1000 atmospheres. It appears, however, from the result of these experiments, that even admitting the elasticities to be as the densities, as Mr. Robins supposes them to be, the initial force of this generated elastic fluid must be at least twenty times greater than Mr. Robins determined it; — for $\frac{468}{1000}$, the density of the elastic fluid in the experiments in question, is to 1, its density when the powder

quite fills the space in which it is confined, as 9431 atmospheres, the measure of its elastic force in the experiments in question, to 20,108 atmospheres ; which, according to Mr. Robins's theory respecting the ratio of
the elasticities to the densities, would be the measure of
its initial force.

But all my experiments tend uniformly to prove, that
the elasticities increase *faster* than in the simple ratio of
the corresponding densities; consequently, the initial
force of the generated elastic fluid *must necessarily* be
greater than the pressure of 20,108 atmospheres.

In one of my experiments, which I have often had occasion to mention, the force actually exerted by the fluid
must have been at least equal to the pressure of 54,752
atmospheres. The other experiments ought, no doubt,
to shew, at least, that it is *possible* that such an enormous
force may have been exerted by the charge made use of;
and this, I think, they actually indicate.

In the first set of experiments, which were made when
the weather was cold, though the results of them uniformly shewed the force of the powder to be much less
than it appeared to be in all the subsequent experiments,
made with greater charges and in warm weather, yet they
all shew that the ratio of the elasticity of the generated
fluid to its density is very different from that which Mr.
Robins's theory supposes; and that this ratio increases
as the density of the fluid is increased.

Supposing (what on many accounts seems to be extremely probable) that this ratio increases uniformly, or
with an equable celerity, while the density is uniformly
augmented; and supposing farther, that the velocity
and limit of its increase have been rightly determined
from the result of the set of experiments, Table I., which

were made with that view; then, from the result of the experiments of which we have just been giving an account (in which 12 grains of powder exerted a force equal to 9431 atmospheres), taking these experiments as a standard, we can, with the help of the theorem $(x^{1\,+\,0.0004x} = y)$ deduced from the former set of experiments, compute the initial force of fired gunpowder, thus : —

The density of the elastic fluid, when 12 grains of powder are used for the charge, being $= 468$, it is $468^{1.1872} = y = 1479.5$; and in order that this value of y may correspond with the result of the experiment, and be expressed in atmospheres, it must be multiplied by a certain coefficient, which will be found by dividing the value of y expressed in atmospheres, as shewn by the experiment, by the number here found indicating its value, as determined by computation.

It is therefore $\frac{9431}{1479.5} = 6.3744$ for the value of this coefficient; and this multiplied into the number 1479.5 gives 9431 for the value of y in atmospheres.

Again, the density being supposed $= 1000$ (or that the charge of powder completely fills the cavity in which it is confined), in that case it will be $1000^{1\,+\,0.4} = y = 15,849$; and this number being turned into atmospheres by being multiplied by the coefficient above found $(= 6.3744)$, gives 101,021 atmospheres for the measure of the *initial force* of the elastic fluid generated in the combustion of gunpowder.

Enormous as this force appears, I do not think it overrated; for nothing much short of such an inconceivable force can, in my opinion, ever explain in a satisfactory manner the bursting of the barrel so often mentioned; and to this we may add, that, as in 7 different experiments, all made with charges of 12 grains of powder, there were no less than 5 in which the weight was *raised with a report;* and as the same weight was *moved* in 3 different experiments in which the charge consisted of less than 12 grains, there does not appear to be any reason whatever for doubt with regard to the principal fact on which the above computation is founded.

There is an objection, however, that may be made to these decisions respecting the force of gunpowder, which on the first view appears to be of considerable importance; but on a more careful examination it will be found to have no weight.

If the force of fired gunpowder is so very great, how does it happen that fire-arms, and artillery of all kinds, which certainly are not calculated to withstand so enormous a force, are not always burst when they are used? I might answer this question by another, by asking how it happened that the barrel used in my experiments, and which was more than 10 times stronger in proportion to the size of its bore than ever a piece of ordnance was formed, could be burst by the force of gunpowder, if its force is not in fact much greater than it has ever been supposed to be? But it is not necessary to have recourse to such a shift to get out of this difficulty; there is nothing more to do than to shew, which may easily be done, that the combustion of gunpowder is less rapid than it has hitherto been supposed to be, and the objection in question falls to the ground.

Mr. Robins's theory supposes that all the powder of which a charge consists is not only set on fire, but that it is actually *consumed* and " *converted into an elastic fluid before the bullet is sensibly moved from its place.*" I have already, in the former part of this paper, offered several reasons which appeared to me to prove that, though the *inflammation* of gunpowder is very rapid, yet the progress of the combustion is by no means so *instantaneous* as has been imagined.   I shall now give an account of some experiments which put that matter out of all doubt.

It is a fact well known, that on the discharge of fire-arms of all kinds, cannon and mortars, as well as mus-kets, there is always a considerable quantity of uncon-sumed grains of gunpowder blown out of them ; and, what is very remarkable, and as it leads directly to a dis-covery of the cause of this effect is highly deserving of consideration, these unconsumed grains are not merely blown out of the *muzzles* of fire-arms ; they come out also by their vents or touch-holes, *where the fire enters to inflame the charge ;* as many persons who have had the misfortune to stand with their faces near the touch-hole of a musket, when it has been discharged, have found to their cost.

Now it appears to me to be extremely improbable, if not absolutely impossible, that a grain of gunpowder, actually in the chamber of the piece, and completely surrounded by flame, should, by the action of that very flame, be blown out of it, without being at the same time set on fire.   But if these grains of powder are *actually on fire* when they come out of the piece, and are afterwards found at a distance from it *unconsumed*, this is, in my opin-ion, a most decisive proof, not only that the combustion of gunpowder is by no means so rapid as it has generally been thought to be, but also (what will doubtless appear quite incredible), that if a grain of gunpowder, actually on fire, and burning with the utmost violence over the whole extent of its surface, be projected with *a very great velocity* into a cold atmosphere, the fire will be extinguished, and the remains of the grain will fall to the ground, unchanged, and as inflammable as before.

This extraordinary fact was ascertained beyond all possibility of doubt by the following experiments. Having procured from a powder-mill in the neighbourhood of the city of Munich a quantity of gunpowder, all of the same mass, but formed into grains of very different sizes, some as small as the grains of the finest Battel powder, and the largest of them nearly as big as large pease, I placed a number of vertical screens of very thin paper, one behind another, at the distance of 12 inches from each other; and loading a common musket repeatedly with this powder, sometimes without, and sometimes with a wad, I fired it against the foremost screen and observed the quantity and effects of the unconsumed grains of powder which impinged against it.

The screens were so contrived, by means of double frames united by hinges, that the paper could be changed with very little trouble, and it was actually changed after every experiment.

The distance from the muzzle of the gun to the first screen was not always the same; in some of the experiments it was only 8 feet, in others it was 10, and in some 12 feet.

The charge of powder was varied in a great number of different ways, but the most interesting experiments were made with one single large grain of powder, propelled sometimes by smaller and sometimes by larger charges of very fine-grained powder.

These large grains never failed to reach the screen; and though they sometimes appeared to have been broken into several pieces, by the force of the explosion, yet they frequently reached the first screen entire; and sometimes passed through all the screens (five in number) without being broken.

When they were propelled by large charges, and consequently with great velocity, they were seldom on fire when they arrived at the first screen, which was evident, not only from their not setting fire to the paper (which they sometimes did), but also from their being found sticking in a soft board, against which they struck, after having passed through all the five screens; or leaving visible marks of their having impinged against it, and being broken to pieces and dispersed by the blow. These pieces were often found lying on the ground; and from their forms and dimensions, as well as from other appearances, it was often quite evident that the little globe of powder had been on fire, and that its diameter had been diminished by the combustion, before the fire was put out, on the globe being projected into the cold atmosphere. The holes made in the screen by the little globe in its passage through them seemed also to indicate that its diameter had been diminished.

That these globes, or large grains of powder, were always set on fire by the combustion of the charge can hardly be doubted. This certainly happened in many of the experiments, for they arrived at the screens on fire, and set fire to the paper; and in the experiments in which they were projected with small velocities, they were often seen to pass through the air on fire; and when this was the case, no vestige of them was to be found.

They sometimes passed, on fire, through several of the foremost screens without setting them on fire, and set fire to one or more of the hindmost, and then went on and impinged against the board, which was placed at the distance of 12 inches behind the last screen.

It is hardly necessary for me to observe, that all these experiments prove that the combustion of gunpowder is very far from being so instantaneous as has generally been imagined. I will just mention one experiment more, in which this was shewn in a manner still more striking, and not less conclusive. A small piece of red-hot iron being dropped down into the chamber of a common horse-pistol, and the pistol being elevated to an angle of about 45 degrees, upon dropping down into its barrel one of the small globes of powder (of the size of a pea), it took fire, and was projected into the atmosphere by the elastic fluid generated in its own combustion, leaving a very beautiful train of light behind it, and disappearing all at once, like a falling star.

This amusing experiment was repeated very often, and with globes of different sizes. When very small ones were used singly, they were commonly consumed entirely before they came out of the barrel of the pistol; but when several of them were used together, some, if not all of them, were commonly projected into the atmosphere on fire.

I shall conclude this paper by some observations on the practical uses and improvements that may probably be derived from these discoveries, respecting the great expansive force of the fluid generated in the combustion of gunpowder.

As the *slowness* of the combustion of gunpowder is undoubtedly the cause which has prevented its enormous and almost incredible force from being discovered, so it is evident, that the readiest way to increase its effects is to contrive matters so as to accelerate its inflammation and combustion. This may be done in various ways, but the most simple and most effectual manner of doing it would, in my opinion, be to set fire to the charge of powder by shooting (through a small opening) the flame of a smaller charge into the midst of it.

I contrived an instrument on this principle for firing cannon, several years ago, and it was found on repeated trials to be useful, — convenient in practice, — and not liable to accidents. It likewise supersedes the necessity of using priming, — vent tubes, — port-fires, — and matches; and on that account I imagined it might be of use in the British navy. Whether it has been found to be so or not I have not heard.

Another infallible method of increasing very considerably the effect of gunpowder in fire-arms of all sorts and dimensions would be to cause the bullet to fit the bore exactly, or without windage, *in that part of the bore, at least, where the bullet rests on the charge;* for when the bullet does not completely close the opening of the chamber, not only much of the elastic fluid generated in the first moment of the combustion of the charge escapes by the sides of the bullet, but, what is of still greater importance, a considerable part of the unconsumed powder is blown out of the chamber along with it, in a state of actual combustion, and, getting before the bullet, continues to burn on as it passes through the whole length of the bore, by which the motion of the bullet is much impeded.

The loss of force which arises from this cause is, in some cases, almost incredible; and it is by no means difficult to contrive matters so as to render it very apparent, and also to prevent it.

If a common horse-pistol be fired with a loose ball, and so small a charge of powder that the ball shall not be able to penetrate a deal board so deep as to stick in

it, when fired against it from the distance of six feet, —
the same ball, discharged from the same pistol, with the
same charge of powder, may be made to pass quite
through one deal board, and bury itself in a second
placed behind it, *merely by preventing the loss of force which
arises from what is called windage ;* as I have found more
than once by actual experiment.

I have, in my possession, a musket, from which, with
a common musket charge of powder, I fire two bullets
at once with the same velocity that a single bullet is discharged from a musket on the common construction,
with the same quantity of powder. And, what renders
the experiment still more striking, — the diameter of
the bore of my musket is exactly the same as that of a
common musket, except only in that part of it where it
joins the chamber, in which part it is just so much con-
tracted that the bullet which is next to the powder may
stick fast in it. I ought to add that, though the bullets
are of the common size, and are consequently considerably less in diameter than the bore, means are used
which *effectually* prevent the loss of force by windage ;
and to this last circumstance it is doubtless owing, in a
great measure, that the charge appears to exert so great
a force in propelling the bullets.

That the conical form of the lower part of the bore,
where it unites with the chamber, has a considerable
share in producing this extraordinary effect, is however
very certain, as I have found by experiments made with
a view merely to ascertain that fact.

I will finish this paper by a computation, which will
shew that the force of the elastic fluid generated in the
combustion of gunpowder, enormous as it is, may be
satisfactorily accounted for upon the supposition that its

force depends *solely* on the elasticity of watery vapour, or steam.

It has been shewn by a variety of experiments made in England, and in other countries, and lately by a well-conducted set of experiments made in France by M. de Betancour, and published in Paris under the auspices of the Royal Academy of Sciences, in the year 1790, that the elasticity of steam is doubled by every addition of temperature equal to 30 degrees of Fahrenheit's thermometer.

Supposing now a cavity of any dimensions (equal in capacity to 1 cubic inch, for instance) to be filled with gunpowder, and that on the combustion of the powder, and in consequence of it, this space is filled with steam (and I shall presently shew that the water, existing in the powder *as water*, is abundantly sufficient for generating this steam), if we know the heat communicated to this steam in the combustion of powder, we can compute the elasticity it requires by being so heated.

Now it is certain that the heat generated in the combustion of gunpowder cannot possibly be less than that of red-hot iron. It is probably much greater, but we will suppose it to be only equal to 1000 degrees of Fahrenheit's scale, or something less than iron visibly red-hot in daylight. This is about as much hotter than boiling linseed oil, as boiling linseed oil is hotter than boiling water.

As the elastic force of steam is just equal to the mean pressure of the atmosphere when its temperature is equal to that of boiling water, or to 212° of Fahrenheit's thermometer, and as its elasticity is doubled by every addition of temperature equal to 30 degrees of the same scale, with the heat of $212° + 30° = 242°$ its elasticity will be equal to the pressure of 2 atmospheres; at the temperature of $242° + 30° = 272°$ it will equal 4 atmospheres;

at $2\overset{\circ}{7}2 + \overset{\circ}{3}0 = \overset{\circ}{3}02$ it will equal 8 atmospheres;
" 302 + 30 = 332 "   "   "   16   "
" 332 + 30 = 362 "   "   "   32   "
" 362 + 30 = 392 "   "   "   64   "
" 392 + 30 = 422 "   "   "   128   "
" 422 + 30 = 452 "   "   "   256   "
" 452 + 30 = 482 "   "   "   512   "
" 482 + 30 = 512 "   "   " 1024   "
" 512 + 30 = 542 "   "   " 2048   "
" 542 + 30 = 572 "   "   " 4096   "
" 572 + 30 = 602

(or 2 degrees above the heat of boiling linseed oil), its elasticity will be equal to the pressure of 8192 atmospheres, or above *eight times* greater than the utmost force of the fluid generated in the combustion of gunpowder, according to Mr. Robins's computation. But the heat generated in the combustion of gunpowder is much greater than that of 602° of Fahrenheit's thermometer, consequently the elasticity of the steam generated from the water contained in the powder must of necessity be much greater than the pressure of 8192 atmospheres.

Following up our computations on the principles assumed, we shall find that,

at the temperature of ⎫ the elasticity will be equal to the pressure of
$6\overset{\circ}{0}2 + \overset{\circ}{3}0 = 6\overset{\circ}{3}2$ ⎬   16,384 atmospheres ;
at 632 + 30 = 662   32,768   "
at 662 + 30 = 692   65,536   "
and at 692 + 30 = 722

the elasticity will be equal to the pressure of 131,072 atmospheres, which is 130 times greater than the elastic force assigned by Mr. Robins to the fluid generated in the combustion of gunpowder; and about one-sixth part greater than my experiments indicated it to be.

But even here the heat is still much below that which is most undoubtedly generated in the combustion of gunpowder. The temperature which is indicated by 722° of Fahrenheit's scale (which is only 122 degrees higher than that of boiling quicksilver, or boiling linseed oil) falls short of the heat of iron which is visibly red-hot in daylight by 355 degrees; but the flame of gunpowder has been found to melt brass, when this metal, in very small particles, has been mixed with the powder; and it is well known that to melt brass a heat is required equal to that of 3807 degrees of Fahrenheit's scale; 2730 degrees above the heat of red-hot iron, or 3085 degrees higher than the temperature which gives to steam an elasticity equal to the pressure of 131,072 atmospheres.

That the elasticity of steam would actually be increased by heat in the ratio here assumed can hardly be doubted. It has absolutely been found to increase in this ratio in all the changes of temperature between the point of boiling water (I may even say of freezing water) and that of 280° of Fahrenheit's scale; and there does not appear to be any reason why the same law should not hold in higher temperatures.

A doubt might possibly arise with respect to the existence of a sufficient quantity of water in gunpowder to fill the space in which the powder is fired with steam, at the moment of the explosion; but this doubt may easily be removed.

The best gunpowder, such as was used in my experiments, is composed of 70 parts (in weight) of nitre, 18 parts of sulphur, and 16 parts of charcoal; hence 100 parts of this powder contain $67\frac{3}{10}$ parts of nitre, $17\frac{3}{10}$ parts of sulphur, and of charcoal $15\frac{4}{10}$ parts.

Mr. Kirwan has shewn, that in 100 parts of nitre there are 7 parts of water of crystallization; consequently, in 100 parts of gunpowder, as it contains $67\frac{3}{10}$ parts of nitre, there must be $4\frac{711}{1000}$ parts of water.

Now, as 1 cubic inch of gunpowder, when the powder is well shaken together, weighs exactly as much as 1 cubic inch of water at the temperature of 55° F., namely, 253.175 grains Troy, a cubic inch of gunpowder in its driest state must contain at least $10\frac{927}{1000}$ grains of water; for it is 100 to 4.711, as 253.175 to 10.927. But besides the water of crystallization which exists in the nitre, there is always a considerable quantity of water in gunpowder, in that state in which it makes bodies *damp* or *moist.* Charcoal exposed to the air has been found to absorb nearly $\frac{1}{8}$ of its weight of water; and by experiments I have made on gunpowder, by ascertaining its loss of weight on being much dried, and its acquiring this lost weight again on being exposed to the air, I have reason to think that the power of the charcoal, which enters into the composition of gunpowder, to absorb water remains unimpaired, and that it actually retains as much water in that state as it would retain were it not mixed with the nitre and the sulphur.

As there are $15\frac{4}{10}$ parts of charcoal in 100 parts of gunpowder, in 1 cubic inch of gunpowder ($= 253.175$ grains Troy), there must be 38.989 grains of charcoal; and if we suppose $\frac{1}{8}$ of the apparent weight of this charcoal to be water, this will give 4.873 grains in weight for the water which exists in the form of *moisture* in 1 cubic inch of gunpowder.

That this estimation is not too high is evident from the following experiment. 1160 grains Troy of apparently dry gunpowder, taken from the middle of a cask, on being exposed 15 minutes in dry air, heated to the temperature of about 200°, was found to have lost 11 grains of its weight. This shews that each cubic inch of this gunpowder actually gave out $2\frac{4}{10}$ grains of water on being exposed to this heat; and there is no doubt but that at the end of the experiment it still retained much more water than it had parted with.

If now we compute the quantity of water which would be sufficient, when reduced to steam under the mean pressure of the atmosphere, to fill a space equal in capacity to 1 cubic inch, we shall find that, either that contained in the nitre which enters into the composition of 1 cubic inch of gunpowder as *water of crystallization,* or even that small quantity which exists in the powder in the state of *moisture,* will be much more than sufficient for that purpose.

Though the density of steam has not been determined with that degree of precision that could be wished, yet it is quite certain that it cannot be less than 2000 times rarer than water, when both are at the temperature of 212°. Some have supposed it to be more than 10,000 times rarer than water, and experiments have been made which seem to render this opinion not improbable; but we will take its density at the highest estimation, and suppose it to be only 2000 times rarer than water. As 1 cubic inch of water weighs 253.175 grains, the water contained in 1 cubic inch of steam at the temperature of 212° will be $\frac{1}{2000}$ part of 253.175 grains, or 0.12659 of a grain.

But we have seen that 1 cubic inch of gunpowder

contains 10.927 grains of water of crystallization, and 4.873 grains in a state of moisture. Consequently, the quantity of water of crystallization in gunpowder is 86 times greater, and the quantity which exists in it in a state of *moisture* is 38 times greater than that which would be required to form a quantity of steam sufficient to fill completely the space occupied by the powder.

Hence we may venture to conclude that the quantity of water actually existing in gunpowder is much more than sufficient to generate all the steam that would be necessary to account for the force displayed in the combustion of gunpowder (supposing that force to depend solely on the action of steam), even though no water should be generated in the combustion of the gunpowder. It is even very probable that there is more of it than is wanted, and that the force of gunpowder would be still greater, could the quantity of water it contains be diminished.

From this computation it would appear, that the difficulty is not to account for the force actually exerted by fired gunpowder, but to explain the reason why it does not exert a much greater force. But I shall leave these investigations to those who have more leisure than I now have to prosecute them.

SUPPLEMENTARY OBSERVATIONS.

ALTHOUGH there is no reason to doubt of the accuracy of M. Betancour's experiments, yet there is one important point which still remains to be ascertained, before the hypothesis I have here endeavoured to establish on the results of those experiments, respecting the force exerted by steam in combustion of gunpowder, can be admitted.

The steam, the elastic force of which was measured in M. Betancour's experiments, *remained constantly in contact with water, in a liquid state.* How far did the presence of this water, and the progressive change of a part of it to steam, as the heat was gradually increased, and the addition to the *density* of the steam which resulted therefrom, contribute to the increase of the elasticity of the steam which was observed?

This is a very important question, and the solution of it must necessarily decide the fate of our hypothesis: and after mature consideration, I am myself inclined to think that I have been precipitate in ascribing too much to the agency of steam in the force exerted by fired gunpowder. I was led into this error, if it be one, on finding the explanation of the cause of the force of gunpowder given by Mr. Robins to be quite inadequate to its effects, as shewn in my experiments. But I did not at first advert to the degree in which one of the suppositions made by Mr. Robins (namely, that respecting the heat of the generated elastic fluid) is gratuitous; nor did I then perceive how very probable it is that he has greatly underrated it.

The supposition of Mr. Robins respecting the heat

was such as enabled him to reconcile the results of *his experiments* with *his theory ;* and as later discoveries have shewn his theory to be unfounded, some of his assumed principles must of necessity have been erroneous.

The most unexceptionable of the suppositions of Mr. Robins relative to the subject under consideration is that respecting the quantity of air, or *permanently elastic fluid*, that is generated from gunpowder in its combustion. It cannot, indeed, with propriety be called a supposition, for it was the result of a well-contrived experiment.

According to Mr. Robins, when any given quantity of gunpowder is fired, the quantity of permanently elastic fluid or fluids generated from it in its combustion is such that, when cooled down to the mean temperature of the atmosphere, it would — under the mean pressure of the atmosphere — fill a space 250 times greater than that which the unfired powder occupied. Consequently, if this fluid were compressed into a space no greater than that occupied by unfired powder, it would, in its endeavours to expand itself, on being so compressed, exert a force 250 times greater than the mean pressure of the atmosphere; or (to use the language, employed in the foregoing paper) its force would be equal to 250 atmospheres.

This is very far indeed from 100,000 atmospheres, — the expansive force we have assigned to fired gunpowder, — but let us see how far *the heat* generated in the combustion of gunpowder may be supposed to increase the expansive force of the elastic fluids which are generated in that process.

From the experiments of the late General Roy, it has been proved that the expansive force of common at-

mospherical air is doubled with an increase of heat indicated by 437 degrees of Fahrenheit's scale; and I was
lately informed by that excellent chemist and natural
philosopher, M. Bertholet, that he has found by repeated experiments, that the expansions with heat of all
the gazes, or different kinds of permanently elastic fluids,
are precisely the same, whatever may be the difference
of their specific gravities, or of their chemical or other
properties.

Supposing now that the permanently elastic fluids
generated in the combustion of gunpowder follow the
same law in their expansions with heat, we can easily
determine, by computation, how much the expansive
force of those fluids will be augmented by any given
augmentation of heat.

If the temperature of air of the atmosphere be 60° F.
when the expansive force of the permanently elastic fluid
generated in the combustion of gunpowder — *being at
that temperature* — is equal to 250 atmospheres; if the
temperature of that fluid be raised 437 degrees, or if it
become 497° of Fahrenheit's scale $(60° + 437° = 497°)$, —
there can be no doubt whatever but its elastic force will
be doubled; or that it will become 500 times greater
than the mean pressure of the atmosphere.

If its temperature be raised 437 degrees higher, or if
it be heated to 934° F., its elasticity will be again
doubled, and will become $= 1000$ atmospheres, which is
the initial force of the elastic fluid generated in the combustion of fired gunpowder, according to Mr. Robins.

But there are many strong reasons for supposing that
the heat generated in the combustion of gunpowder is
vastly higher than that indicated by 937° of Fahrenheit's
scale.

If the heat be only that indicated by 3996° F. (which is many degrees below that at which either copper, silver, or gold melts), that heat will be sufficient to double the expansive force last found (= 1000 atmospheres) *seven times*, which will make it equal to the pressure of *one hundred and twenty-eight thousand atmospheres;* a degree of elastic force considerably more than sufficient to account for the results of all the experiments mentioned in this paper.

A SHORT ACCOUNT

OF SOME

EXPERIMENTS MADE WITH CANNON,

AND ALSO OF

SOME ATTEMPTS TO IMPROVE FIELD ARTILLERY.

DURING my residence in Bavaria, I had an opportunity of verifying, upon a large scale, the method proposed in my first Paper on Gunpowder, for measuring the velocities of bullets by the recoil of the gun, and I had also opportunities of making several other interesting experiments connected with that subject. In the spring of the year 1791, a large building was erected for the express purpose of pursuing these investigations, in the neighbourhood of Munich, on the ground destined for the exercise of the artillery, where a most complete apparatus was put up for measuring the velocities of cannon bullets by the recoil of the gun, and also by the pendulum at the same time; and with this apparatus a great number of interesting experiments were made under my direction, and most of them in my presence. I should long ago have laid an account of them before the public had I not been induced to postpone their publication by a desire that they might make a part of a work on artillery, yet unfinished, but which I hope, at some future period, to be able to send to the press.

In this work I shall give a detailed account, illustrated by accurate plans (which are now ready for the engraver), of all the changes in the construction of the Bavarian artillery, which were introduced in my attempts to improve it, during the time the military affairs of that country were under my direction. In the mean time I have thought it advisable to give, in this place, a short account of such of my experiments as are most intimately connected with the subjects of the two preceding papers; and this I shall now do in as few words as possible.

Pieces of brass ordnance, of three different calibres, viz. 3 pounders, 6 pounders, and 12 pounders, having been suspended, in an horizontal position, by long pendulous rods, or bars of iron, in the manner described in one of the foregoing papers, these guns were fired in this situation, with different charges of powder; with, and also without bullets; and sometimes with two and with three fit bullets at the same time; and the velocity of the gun in its recoil having been determined, in each experiment, by the length (measured by means of a ribband) of the chord of the ascending arc of its first vibration, from that velocity, and the known weights of the gun and of the bullet, the velocity of the bullet was computed.

The gun having been pointed against the center of a very large heavy pendulum, constructed of strong timbers, well fastened together with iron, the bullets lodged in that pendulum; and their velocities were determined, according to Mr. Robins's method, by the arcs of the vibration of the pendulum; and these two methods of ascertaining the velocities of the bullets were found to agree with great accuracy.

This pendulum, although it was made very strong,

was, however, soon destroyed by the bullets; but it was not rendered useless till after a sufficient number of experiments had been made with it to establish, beyond all doubt, the accuracy of the proposed method of determining the velocities of cannon bullets by the recoil of the gun. As soon as this was done, the pendulum, being no longer wanted, was removed, and the bullets were fired into a mound of earth, which had been thrown up to receive them.

The general results of this course of experiments were as follows: With the same charge of powder, the velocities of *two* and *three* fit bullets, discharged at once from the cannon, were found to be greater than the velocity of a *single bullet*, impelled by the given charge, in a proportion considerably higher than that determined by Mr. Robins.

Means were employed, which prevented entirely the escape, by windage, of the elastic fluid generated from the powder in its combustion, and this added very considerably to the apparent force of the charge.

The force of the charge was always sensibly increased when the gun was discharged by firing a pistol (constructed for that use) into the vent, instead of using a priming and a common match for firing off the gun.

As I have entered upon this subject, and as it is possible that I may never find leisure to finish the work on Artillery, which, for many years, I have had in hand, I cannot resist the inclination I feel to avail myself of this opportunity to submit to the public — but more especially to professional men — some of the principal results of my experiments and meditations in the prosecution of my inquiries relative to the improvement of artillery.

Those who are engaged in these researches may, perhaps, derive some advantage from the hints, however
cursory they may be, of a person who has long been in
a habit of observing; and who has had many opportunities of making interesting experiments.

When I was called to take the direction of the military affairs of the late Elector Palatine, Duke of Bavaria, the army was destitute of a well-organized train of
field artillery; and there was no Cannon Foundry in Bavaria that was in a condition to be used. The arsenal at Munich was filled with cannon, but by far
the greater part of them were perfectly useless, being
very ancient, and too heavy and unwieldy to be moved.
There was a very good Cannon Foundry at Manheim,
the capital of the Elector's dominions upon the Rhine;
but the distance between Munich and Manheim is so
great that it would have cost more to have sent the Bavarian guns to Manheim to be refounded, and to have
brought them back by land carriage, than was required
to defray the expence of establishing a new manufactory
for the construction of artillery in Bavaria.

A Foundry was accordingly established at Munich,
and neither pains nor expence were spared to make it as
perfect as possible; and a most excellent machine was
erected for boring cannon; with work-shops adjoining
to it for the construction of gun-carriages and ammunition waggons.

With these advantages, and with a set of good workmen at my command in all the different branches of
mechanics that are concerned in the construction of artillery, it will readily be believed, by those who know
how much my attention had been employed on that
subject, that I did not neglect to avail myself of so

favourable an opportunity to make trial of some of the plans for the improvement of artillery which had been recommended by professional men of eminence ; or that had been the result of my own experiments and meditations.

The following *Memoir,* that accompanied a model of a Bavarian field piece, with its ammunition waggon, which, with the permission of the late Elector, I had the honour to present to the United States of North America (my native country), will give the reader a general idea of some of the alterations that were introduced, in the construction of that species of ordnance, in my attempts to improve Field Artillery.*

The model above mentioned was upon a large scale, being *one quarter of the full size* in length, diameter, &c., and it was finished, and mounted in the most complete manner, and fitted for actual service or experiment. I brought it with me to England, from Bavaria, in the autumn of the year 1798, and before it was shipped for America, I had the honour to shew it to his Royal Highness the Duke of York, commander-in-chief of his Majesty's forces in Great Britain ; and to leave it several months for the inspection of the officers of the Royal Artillery.

" MEMOIR, *in which some account is given of the new Bavarian Field Pieces, lately constructed at Munich, under the direction of Lieutenant-General Count* Rumford.

" In contriving these guns (which are 6 pounders, 18 calibres in length), the following objects were had in view : —

* This gun, with all the details of its carriage, drawn to a scale, are represented in the (annexed) Plates VII., VIII., and IX.

" 1. To construct them in such a manner as to render them capable of being used occasionally as flying or horse artillery.

" Provision is made for carrying occasionally all the men belonging to the gun, upon the limber, and upon the ammunition waggon, where safe and commodious seats are provided for them.

" To save time in getting the gun into action, the two men who ride upon the limber jump down from their seat the instant the gun arrives upon the ground where it is to be posted, and unlimber, while the other men who ride on the ammunition waggon are coming up.

" The two long pieces of ash timber, which form the principal part of the body of the ammunition waggon (uniting the fore wheels to the hind), act as springs by their elasticity ; and, in order that their action may be as free as possible, they should not be shod with iron, nor should they be made too bulky.

" The long chest in which the greater part of the ammunition is carried, and upon which five men occasionally ride, is so slung and confined by strong side braces, that if the ammunition waggon should be overturned, the men who are upon this chest — upon which they are seated astride — would be in no danger of its falling upon them.

" Although provision is made for carrying the men belonging to these guns in cases of necessity, and transporting them with celerity from one place to another, yet it is not meant that they should be allowed to ride at all times ; but merely when the guns are used as flying artillery.

" 2. One principal object had in view was to render the gun-carriage as strong and durable as possible, without increasing its weight.

Scale of 6 Inches to the Inch Rhineland Measure

100 Rhineland feet are equal to 103 English feet

PLATE VII.

" A bare inspection of this carriage, and a comparison of it with the carriages of field pieces on the common construction, will shew the various means that have been used to attain this important end; and that these means have been effectual has been abundantly proved by the uncommon strength which those carriages evinced when they were submitted to the most severe trials. Several of these 6 pounders were fired repeatedly with 3 lbs. of the best powder and three fit bullets, without receiving the smallest injury; while other 6 pounders of the same weight, mounted according to the common method, seldom failed to break and disable their carriages, when exposed to this trial, although the common carriage was 100 lbs. heavier than the new Bavarian carriage, — namely, 80 lbs. in iron, and 20 lbs. in wood.

" The flasks of the carriages of field pieces are commonly much weakened by being made crooked; and also by the number of holes that are bored in them; but the new Bavarian carriage is free from both these defects. The Bavarian carriage is moreover much preserved by the collars of thick sole leather, which surround and cover the trunnions of the gun and the pivots of the elevating machine; for this soft and elastic substance, being interposed between the gun and the carriage, serves to deaden the blow of the gun against its carriage in the recoil.

" 3. Several new contrivances were introduced with a view to expedite the management of the gun in service; and to prevent accidents and mistakes in the use of the handspikes, ram-rods, &c.

" The handspikes (of which there are two, in order that one may remain if the other is shot away) are at-

PLATE VIII.

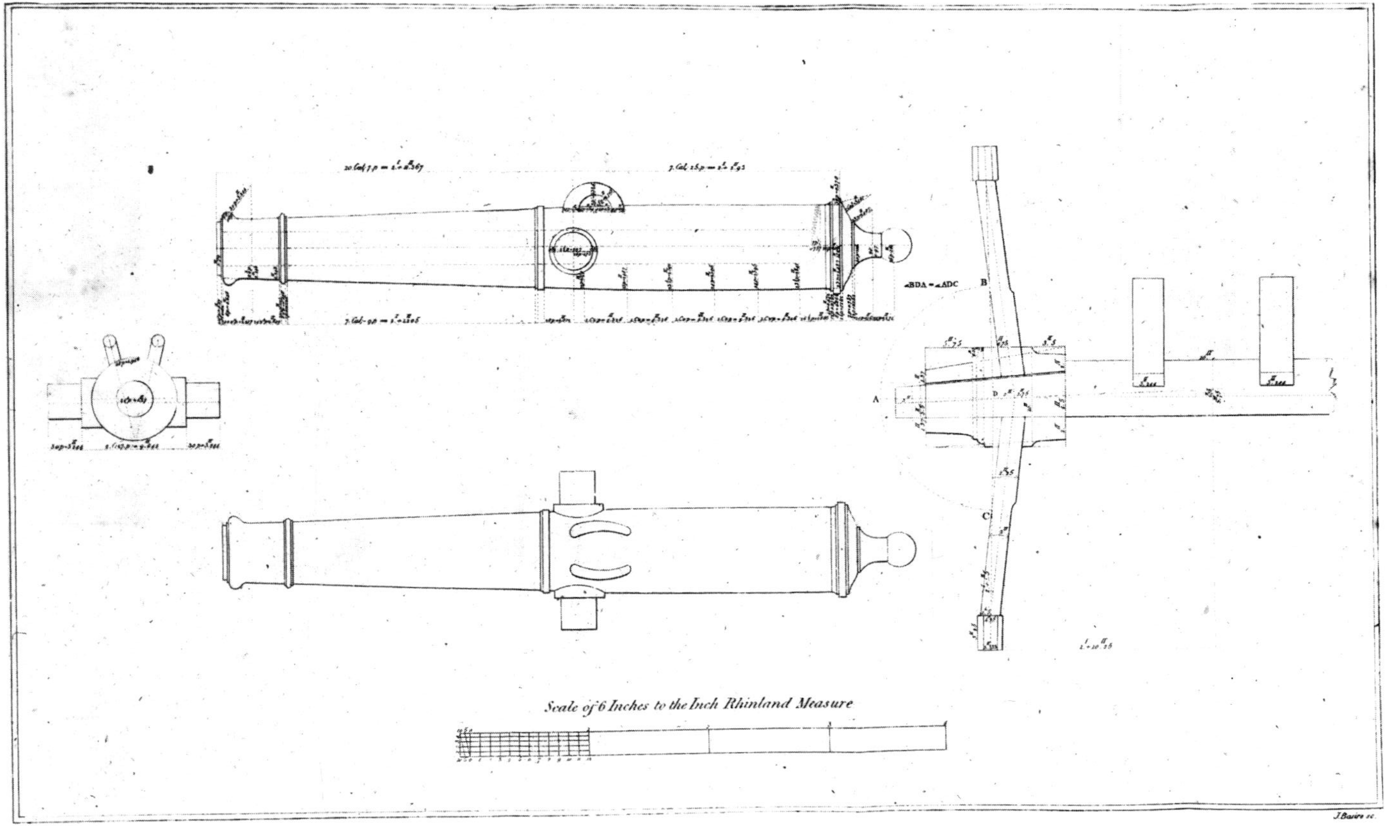
∠BDA = ∠ADC
A
B
C
D
Scale of 6 Inches to the Inch Rhinland Measure
J. Basire sc.

tached to the gun-carriage, and consequently cannot be
misplaced nor lost, through carelessness, nor in the
hurry of action.   There are no buckles to unfasten, nor
cords to loosen and untie, in preparing the gun for action. — The ram-rod is fastened to the carriage in a safe
and simple manner, and may be detached from it in
an instant, when wanted ; and the tompion of the gun,
and the stopper that closes the vent, may be removed,
or put into their places, with the greatest expedition.

" Upon a comparative trial of one of these new-in-
vented guns, with a field piece on the common construction (which trial was made in the presence of the late
Elector Palatine, reigning Duke of Bavaria), it was
found that, when both guns arrived on the ground at
the same moment, the new gun commonly unlimbered
and fired from four to six rounds before the old gun
could be got ready to be fired once.

" 4. In the mounting of this new gun, care was taken
to provide for the pointing and elevating of it, in the
most expeditious manner, and for the confining of it at
any given elevation.

" 5. To make provision for elevating it, to any given
number of degrees or minutes, above the object against
which it is pointed, without the assistance of any quadrant, plumb-line, or other instrument.

" The elevating machine, belonging to this gun, will be
found to answer perfectly for all these purposes.   The
thread of the elevating screw may, in all cases, be so
chosen, that one turn of the screw shall elevate the gun a
certain number of minutes, — as 60, for instance, — when
the gun, being previously pointed directly at the object,
may be elevated to any required number of degrees or
minutes above it, merely by keeping an account of the

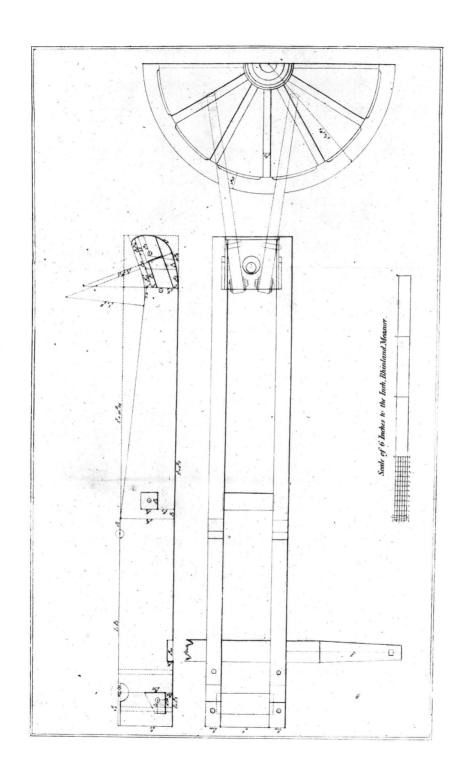

Scale of 6 Inches to the Inch, Rhinland Measure.

number of revolutions, and parts of revolutions, of the elevating screw that answer to the given elevation.

"6. In order to facilitate the pointing of the gun, when the wheels of the gun-carriage happen to be placed upon uneven ground, there are two lines of sight drawn upon the gun (one on each side of it), which are both perfectly parallel with the axis of its bore.

"The utility of these lines must be evident to those who know how difficult it is to point a gun at a given object when one of the wheels of its carriage is higher than the other; and how much, under this circumstance (of uneven ground), a gun is necessarily thrown out of its true direction, by pointing it by means of fixed sights, or notches, situated on the upper part of the gun.

"By means of the lines of sight, *parallel to the bore*, which are marked on these guns, the pointing of the gun may at any time be examined and corrected; for whenever the gun is properly pointed, either of the lines of sight will carry the eye either against the object (namely, in very small distances) or perpendicularly over it.

"7. As it frequently happens that the wheels of gun-carriages are wounded and disabled in action, in order that a speedy remedy may be applied in those cases, in the Bavarian artillery, the wheels of the gun-carriages of the field pieces are of the same form and dimensions, precisely, as the wheels of their limbers, and the hinder wheels of their ammunition waggons, in order that these last may be taken occasionally to replace the former.

"8. In the construction of the new Bavarian artillery, all useless reinforce rings upon the gun have been omitted, and pains have been taken to make its form as simple as possible.

(Signed,)   "RUMFORD.

"BROMPTON, 26th August, 1799."

But my attempts to improve artillery were not confined to the *form* of the gun, and its carriage; — the change that might be made, with advantage, in the *material* employed in constructing cannon for the land service, was likewise a subject of experiment which engaged my attention.

Happening to be present many years before, when the late Admiral Darby, in a large company of Admirals and Captains of the navy, expressed his *great satisfaction* at having *at length* succeeded in his attempts *to get rid of the brass guns*, which, for many years after iron ordnance had been generally substituted for brass, in the navy, the Britannia (the Admiral's ship) had continued to carry, on her lower gun-deck : the conversation to which this incident gave rise, concerning the relative merit of iron and brass guns, made a lasting impression on my mind; and as soon as it was in my power, I did not neglect to make such experiments as I conceived would be sufficient to determine a question that appeared to me to be of very great magnitude indeed.

I had conceived an idea that IRON ordnance might, with much advantage, be substituted instead of BRASS, for field artillery, and in general for all kinds of artillery.

I made some experiments with a view to the ascertaining of that fact, during the time I served with my regiment in the American war, but these were upon too confined a scale to be decisive ; as far, however, as they went, they tended to confirm the favourable opinion I had conceived of the usefulness of iron guns in the land service. The Hon. Admiral Digby, having been so kind, at my solicitation, as to lend me two *twelve pounder* carronades, I mounted them as howitzers, and found them to be very useful guns, especially when they were fired with a *grape* composed of 6 or of 9 *pound balls;* but at Munich these experiments were made on a much more extensive scale.

It had been asserted by those who did not approve of the introduction of iron ordnance for the land service, that, although iron guns of a very large calibre, such as are used on shipboard, are found to be sufficiently strong, yet smaller guns, such as would be proper for field artillery, would be very liable to burst, if they were not made much heavier than brass guns of the same bore; which would render them unwieldy, and unfit for those rapid movements which are often so decisive on a day of action.

Were this objection founded, it would undoubtedly be decisive against the general introduction of iron guns; but from all the inquiries I could make I thought there was reason to conclude that *want of strength*, which was certainly very apparent in iron guns of inferior dimensions, arose from accidental circumstances; and that an effectual remedy might easily be found for that imperfection.

Until iron guns were cast *solid*, or without a core, no hopes could reasonably be entertained of being able to cast small guns of that metal so sound, and to render their texture so uniform throughout, as to enable them to resist the force of their customary charges, without reinforcing them with an unusual quantity of metal; and even after iron guns of all calibres were cast solid, yet, as the strength, or toughness, of cast-iron depends much on the *slowness with which it cools in the mould;* and as small masses cool more rapidly than larger ones, it is evident that guns of a small size would be much more likely to be wanting in strength than larger cannon of a similar form ; but I never could see any reason for supposing that a small piece of iron ordnance would be wanting in strength, if means were employed for pressing the metal with a considerable weight while it remains in the mould in a fluid state ; and for prolonging the time of its cooling.

When cannon are cast of gun-metal, or brass, the solid cylinder, or rather cone, which, when bored, constitutes the gun, is cast at least 2 feet longer than it is intended that the gun should be. The additional piece of metal beyond the end of the muzzle, which is cut off before the gun is bored (and thrown away, or rather preserved and melted again), serves to compress the fluid mass in the lower part of the mould, and to force upwards those bubbles of air that are frequently carried down into the mould with the descending current of melted metal ; and which, if they were not expelled, would form what are called *honeycombs* in the metal ; and would render the gun unsound and unserviceable.

The mould is always placed in a vertical position, with that end upwards which is to be the muzzle of the gun, in order that the soundest part of the metal — namely, that which, having sustained the greatest pressure while the metal remained in a fluid state, is most effectually freed of air-bubbles — may be in the neighbourhood of the chamber of the piece, where strength and soundness are most wanted.

The utility of these precautions being evident, they were not neglected in casting the iron guns that were constructed for my experiments ; and means were used for prolonging the time of the cooling of the metal in the mould.

The guns cast were 1 pounders, 3 pounders, 6 pounders, 12 pounders, and one 18 pounder; and to make the comparison with brass artillery the more striking and satisfactory, they were all — except the 1 pounders and the 18 pounder — made of the same lengths, and of the same weight, as brass guns of the same calibres.

These iron guns were all *cast solid*, and were bored in an horizontal position; and while the gun was boring, the swelling of its muzzle, and the first reinforce ring (at the breech) were neatly turned. The forms of all these guns were simple, and not inelegant. Their trunnions were placed in such a manner that a line passing through their axes meets the axis of the bore of the gun, and cuts it at right angles. The trunnions were *turned*, and their forms and dimensions made perfectly true, by means of a particular machine, contrived for that purpose.

To protect the trunnions and the gun-carriage from the violence of the blow which the carriage receives from the gun in its recoil, the trunnions were covered with thick sole leather, greased with tallow; and the trunnion plate was made to fit the trunnion — when thus covered with leather — as accurately as possible. The elevating screw was so attached to the cascable that the gun was completely confined, and prevented from kicking up, which probably contributed not a little to the protection of the carriage.

When these iron guns were mounted, — and not before,* — they were *proved*; and they all sustained, with-

---

* As it is not common to mount guns before they are proved, it is right that the reader should know why this usual and necessary precaution was neglected in this instance. It was done to surprise and confound those who were disposed to criticise, and prepared to oppose. It was, no doubt, a bold measure, but bold measures are sometimes the most prudent. The 18 pounder was not submitted to these severe trials.

out the smallest injury, the most severe proof that ever had been given to brass guns of the same weights, lengths, and calibres. They were then *fired, quick*, at the shortest possible intervals, with half the weight of their bullets in powder, and three fit bullets, one upon the other, but *not one of them burst in these severe trials;* nor were any of their carriages injured. One of the 6 pounders, 16 calibres in length, and weighing 720 lbs., was then taken from its carriage, and being laid on the ground, was twice fired, once with 6 lbs. of powder and two bullets; and once with the same charge of powder and three bullets; — but these attempts to burst it were fruitless.

The result of these experiments having removed all the doubts that were entertained respecting the strength of these guns, their accuracy in shooting was now tried. They were repeatedly fired both with round, and with cannister-shot against a mark, placed at different distances; and they were unanimously declared by all present at these trials, to be quite equal, for accuracy, to the best brass ordnance.

Several of them were afterwards used in actual service, and were found to be as complete and as useful guns as any in the service.

The 1 pounders — which were on a peculiar construction — were much used in the defence of Manheim; and they became at last such favourites with the corps of artillery, that the men on duty actually made interest with their officers to be stationed at them. These small guns were about 4 feet long in the bore; and although their calibre was that of an *one pound* iron bullet, they weighed as much as one of the 3 *pounders*, and were commonly fired, in service, with *three* bullets at a time, which they carried with surprising accuracy.

When the object at which they were pointed was at a great distance, single leaden bullets were used, which, in order that they might fit the bore with greater precision, were wrapped up in thin leather, greased with tallow, or soaked in oil.

The carriage of this gun was extremely simple, being a single piece of elm timber, fastened to an iron axle. The wheels were of the same height and strength as those used for the carriages of 3 pounders.

From this description it will be evident that this little gun bears a near resemblance to the *Ammusette* invented by the late Lieutenant-General Desaguliers, and constructed at Woolwich. The fact is, that they were copied, with a few trifling alterations, from that piece of ordnance, being made after a drawing of it which was given me by the Lieutenant General three and twenty years ago. He, no doubt, took the idea of this gun from the reveries of Marshal Saxe.

The iron 18 pounder constructed at Munich — which was intended merely as an experiment — was very short, being only 10 calibres in length, and it was mounted in a very singular manner. It was intended for covering troops retreating before an advancing enemy, and is so contrived that it can be fired without stopping, or while it is *in full march*. It has indeed often been fired, and very quick too, while the horses which drew it were in full gallop. The carriage, which is upon four wheels, serves at the same time as an ammunition waggon ; and also for carrying the men who serve the gun. These, however, are only *three* in number, and more are not wanted.

After discharging the piece, upon pulling a strap, the gun, of itself, falls into a vertical position, with its muzzle upwards. The cartridge is then put into it, and by its weight falls into its place; the ball, grape, or cannister, with which the gun is loaded, falling into the conical opening of the chamber, there sticks fast, and is firmly fixed and confined in its place. By means of another strap, or rope, the breech of the gun is raised, with the strength of one man, and the piece is brought again into an horizontal situation (or to any given elevation); where, by means of a rack (in the form of the limb of a quadrant) and a catch, it is confined, and ready to be again discharged. Upon drawing back this catch, after the piece has been fired, the gun falls again into a vertical position.

The carriage is so constructed that the gun may, with great facility, be pointed several degrees, either to the right or to the left of the line of the direction of the march, without altering the direction in which the horses are going on.

The gun requires no priming, being fired by means of a pistol, constructed for that purpose; the flame of which is impelled with such violence through the vent of the gun, that it never fails to pierce the thick woollen bag, which contains the powder, and to set fire to the charge.

This piece carries cannister-shot with great effect, but the charge, which to me appeared to be most formidable, and best calculated to intimidate an enemy, was a grape, consisting of 9 *two pound* iron bullets; for as these balls are sufficiently large to rebound from the ground, or *recocheter*, several times, especially when the gun is not much elevated, they bound on to a great distance; and as they exhibit all the appearances of cannon bullets to the spectators who see them arrive among them, and produce nearly the same effects as much larger bullets, where they take place against either cavalry or infantry, it is very likely, I think, that two or three of these guns, well plied with this grape, would make an advancing column of very brave troops hesitate, even though they should come on flushed with victory.

I had contrived a gun, on these principles, that could be fired *advancing*, as well as *retreating*, in full march; but as I am not now writing a treatise on artillery, it would be improper for me to enlarge farther on the subject.

I cannot finish this Paper, without just observing, with respect to iron guns, that if any country could safely venture to substitute iron ordnance instead of brass, for field artillery, it would be Great Britain; for the manufacture of cast-iron is now carried to such perfection in this island that it is made, at pleasure, of almost any degree of hardness or softness; and if the saving of copper can *anywhere* be an object of public importance, it must be here, where so much of that metal is used in covering ships.

For my own part, I do not hesitate to say, that I think iron guns better than brass guns, in every respect; when the metal is as good as it may be easily made; and they are certainly much more durable, and cost incomparably less. They are likewise more easily destroyed and rendered useless (by knocking off their trunnions) when it becomes necessary to abandon them.

I well know that these opinions will not meet with the general approbation of those who, no doubt, ought to be considered as the proper and only competent judges in matters of this kind; yet I may be permitted to say that my opinions have not been lightly taken up, nor hastily formed. I submit them to professional men, with that deference which is due from an individual to so numerous and so respectable a corps of gentlemen.

FACTS

OF

PUBLICATION

EXPERIMENTS ON THE RELATIVE INTENSITIES OF THE
LIGHT EMITTED BY LUMINOUS BODIES

In two letters to Sir Joseph Banks. Read before the Royal
Society, February 6, 1794.
Philosophical Transactions of the Royal Society of London 84
(London, 1794), 67–106.
Sir Benjamin Thompson, Count of Rumford, *Philosophical
Papers* (London: T. Cadell, jr. and W. Davies, 1802), I, 270–318.
Bibliothèque Britannique (*Science et Arts*), edited by Auguste
Pictet, Charles Pictet, and F. G. Maurice (Geneva, 1796), I,
339–372.
Neues Journal der Physik, edited by D. Friedrich Ulbrecht
(Leipzig: Carl Gren, 1795), II, 15–57.
The Complete Works of Count Rumford (Boston: American
Academy of Arts and Sciences), IV (1875), 1–47.

AN ACCOUNT OF SOME EXPERIMENTS ON COLOURED
SHADOWS

In a letter to Sir Joseph Banks. Read before the Royal
Society, February 20, 1794.
Philosophical Transactions of the Royal Society of London 84
(London, 1794), 107–118.
Sir Benjamin Thompson, Count of Rumford, *Philosophical
Papers* (London: T. Cadell, jr. and W. Davies, 1802), I, 319–332.

A Journal of Natural Philosophy, Chemistry and the Arts: Illustrated with Engravings, edited by William Nicholson (London, 1797), I, 101–106.

Neues Journal der Physik, edited by D. Friedrich Ulbrecht (Leipzig: Carl Gren, 1796), III, 271–277.

The Complete Works of Count Rumford (Boston: American Acadmy of Arts and Sciences), IV (1875), 49–62.

CONJECTURES RESPECTING THE PRINCIPLES OF THE HARMONY OF COLOURS

Sir Benjamin Thompson, Count of Rumford, *Philosophical Papers* (London: T. Cadell, jr. and W. Davies, 1802), I, 333–340.

The Complete Works of Count Rumford (Boston: American Academy of Arts and Sciences), IV (1875), 63–71.

AN INQUIRY CONCERNING THE CHEMICAL PROPERTIES THAT HAVE BEEN ATTRIBUTED TO LIGHT

Read before the Royal Society of London, June 14, 1798.

Philosophical Transactions of the Royal Society of London 88 (London, 1798), 449–468.

Sir Benjamin Thompson, Count of Rumford, *Philosophical Papers* (London: T. Cadell, jr. and W. Davies, 1802), I, 341–365.

Bibliothèque Britannique (Science et Arts), edited by Auguste Pictet, Charles Pictet, and F. G. Maurice (Geneva, 1799), X, 93–118.

A Journal of Natural Philosophy, Chemistry and the Arts: Illustrated with Engravings, edited by William Nicholson (London, 1799), II, 400–405, 453–457.

Chemische Annalen fur die Freunde der Naturlehre Arzney Gelahrtheit, Haushaltungskunst und Manufacturen, edited by D. Lorenz Crell (Helmstädt: C. G. Fleckeisen, 1799), 65–74, 120–137.

Allgemeines Journal der Chemie, edited by Alexander Nicolaus Scherer (Berlin: H. Frölich, 1799), II, 3–20.

The Complete Works of Count Rumford (Boston: American Academy of Arts and Sciences), IV (1875), 73–97.

OF THE MANAGEMENT OF LIGHT IN ILLUMINATION

Read before the First Class of the Institut de France, June 24, 1811.

Published separately (London: T. Cadell, jr. and W. Davies, 1812).

Published separately (Paris: Chez Firmin Didot, 1811).

Annalen der Physik, begun by F. A. C. Gren, continued by L. W. Gilbert (Halle, 1813), XLV, 365–385; supplement by Professor Lüdicke, 386–390.

Sir Benjamin Thompson, Count of Rumford, *Essays, Political, Economical and Philosophical* (London: T. Cadell, jr. and W. Davies, 1812), IV, 1–126.

The Complete Works of Count Rumford (Boston: American Academy of Arts and Sciences), IV (1875), 99–205.

OBSERVATIONS ON THE DISPERSION OF THE LIGHT OF LAMPS BY MEANS OF SHADES OF UNPOLISHED GLASS, SILK, &C.; WITH A DESCRIPTION OF A NEW LAMP

Read at the Institut de France, March 24, 1806.

Mémoires de la classe des Sciences, Mathématiques et Physiques de l'Institut de France (Paris: Baudouin, Imprimeur de l'Institut de France, 1807), VIII, i, 223–246; supplement, 246–248.

A Journal of Natural Philosophy, Chemistry and the Arts: Illustrated with Engravings, edited by William Nicholson (London, 1806), XIV, 22–38.

AN INQUIRY CONCERNING THE SOURCE OF THE LIGHT WHICH IS MANIFESTED IN THE COMBUSTION OF INFLAM-MABLE BODIES

Read before the Royal Society, January 16, 1812.

Bibliothèque Britannique (Science et Arts), edited by Auguste Pictet, Charles Pictet, and F. G. Maurice (Geneva, 1813), LIV, 3–26, where the date is given as January 23, 1812.

Sir Benjamin Thompson, Count of Rumford, *Essays, Political, Economical and Philosophical* (London: T. Cadell, jr. and W. Davies, 1812), IV, 127–152.

The Complete Works of Count Rumford (Boston: American Academy of Arts and Sciences), IV (1875), 207–228.

EXPERIMENTS ON THE PRODUCTION OF AIR FROM WATER, EXPOSED WITH VARIOUS SUBSTANCES TO THE ACTION OF LIGHT

In a letter to Sir Joseph Banks. Presented to the Royal Society, February 15, 1787.

Philosophical Transactions of the Royal Society of London 77 (London, 1787), 84–124.

Sir Benjamin Thompson, Count of Rumford, *Philosophical Papers* (London: T. Cadell, jr. and W. Davies, 1802), I, 218–263.

The Complete Works of Count Rumford (Boston: American Academy of Arts and Sciences), I (1870), 191–231.

AN ACCOUNT OF SOME EXPERIMENTS UPON GUN-POWDER

Read before the Royal Society, March 29, 1781.

Philosophical Transactions of the Royal Society of London 71 (London, 1781), 229–328.

Sir Benjamin Thompson, Count of Rumford, *Philosophical Papers* (London: T. Cadell, jr. and W. Davies, 1802), I, 1–114.

French translation by M. Reiffel, Professeur aux écoles d'artillerie, *Expériences sur la poudre-à-canon faites en 1778* (Paris: Librairie Militaire, Maritime et Polytechnique de J. Correard, 1857), 8vo., 154.

The Complete Works of Count Rumford (Boston: American Academy of Arts and Sciences), I (1870), 1–97.

EXPERIMENTS TO DETERMINE THE FORCE OF FIRED GUNPOWDER

Read before the Royal Society, May 4, 1797.

Philosophical Transactions of the Royal Society of London 87 (London, 1797), 222–292 (does not include the supplement).

Sir Benjamin Thompson, Count of Rumford, *Philosophical Papers* (London: T. Cadell, jr. and W. Davies, 1802), I, 115–194; supplement, 194–197.

The Complete Works of Count Rumford (Boston: American Academy of Arts and Sciences), I (1870), 98–172.

A SHORT ACCOUNT OF SOME EXPERIMENTS MADE WITH CANNON, AND ALSO OF SOME ATTEMPTS TO IMPROVE FIELD ARTILLERY

Sir Benjamin Thompson, Count of Rumford, *Philosophical Papers* (London: T. Cadell, jr. and W. Davies, 1802), I, 198–217.

The Complete Works of Count Rumford (Boston: American Academy of Arts and Sciences), I (1870), 173–190.

INDEX

accommodation of eye, 100
air
  produced from water by
    cotton-wool, 263; eider-
    down, 263; exposure to
    light, 251; fur of a
    Russian hare, 263;
    human hair, 263; poplar-
    cotton, 271; ravelings of
    fine linen, 263; sheep's
    wool, 263; silk, 252
  transparency of, 20
ammusette, 490
Argand, François Pierre
  Aimé (1755–1803), 207
Argand's lamp, 16, 23, 33,
  56, 102, 236

Bale, Reverend Mr., 293
ballistic pendulum, 299
Bernoulli, Daniel (1700–
  1782), 396
Berthollet, Count Claude
  Louis (1748–1822), 470
Betancour, M. de, 462, 468
Blagden, Sir Charles (1748–
  1820), 429
Boerhaave, Hermann (1668–
  1738), 331
Bouguer, Pierre (1698–1758),
  27
bullets, velocity of, 299, 320,
  344
  related to weight, 370
  relative to charge of
    powder, 335

Cadell, W. A. (publisher), 206
caloric, 406, 423
candle, standard, 17, 187
cannon
  Bavarian, 477, 479
  experiments with, 473
  as steam-engine, 407
Charles, Jacques Alexander
  César (1746–1823), 247
color
  complementary, 66
  harmony, 63, 65
  imaginary, 66
  of shadows, 53

Darby, Admiral, 485
Desaguliers, General John
  Theophilus (1683–1744),
  306, 408, 490
diffusion of light, 102, 206
Douglas, Sir Charles (died
  1789), 408

Elector Palatine, Carl
  Theodor (1724–1799),
  97, 412, 476, 482
éprouvettes, 363, 412, 415
eudiometer, 253
Euler, Leonhard (1707–1783),
  321
explosive force, Aurum
  Fulminans, 386

field artillery, 477
fire-arms without windage,
  461

flame, transparency of, 39
flame-thrower, 393
Florence, 69
Fraser, Mr. (instrument
    maker), 299
fuel consumed in lighting, 35,
    201
Fulhame, Mrs., 82

Gay-Lussac, Joseph Louis
    (1778–1850), 247
Germain, Lord George (1716–
    1785), 292
green matter, 252, 284, 291
ground glass for windows,
    175
gun
    momentum of, 344
    heated on firing, 326
    iron, 492
    on ships, 409
gun-carriage, 303
gunpowder, 293
    battle, 369
    charges of, 322
    effect of heat upon force,
        323
    effect of ramming, 334
    force of, 389, 395, 412, 428
    proving, 363
    specific gravity of, 388
    value of, 368

Hardy, Admiral Sir Charles
    (1716–1780), 408
heat in firing guns, 332
houses of industry, 97
Hutton, Charles (1737–1823),
    321, 367, 371

illumination, 97, 189
    Chinese system, 102
illuminator, 108
    balloon, 109, 134, 179, 246
    dining-room, 109

pendulous, 110, 179, 222,
    225
table, 109, 126
wall, 170
Ingen-Housz, Jan (1730–
    1799), 251, 254, 267, 284,
    291
instrument, shadow
    photometer, 1
Kirwan, Richard (1733–1812),
    465
lamp (*see also* illuminator)
    polyflame, 110, 248
    portable, 123, 136
    secondary reservoir, 144
    with circular reservoir, 106,
        126
    with flat ribbon wicks, 33,
        238
    with glass chimney, 239
Laplace, Pierre Simon de
    (1749–1827), 27
Lavoisier, Antoine Laurent
    (1743–1794), 406
light, as substance, 231, 244
    as vibration, 232
    by lamps of different sizes,
        193
    chemical properties of, 73
    degrees of, 235
    dispersion of, 173, 219
    fluctuations of, 35
    from Argand lamp, 34
    from combustion, 233
    from wax candle, 34
    in passage through glass,
        27, 210
    intensities of, 1
    loss on reflection from a
        mirror, 30
    scale of, 181, 186
    source of, 231
    standard, 17, 181
    transparency of air, 20
luminous bodies, 1

Macbride, Admiral, 408
Micheli, M., 247

National Institute of France,
    lighting, 176
Newton, Isaac (1642–1727),
    357, 375

oil consumption in lighting,
    33

Palmerston, Lord (1739–
    1802), 69
phlogiston, 261
photochemical effects, 73
photometer, 7, 12, 42, 98, 162,
    181, 212, 234
photosynthesis, 252, 285
Pictet, Marc Auguste (1752–
    1825), 247
Priestley, Joseph (1733–1804),
    55, 279, 281, 284

Ramsden, Mr. (instrument
    maker), 31
Ravrio, M. (instrument
    maker), 115
recoil of guns, 308
Reichenbach, Mr., 434
robbery, 430

Robins, Benjamin (1707–
    1751), 294, 299, 302, 321,
    338, 355, 362, 367, 370,
    386, 388, 396, 405, 409,
    442, 452, 460, 468, 474
Roy, General, 469
Royal Institution of Great
    Britain, lighting, 106
Royal Society, Museum, 429
Russell, Mr., 247

Saxe, Hermann Maurice de
    (1696–1750), 490
Scheele, Karl Wilhelm (1742–
    1786), 261
Senebier, Jean (1742–1809),
    267
shadows, colored, 53
silvering ivory, 94
Spreti, Count, 434
standard candle, 17, 181
Stewart, Keith, 408

United States of America, 477

vent, gun, 312, 330, 338

windage, gun, 312
Wogdon, Mr. (gunsmith), 294

York, Duke of, 477